International Perspectives on Early Childhood Education and Development

Volume 16

Early childhood education in many countries has been built upon a strong tradition of a materially rich and active play-based pedagogy and environment. Yet what has become visible within the profession, is, essentially a Western view of childhood, preschool education and school education.

It is timely that a series of books be published which present a broader view of early childhood education. This series seeks to provide an international perspective on early childhood education. In particular, the books published in this series will:

- Examine how learning is organized across a range of cultures, particularly indigenous communities
- Make visible a range of ways in which early childhood pedagogy is framed and enacted across countries, including the majority poor countries
- Critique how particular forms of knowledge are constructed in curriculum within and across countries
- Explore policy imperatives which shape and have shaped how early childhood education is enacted across countries
- Examine how early childhood education is researched locally and globally
- Examine the theoretical informants driving pedagogy and practice, and seek to find alternative perspectives from those that dominate many Western heritage countries
- Critique assessment practices and consider a broader set of ways of measuring children's learning
- Examine concept formation from within the context of country-specific pedagogy and learning outcomes

The series covers theoretical works, evidence-based pedagogical research, and international research studies. The series also covers a broad range of countries, including majority poor countries. Classical areas of interest, such as play, the images of childhood, and family studies, will also be examined. However, the focus is critical and international (not Western-centric).

More information about this series at http://www.springer.com/series/7601

Nadine Ballam • Bob Perry • Anders Garpelin
Editors

Pedagogies of Educational Transitions

European and Antipodean Research

 Springer

Editors
Nadine Ballam
University of Waikato
Hamilton, New Zealand

Anders Garpelin
Mälardalen University
Västerås, Sweden

Bob Perry
Research Institute for Professional Practice,
  Learning and Education (RIPPLE)
Charles Sturt University
Albury, NSW, Australia

International Perspectives on Early Childhood Education and Development
ISBN 978-3-319-43116-1   ISBN 978-3-319-43118-5   (eBook)
DOI 10.1007/978-3-319-43118-5

Library of Congress Control Number: 2016952420

Printed on acid-free paper

This Springer imprint is published by Springer Nature
The registered company is Springer International Publishing AG Switzerland

Contents

Contributors

Nadine Ballam is a Lecturer in the Faculty of Education at the University of Waikato, New Zealand. She has recently completed her PhD, investigating the lived experiences of gifted young people from low socioeconomic backgrounds, which is a key research interest. Other research interests include gifted and talented education, risk and resilience, transitions across the lifespan and human development. Nadine has a passion for travel and has spent several years living, working and exploring overseas.

Amanda Bateman is a Senior Lecturer in early childhood education at the University of Waikato, New Zealand. She has led various research projects where she uses conversation analysis to explore peer-peer relationships and teacher-child interactions and is currently working on a Teaching and Learning Research Initiative-funded project investigating children's storytelling in early childhood through primary school. Amanda has several publications from her projects, including her recent book *Conversation Analysis and Early Childhood Education: The Co-Production of Knowledge and Relationships*, and is the lead author for an edited book *Children and Knowledge-in-Interaction* that will be published in September 2016.

Jessamy Davies is currently completing her doctoral studies at Charles Sturt University (CSU), Albury-Wodonga, Australia. Jessamy's doctoral research focuses on pedagogies of educational transitions in rural areas. The study explores transition to school as the point at which different contexts, curricula, policies and approaches meet, and opportunities are provided for educators to generate new pedagogies of transitions as they negotiate these intersections. The impact of Australia's policy reforms, specifically the two new curriculum documents for the prior-to-school and school sectors, as well as the impact of rurality is considered. Jessamy previously completed her Bachelor of Education (Early Childhood) (Honours) at Charles Sturt University. She lives in Wodonga with her son Rory.

Lysa Dealtry has a Bachelor of Early Childhood Education with Honours from Charles Sturt University (CSU). She is currently in the final stages of her doctoral candidacy at CSU. Lysa's research explores a positive start to school from the perspectives of Aboriginal children, their families and educators, living in an urban community. Lysa has been a casual academic at CSU since 2009. Her current teaching areas and interests include transitions in the early years, social justice pedagogies, Indigenous education studies and play and learning. Prior to joining the team at CSU, Lysa was an early-year classroom teacher. Lysa lives in Albury-Wodonga, Australia, with her partner Chris and children Kristian and Joanna and surrounded by wonderful extended family and friends.

Sue Dockett is a Professor of Early Childhood Education at Charles Sturt University, Albury, Australia. Sue has researched in the area of educational transitions for many years. She continues this focus with current projects exploring pedagogies of educational transition, continuity and change at times of educational transition, curriculum connections and strategies to support positive transitions. Other areas of research interest include children's play and mathematics.

Aline-Wendy Dunlop, MBE is an Emeritus Professor in the School of Education, Faculty of Humanities and Social Sciences, University of Strathclyde, Glasgow, Scotland. In this role, Aline-Wendy has chosen to focus her current research, conference, networking and writing interests on educational transitions across the lifespan, autism, family engagement in education, the very youngest children, practitioner beliefs and practices and arts-related childhood experiences. She is the Scottish Project Coordinator for the POET (Pedagogies of Educational Transitions) International Research Staff Exchange Scheme. She chaired the Autism Network Scotland, and for many years, she worked in the field of autism and continues to work with the Asperger Forum: a group of writers on the autism spectrum. Her work-life balance allows for family time, travel and much-loved hobbies of pottery, the arts, walking, film and reading widely. She believes passionately in the importance of the Early Years in Scotland.

Johanna Einarsdóttir is a Professor of Early Childhood Education and the Dean of the School of Education, University of Iceland. She has been involved in several international research projects as a researcher and a consultant in her areas of expertise and published together with international colleagues. Professor Einarsdóttir is an editor of several books published in Icelandic and English. She has presented numerous papers and research results on early childhood education and educational transitions to professional and community groups nationally as well as internationally. Recently, she has been conducting research on children's views on their preschool education and transition and continuity in early childhood education.

Kenneth Ekström is a Senior Lecturer (Associate Professor) in the Department of Applied Educational Science at Umeå University, Umeå, Sweden, a researcher and a lecturer in the preschool teacher programme and part time researcher at Mälardalen

University. Kenneth's research interest is about how preschool practices are influenced by societal factors such as policy and economy. The ongoing projects are about transitions between preschools and preschool class and also how emergent science in preschools is facilitated.

Bryndís Garðarsdóttir works as a Lecturer and researcher at the School of Education, University of Iceland. She completed her master's degree in ECE from Queen Maud University College and the Norwegian University of Science and Technology. Her current research interests include teachers' roles in supporting children's well-being and learning, continuity in children's learning across school levels, learning stories in preschools and professionalism. Currently, she is taking part in projects and research involving documentation and assessment in preschools and transition from preschool to primary school.

Anders Garpelin is a Professor of Education/Special Needs Education and the principal scientific officer of Educational Sciences at Mälardalen University, Västerås, Sweden. His research concerns the meaning of educational transitions, also from a life perspective, for children and young people, with their diverse abilities and experiences. His current research deals with transitions that young children encounter between three school forms – preschool, preschool class and school – with a special focus on learning and participation. Anders and his wife Merja live in a family where different cultural perspectives meet daily. The mother-tongues, Finnish, Hungarian and Swedish, are present almost daily with their children and grandchildren.

Robyn Gerrity is the Senior Teacher/Centre Director at the Carol White Family Centre based on the Selwyn College in Kohimarama, Auckland, New Zealand. Robyn has been based in this centre for the past 12 years and was previously at the Mangere Refugee Reception Centre. She has a total of 18 years working alongside refugee families in New Zealand and around 30 years teaching and being involved in diverse aspects of New Zealand early childhood education. Robyn has a strong interest in centre hospitality, social justice and family-centred education. Robyn and husband John live in Auckland and have three children residing, respectively, in Auckland, London and Tokyo and three grandchildren in Tokyo.

Tina Hellblom-Thibblin works as a Senior Lecturer at the School of Education, Culture and Communication at Mälardalen University in Västerås. Tina's current research interests include transitions from preschool and preschool class to school, children's diversity in different school settings and implications for children with diverse qualifications and experiences in school. Her focus is also on conceptualisation and how concepts are used in educational settings, especially regarding pupils with special needs and also the relationship between the concepts used and educational settings. Educational challenges regarding mathematics in compulsory school and school for intellectually disabled are also of interest.

Margie Hohepa affiliates to Te Māhurehure, Ngāpuhi Nui Tonu and Te Ātiawa in the North Island of Aotearoa, New Zealand. She is an Associate Professor and Associate Dean Māori in Te Kura Toi Tangata Faculty of Education at the University of Waikato. Primary trained, Margie has taught in English medium and Māori medium settings. Her research focuses on Māori medium education. Her three children are graduates of kohanga reo and attended kura kaupapa Māori. One now teaches in a kura, and four of her grandchildren have begun their Māori medium education journeys.

Pernilla Kallberg is a Lecturer in Early Childhood Teacher Education and a doctoral student in the Department of Education, Culture and Communication at Mälardalen University, Västerås, Sweden. Her doctoral work and research interests are around teachers' professional work with social relationships in the transitions between and within school forms in early years. Her research has a particular focus on issues that relate to teachers' representations of social relationships and transitions to compulsory school in a Swedish context. She is enjoying life with her family, where her sons Elliot and Alvin are a great inspiration, and she finds sport activities like floorball a big energy boost.

Kristín Karlsdóttir works as a Lecturer and researcher at the School of Education, University of Iceland. In 2001, she completed her M.Ed. degree in Education from the Teacher University and currently is working on the final steps in her doctoral thesis. The thesis gives detailed description of children's learning processes in their daily lives and explores the multiple factors affecting young children's learning while participating in two different early childhood curricular contexts. Her teaching and research touch upon preschool teachers' reflections and professional development, children's participation in play and learning and children's perspectives, well-being and learning dispositions. Currently, she is taking part in projects and research involving documentation and assessment in preschool education and transition from pre- to primary school.

Anne Lillvist works as a Senior Lecturer in Education at the School of Education, Culture and Communication at Mälardalen University in Västerås, Sweden. Her research interests include quality in preschool education and participation and social interaction of preschool children in need of special support. She is currently involved in a research project on the educational transitions of young children with intellectual disabilities with a specific focus on stakeholder collaboration and learning journeys.

Leonie McIntosh is a proud Wiradjuri woman living on Wiradjuri country. She is an Indigenous Academic Fellow at Charles Sturt University, Albury, and is working on her PhD which is looking at transitions for Indigenous children moving from preschool to formal education, with particular emphasis on how the child, the family and the community move together into the next stage of education. Leonie has two children – a teenager and a preschooler – and is currently having a little bit of a break from work but, hopefully, will be back there soon.

Helen Marwick is a Developmental Psychologist and Senior Lecturer, who lectures on child development and autism, and has researched extensively on social interactions, communicative development and interpersonal understanding. She is currently involved in research on intersubjectivity, conceptual development and relational identity, for both typically developing children and children with autism spectrum disorders, and has developed the Joint-Play Intersubjectivity Assessment Method (JPIAM), also known as 'playboxes', which promotes and assesses active interpersonal engagement and communication and which is being used widely in school settings. Helen is a member of international research groups investigating neurodevelopmental disorders and social communication.

Linda Mitchell is an Associate Professor and Director of the Early Years Research Centre at the University of Waikato, Hamilton, New Zealand. Linda's current research focuses on early childhood education policy, teaching and learning in culturally and linguistically diverse early childhood settings, assessment practices and relationships with parents, whānau and community. She is interested in democratic policies and practices in early childhood education and is critical of the market approach to early childhood provision. Linda has three children and four grandchildren, one of whom lives in London and the others in New Zealand.

Htwe Htwe Myint is from Burma and her home language is Burmese. She came to New Zealand from Burma in 1992. She is a fluent speaker and writer of Burmese and English and has completed a Bachelor of Science in Chemistry at Mandalay University, Burma. After she gained her Science degree, she worked as an intermediate schoolteacher in Burma. In New Zealand, she worked at primary school as a language support teacher for a year and 5–6 years in an ECE centre. After finishing her Bachelor of Teaching (ECE), she became supervisor of the Carol White Family Centre. She works as a bilingual teacher, cultural broker, trusted interpreter and community representative and uses her knowledge, experience and skills to support children and families of all communities. Htwe Htwe believes that home language is very important and that any time is the right time to use it as a communication tool for fostering cultures and mediating identity and learning.

Sara Margrét Ólafsdóttir is a doctoral student at the University of Iceland, School of Education. In her doctoral study, she is researching with children, exploring their perspectives on play and learning in preschools. In addition, the study aims to gain a better understanding of how children see the role of adults in their play. Other research interests include children's well-being and transitions in early education. In her spare time, Sara likes running and hiking and, of course, spending time with her family, her husband and their three children.

Vanessa Paki affiliates to Ngāti Mahuta and Te Atiawa in the North Island of Aotearoa, New Zealand, and is a Lecturer at the University of Waikato, Te Oranga School of Human Development and Movement Studies. Vanessa is early childhood trained, and her primary research interests focus around kaupapa Māori issues and perspectives in early childhood, research and ethics, transitional pedagogies and human development over the lifespan.

Guðbjörg Pálsdóttir works in the University of Iceland, School of Education. She started her career as a compulsory schoolteacher in mathematics and social science but over the last 20 years has been involved in teacher education and curriculum development in mathematics. Her research interests include preschool mathematics, teacher education and curriculum resources.

Bob Perry recently retired from Charles Sturt University, Albury-Wodonga, Australia, after 45 years in tertiary education. He is currently the director of a small educational consultancy. Bob's research interests include powerful mathematics ideas in preschool and the first years of school; ethical tensions in researching with children; transition to school, with particular emphasis on starting school within families with complex support needs; preschool education in remote Indigenous communities; and evaluation of educational programmes. Bob shares a happy and fulfilling life with his partner, Sue Dockett, and their son, Will.

Sally Peters is an Associate Professor and Head of Te Oranga School of Human Development and Movement Studies at the University of Waikato, New Zealand. She is also an Associate Director of the University of Waikato's Early Years Research Centre. Sally's current research interests include many aspects of transition experiences as well as understanding more about young children's thinking, working theories and social development. Before joining the university, Sally was an early childhood teacher. Many of her projects now involve working in partnership with teachers in schools and early childhood settings to look at ways to enhance and support learning over time.

Gunilla Sandberg works as a Senior Lecturer in special needs education at the School of Education, Culture and Communication, Mälardalen University, Sweden. Her research has a focus on children's transitions to Grade 1 of primary school, with a particular interest directed towards children's reading and writing processes and inclusive education. This interest is based on a long experience of working as a primary school teacher and as a special needs educator. Gunilla lives in the countryside outside Uppsala with her husband Per. Her three children and their families live nearby.

Jenny Wilder is an Associate Professor in special needs education at Mälardalen University, Västerås, Sweden. Jenny's research interests include communication, interaction and participation of children with severe disabilities and the support system for children and families of children with disabilities. Her current research project deals with collaboration and learning in transitions from preschool into forms of special schools for children with intellectual disabilities.

Chapter 1
International Perspectives on the Pedagogies of Educational Transitions

Nadine Ballam, Bob Perry, and Anders Garpelin

There has been a great deal written recently about children starting school, particularly primary school. All of the stakeholders in these transitions to school have been considered, along with matters of readiness – for the child, family, educators, schools and communities; adjustment and adaptation; continuity and change in curricula and learning; and the opportunities, aspirations, expectations and entitlements encompassed in the transformation of roles involved. As the children move from their prior-to-school experiences – preschool, child care, home, other out-of-home care – to school, they experience many changes. One of these is often a change from a primarily play-based pedagogical approach in the prior-to-school setting to perhaps a more structured, even formal pedagogy in school. But what about the pedagogies of the transitions themselves? Children do not stop learning and teachers do not stop teaching as children are in the process of transition to school. There are pedagogies of transition employed. This book explores these pedagogies through the work of an international alliance of transitions to school researchers from five countries – Iceland, Scotland and Sweden (European) and Australia and New Zealand (Antipodean). This alliance is named Pedagogies of Educational Transitions – POET.

N. Ballam (✉)
University of Waikato, Hamilton, New Zealand
e-mail: nballam@waikato.ac.nz

B. Perry
Research Institue for Professional Practice, Learning and Education (RIPPLE),
Charles Sturt University, Albury, NSW, Australia

A. Garpelin
Mälardalen University, Västerås, Sweden

© Springer International Publishing Switzerland 2017
N. Ballam et al. (eds.), *Pedagogies of Educational Transitions*, International
Perspectives on Early Childhood Education and Development 16,
DOI 10.1007/978-3-319-43118-5_1

1.1 Introduction

The transition to school has increasingly become a focus of attention for researchers, policymakers, practitioners, parents and others with an interest in children's lives. This focus has developed, in part, out of a growing recognition of the importance of early experiences and their influence on positive outcomes in later years (Australian Institute of Health and Welfare 2015; Dockett and Perry 2007; Dockett et al. 2014; Organisation for Economic Co-operation and Development [OECD] 2012; Perry et al. 2015; United Nations Children's Fund [UNICEF] 2012).

Increased interest in any field tends to stimulate provocative discussion and debate and the area of educational transitions has not escaped this. Transition itself is a contested phenomenon that has no universally accepted definition (Dockett et al. 2014); what is considered a successful transition might well differ between stakeholders in diverse contexts and cultures and across time. However, there is general agreement that a child's sense of belonging in the new setting marks an optimal transition to school (Brooker 2008; Bulkeley and Fabian 2006; Dockett and Perry 2004). While there is less agreement about how a sense of belonging or a positive transition might be achieved or measured, the discussion and debate exposes the many ways in which it might be conceptualised.

The transition to school is experienced and understood in varied ways in different contexts, many of which are captured in this book. Many years of transitions research have presented ideas including readiness (Dockett and Perry 2009; Graue 2006; Graue and Reineke 2014), continuity (Brooker 2008; Einarsdóttir 2007), adjustment (Margetts 2014) and adaptation (Woodhead and Brooker 2008). All of these ideas are, and should be, continually questioned, challenged, teased out and reshaped into further notions about children's transitions to school.

1.2 Transition-to-School Theories

While '[M]ost researchers see theory as an important aspect of educational research' (Einarsdóttir 2014, p. 21), others point out that there are dangers in adhering too closely to a particular theory. While not always explicitly stated, all of the chapters in this book that report on particular research studies are based in a theory or, perhaps, some combination of theories. The major theories used are identified briefly in this section.

Just as there are many ways for children and other stakeholders to experience transition to school, there are many different theoretical underpinnings utilised in transition-to-school research (Dockett et al. 2014). Much of the work in this book utilises the work of Bronfenbrenner, either through his early conceptualisations of ecological transitions (Bronfenbrenner 1979; Dunlop 2014) or his later bioecological theory, particularly the process-person-context-time (PPCT) model

(Bronfenbrenner and Morris 2006) with its emphasis on proximal processes. Dockett et al. (2014, p. 4) note that:

> The PPCT model provides a great deal of flexibility in researching transition to school. When applied in full, it prompts attention to the relationships and interactions associated with starting school, the characteristics and resources each individual (be they a child, family member, or educator) brings with them to the transition, recognition of the various systems or contexts in which children and families are located, as well as attention to specific events, patterns of interactions and historical context. It provides potential to explore issues of continuity and change, in terms of the individuals, the nature of experiences and interactions they have, the people with whom they interact and the contexts in which they are located. It also recognises that social and cultural contexts are dynamic, affected by processes of continuity and change.

Building on Bronfenbrenner's theories and using other conceptualisations of transition to school is a feature of the book. For example, the conceptualisation of transitions to school using van Gennep's (1960) 'rites of passage' invokes a three-phase vision of transitions in terms of preliminal, liminal and postliminal times and spaces and the ambiguity that children and other stakeholders may find as they move through these phases. Notions of 'bridges' (Garpelin 2014; Huser et al. 2015), 'chasms' (Garpelin 2014) or 'borderlands' (Giroux 2005; Peters 2014) are all invoked from such a conceptualisation.

Elder's (1996) 'life course' theory, which emphasises human agency over time, can be utilised in conjunction with bioecological theory to place transition to school as part of a person's life history. This is particularly useful in studies that reflect on past transitions to school and in the development of the notion of 'transitions capital' (Dunlop 2014).

Many of the chapters in the book utilise a critical theoretical stance. Such a stance goes beyond the nested systems of ecological theory or the location of the child at the centre of the transition process to consider the social, economic and political contexts involved. Critical theory is particularly important in the chapters considering issues of diversity in children's transition to school. In particular, when researching the starting school experiences of Indigenous children, families and communities, both *Kaupapa Māori* research approaches (Pihama 2010) and critical Indigenous research methodology (CIRM) (Brayboy et al. 2011) are brought to bear as culturally appropriate, respectful protocols that are 'rooted in Indigenous knowledge systems, [are] anticolonial and [are] distinctly focused on the needs of communities' (Brayboy et al. 2011, p. 423). The construct of 'cultural interface' (Nakata 2007) also allows a critical, anticolonial theoretical stance on researching children's transition to school that has not been used in previous transition-to-school research.

Underlying each study reported in this book, there is (or are) one or more theories about researching children's start to school. Some of the major ones have been outlined but others are also used. These are not always explicitly stated nor explicitly applied throughout the studies but are there guiding the studies and their reporting. Einarsdóttir (2014) explains her process, which has inspired many of the researchers who have reported their work in this book:

Theories are an important part of educational research. I use theory as a tool to develop research questions and to shed light on the generated data. Theory helps me see what is visible in a new light, notice novel things, and reveal new understandings. I also use it to help me understand the reality that I am investigating and explain what I see, why I see it, and what it means. However, I usually do not explicitly start a study with a specific theory; rather, I let the data help me decide which theory to use. I find that determining the theory beforehand could become restricting and could limit what I see, and how I analyze and interpret what I see. On the other hand, I am well aware that my implicit theories and beliefs about children, childhood, and education influence my decisions about what to study, the design of the study, what I see, and how I interpret it. In that way theory is also a foundation for the study design. (pp. 28–29)

1.3 Pedagogies of Educational Transitions

This book is about pedagogies of educational transitions, particularly those developed and used as children start school. Transition to school provides opportunities for the study of pedagogies as it incorporates spaces and times where (often) different approaches to curriculum, teaching and learning are invoked. It is critical that there is an understanding of the meaning that the editors and authors of this book are using for 'pedagogies of educational transition'. This is a new term that must be defined in a way that is meaningful, but flexible enough to allow its application in many different national, personal, political and cultural contexts.

The working definition of pedagogy for the longitudinal studies undertaken by Sylva, Siraj-Blatchford and their colleagues is:

> … that set of instructional techniques and strategies which enable learning to take place and provide opportunities for the acquisition of knowledge, skills, attitudes and dispositions within a particular social and material context. It refers to the interactive process between teacher and learner and to the learning environment. (Siraj-Blatchford et al. 2002, p. 10)

In 2005, Learning and Teaching Scotland defined 'pedagogy' in the following way:

> Pedagogy is about learning, teaching and development, influenced by the cultural, social and political values and principles we have for children in Scotland, and underpinned by a strong theoretical and practical base. (p. 9)

The equivalent statement in the Australian Early Years Learning Framework defines 'pedagogy' as:

> … early childhood educators' professional practice, especially those aspects that involve building and nurturing relationships, curriculum decision-making, teaching and learning. (Department of Education, Employment and Workplace Relations 2009, p. 9)

These definitions have influenced the authors in this book as they consider pedagogies in educational transitions.

In 2011, the Educational Transitions and Change (ETC) Research Group published the *Transition to School: Position Statement* following intensive work from transitions to school researchers from many countries (Dockett and Perry 2014b). This statement characterised transition to school as a time of opportunities, aspirations, expectations and entitlements for all involved. These constructs, linked to previous definitions of pedagogies in early childhood education, have led Davies (2014) to define 'pedagogies of educational transition' as:

> ... the interactive processes and strategies that enable the development of opportunities, aspirations, expectations and entitlements for children, families, educators, communities and educational systems around transition to school, together with the theories, beliefs, policies and controversies that shape them. (p. 25)

It is this definition which implicitly underlies the chapters in this book and which is explicitly developed in Chap. 12.

1.4 POET International Alliance

This book is the first consolidated publication arising from the Pedagogies of Educational Transitions (POET) international alliance. It is planned to be the first of many such publications.

The POET international alliance was originally developed by six experienced transition-to-school researchers from the five countries involved: Sue Dockett (Charles Sturt University, Australia), Aline-Wendy Dunlop (University of Strathclyde, Scotland), Jóhanna Einarsdóttir (University of Iceland, Iceland), Anders Garpelin (Mälardalen University, Sweden), Bob Perry (Charles Sturt University, Australia) and Sally Peters (University of Waikato, New Zealand). Each of these researchers had many years of experience in the development and implementation of quality research in the area of educational transitions and had published widely. While they had not worked together extensively, they had met at a number of conferences such as those of the American Educational Research Association (AERA), the European Educational Research Association (EERA) and the European Early Childhood Education Research Association (EECERA), including some joint presentations. All were members of the EECERA Special Interest Group, which had been initially co-chaired by Aline-Wendy Dunlop and, since 2011, has been co-chaired by Sue Dockett. Over the last 4 years, between 2012 and 2016, these researchers along with a total of more than 100 of their colleagues have engaged in a series of biannual exchanges focused on educational transitions, as part of the European Union Marie Curie International Research Staff Exchange Scheme (IRSES). Further details about the genesis, vision, purpose, structure, activities and funding of POET are provided in an appendix to this book. For the time being, however, we focus on the product.

1.5   Structure of the Book

This book contains five sections, each of which reflects lenses through which the transition to school is conceptualised by current international scholars.

1.5.1   *Diversity and Inclusion in Transition to School*

Diversity and inclusion have increasingly become central to educational policy documents around the globe (OECD 2012; UNICEF 2012; Woodhead and Moss 2007), with an emphasis on groups of children who might be perceived to be at a disadvantage in many areas, including in their schooling. These groups are consistently reported to include children with learning difficulties or disabilities, children from low socio-economic households, children from ethnic minorities and increasingly, refugee children. Part I of the book considers the transition to school for children from many of these groups.

Hellblom-Thibblin and Marwick (Chap. 2) open this section with an overview of ideas about diversity and educational transitions, written with the background of the authors' own countries – Sweden and Scotland. The authors contend that the way diversity is conceptualised and inclusion is enacted directly influences the way children are perceived and received in educational contexts.

The following three chapters in Part I examine specific groups of children and their transitions into the school setting. Mitchell et al. (Chap. 3) outline a study undertaken with refugee families in New Zealand, exploring the transition from home into an early childhood setting. Their study indicated that an important transitional element for these families was not only bridging oral language but also aspirations, values and beliefs. The findings provide valuable considerations for families, educators and other professionals involved in the transition of refugee children from early childhood to school settings.

In their move from preschool to primary school, many Swedish children transition through preschool class, providing an important context for the study reported in Chap. 4. In this chapter, Hellblom-Thibblin et al. use an ecological model to consider the obstacles and challenges associated with these transitions for children who have learning difficulties and disabilities.

Wilder and Lillvist (Chap. 5) also explore educational transitions for young children with special learning needs, presenting preliminary findings from an ongoing study undertaken with children transitioning from preschool to compulsory school for students with intellectual disabilities (CSSID). Aspects such as the transfer of knowledge, teacher attitudes and collaboration between home and school provide insights into the continuity of learning over the transition period for these children.

1.5.2 Transition to School for Indigenous Children

The theme of diversity and inclusion continues in Part II of this book, with a special focus on Indigenous children from Aotearoa New Zealand, and Australia. In Chap. 6, Hohepa and McIntosh, both Indigenous researchers from Aotearoa New Zealand, and Australia, respectively, provide an overview chapter that considers research related to the transition to school for Indigenous children in these two countries, Indigenous research approaches and the implications of these for educational transitions. The chapter adopts a critical post-colonial lens and demonstrates the importance of critical Indigenous research paradigms.

Hohepa and Paki (Chap. 7) follow with an outline of the history of educational provisions for Māori, the Indigenous people of Aotearoa, New Zealand. With an emphasis on the regeneration of language, cultural identity and values that are important to Māori communities, these authors outline elements that underpin effective transitions for Māori children into both Māori immersion and mainstream educational settings.

In the final chapter of Part II (Chap. 8), Dealtry et al. report on a study that draws from a larger multidisciplinary research project with an Aboriginal community in Australia. The smaller study reported in this chapter takes a social justice view of the way educators conceptualise and engage with Aboriginal children as they transition to school. The authors offer particular insights into the complexities of notions of diversity.

1.5.3 Continuity and Change as Children Start School

Part III of the book explores the notion of continuity, which has been widely debated in terms of its role in the transition to school (Dockett et al. 2014; Dunlop and Fabian 2002). The chapters in this section present continuity and change as being not only about academic learning but also about relationships, pedagogy and practice, curriculum, resources and support (Dockett and Perry 2014a).

Dockett and Einarsdóttir open Part III of this book with a comprehensive overview of research and literature related to continuity and change in educational transitions (Chap. 9). There is critical coverage of the debate around the role of these elements in transitions, and Dockett and Einarsdóttir urge readers to consider the opportunities that both continuity and change offer children, families and other stakeholders in the transition to school.

The other four chapters in this section each explore different aspects of continuity and change in educational transitions. Garðarsdóttir and Ólafsdóttir (Chap. 10) report on a study undertaken collaboratively with preschool educators in Iceland. This study focused on the implementation of the curriculum learning area, 'health and well-being', in the early childhood context and the way this might then be experienced by children when they transition into primary school settings. In Chap. 11, also based on studies in Iceland, Karlsdóttir and Perry explore the role of play in the pedagogies of educational transitions as children move from preschool to primary school. In particular, these authors consider how children and their teachers can use children's participation repertoires (Carr 2001) to promote continuity across the transition.

Curriculum and pedagogy provide the focus for Chap. 12, in which Dockett et al. provide a preliminary analysis of the influence of two recent curriculum reforms in the Australian context. In this analysis, the continuity between curriculum documents for early childhood and school sectors is investigated, and the authors consider what this might mean for children's transitions between these settings. The final chapter of Part III (Chap. 13) describes a study undertaken in Iceland, which focused on mathematics and play. Garðarsdóttir et al. worked with educators in both a preschool and a primary school to establish pedagogical continuity in mathematics learning across the two settings. This study highlights some of the common and differing perspectives between educators in these settings and the way these influence children's transition experiences.

1.5.4   Borderlands, Bridges and Rites of Passage

Transition to school can be explored through the lens of 'crossing borders' (Brooker 2002; Garpelin 2011; Hartley et al. 2012; Peters 2004, 2014). Dockett et al. (2014) reflected that conceptualising the transition to school in this way raises a number of questions about both the border and the borderlands surrounding it and all those involved in ensuring safe passage for children through transition spaces. This section also draws on the work of van Gennep (1960), who conceptualised the transition to school as a 'rite of passage'.

In the opening chapter for Part IV (Chap. 14), Peters and Sandberg consider ways in which educational transitions have been theorised and conceptualised. These authors outline several studies that have used the concepts of traversing borders, crossing bridges and rites of passage to explore points of transition in various ways.

In Chap. 15, Sandberg et al. discuss the implications of pedagogy and practice in Sweden across preschool, preschool class and primary school for children's learning journeys. The authors draw on studies they have undertaken that focus on the activities in each of the three settings, as well as some of the associated challenges for children in their transition through the three school forms in their early years.

1.5.5 Into the Future

Part V explores future directions in educational transitions research. Dunlop (Chap. 16) introduces the idea of transitions as a tool for change, a perspective generated by the Scottish POET team through their ongoing projects. From this perspective, there is less focus on problematising transitions and more on demonstrating that successful transitions can result in positive, transformative changes for all stakeholders.

In Chap. 17, the POET project team leaders from each participating country bring the book to a close with a synthesis of themes emanating throughout the book and suggestions for future research in the field of educational transitions. Dockett et al. emphasise that commonalities from research undertaken in each of the five participating POET alliance countries have the potential to contribute significantly to addressing some of the challenges faced in this area.

1.6 Using This Book

The POET project has been one where some members have been able to sustain their involvement throughout the project's duration from 2012 to 2016, while others have visited the activities intermittently, as their circumstances allowed. In every case, each POET member has received some benefit from his or her involvement and engagement. To a large extent, readers of this book, which has emanated from the POET activities and underlying country projects, will be able to choose their level of engagement with the book – some will want to read it from cover to cover, while some will want to visit only certain sections or even single chapters. The editors and the authors have tried to ensure that these various levels of engagement are possible.

The editors believe that this book reflects the vision of the POET international alliance through collaborative writing and the wide scope of projects reported. While much of the book addresses educational transitions to primary school, there are considerations around educational transitions that are much broader than this. Hence, while the various chapters do consider important challenges and issues around transition to school, we hope that the agenda can be broadened substantially using the information in the book as a base.

From the individual projects reported in this book, the editors and authors know that their work is well received by others. This book is written for educational transitions researchers, policymakers, higher degree candidates and practitioners, in the hope that it will assist them in their own work, as we all strive for optimal educational transitions for all children, families, educators and other stakeholders.

As Dockett et al. highlight in Chap. 17, there is still much to be done and many new and interesting pathways to be explored through further quality research. Some of that will undoubtedly occur as a direct result of the POET international alliance and will be undertaken by POET members. Much of this will be reported in other planned publications from the POET group. However, it is the editors and authors' hope that this book will inspire researchers, policymakers and practitioners beyond POET to choose their pathways and to assist all stakeholders in educational transitions to reach their optima.

Acknowledgements In order for the POET project to function, funding was required. A large part of this funding, allowing exchange of European POET members, came from the Marie Curie International Research Staff Exchange Scheme FP7, conducted by the European Commission. The funding for the New Zealand members, through the New Zealand-EU International Research Staff Exchange Scheme, was supported by government funding and administered by the Royal Society of New Zealand. A small amount of the funding for the Australian contingent was provided by Charles Sturt University. All of these funding sources are gratefully acknowledged. Individual research project funding from many sources will be acknowledged in the relevant chapters.

The editors would also like to acknowledge all of their POET colleagues who not only wrote chapters for this book but also helped in the reviewing of the manuscript and generally provided encouragement during the difficult times that inevitably occur in the editing of such a complex book. Thank you for providing the opportunity for us to bring your work together and showcase what we have achieved in POET over the last 4 years.

A special vote of gratitude goes to Professor Sue Dockett who not only led the writing of a number of the chapters in the book but also provided great support to the editors through her reviewing of all the chapters and provision of advice on structure and approach.

1.7   Collaboration Between Editors

A secret to sustainable and effective research activity in any field of work is for those more experienced to have a willingness to nurture those less experienced and then to put this into practice. At the heart of the POET alliance is the notion of mentoring less experienced colleagues. This notion is tangibly implemented within the context of POET through the promotion of collaboration between researchers at varying stages in their careers and consequently transmission of skills, knowledge and understanding.

In a number of ways, the editorship of this book exemplifies the underlying intention of the POET alliance to be a platform for mentoring. The first editor of this book, Nadine Ballam, is an early-career researcher. The willingness of more experienced researchers, Bob Perry and Anders Garpelin, to take on mentoring roles in this editorial team reflects, in action, precisely what was conceived in the initial planning of the POET collaboration. The existing partnership between these two experienced researchers has provided a safe, dependable foundation upon which someone less experienced can learn. This is significant and exemplifies that it is not only theoretical knowledge and understandings that are being transferred as part of the POET alliance but also the art of research and scholarship.

References

Australian Institute of Health and Welfare. (2015). *Literature review of the impact of early childhood education and care on learning and development: Working paper.* Canberra: Author.

Brayboy, B. M. J., Gough, H. R., Leonard, B., Roehl, R. F., II, & Solyom, J. A. (2011). Reclaiming scholarship: Critical Indigenous research methodologies. In S. D. Lapan, M. T. Quartaroli, & F. J. Riemer (Eds.), *Qualitative research: An introduction to methods and designs* (pp. 423–450). Hoboken: Wiley.

Bronfenbrenner, U. (1979). *The ecology of human development: Experiments in nature and design.* Cambridge, MA: Harvard University Press.

Bronfenbrenner, U., & Morris, P. A. (2006). The bioecological model of human development. In W. Damon & R. M. Lerner (Eds.), *Handbook of child psychology, Vol. 1: Theoretical models of human development* (6th ed., pp. 793–828). New York: Wiley.

Brooker, L. (2002). *Starting school: Young children learning cultures.* Buckingham: Open University Press.

Brooker, L. (2008). *Supporting transitions in the early years.* Maidenhead: Open University Press/McGraw-Hill.

Bulkeley, J., & Fabian, H. (2006). Well-being and belonging during early educational transitions. *International Journal of Transitions in Childhood, 2,* 18–31.

Carr, M. (2001). *Assessment in early childhood settings: Learning stories.* London: Sage.

Davies. J. (2014). *Pedagogies of educational transitions: Continuity and change as children start school in rural areas.* Unpublished research proposal. Charles Sturt University.

Department of Education Employment and Workplace Relations (DEEWR). (2009). *Belonging, being and becoming: The early years learning framework for Australia.* Department of Education Employment and Workplace Relations. https://docs.education.gov.au/system/files/doc/other/belonging_being_and_becoming_the_early_years_learning_framework_for_australia.pdf. Accessed 26 Feb 2015.

Dockett, S., & Perry, B. (2004). What makes a successful transition to school? Views of Australian parents and teachers. *International Journal of Early Years Education, 12*(3), 217–230.

Dockett, S., & Perry, B. (2007). *Starting school: Perceptions, expectations and experiences.* Sydney: UNSW Press.

Dockett, S., & Perry, B. (2009). Readiness for school: A relational construct. *Australasian Journal of Early Childhood, 34*(1), 20–26.

Dockett, S., & Perry, B. (2014a). *Continuity of learning: A resource to support effective transition to school and school age care.* Canberra: Australian Government Department of Education.

Dockett, S., & Perry, B. (2014b). Research to policy: Transition to School Position Statement. In B. Perry, S. Dockett, & A. Petriwskyj (Eds.), *Transitions to school: International research, policy and practice* (pp. 277–294). Dordrecht: Springer.

Dockett, S., Petriwskyj, A., & Perry, B. (2014). Theorising transition: Shifts and tensions. In B. Perry, S. Dockett, & A. Petriwskyj (Eds.), *Transitions to school: International research, policy and practice* (pp. 1–18). Dordrecht: Springer.

Dunlop, A.-W. (2014). Thinking about transitions: One framework or many? Populating the theoretical model over time. In B. Perry, S. Dockett, & A. Petriwskyj (Eds.), *Transitions to school: International research, policy and practice* (pp. 31–46). Dordrecht: Springer.

Dunlop, A.-W., & Fabian, H. (2002). Conclusions. In H. Fabian & A.-W. Dunlop (Eds.), *Transitions in the early years: Debating continuity and progression for children in early education* (pp. 146–154). London: Routledge/Falmer.

Educational Transitions and Change (ETC) Research Group. (2011). *Transition to school: Position statement.* Albury-Wodonga: Research Institute for Professional Practice, Learning and Education, Charles Sturt University. http://www.csu.edu.au/faculty/educat/edu/transitions/publications/Position-Statement.pdf. Accessed 9 Aug 2015.

Einarsdóttir, J. (2007). Children's voices on the transition from preschool to primary school. In A.-W. Dunlop & H. Fabian (Eds.), *Informing transitions in the early years: Research, policy and practice* (pp. 74–91). Maidenhead: Open University.

Einarsdóttir, J. (2014). Reading of media accounts of transition to school in Iceland. In B. Perry, S. Dockett, & A. Petriwskyj (Eds.), *Transitions to school: International research, policy and practice* (pp. 21–30). Dordrecht: Springer.

Elder, G. H., Jr. (1996). Human lives in changing societies: Life course and developmental insights. In R. B. Cairns, G. H. Elder Jr., & E. J. Costello (Eds.), *Developmental science* (pp. 31–62). New York: Cambridge University Press.

Garpelin, A. (2011). *Borderlands, bridges and rites of passage: Understanding children's learning journeys from preschool into school.* Application. Swedish Research Council, VR: Västerås: Mälardalen University.

Garpelin, A. (2014). Transition to school: A rite of passage in life. In B. Perry, S. Dockett, & A. Petriwskyj (Eds.), *Transitions to school: International research, policy and practice* (pp. 117–128). Dordrecht: Springer.

Giroux, H. A. (2005). *Border crossings* (2nd ed.). New York: Routledge.

Graue, E. (2006). The answer is readiness – Now what is the question? *Early Education and Development, 17*(1), 43–56.

Graue, E., & Reineke, J. (2014). The relation of research on readiness to research/practice of transitions. In B. Perry, S. Dockett, & A. Petriwskyj (Eds.), *Transitions to school: International research, policy and practice* (pp. 159–173). Dordrecht: Springer.

Hartley, C., Rogers, P., Smith, J., Peters, S., & Carr, M. (2012). *Across the border: A community negotiates the transition from early childhood to primary school.* Wellington: NZCER.

Huser, C., Dockett, S., & Perry, B. (2015). Transition to school: Revisiting the bridge metaphor. *European Early Childhood Education Research Journal.* doi:10.1080/1350293X.2015.1102414.

Learning and Teaching Scotland. (2005). *Let's talk about pedagogy.* Edinburgh: Scottish Executive. http://www.educationscotland.gov.uk/images/talkpedagogy_tcm4-193218.pdf. Accessed 17 May 2016.

Margetts, K. (2014). Transition and adjustment to school. In B. Perry, S. Dockett, & A. Petriwskyj (Eds.), *Transitions to school: International research, policy and practice* (pp. 75–87). Dordrecht: Springer.

Nakata, M. (2007). *Disciplining the savages: Savaging the disciplines.* Canberra: Aboriginal Studies Press.

Organisation for Economic Co-operation and Development (OECD). (2012). *Education today 2013: The OECD perspective.* Paris: OECD Publishing.

Perry, B., MacDonald, A., & Gervasoni, A. (2015). Mathematics and transition to school: Theoretical frameworks and practical implications. In B. Perry, A. MacDonald, & A. Gervasoni (Eds.), *Mathematics and transition to school: International perspectives.* Singapore: Springer.

Peters, S. (2004). *"Crossing the border": An interpretive study of children making the transition to school.* Unpublished PhD thesis. University of Waikato, New Zealand.

Peters, S. (2014). Chasms, bridges and borderlands: A transitions research 'across the border' from early childhood education to school in New Zealand. In B. Perry, S. Dockett, & A. Petriwskyj (Eds.), *Transitions to school: International research, policy and practice* (pp. 105–116). Dordrecht: Springer.

Pihama, L. (2010). Kaupapa Māori theory: Transforming theory in Aotearoa. *He Pukenga Kōrero: A Journal of Māori Studies, 9*(2), 5–14.

Siraj-Blatchford, I., Sylva, K., Muttock, S., Gilden, R., & Bell, D. (2002). *Researching effective pedagogy in the early years.* London: Department for Education and Skills.

United Nations Children's Fund (UNICEF). (2012). *The state of the world's children: Children in an urban world.* New York: UNICEF.

van Gennep, A. (1960). *The rites of passage* (B.V. Minika & G. L. Caffee, Trans.). London: Routledge/Kegan Paul.

Woodhead, M., & Brooker, L. (2008). A sense of belonging. *Early Childhood Matters, 111,* 3–6.

Woodhead, M., & Moss, P. (2007). *Early childhood and primary education: Transitions in the lives of young children.* Milton Keynes: The Open University.

Part I
Diversity and Inclusion in Transition to School

Chapter 2
Diversity and Pedagogies in Educational Transitions

Tina Hellblom-Thibblin and Helen Marwick

This chapter presents issues regarding diversity and inclusion from different perspectives, involving various aspects of children and young people's learning and development related to educational transitions and practices. Several factors and conditions are highlighted as part of the explanation of how diversity can be understood and addressed pedagogically in different educational transitions. The chapter takes into account important issues on meeting diversity from an inclusive perspective with regard to the variety of cultural, socio-economic and individual conditions relating to young children's learning and development.

2.1 Introduction

All children have individual backgrounds, and, during their learning journeys from preschool to compulsory school, they can encounter different educational environments with new cultures, rules, norms and relationships (Corsaro and Molinari 2006; Flum and Kaplan 2012). These journeys may pose challenges and difficulties (Fabian and Dunlop 2006).

Peters (2014) emphasised the importance of recognising diversity within groups, with the focus being placed on observing different transitions and taking into account the complexity of children's learning journeys from early childhood to later school years. Diversity includes different cultures, social backgrounds, ethnic origins and languages. Other aspects of diversity include children's development in

T. Hellblom-Thibblin (✉)
Mälardalen University, Västerås, Sweden
e-mail: tina.hellblom-thibblin@mdh.se

H. Marwick
University of Strathclyde, Glasgow, UK

© Springer International Publishing Switzerland 2017
N. Ballam et al. (eds.), *Pedagogies of Educational Transitions*, International
Perspectives on Early Childhood Education and Development 16,
DOI 10.1007/978-3-319-43118-5_2

different pedagogical settings, socialisation and identity development (Flum and Kaplan 2012; Lago 2014). The competence of teachers appears to be of great value in order to be able to meet children's needs successfully (Dockett and Perry 2009). It is thus valuable to look at inclusive schools from the perspective of different pedagogical ideas and traditions (Göransson 2006).

An ecological approach to a child's development (Bronfenbrenner and Morris 2006) makes it clear that children's individual experiences in different educational settings result from interactions between children and adults, requirements and expectations. Children, families and teachers may experience changes in relationships when entering the school context. For some children, entering school may present difficulty and even a feeling of anxiety (Dockett et al. 2011). Therefore, pedagogies are important for creating inclusive environments for all children's needs and requirements and are significant in educational transitions. This chapter introduces issues that are discussed in more detail in the following chapters in this section.

2.2   Diversity in Educational Settings

Diversity is an overarching concept, often used to describe the differences between children in educational settings. This term is also used when discussing the social backgrounds of individuals and their varying cultural, ethnic and language origins, as well as their learning and behaviour-related difficulties (Hjörne and Säljö 2014; Margetts 2002; Nusbaum 2013; Petriwskyj 2010). Other aspects of diversity include children's development in different pedagogical settings, socialisation and identity development (Flum and Kaplan 2012; Lago 2014). It is clear that the concept of diversity covers more than traditions and cultural expressions (Lunneblad 2006).

In recent years, diversity has been conceptualised as encompassing an increasing range of varied circumstances in relation to the needs and identities of individual children. Valuing these differences is central to promoting and achieving equality of opportunity and positive relations in the teaching and learning environment. The diversity of children in different educational activities can be perceived as either an asset or a challenge. Despite diversity often being associated with positive values, it is not an unproblematic concept (Hjörne and Säljö 2014). In other words, the term can be discussed from different points of departure and perspectives. One of the problems associated with discussions about diversity is the question of who decides or defines the differences and on what grounds (Lahdenperä 2011). The term can therefore be understood in different ways; it could be based on notions that are conceptualised in discussions about children in different educational environments, such as preschool and school (Markström 2005). The ways children are discussed and perceived influence how they are received (Hacking 1999; Harwood and Allen 2014; Mowat 2010).

Despite its potentially positive meaning, the term 'diversity' is often associated with problems and difficulties. There are different circumstances to be considered when exploring this issue. The ways children's differences are viewed can be linked, during various periods, to society's actual ideals and attitudes towards deviation. During the course of history, different terms have been used to represent the concept of diversity. What was regarded at the beginning of the twentieth century as child-rearing problems or moral 'aberrations' are increasingly becoming seen as phenomena or conditions related to social factors or as states of ill health or syndromes (Hellblom-Thibblin 2004). The ideals that emerge during different periods can affect people's views and, thereby, understanding of differences and diversity.

Another concern is the way children's different preconditions for learning acquire significance in the transitions from preschool to the different levels of compulsory school. All children, with their individual backgrounds, need to be provided with opportunities in preschool and compulsory school to develop and feel the joy of learning and overcoming difficulties. Hellblom-Thibblin (2004) argued that knowledge and understanding about children's different abilities and experiences can contribute to a variety of educational measures on both an individual basis and at a more general organisational level.

2.3 Educational Transitions and Pedagogical Approaches

Teaching professionals, parents and children's perceptions of the transition period are of great importance, as are the clear gathering of information, effective communication, a responsive environment and inclusive pedagogy for all children entering into an educational setting (Dunlop et al. 2008). The term 'transition' can be understood as a phenomenon 'involving a range of interactions and processes over time, experienced in different ways by different people in different contexts' (Dockett et al. 2014, p. 3). The transitions from a home environment to a preschool environment and then to formal schooling are important events in a child's learning journey (Ainscow and Miles 2008; Garpelin 2014). Moving to the first year at school is also an important educational transition for children (Einarsdóttir 2006; Sandberg 2012) and can have consequences for future transitions in school (Dockett et al. 2011). Knowledge of the variation in children's needs is important for developing different pedagogies in educational transitions (Dockett and Perry 2009; Peters 2014).

Transitions to school can be complex. In school settings, children of various backgrounds come together. Peers and Fleer (2014) emphasised the value of understanding how group affiliations or the sense of belonging to a group can alter and vary for a child in relation to transitions from preschool and first grade in primary school.

Teachers' knowledge and pedagogical strategies are important for supporting successful transitions to school (Petriwskyj et al. 2014). The ways in which children with various conditions are received, and the opportunities created for their participation in different groups, are important in developing a sense of belonging (Ackesjö 2014). While transition can be a point of stress and vulnerability for children and families, it can also be a potential tool or opportunity for change (Fabian 2007). Transitions can be related to specific events or substantial roles or identities in a society (Garpelin 2003). Several studies have highlighted the teacher's role in successful transitions and for learning (Dockett and Perry 2004), as well as educational leaders' views on how to work with children who need additional support in preschool and school (Lindqvist and Nilholm 2013).

Educational transitions between preschool and school can pay attention to relationships (Corsaro and Molinari 2008) or processes. Lago (2014) regarded identity, culture, status and role as parts of these processes, while Noel (2010) saw the relationship between the preschool and the primary school, as well as other stakeholders, as important in the transition to school. Thomas and Dykes (2011) called for new practical and relevant proposals to promote successful transitions for all pupils. The importance of a well-established plan for the transition from preschool to primary school has been highlighted in several studies (Margetts 2002; Rimm-Kaufman et al. 2000). A transition-to-school programme may include planned activities or processes in which a number of people collaborate to contribute to a successful transition. Teachers' knowledge is a key factor in educational transitions and hence for educational strategies (Peters 2014).

2.4   A Dynamic Ecological Approach to Transitions

In current research there is consensus that development occurs through the interaction of many different factors. A dynamic ecological approach notes the importance of early transitions for later school success (Dockett and Perry 2004). The ecological systems model (Bronfenbrenner and Morris 2006) provides a framework for understanding multiple levels of influence on children's learning and development, such as those in various educational transitions. According to transitions researchers, there are several interactive variables to consider, such as the interactions between individuals and the contexts in which relationships are created (Corsaro and Molinari 2006; Dockett et al. 2014; Peters 2014):

> The combination of interactions, change and time sets up a dynamic model in which the transition to school can be explored by focusing on the overlapping or intersecting contexts of children's experience. (Dockett et al. 2014, p. 5)

Learning can be regarded as a social activity arising from interactions between individuals and the environment. Research shows that learning, inclusion and diversity interact with one another (Aalsvoort et al. 2012). Learning is a process in which identities are formed, and, during transitions from one school form to another, these identities can change and develop (Mowat 2014). To promote learning and development for all children, it is important to consider their different backgrounds in order to adapt successfully to their needs and hence provide opportunities to experience meaningfulness, comprehensibility and context in their educational lives (Antonovsky 1979; Krasny et al. 2010). In a study undertaken by Mowat (2014), issues of the stigmatisation of pupils with emotional and behaviour-related problems were reported. The study demonstrated the need for a deeper understanding of the variables affecting children's group identification and interactions with one another, in order to create a feeling of inclusion rather than a feeling of social isolation in educational settings.

The diagnostic process encompasses a form of identification, mapping and assessment, implying a categorisation. To understand the emergence of certain categorisations, Hacking (1999) takes his point of departure from a model he calls the 'ecological metaphor'. 'Ecological' refers to the fact that there are different conditions in the environment that are significant in a categorisation process. The model focuses on medical, biological and social conditions. Based on this perspective, it is likely that many factors are important for learning.

2.5 The Implementation of Inclusion in Practice Regarding Children with Special Educational Needs

Since the beginning of the twenty-first century, the concept of inclusion in education for children with special educational needs has become widely recognised, and the 'presumption of mainstreaming' entered legislation in 2003 in Scotland, following the Standards in Scotland's Schools etc. Act (Scottish Government 2000). The concept of inclusion focused attention on understanding the needs of children with disabilities and the importance of the responsiveness of the education environment in promoting mental well-being in, and encouraging active participation from, these children.

In several studies, inclusion is described as a process rather than a fixed condition, with the key objective of offering education to all children (United Nations Educational Science and Cultural Organisation [UNESCO] 1994, 2007). The emphasis on inclusion of all children and young people in mainstream schools presents major challenges for all teachers and marks a new agenda in the perception of diversity (Ferguson 2008; Petriwskyj 2010). According to Ainscow and Miles (2008), inclusion implies (based on the purpose of providing effective education for all children and young people) the biggest challenge yet seen for the schools of our time. These authors noted the importance of paying attention to strategies that may be causing barriers in children's learning and participation and of studying the underlying ideas of the approach adopted in inclusive educational practice. They argued that the implementation of inclusion in practice requires a regard for diversity.

Arguments remain about the effectiveness of inclusion of all children with special educational needs, and opinions on how inclusion can be achieved vary widely (Obiakor et al. 2012). An important outcome when examining inclusive practices is the focus on considering the needs of all children in an educational setting and the appreciation that for any child, a need for support can arise from a range of factors.

These may include a temporary illness or transient family circumstances, as well as long-term health conditions. This understanding informs the concept of additional support needs (ASNs) in Scotland, which acknowledges that the need for additional support can arise from multiple situational factors, which may be short or long term in nature and can occur for any children at different points in their experience.

It is important to create opportunities for all children and young people to learn and develop in spite of their diverse backgrounds. Teachers' knowledge of children's different learning conditions and development can contribute to pedagogical strategies to meet the variety of learning approaches of different children. The view of a child's different capabilities may be relevant to the pedagogies to which teachers contribute with regard to inclusion and educational transitions.

2.6 Pedagogies in Inclusive Educational Settings

In an inclusive school, it is assumed that all children and young people, regardless of disability or other potential obstacles, are to be integrated into the school community. Current research shows that the teacher's role is of great importance when working towards achieving inclusion and when working to create learning opportunities for all children. Language and communication are important aspects to consider in studies dealing with transitions from preschool to school (Ackesjö 2014).

A study conducted by Göransson et al. (2015), in which students with intellectual disability and students with no disabilities participated together in lessons in mathematics, showed that children with varying abilities could attend the same class and learn together. This demonstrates the importance of creating conditions for collaboration between different educational settings (Peters 2010). The educational models to which this applies imply both inclusion and peer learning (Vygotsky 1978). Research has also shown that it is relevant to observe children or pupils in their everyday environment in order to be able to gain in-depth knowledge regarding their needs (Westman Andersson 2013). Studies have highlighted the importance of teachers' knowledge of a child as a pedagogical asset in meeting all children's different needs sufficiently and efficiently (Harwood and Allen 2014), especially in connection with transitions and inclusion (Ferguson 2008; Petriwskyj 2010).

Achieving positive results at school is a challenge for many young people, especially those with disabilities. Transitions to school should be based on cooperation between those involved in this process, to ensure that children have positive experiences during their time in school (Ainscow and Miles 2008). A study conducted by Dunlop and colleagues (2008) found that communication between parents and teachers was essential in supporting a positive transition experience for children entering formal schooling. The study also pointed out the importance of creating an engaging and welcoming environment when working towards the aim of successful inclusion for all in the educational setting. This is believed to have a positive impact on the sense of belonging experienced both by the children and their parents. It is clear from the results of a study undertaken by Moen (2008) that the ways in which teachers invite children to learn are of importance to the children and thereby also for children's continued learning journeys.

Children develop different strategies for dealing with school requirements, which means that their experiences of schooling and learning journeys can vary. Bronfenbrenner and Morris (2006) stressed the importance of the interaction between adults and children in creating opportunities for 'healthy' development. Students' well-being has an impact on their learning as well as on their social development (White et al. 2013). Research has shown there is a need for deeper understanding of what different school environments and transitions could actually mean for various children's learning and development, especially in the early school years. The idea of inclusion is based on understandings about, and moves for, prevention of social isolation. This is something Slee (2013) identified as a challenge. He problematised the way inclusion works in practice and argued that more focus needs to be placed on the way children in need of special additional support can be provided with opportunities for involvement and participation in class activities. He called for the implementation of learning communities that can accommodate all children working in an inclusive school.

2.7 Vulnerability of Children and Inclusive Educational Settings

The number of diagnoses of children with special needs in educational settings, and therefore categorisations of children's needs, is increasing. This has an impact on the way these children are met in various educational transitions. Studies of inclusive practices have highlighted the importance of educators' attitudes and beliefs about disability. Children's behaviour problems are often described in terms of difficulties in concentration, problems in attentiveness or interaction difficulties, but also more specifically as part of a medical condition, such as ADHD, ADD or other syndrome diagnoses (Jacobsson 2004). These diagnostic terms have been prominent in various debates in the educational world during the last few decades (Mooij and Smeets 2009).

Getting it right for every child (GIRFEC) (Scottish Government 2016) is an approach that provides support for children and young people and their families through the integrated involvement of all people working with the child. A process of staged intervention is outlined, to enable support for a child to be in place at the earliest point of concern, rather than when a crisis has arisen. Issues remain, however, for supporting all children in reaching their potential and experiencing positive well-being in their school environments. Research has, for example, indicated the vulnerability to bullying of children on the autism spectrum, when attending mainstream educational settings (Humphrey and Hebron 2015).

Additionally, a child's social background and communication environment have been found to significantly affect later language development outcomes and school 'readiness' (Roulstone et al. 2011). In Scotland, for example, a marked gap in attainment has been identified for children from economically disadvantaged backgrounds in comparison to children from more economically advantaged backgrounds (Sosu and Ellis 2014), and this gap widens as children move further through the school system. Household income and parental educational attainment level are two other factors that have been found to be associated with distinct discrepancies in language development and cognitive abilities in children at the ages of 3 years and 5 years (Bradshaw 2011).

Almost 10 % of children in UK schools are reported to have a mental health diagnosis (Layard and Dunn 2009; Scottish Government 2008), and a focus is being placed on supporting children's mental health (HM Inspectorate of Education [HMIE] 2011). Marwick and Sosu (2014) found that the most frequently identified type of ASN for 6-year-old children in Scottish schools was 'social and behavioural' needs, and this ASN was linked strongly to parental perceptions of hyperactivity and difficulties in conduct and peer relationships in the children at the ages of 4 and 5 years. Social, emotional and behavioural difficulties (SEBD) describe a range of difficulties that children might experience that can be understood to be the result of nonoptimal early experiences, difficult family relationships, lack of effective behaviour management or lack of ways of engaging children effectively within the school.

All of these aspects point to the importance of creating conditions that are effective for supporting all children's development and learning, based on the idea of an inclusive education. Research has shown that despite inclusion, it is difficult to avoid categorising children's abilities, especially those with challenging behaviour, as a basis for special educational efforts (Graham and Harwood 2011).

2.8 The Link Between Inclusion, Pedagogies in Transitions and Diversity

The importance of teachers' pedagogies regarding diversity, inclusion and learning is evident in research today. Teachers have an important role in building knowledge about the different needs of children and creating the prerequisites for diverse learning communities (Slee 2013). It is clear that the challenges and dilemmas related to transitions have a common starting point in the task of meeting the diverse needs of children. Several studies have made connections between inclusion and diversity and children's sense of belonging (Crouch et al. 2014; Leggett and Ford 2015; Mineur 2013; Peers and Fleer 2014). Research has shown the need for a special focus on pedagogical changes associated with transition to school and diversity (Petriwskyj et al. 2014). The learning environment is key in supporting the diverse needs of children, and it should include flexibility of curricular arrangements and appropriate approaches to teaching and learning (Scottish Government 2009). An inclusive pedagogy approach in classroom practice should respond effectively to the diverse needs of all children (Moscardini 2014).

Inclusion means that all children, regardless of their different capabilities and experiences, should be able to be active participants in a community. Differences are regarded as an asset or as a natural variation among different individuals. The work of developing an inclusive school means deepening the knowledge of obstacles in the environment for those with disability, how these obstacles can be addressed, and highlighting the importance of different types of disabilities in relation to 'inclusive measures' (Bines and Lei 2011). Issues relating to these areas are complex. Studies have highlighted the need for teachers' skills and knowledge about different disabilities and the different needs of children to be developed in order to create conditions that enable successful transitions (Petriwskyj et al. 2014).

2.9   Conclusion

The issues and areas highlighted in this chapter include conditions that are significant for understanding opportunities associated with pedagogies in educational transitions. The question still remains as to how understanding can be deepened to address diversity from an inclusive perspective, regarding individual capabilities and experiences.

Various explanations, theories and perspectives contribute to views about how diversity can be understood and met within pedagogical approaches. The different perspectives referred to in this chapter show the complexity of educational transitions, diversity and pedagogies. Knowledge regarding how to create and evolve relevant pedagogies in different educational transitions is required by those who work with children. In summary, current research highlights both challenges and obstacles based on equivalent aspects and democratic conditions in the inclusive school that children can be faced with during their development.

As presented in this overview, recent research has shown a clear link between children's diversity, ambitions for inclusion and teachers' pedagogical strategies in supporting children in their transitions between the different stages at school. Well-established planning is crucial for giving children the best opportunities to make these transitions a positive experience. In an inclusive school, children's different prerequisites and experiences are of importance and special attention is paid to this in early transitions. Research has shown that a successful transition experience has a positive impact on a child's continued learning journey.

Pedagogies in educational settings deal with attitudes, environmental accommodations, learning opportunities, teachers' knowledge and collaboration strategies. In this section, several chapters have examined the key areas of studies within inclusive criteria, such as cultural identity, poverty, disability and teaching professionals' perceptions of inclusion and diversity. There are many challenges in trying to gain in-depth knowledge, based on relevant pedagogies, for the purpose of creating good conditions for all children in their learning journeys in educational transitions.

References

Aalsvoort, G. M., Abreu, G., & Hjörne, E. (Eds.). (2012). *Learning, social interaction and diversity exploring identities in school practices*. Rotterdam: Sense.

Ackesjö, H. (2014). *Barns övergångar till och från förskoleklass. Gränser, identiteter och (dis) kontinuiteter* [Children's transitions to and from preschool class. Borders, identities and (dis) continuities]. Thesis in Pedagogic. Kalmar: Linnéuniversitetet.

Ainscow, M., & Miles, S. (2008). Making education for all inclusive: Where next? *Prospects, 38*, 15–34.

Antonovsky, A. (1979). *Hälsans mysterium* [The mystery of health]. Stockholm: Natur och Kultur.

Bines, H., & Lei, P. (2011). Disability and education: The longest road to inclusion. *International Journal of Educational Development, 31*, 419–424.

Bradshaw, P. (2011). *Growing up in Scotland: Changes in child cognitive ability in the pre-school years*. Edinburgh: Scottish Government.

Bronfenbrenner, U., & Morris, P. (2006). The bioecological model of human development. In W. Damon & R. M. Lerner (Eds.), *Handbook of child psychology Vol 1. Theoretical models of human development* (6th ed., pp. 793–828). New York: Wiley.

Corsaro, W. A., & Molinari, L. (2006). *I Compagni: Understanding children's transition from preschool to elementary school*. New York: Teachers College Press.

Corsaro, W. A., & Molinari, L. (2008). Policy and practice in Italian children's transition from preschool to elementary school. *Research in Comparative and International Education, 3*(3), 250–265.

Crouch, R., Keys, B., & McMahon, S. (2014). Student–teacher relationships matter for school inclusion: School belonging, disability, and school transitions. *Journal of Prevention & Intervention in the Community, 42*(1), 20–30.

Dockett, S., & Perry, B. (2004). What makes a successful transition to school? Views of Australian parents and teachers. *International Journal of Early Years Education, 12*(3), 217–230.

Dockett, S., & Perry, B. (2009). Readiness for school: A relational construct. *Australasian Journal of Early Childhood, 34*(1), 20–27.

Dockett, S., Perry, B., & Kearney, E. (2011). Starting school with special needs: Issues for families with complex support needs as their children start school. *Exceptionality Education International, 21*(2), 45–61.

Dockett, S., Petriwskyj, A., & Perry, B. (2014). Theorising transition: Shifts and tensions. In B. Perry, S. Dockett, & A. Petriwskyj (Eds.), *Transitions to school: International research, policy and practice*. Dordrecht: Springer.

Dunlop, A.-W., Lee, P., Fee, J., Hughes, A., Grieve A., & Marwick, H. (2008). *Positive behaviour in the early years: Perceptions of staff, service providers and parents in managing and promoting positive behaviour in early years and early primary settings*. Full report. http://www.scotland.gov.uk/238252. Accessed 18 Mar 2015.

Einarsdóttír, J. (2006). From preschool to school. When different contexts meet. *Scandinavian Journal of Educational Research, 50*(2), 165–184.

Fabian, H. (2007). Informing transitions. In A.-W. Dunlop & H. Fabian (Eds.), *Informing transitions in the early years. Research, policy and practice*. Maidenhead: Open University Press.

Fabian, H., & Dunlop, A.-W. (2006). *Outcomes of good practice in transition processes for children entering primary school*. Paris: UNESCO.

Ferguson, D. (2008). International trends in inclusive education: The continuing challenge to teach each one and everyone. *European Journal of Special Needs Education, 23*(2), 109–120.

Flum, H., & Kaplan, A. (2012). Identity formation in educational settings: A contextualized view of theory and research in practice. *Contemporary Educational Psychology, 37*(3), 240–245.

Garpelin, A. (2003). *Ung i skolan. Om övergångar, klasskamrater, gemenskap och marginalisering* [Young in school: About transitions, classmates, community, and marginalization]. Lund: Studentlitteratur.

Garpelin, A. (2014). Transition to school: A rite of passage in life. In B. Perry, S. Dockett, & A. Petriwskyj (Eds.), *Transitions to school: International research, policy and practice.* Dordrecht: Springer.

Göransson, K. (2006). Pedagogical traditions and conditions for inclusive education. *Scandinavian Journal of Disability Research, 8*(1), 67–74.

Göransson, K., Hellblom-Thibblin, T., & Axdorph, E. (2015). A conceptual approach to teaching mathematics to students with intellectual disability. *Scandinavian Journal of Educational Research, 59*(1), 1–19.

Graham, L. J., & Harwood, V. (2011). Developing capabilities for social inclusion: Engaging diversity through inclusive school communities. *International Journal of Inclusive Education, 15*(1), 135–152.

Hacking, I. (1999). *The social construction of what?* Cambridge, MA: Harvard University Press.

Harwood, V., & Allen, J. (2014). *Psychopathology at school. Theorizing mental disorders in education.* New York: Routledge.

Hellblom-Thibblin, T. (2004). *Kategorisering av barns "problem" i skolans värld: en undersökning av skolhälsovårdsrapporter läsåren 1944/45-1988/89* [Categorization of children's problems in school. A study of health care reports]. Doctoral thesis, Uppsala university, Acta Universitatis Upsaliensis. Uppsala Studies in Education, 106.

Hjörne, E., & Säljö, R. (2014). Representing diversity in education: Student identities in contexts of learning and instruction. *International Journal of Educational Research, 63,* 1–4.

HM Inspectorate of Education (HMIE). (2011). *Count us in: Mind over matter. Supporting and promoting mental and emotional wellbeing.* http://www.hmie.gov.uk/documents/publication/mom-01.pdf. Accessed 22 Mar 2015.

Humphrey, N., & Hebron, J. (2015). Bullying of children and adolescents with autism spectrum conditions: A 'state of the field' review. *International Journal of Inclusive Education, 19*(8), 845–862.

Jacobsson, I. -L. (2004). *Diagnosen I skolan. En studie av skolsituationer för elever med syndromdiagnos* [Diagnosis at school – A study of school situations of pupils with a syndrome-diagnosis]. Doctoral thesis. Acta Universitatis Gothoburgensis. Göteborg Studies in Educational Sciences, 185, Göteborgs universitet.

Krasny, M. E., Lundholm, C., & Plummer, R. (2010). Environmental education, resilience, and learning: Reflection and moving forward. *Environmental Education Research, 16*(5), 665–672.

Lago, L. (2014). *"Mellanklass kan man kalla det". Om tid och meningsskapande vid övergången från förskoleklass till årskurs ett* ["You could say in-between class": Time and meaning-making in the transition from preschool class to first grade]. Doctoral thesis. Linköping: Linköping universitet.

Lahdenperä, P. (2011). Mångfald, jämlikhet och jämställdhet – interkulturellt lärande och integration. I P. Lahdenperä (Red.), Forskningscirkel – arena för verksamhetsutveckling i mångfald (s. 15–43) [Diversity, equality and equal opportunities – intercultural learning and integration]. *Studies in Social Sciences, Forskningsrapport,* 1. Västerås: Mälardalens högskola.

Layard, R., & Dunn, J. (2009). *A good childhood: Searching for values in a competitive age. The landmark report for the children's society.* London: Penguin.

Leggett, N., & Ford, M. (2015). Group time experiences: Belonging, being and becoming through active participation within early childhood communities. *Early Childhood Education Journal.* doi:10.1007/s10643-015-0702-9.

Lindqvist, G., & Nilholm, C. (2013). Making schools inclusive? Educational leaders' views on how to work with children in need of special support. *International Journal of Inclusive Education, 17*(1), 95–110.

Lunneblad, J. (2006). *Förskolan och mångfalden. En etnografisk studie på en förskola i ett multietniskt område* [Preschool and diversity: An ethnographic study of a kindergarten in a multi-ethnic area]. Acta Univeristatis Gothoburgensis, Göteborg Studies in Educational Sciences 247, Göteborgs universitet.

Margetts, K. (2002). Transition to school: Complexity and diversity. *European Early Childhood Education Research Journal, 10*(2), 103–114.

Markström, A.-M. (2005). *Förskolan som normaliseringspraktik: en etnografisk studie* [Preschool as a normalizing practice – An ethnographic study]. Doctoral thesis. Linköping: Linköpings universitet.

Marwick, H., & Sosu, E. (2014). *Predictors of additional support needs (ASN) in Scottish schools.* Paper presented at the European Early Childhood Educational Research Association annual conference. Crete, Greece.

Mineur, T. (2013). *Skolformens komplexitet – elevers erfarenheter av skolvardag och tillhörighet i gymnasiesärskolan* [The complexity of a special type of school – Pupils' experiences of everyday life and sense of belonging in upper secondary schools for pupils with intellectual disability]. Studies from the Swedish Institute for Disability Research, *51*. Örebro: Örebro universitet.

Moen, T. (2008). Inclusive educational practice: Results of an empirical study. *Scandinavian Journal of Educational Research, 52*(1), 59–75.

Mooij, T., & Smeets, E. (2009). Towards systemic support of pupils with emotional and behavioural disorders. *International Journal of Inclusive Education, 13*(6), 597–616.

Moscardini, L. (2014). Developing equitable elementary classroom through teachers learning about children's mathematical thinking: Cognitively guided instruction as an inclusive pedagogy. *Teaching and Teacher Education, 43*(10), 69–79.

Mowat, G. J. (2010). Towards the development of self-regulation in pupils experiencing social and emotional behavioural difficulties (SEBD). *Emotional and Behavioural Difficulties, 15*(3), 189–206.

Mowat, G. J. (2014). 'Inclusion – That word!' Examining some of the tensions in supporting pupils experiencing social, emotional and behavioural difficulties/needs. *Emotional and Behavioural Difficulties.* doi:10.1080/13632752.2014.927965.

Noel, A. (2010). Perceptions of school readiness in one Queensland primary school. *Australasian Journal of Early Childhood, 35*(2), 28–35.

Nusbaum, E. A. (2013). Vulnerable to exclusion: The place for segregated education within conceptions of inclusion. *International Journal of Inclusive Education, 17*(12), 1295–1311.

Obiakor, F. E., Harris, M., Mutua, K., Rotatori, A., & Algozzine, B. (2012). Making inclusion work in general education classrooms. *Education and Treatment of Children, 35*(3), 477–490.

Peers, C., & Fleer, M. (2014). The theory of 'belonging': Defining concepts used within belonging, being and becoming: The Australian Early Years Learning Framework. *Educational Philosophy and Theory: Incorporating ACCESS, 46*(8), 914–928.

Peters, S. (2010). Shifting the lens: Re-framing the view of learners and learning during the transition from early childhood education to school in New Zealand. In D. Jindal-Snape (Ed.), *Educational transitions: Moving stories from around the world* (pp. 68–84). New York: Routledge.

Peters, S. (2014). Chasms, bridges and borderlands: A transitions research 'across the border' from early childhood education to school in New Zealand. In B. Perry, S. Dockett, & A. Petriwskyj (Eds.), *Transition to school: International research, policy and practice* (pp. 105–116). Dordrecht: Springer.

Petriwskyj, A. (2010). Diversity and inclusion in the early years. *International Journal of Inclusive Education, 14*(2), 195–212.

Petriwskyj, A., Thorpe, K., & Tayler, C. (2014). Towards inclusion: Provision for diversity in the transition to school. *International Journal of Early Years Education, 22*(4), 359–379.

Rimm-Kaufman, S. E., Pianta, R., & Cox, M. J. (2000). Teachers' judgements of problems in the transition to kindergarten. *Early Childhood Research Quarterly, 15*(2), 147–166.

Roulstone, S., Law, J., Rush, R., Clegg, J., & Peters, T. (2011). *Investigating the role of language in children's early educational outcomes*. UK Government. https://www.gov.uk/government/uploads/system/.../DFE-RR134. Accessed 2 May 2015.

Sandberg, G. (2012). *På väg in i skolan. Om villkor för olika barns delaktighet och skriftspråks-slärande* [On their way into school. About conditions for participation and learning] (Studia Didactica Upsaliensia 6). Uppsala: Acta Universitatis Upsaliensis.

Scottish Government. (2000). *Standards in Scotland's schools etc. Act 2000*. http://www.gov.scot/Resource/Doc/46922/0024040.pdf. Accessed 2 May 2015.

Scottish Government. (2008). *Support for change: Approaches and models for the development of provision for children and young people's mental health*. http://www.scotland.gov.uk/Resource/Doc/924/0079270.pdf. Accessed 2 May 2015.

Scottish Government. (2009). *Additional Support for Learning Act 2004 – amended 2009*. http://www.scotland.gov/Publications/2009. Accessed 2 May 2015.

Scottish Government. (2016). *Getting it right for every child (GIRFEC)*. http://www.gov.scot/Topics/People/Young-People/gettingitright/what-is-girfec. Accessed 31 Jan 2016.

Slee, R. (2013). How do we make inclusive education happen when exclusion is a political predisposition? *International Journal of Inclusive Education, 17*(8), 895–907.

Sosu, E., & Ellis, S. (2014). *Closing the attainment gap in Scottish education*. York: Joseph Rowntree Foundation. http://www.jrf.org.uk/files/jrf/education-attainment-scotland-summary.pdf. Accessed 2 May 2015.

Thomas, S., & Dykes, F. (2011). Promoting successful transitions: What can we learn from RTI to enhance outcomes for all students? *Preventing School Failure, 55*(1), 1–9.

United Nations Educational, Scientific and Cultural Organization (UNESCO). (1994). *Final report: World conference on special needs education: Access and quality*. Paris: UNESCO.

United Nations Educational, Scientific and Cultural Organization (UNESCO). (2007). *EFA global monitoring report: EFA strong foundations: Early childhood care and education*. Paris: UNESCO.

Vygotsky, L. S. (1978). *Mind in society*. London: Harvard University Press.

Westman Andersson, G. (2013). *Autism in preschoolers: Assessment, diagnostic and gender aspects*. Doctoral thesis. University of Gothenburg, Göteborg.

White, J., Connelly, G., Thompson, L., & Wilson, P. (2013). Assessing wellbeing at school entry using the strengths and difficulties questionnaire: Professional perspectives. *Educational Research, 55*(1), 87–98.

Chapter 3
Bridging Transitions Through Cultural Understanding and Identity

Linda Mitchell, Amanda Bateman, Robyn Gerrity, and Htwe Htwe Myint

Internationally, there is a commitment to helping refugees resettle in a new country. However, few studies have explored the role that might be played by early childhood education and care (ECEC) to support these transitions. This chapter draws on research investigating teaching and learning in an early childhood centre for refugee children and families in New Zealand. The study gathered data on teaching and learning practices through documentation and video recording of intercultural episodes. Through interviews, the researchers investigated the perspectives of teachers and families. The chapter concludes by arguing for values of respect, social justice and dialogue as a basis for creating a community based on a sense of belonging and well-being. Through providing opportunities for families and children to contribute and communicate in ways that they feel are meaningful, early childhood teachers bridge the transition process between home cultures and the culture of the early childhood centre.

3.1 Background

In 2013, the United Nations High Commissioner for Refugees (UNCHR) (2014, pp. xi–x) reported that there were 11.7 million refugees worldwide. At the time of writing, New Zealand was accepting 750 refugees each year, many of them young children. In the period from 2013 to 2014, 204 of the refugees who came to New Zealand (27 % of the total) were under 12 years (Ministry of Immigration 2014).

L. Mitchell (✉) • A. Bateman
Early Years Research Centre, University of Waikato, Hamilton, New Zealand
e-mail: lindamit@waikato.ac.nz

R. Gerrity • H.H. Myint
Carol White Family Centre, Auckland, New Zealand

© Springer International Publishing Switzerland 2017
N. Ballam et al. (eds.), *Pedagogies of Educational Transitions*, International
Perspectives on Early Childhood Education and Development 16,
DOI 10.1007/978-3-319-43118-5_3

McMillan and Gray (2009), in their annotated bibliography of New Zealand and international literature on the long-term settlement of refugees, reported difficulties for refugee students in acquiring a second language, in meeting with racism and prejudice and in settling into a next culture. Female refugees with young children face particular challenges in accessing education opportunities for themselves and having opportunities to socialise (McMillan and Gray 2009). We are surprised at the lack of research on refugee families' ECEC experiences, given the importance of the early years to children's learning and development (McCain and Mustard 1999; Mitchell et al. 2008; Shonkoff 2010) and the value of pretend play and talk in early childhood centres to help children come to terms with traumatic experiences (Bateman et al. 2013a, b). The role that ECEC might play in offering wider family support and opportunities for social and cultural networking is another reason for asking what opportunities ECEC centres might provide in bridging the process of refugee children and their families stepping out into a new culture, while also supporting them in retaining their own cultural identity and overcoming trauma. Such transitions are the focus of this chapter.

Prior research (Mitchell and Ouko 2012) that involved Congolese refugee families found out about their aspirations for children and experiences of early childhood education in New Zealand. Early childhood education was highly regarded by these families, but they reported a range of barriers that made it hard for them to access culturally responsive ECEC and for families to be understood and contribute in ways that they wanted. Overall, these families wanted ECEC to offer space for them and their children to meet socially with others and to sustain cultural connections. The greatest barrier in resettling in New Zealand was experienced by families who were not fluent in English. These families would have liked educational institutions to offer opportunities for them and their children to learn English. They also wanted ECEC to support a sense of agency so that they and their children could contribute to society. Underlying these aspirations was an ideal of a 'good' ECEC centre as a place where families belong, which generates a sense of community and in which language and culture are understood and reinforced.

Recently, writers (Gundara and Portera 2008; Guo 2012; Miller and Petriwskyj 2013; Portera 2008) have argued for a focus on intercultural education that challenges deficit assumptions about students from minority groups. Portera (2008) states: 'Intercultural education offers the opportunity to "show" real cultural differences, to compare and exchange them, in a word, to *interact*: action in the activity; a compulsory principle in every educational relationship' (p. 488). Likewise, Miller and Petriwskyj (2013) argued that approaches to intercultural education require 'deep engagement with diverse cultures and world views to enrich children and the society' (p. 253). How teachers might adopt an intercultural focus and thereby support the transitions of refugee families and children is a question of significant importance.

This chapter draws on empirical evidence from a research study (Mitchell et al. 2015) of teaching and learning in three culturally diverse ECEC centres in New

Zealand. One of these, the Carol White Family Centre, which caters for refugee families, is the focus of this chapter. The values and teaching and learning practices are examined to highlight factors that supported refugee children and families in their transition to a new society. In doing so, we explore transitions in two ways: the ways in which refugees transition from their home country to a new country, which is an irreversible change, and a closer analysis of the cultures of the home and the early childhood institution.

3.2 Funds of Knowledge and Participation

Children's transitions can be viewed within a sociocultural frame that analyses the linkages between the familiar worlds of home and community and the world of the ECEC centre. A level of continuity between these worlds in a child's life can support a sense of belonging, while discontinuity and contradictions are likely to create difficulties for the child as well as the family. Belonging, *Mana Whenua*, is one of the five strands of *Te Whāriki*, the New Zealand early childhood curriculum (Ministry of Education 1996), which is strengthened when:

> Children and families experience an environment where:
>
> • connecting links with the family and wider world are affirmed and extended;
> • they know they have a place;
> • they feel comfortable with the routines, customs and regular events;
> • they know the limits and boundaries of acceptable behaviour. (p. 54)

Participation is a core idea in *Te Whāriki's* portrayal of belonging – 'that children know that what they can do can make a difference and that they can explore and try out new activities' and that 'The families of all children should feel that they belong and are able to participate in the early childhood education programme and in decision-making' (Ministry of Education 1996, p. 54). These ideas were useful framings for our analysis of the wider context of effective, culturally responsive teaching and learning for all participating members.

Another useful theoretical understanding was the idea of 'funds of knowledge', described by Gonzalez et al. (2005) as follows:

> The concept of funds of knowledge is based on a simple premise: people are competent, they have knowledge and their life experiences have given them knowledge. … A funds of knowledge approach facilitates a systematic and powerful way to represent communities in terms of resources, the wherewithal they possess, and how to harness these resources for classroom teaching. (pp. ix–x)

A funds of knowledge frame contributed to our development of the research questions and our investigation of the way teachers accessed the values and practices of diverse families and integrated these within the curriculum (our second question). It also contributed to the way the project was set up as a partnership with teachers who participated as collaborators in the project.

3.3   Methods and Analysis

This study analysed what pedagogic interactions were taking place in three culturally diverse ECEC centres and how teachers found out about, and used, the funds of
knowledge of families and communities to enrich the education and respond to
children's interests and experiences. In this section we provide details about the
focus ECEC centre, the Carol White Family Centre, and outline the research methods and analytic approach.

The Carol White Family Centre is a refugee family centre in Auckland, the only
one of its kind in New Zealand. Children attending the Centre have diverse nation-
alities: Burmese, Sudanese, Afghani, Iraqi, Ethiopian, Burundian, Iranian, Japanese,
Kurdish, European and Nigerian. Within the same ethnic group, families may be
from different religions. Their levels of education in their home countries vary, from
some parents (mainly mothers) who have not had a chance to go to school and who
cannot read or write to others with formal educational experiences. Educational
experiences for all participants are very different from those in New Zealand. The
families have all come to New Zealand as United Nations quota refugees and spent
6 weeks of orientation at the Mangere Refugee Resettlement Centre on their arrival.
After this, they are located in one of five New Zealand cities, Auckland being the
largest.

The Carol White Family Centre, established in 2004, was the vision of the then
principal of Selwyn College (Carol White), where the Centre is located. Having
observed the situation of Kosovar refugees using Selwyn College in the 1980s, she
saw a need for a holistic programme for refugee families that offered opportunities
for adults (including English language learning) and early childhood education for
children. Operating in a building alongside the ECEC centre is the Refugee
Education and Families (REAF) programme, which most families attend. Here, parents learn English and attend community classes on a range of subjects – cooking,
sewing, gardening, Zumba, self-defence, games, sports, citizenship classes and
computing. The school library is a favourite place for children to visit, and they go
there once a week, bringing their own portfolios of learning stories and reading with
the secondary school librarian.

Research participants from the Carol White Family Centre were two teachers
and three case study children and their families. The two teacher participants were
Robyn Gerrity (the senior teacher and director) and Htwe Htwe Myint (the supervisor). Robyn is a highly experienced, registered ECEC teacher who has been teaching for over 30 years and has worked with refugee families for 17 years. Htwe Htwe
is a fluent speaker and writer of Burmese, whose role is 'bilingual teacher, cultural
broker, trusted interpreter and community representative' (Mitchell et al. 2015,
p. 38). The three children were Thamee, Tharthar and Nyandie (pseudonyms), all
aged 4 years. Thamee's parents are Mon from Burma and speak Mon and Burmese
at home. Tharthar's parents are Mon Tavoy from Burma; his father speaks Mon and
Burmese and his mother speaks Tavoy and Burmese. Nyandie's family is Sudanese
and speaks Dinka at home. Adult family members also speak Kiswahili.

The teachers had a dual role in the research process, in which they were identified as 'teacher-researchers', a role that was agreed on prior to the beginning of the project. Including early childhood teachers as active members of research projects has been well documented as a valuable addition to educational research in New Zealand, as their experience and knowledge of everyday early childhood teaching practice provides an insightful analytical layer when engaging in data analysis (Meade 2009). Student teachers and practising teachers are encouraged to be reflective practitioners, analysing their developing practice to see what they are doing well and where their practice can be improved. Similar analytical rigour is then applied to research projects when they take the role of teacher-researchers (Meade 2009).

The project was subject to the University of Waikato's ethics procedures, stipulated in the *Ethical Conduct in Human Research and Related Activities Regulations* (University of Waikato 2008). Research ethics approval was granted by the Faculty of Education Research Ethics Committee. Adult participants were given information sheets, and these were translated and explained through teacher interpreters where appropriate, to ensure understanding. Particular care was taken to explain issues of confidentiality and anonymity for this group of participants, to enable them to make a thoroughly informed decision on whether to use their real names or pseudonyms. The teacher participants gave signed consent for their real names to be used. Participating parents gave written consent for video recording of their child, their own interview and the gathering of learning stories about their child. The teachers explained the project to the children and invited them to participate and to give their assent for video recording and use of their learning stories and drawings. Signed consent was given by parents for specific documentation about their child to be used in the report. Teachers gave written consent for video recording of teaching and learning episodes and their own interview and chose and agreed to the use of learning stories. The children were given pseudonyms to protect their identities and their parents were not named in this chapter.

The teachers presented information about their centres and their values and practices at an initial workshop with all participating centres and university researchers. The selected children and teachers were video recorded for 1–2 h each: the children during their free play and the teachers on arrival of families and during interactions with children. Family members of the case study children were then invited in an interview to watch their child's video footage and comment on the learning that was valued, family funds of knowledge and continuity between the Centre and home. Teachers were interviewed about the children's video recordings, as well as their own. In these interviews, teachers were asked to comment specifically on episodes relating to belonging, communication, language and culture. These interviews enabled understanding of the wider context of effective, culturally responsive teaching and learning for all participating members.

Following the teacher and parent analysis of the video recorded episodes, the process of building stories of teaching and learning in context through further analysis of videotaped episodes, interview data and documentation (wall displays, information and children's learning stories) was initiated. This additional information provided illustrations of particular practices and philosophies in which teachers were demonstrably responsive to cultural diversity and supporting transitions.

In a more detailed analysis of talk and play within the Centre, conversation analysis (Sacks et al. 1974) and membership categorisation analysis were used to investigate the systematic ways in which videoed interactions were co-produced. Through such detailed analysis, specific aspects that were significant to the participants themselves were also revealed.

3.4   Managing Cultural Transitions in Everyday Practice

3.4.1   Alignment of Cultural Values: Hospitality and Community Connectedness

A foundation for intercultural understanding at the Carol White Family Centre is the alignment of cultural values that are upheld in the ECEC centre and home. When we discussed values with the Centre director, Robyn Gerrity, she commented that hospitality was a significant early pathway into belonging, communication and contribution. She called hospitality a 'global value' that was experienced in everyday interactions with people at the Centre. Identifying hospitality as a value brought an awareness of how deeply it was embedded within the daily practice of the Centre. Hospitality is enacted every day in the morning tea custom of serving food from the countries of the families, enjoyed by teachers, children and the parents who come over from their REAF programme to participate. A further demonstration of the way the families practised hospitality as they operated as communities was evident when we undertook family interviews for the research project. The interviews were attended not only by the child's parents but also their wider *whānau* (extended family) of relations and friends; the families insisted that we came to their home, where they offered wonderful hospitality and food.

Another indication of hospitality and community connectedness is that teachers are invited to participate in special ceremonies in the community with families from the Centre, such as the closing ceremony of the Mon Summer School, where the Mon teaching team encourage Burmese children to learn to speak and write in their home language, Mon. Htwe Htwe reinforced their work and the value of language and culture in the photographic and written documentation she made of this ceremony:

> Thank you to Mon community for giving us an opportunity to participate in this special ceremony. You have done a wonderful job for the children with their learning home language in writing and speaking. Especially away from home land, away from family, we the adults have a big responsibility to pass on our home language, culture and traditions to our children (future generation).

The alignment of cultural values was identified as significant by Thamee's dad after he had watched the video recording of Thamee's block play. He was surprised at how much his child knew, had learnt and was capable of doing. He commented on his child's sense of belonging, understanding and kindness as well as the breadth of learning he saw in her play as she built a temple and road with blocks:

> This is the first video clip I have ever seen of my child. It brings out the bigger picture of my child's learning and development. My child is wonderful; she is making a big road and playing with her friends … I saw my child play really comfortably at the Centre. She feels she belongs there. I have the responsibility of supporting my child's learning. In the video, I can recognise which area to support my child in. … I like the way she builds the road. She is not distracted and copes with the other children who are destroying her work. She has a kindness inside and she is able to understand that the destructive children are younger and they do not upset her.

In commenting on this same excerpt, both Htwe Htwe and Robyn spoke of the child's understanding and her inner qualities. 'The child can problem solve without conflict because she understands the spiritual learning of happiness and content-ment' (Htwe Htwe). 'The child is not angry or upset by the destruction of her work because she understands [the younger child's] stage of development; her mind-set is very open' (Robyn). Underlying these examples were emphases of contribution, the child as a person participating in a social practice and belonging through connec-tions made with cultural identity, home languages, funds of knowledge and interests from home (Ministry of Education 2012). Communication was also a key factor here, as the child communicated her willingness to be patient, open and accepting of her peers in her response to the actions of others who were sharing the environ-ment with her.

3.4.2 Communication and Contribution

In early childhood education in New Zealand, communication is interpreted in the broader sense that encompasses verbal and non-verbal skills or multimodal ways of communicating (Haggerty et al. 2007; Simonsen et al. 2010). Te Whāriki states that for children to develop communication skills:

> Children experience an environment where:
>
> - they develop non-verbal communication skills for a range of purposes;
> - they develop verbal communication skills for a range of purposes;
> - they experience the stories and symbols of their own and other cultures;
> - they discover and develop different ways to be creative and expressive. (Ministry of Education 1996, p. 16)

This emphasis on multimodal communication aligns well with the cultural bridg-ing between the child's knowledge of their own cultural ways of being and that of their early childhood centre, as they are encouraged to communicate in a range of ways and with a range of people from different cultural backgrounds. In the Carol White Family Centre, the children and their families are encouraged to contribute wherever possible. The connection that the Centre staff has with the families is so strong that a Burmese father said he felt the Centre was perfect and could not be improved and was willing to offer his services to do anything that the Centre staff needed him to do. Placing value on cultural connectedness was observed as being practised through the everyday process of contribution and communication, with family participation in the Centre encouraged and appreciated.

In the video footage of teacher-child interactions, the teachers were observed noticing, recognising and responding to the individual needs of the children; when children communicated an interest in connections to their home culture, the teachers responded in ways that promoted and extended these interests. This was displayed when Htwe Htwe noticed children's particular interest in traditional Burmese music and dance and responded by turning up the volume of the music and engaging in the traditional dance with the children, guiding their movements to ensure accuracy (Mitchell et al. 2015). These multimodal ways of displaying communicative competence, supported by teachers, assisted in bridging cultural values as they aligned with promoting home cultures and the New Zealand early childhood curriculum.

Literacy practices that were engaged in every day at the Carol White Family Centre also aided the process of bridging cultural values. A video excerpt showed Htwe Htwe sitting with one of the Burmese children, Tharthar, as they read a storybook together. During this interaction, Htwe Htwe used three languages – Burmese, te reo Māori and English – as she read and explained the story to Tharthar. The importance of the linguistic and cultural diversity of the teachers is acknowledged here as being imperative for the practical implementation of bridging cultural values between the home and early childhood centre, due to the rich intercultural understandings that the teachers bring with them, as they, too, belong to another culture and live in New Zealand. When interviewed, Htwe Htwe spoke about the importance of being able to communicate with children on a 'deep level', and this involved being able to speak their home language. Through being able to engage in a range of languages when storytelling with children, the teachers were able to introduce the language of the 'new' culture while also offering reassurance to the child and their family that their home language was not being lost or forgotten.

Having the opportunity to share in storytelling with linguistically skilled teachers not only encourages an environment where other languages can be introduced but also affords a means through which cultural symbols can be explored with a knowledgeable other. This rich teaching and learning context is written about and transcribed here by Htwe Htwe Myint to demonstrate the way the transfer of knowledge that was present during this storytelling activity was evident through her use of the three different languages:

Tharthar chose a te reo book for reading with me, He Kauri, which enables us to learn about colour in Māori.

Htwe:	Let's read about colour (in Burmese). He porowhita whero.
Tharthar:	Whero.
Htwe:	Do you know what it is? It's Māori language.
	Whero is red (in English), whero = red (in Burmese).
Tharthar:	Whero is red (in English). Whero = red (in Burmese). This colour is red (in Burmese)?
Htwe:	You're right. It's red (in English), red (in Burmese). What's next (in Burmese)?
Tharthar:	Star (in English).

Htwe:	Star in Burmese star (in Burmese). What colour of the star?
Tharthar:	Purple (in English).
Htwe:	Purple (in English), purple (in Burmese). The next one is … You know very well for the next one.
Tharthar:	Blue. This colour (in Burmese)? (as he pointed on his shirt).
Htwe:	Yes, blue. The same blue that you're wearing (in Burmese).
Htwe & Tharthar:	Red, purple, blue (in English).
Htwe:	Then, kakariki green (in English).
Tharthar:	Kakariki green.
Htwe:	Kowhai yellow.
Tharthar:	Kowhai yellow.
Htwe:	Karaka orange.
Tharthar:	Ka rrr … orange.
Htwe:	Ka ra ka.
Tharthar:	Ka r aka.
Htwe:	Kowhai yellow.
Tharthar:	Kawhai yellow.
Htwe:	Kowhai yellow (in English), yellow (in Burmese).
Tharthar:	Yellow (in Burmese).
Htwe:	This is (in Burmese)?
Tharthar:	Orange (in English).
Htwe:	In Burmese?
Tharthar:	Orange (in Burmese).
Htwe:	Shall we say the name of the colour in Burmese? This is red. Remember? Ok (in Burmese)?
Htwe & Tharthar:	Red, purple, blue, green (in English).
Tharthar:	Green (in Burmese), green (in English).
Htwe:	Do you like green (in Burmese)? What colour do you like (in Burmese)?
Tharthar:	Blue (in English). Here is my blue (in Burmese).
Htwe:	Yes, it's blue.
Htwe & Tharthar:	Blue (in English), blue (in Burmese).
Htwe:	Where is the red go (in Burmese)?
Tharthar:	On my toy (Lego man).
Htwe:	On your toy?
Tharthar:	Here red (in English).
Htwe:	This is the colour from my salong (in Burmese).
Tharthar:	Purple (in English), purple (in Burmese).
Htwe:	Yes, purple. Ok, I take purple (in Burmese).
Tharthar:	I take blue (in Burmese).
Htwe:	What more colour do you like to take (in Burmese)?
Tharthar:	Blue and red … (in English). More colour for my toy (in Burmese).
Htwe:	You need more for your shirt.
Tharthar:	Blue (in English), blue (in Burmese), and then red (in English), red (in Burmese).

3.4.3 Aspirations for Education

Our next example illustrates the teachers' deep understanding of families' aspirations for their children's early education and the ways the teachers accommodate these aspirations within the education programme. Nyandie, aged 4 years and part of a family of nine children, came to New Zealand from Southern Sudan with her mother and two older siblings. When she first came to New Zealand, the mother did not know any English – she learned English at the Carol White Family Centre.

One of our video excerpts shows Nyandie's aunty sitting on a rug on the floor holding Nyandie's baby brother. The aunty was pointing to pictures in the book and asking Nyandie to name the images. When she finished the book, at her aunty's request, Nyandie chose another book from the shelf and returned to the rug. She opened the book, holding it so that her baby brother could see as well. The aunty continued to point and ask: 'What word is that?' Nyandie pointed and named. In Sudanese culture, the family is respected as the first teacher for the child; here, the aunty was recorded taking an active role in teaching Nyandie.

In watching this episode, the teachers observed the cooperation, kindness and respect in the interactions amongst the family members. Early literacy was evident as Nyandie read a story to her young brother, holding the book the right way up. She knew that literacy was an important part of her family values and the teachers acknowledged and respected the same. As well, the baby brother was already involved in literacy. It is culturally normal for Sudanese families to operate from the floor in their home environments and that is acknowledged and respected by the teachers. Through affording opportunities for family participation in the programme in ways such as those illustrated here, teachers not only cater for the educational aspirations of their families but also signal that family contribution is welcomed.

Further, the teaching team at the Carol White Family Centre has consciously adapted the teaching environment to meet family aspirations. This was particularly evident with regard to structured teaching opportunities, which many families desired:

> We make sure that we have some formality in here to meet [parent needs], especially the writing and reading expectations. So we make sure that everything is available – lined paper, pencils for more formal [writing] and models of letters … but we would have that anyway because we have a whole range [of activities]. And parents, we invite them [to teach] so they will sit with their children when they come, and do ABC. (Robyn)

The following learning story, 'Nyandie is a writer', highlights Nyandie as 'becoming an expert' in writing, thereby reinforcing Nyandie's identity as a writer with a 'mastery orientation' – she practises and practises. The story is positive about the teaching role of Nyandie's mum and makes connections to the way children learn within a social context, from learning that has interest and meaning for them.

Nyandie is a writer

March 2012

> Today as I find you at our writing table Nyandie, I notice you have written two letters as some letter Os and also some Cs. We have some letter N templates so we have a look at how capital letter N goes. You are writing very competently, Nyandie, just three years old; you are a confident learner and today you showed me just what you can do. Your mum is a very good teacher and she helps you with all of your letters. You have become very interested in writing lately. This seems to be when you arrive and you and your mum spend some time together practising many letters. Every day you are practising and practising. "Look aunty Robyn, I can do C," you tell me. C for cat. You are becoming an expert, Nyandie.

> I look forward to us working together and discovering more letters that interest you. We should try M for mummy and T for [Name], your mummy's name.
> *Te Whāriki* reminds us that children enjoy their learning when it is in a social context, when they are interested and when their learning has meaning for them. Nyandie knows she is a writer and she knows A B C and now she is writing those letters.
> Love to you from Teacher Robyn.

More generally, Nyandie is developing an identity that is positive about learning and able to support further learning. Siraj-Blatchford (2004) described mastery orientation as children tending, after a setback, to 'focus on effort and strategies instead of worrying that they are incompetent' (p. 11), as well as problem solving.

When asked, Nyandie's mum identified a broad range of learning for Nyandie through her participation in the Carol White Family Centre, including literacy and cooking, drawing, socialising and living in New Zealand:

> She knows how to cook, knows all the ingredients and she knows how to play with other children. She knows how to read the book and how to write. When she goes to school it will be easy for her to do her reading and even draw. One day she showed me a drawing of all her teachers. I asked her, "Who drew your teachers?" "I draw my teachers all by myself." She responded. ... She knows that you do not hit your friends and if they hit you, you report to your teacher. In my country if a child of the same age punches you, then you punch back, but my daughter knows we do not do that in New Zealand. I know the attitude of the child is very important. (Nyandie's mum)

Through discussion, participants came to understandings about education in each other's countries and education in a New Zealand context:

> They talk about their own experiences of education so it's very different and some people are very, very happy with what's here and other people are a little bit skeptical because they think we're too soft. They're used to being hit, they're used to being very [*tut tuts*] ... so many, many, like, not tensions but many ideas flowing for us to talk about how it works and for them to tell us how it was for them. (Robyn)

Htwe Htwe was able to understand and compare education in Burma and education in New Zealand, as well as explain to Burmese parents the very different idea of learning through play, which happens in New Zealand settings:

> So between them, I just make it balanced and then talk to them what is in our New Zealand culture of teaching and learning, [how it's] different in Burma, teaching and learning is different. So make it balanced and this is also the way we're learning, not only sit and write. So yeah, [... play] or painting is a part of learning, you know? So there's a freedom of learning here so ... slowly, slowly they can [take it on board].

The generated discussion was meaningful and two way: each party learning through listening to the other and taking action on the learning. Hence, in interview, Nyandie's mum described her liking for the Carol White Family Centre because 'the teachers know our language and protect our culture'. She described the process of teachers finding out about culture as open and respectful: 'They ask about our culture and we explain to them. They say 'okay' and then follow the culture'.

3.5 Conclusion

In our research project, we found that bridging transitions between cultures lies not only with transferring oral language (although this is indeed a significant strategy) but also with the everyday practices that are embedded as part of daily life within the Centre, where shared values were jointly respected by each party. This was evident through such multimodal communication as regularly engaging in traditional dance and sharing of food and the appreciation of each person contributing in acts of hospitality and shared cultural values. For these interactions to be meaningful in the process of bridging cultures, the teachers, children and family members engaged in conversations every day, with the teachers making a conscious effort to ask about and listen to the aspirations of the child's family and to learn about ways that they could effectively implement family cultural values into their everyday practice. Through such regular interactions, an authentic support for the transition between two cultures becomes achievable and respectful communities are developed.

The discussions and practices occurring within the Carol White Family Centre create possibilities for constructing an early childhood centre that reflects the values and beliefs of both the refugee families and the new country in which they have resettled. Internationally, writers have argued for such discussion to occur widely so that values for children and childhood, and for what an early childhood service might possibly be, are given priority. Moss and Petrie (2002) advocated public debate about fundamental questions and issues concerning aspirations for children, values about childhood and the place of children and childhood in society and relationships between children, parents and society. They suggested that as community institutions, early childhood centres can provide the opportunity for a wide range of participants to be engaged in debating such issues. Dahlberg et al. (1999) described the development of a partnership between First Nations' elders and the University of Victoria, Canada, where a 'forum' for learning, involving elders, students, instructors, community members and written texts, enabled diverse views and voices to be heard. In their study of listening to the voices of immigrant parents, Adair and Tobin (2008) argued that dialogue amongst all participants is a basis for developing early childhood programmes that cater well for immigrant families.

In the New Zealand context, early childhood centres work within the sociocultural framework of their national curriculum, *Te Whāriki* (Ministry of Education 1996), which encourages the co-production of teaching and learning between children, teachers and families. In relation to interculturalism, this framework affords opportunities for the funds of knowledge of each person to be shared and explored at ground level through everyday interactions, both verbal and non-verbal. For the Carol White Family Centre, the teachers, families and children were indeed observed co-producing such rich teaching and learning contexts where funds of knowledge were contributed, valued and respected by each person present.

Brooker (2014) described children's transitions as 'a process in which a primary task is to develop a sense of belonging, of membership, of *feeling suitable* in the new space' (p. 32). In our study, we found that the values and practices embedded within the Carol White Family Centre, of social justice and listening to families, laid a foundation for participants to create a community to which they had a sense of belonging and in which their well-being was ensured. The teaching practices and family contributions bridged the process of children stepping out into a next culture while also supporting them to learn and retain their own. These practices lay a foundation for a confident transition to a culture additional to their own.

References

Adair, J., & Tobin, J. J. (2008). Listening to the voices of immigrant parents. In C. Genishi & A. L. Goodwin (Eds.), *Diversities in early childhood education* (pp. 137–150). New York: Routledge.

Bateman, A., Danby, S., & Howard, J. (2013a). Everyday preschool talk about Christchurch earthquakes. *Australian Journal of Communication Special Issue: Disaster Talk, 40*(1), 103–133.

Bateman, A., Danby, S., & Howard, J. (2013b). Living in a broken world: How young children's well-being is supported through playing out their earthquake experiences. *International Journal of Play. Special Issue on Play and Well Being, 3*(3), 202–219.

Brooker, L. (2014). Making this my space: Infants' and toddlers' use of resources to make a day care setting their own. In J. Sumsion & L. J. Harrison (Eds.), *Lived spaces of infant-toddler education and care* (pp. 29–42). Dordrecht: Springer.

Dahlberg, G., Moss, P., & Pence, A. (1999). *Beyond quality in early childhood education and care. Post modern perspectives*. London: Falmer Press.

Gonzalez, N., Moll, L., & Amanti, C. (2005). Preface. In N. Gonzalez, L. Moll, & C. Amanti (Eds.), *Funds of knowledge. Theorizing practices in households, communities, and class-rooms* (pp. ix–xii). New York: Routledge.

Gundara, J., & Portera, A. (2008). Theoretical reflections on intercultural education. *Intercultural Education, 19*(6), 463–468. doi:10.1080/14675980802568244.

Guo, K. (2012). Chinese immigrants in New Zealand early childhood settings. *Early Childhood Folio, 16*(1), 5–9.

Haggerty, M., Simonsen, Y., Blake, M., & Mitchell, L. (2007). Investigating multiple literacies: Wadestown Kindergarten COI. *Early Childhood Folio, 11*, 15–20.

McCain, M., & Mustard, J. (1999). *Early years study: Reversing the brain drain*. Final report to Government of Ontario, Toronto, Canada. www.childsec.gov.on.ca. Accessed 29 Feb 2014.

McMillan, N., & Gray, A. (2009). *Long-term resettlement of refugees: An annotated bibliography of New Zealand and international literature. Quota refugees ten years on series*. Wellington: Department of Labour.

Meade, A. (2009). *Generating waves*. Wellington: NZCER Press.

Miller, M., & Petriwskyj, A. (2013). New directions in intercultural early education in Australia. *International Journal of Early Childhood, 45*(2), 252–266. doi:10.1007/s13158-013-0092-3.

Ministry of Education. (1996). *Te Whāriki*. Wellington: Learning Media.

Ministry of Education. (2012). *Working paper. Strengthening the learning: Outcomes in Aotearoa New Zealand early childhood education. Draft ECE Learning Outcomes Framework*. Wellington: Ministry of Education.

Ministry of Immigration. (2014). *Refugee quota branch arrivals by category, age and gender*. Wellington: Ministry of Immigration.

Mitchell, L., & Ouko, A. (2012). Experiences of Congolese refugee families in New Zealand: Challenges and possibilities for early childhood provision. *Australasian Journal of Early Childhood, 37*(1), 99–107.

Mitchell, L., Wylie, C., & Carr, M. (2008). *Outcomes of early childhood education: Literature review. Report to the ministry of education*. Wellington: Ministry of Education.

Mitchell, L., Bateman, A., Ouko, A., Gerrity, R., Lees, J., Matata, K., et al. (2015). *Teaching and learning in culturally diverse early childhood settings*. Hamilton, New Zealand: Wilf Malcolm Institute of Educational Research, University of Waikato.

Moss, P., & Petrie, P. (2002). *From children's services to children's spaces*. London: Routledge Falmer.

Portera, A. (2008). Intercultural education in Europe: Epistemological and semantic aspects. *Intercultural Education, 19*(6), 481–491. doi:10.1080/14675980802568277.

Sacks, H., Schegloff, E. A., & Jefferson, G. (1974). A simplest systematics for the organisation of turn-taking for conversation. *Language, 50*, 696–735.

Shonkoff, J. P. (2010). Building a new biodevelopmental framework to guide the future of early childhood policy. *Child Development, 81*(1), 357–367.

Simonsen, Y., Blake, M., LaHood, A., Haggerty, M., Mitchell, L., & Wray, L. (2010). *A curriculum whāriki of multimodal literacies*. Wellington: Ministry of Education.

Siraj-Blatchford, I. (2004). Educational disadvantage in the early years: How do we overcome it? Some lessons from research. *European Early Childhood Education Research Journal, 12*(2), 5–19.

United Nations High Commissioner for Refugees (UNHCR). (2014). *Mid year trends 2014*. http://unhcr.org/54aa91d89.html. Accessed 14 Mar 2015.

University of Waikato. (2008). *Ethical conduct in human research and related activities regulations*. http://calendar.waikato.ac.nz/assessment/ethicalConduct.html. Accessed 14 Mar 2015.

Chapter 4
Obstacles and Challenges in Gaining Knowledge for Constructing Inclusive Educational Practice: Teachers' Perspectives

Tina Hellblom-Thibblin, Gunilla Sandberg, and Anders Garpelin

In this chapter we explore teachers' perceptions of children's diversity in different educational settings. Using interviews with teachers from Swedish preschools, preschool classes and the first grade in primary school, we aim to study transitions in school from the perspectives of several actors. The theoretical framework we employ is influenced by an ecological approach to understanding children's needs in educational transitions. The teachers' reflections on these three transitions emphasised the importance of context when responding to children's needs. The teachers also described transitions as dynamic processes in which factors and conditions at different levels interact.

4.1 Introduction

Children's transitions from preschool to primary school pose new challenges and new conditions for interactions and for forming relationships (Rimm-Kaufman et al. 2000). Activities that take place in preschool are important for children's later school experiences (Corsaro and Molinari 2000). A transition from preschool to school therefore involves both opportunities and challenges (Fabian and Dunlop 2006).

Exchanges of educational experiences can be shared in discussions between the actors who encounter children in their lives, and these exchanges can contribute to a deeper understanding of how different children are identified and met during their learning journeys and transitions. However, research shows a lack of educational arenas for such educational discussions (Peters 2010). There are several interactive

T. Hellblom-Thibblin (✉) • G. Sandberg • A. Garpelin
Mälardalen University, Västerås, Sweden
e-mail: tina.hellblom-thibblin@mdh.se

© Springer International Publishing Switzerland 2017
N. Ballam et al. (eds.), *Pedagogies of Educational Transitions*, International
Perspectives on Early Childhood Education and Development 16,
DOI 10.1007/978-3-319-43118-5_4

43

variables to consider with regard to transitions, such as the interaction between individuals and the context of learning (Corsaro and Molinari 2008). Additionally, consideration is needed regarding children's individual capabilities and experiences for their different learning journeys. It is therefore relevant to try to understand how teachers in preschool, preschool class and primary school perceive children's different experiences and needs during transitions to the different school forms. The way in which diversity is communicated and understood in educational settings seems to be a key question that is important to address (Hjörne and Säljö 2014).

In this chapter, we report a study that aimed to deepen the understanding of how children, with their unique capabilities and experiences, are perceived and understood when going through different stages in school, from the teachers' perspectives and with special reference to obstacles and challenges. This can contribute valuable knowledge to professionals involved in children's learning journeys and transitions from preschool to primary school.

4.2 Background

The study described in this chapter was part of two research projects: Garpelin (2011) and Garpelin et al. (2010). The empirical data that informed this chapter were collected in 2011 and 2012.

4.2.1 Inclusion and Diversity in Educational Settings

The diversity of children making the transition from preschool to school necessitates a focus on inclusion (Petriwskyj et al. 2014). 'Inclusion' is a complex concept that can be understood in several ways (Clark et al. 1998). Although the term 'inclusion' can have different meanings, a common starting point is that all children, regardless of their conditions and needs, should be given the same opportunities to participate in a school community (Heimdahl Mattson and Malmgren Hansen 2009).

In Sweden, the idea of an inclusive school began taking form after the Salamanca Declaration (United Nations Educational Scientific and Cultural Organisation [UNESCO] 1994). Inclusion may focus on the educational environment supporting children with disabilities and those in need of additional support. Children's behaviour, abilities and motivation are all influenced by the expectations of those around them and the number and nature of opportunities that their teachers give them to address their problems. Attitudes towards people with disabilities and their capabilities have changed in recent years, with an increasing emphasis placed on inclusion (Bines and Lei 2011). Children, all with different abilities and experiences, inevitably encounter their environments in different ways. The concept of 'affiliation' or 'belonging' is also addressed in the context of studies on inclusion (Nilholm and Alm 2009).

It is important to look at what teachers identify as barriers for children and their learning. Studies of inclusive practices raise the importance of educators' attitudes and beliefs about disability. Thus, there are reasons to consider how diversity can be represented, understood and adapted in different learning environments (Hjörne and Säljö 2014). In relation to the idea of inclusion, diversity can be considered from a range of perspectives about children's differences (Clark et al. 1998). Regardless of the approach taken, it is necessary for teachers to be aware of the diverse needs of children entering the school system. These needs may be due to a specific disability or may derive from certain aspects of the child's background, such as having a certain cultural background or being from a disadvantaged family.

The immense variety in children's development and experiences makes each child's transition to school unique. Children commence school with a diversity of skills, family and cultural backgrounds and early childhood experiences (Margetts 2002).

4.2.2   Educational Transitions and Children's Learning Opportunities

There is a growing interest in trying to understand what it means to start school and preschool (Dockett and Perry 2004; Shevlin et al. 2008). Several issues are relevant, such as understanding the different ways in which children face school and the consequences of children's different capabilities (Sandberg 2012). In this context, 'children with special educational needs' are often discussed in connection to interventions, with reference to exclusion and inclusion (Haug 2014; Moen 2008).

The process of transitioning to school is influenced by many factors, including the readiness of children, families, schools and communities (Dockett et al. 2011). Communication is perceived as a central part of the transition process. Activities that take place in preschool can influence children's later school experiences (Corsaro and Molinari 2000).

Socialisation processes and contextual factors are of particular importance for the child's learning in different educational settings (Ackesjö 2014; Bjervås 2011). The child's development is also influenced by teachers' views on knowledge and learning. According to a study by Bulkeley and Fabian (2006), a sense of belonging and social and emotional well-being are important factors in children's early educational transitions. Discussions on how to organise transitions between different school forms have been highlighted in several studies, focusing particularly on teachers' understandings of transitions (Ackesjö 2014; Garpelin et al. 2010; Lago 2014). Different concepts can be related to transition activities, such as 'priming events', which are central to children's social development (Corsaro and Molinari 2000). The concept of 'rites of passage' is also discussed as playing a central role in the research on transitions (Garpelin 2014). Focus is also placed on identity processes, which have been described as potential problems for children with disabilities (Renshaw et al. 2014). The roles that children take on and the social relationships that they develop are of importance when trying to understand the different ways in which school environments can promote children's learning and development in transitions (Corsaro and Molinari 2006). Negative expectations about a new transition can lead to problems (Ackesjö 2014). Such expectations can come from many sources – including from teachers.

Teachers' conversations about children's learning opportunities are given particular attention in studies that emphasise the importance of context. Inclusive school activities for children and their learning are characterised by both organisational features and certain fundamental values (Göransson et al. 2011). The way we talk about children's capabilities and experiences has an effect on the way we meet and interact with them (Harwood and Allen 2014; Hellblom-Thibblin et al. 2012). The tendency to place a child into a category that labels their personality or capabilities can lead to issues with identity formation (Mowat 2014). This practice of pigeon-holing children, based on assumptions, often results in false interpretations. Thus, the categorisation process can, in some respects, be seen as going hand in hand with an identification process (Hacking 1999; Hjörne and Säljö 2014; Renshaw et al. 2014). Research shows that teachers' attitudes, values and other conditions in the school environment can all contribute to the way that children and young people are perceived in different learning environments (Harwood and Allen 2014).

In summary, the current review of studies on children's transitions between different school forms focuses on the ways in which teachers talk about and create transitions from an inclusive perspective.

4.3   Theoretical Framework

The theoretical framework used in the study reported in this chapter is influenced by an ecological perspective. In this way, we try to understand children's needs when considering diversity and educational transitions. Children are a part of a complex reality in which many different variables influence the opportunities and obstacles that may arise (Hacking 1998). The theoretical starting point for this study is based on an ecological model presented by Hacking (1998; also cf. Hellblom-Thibblin 2004), with its focus on the following components: medical taxonomy, observability, power and cultural polarity. Inspired from this, a new model was developed by Hellblom-Thibblin in order to enable deeper analyses of the empirical data. Four components were used: observability, activity, steering documents and effect, all important in identifying the needs of individuals in different settings. The starting point of the study was teachers' conversations about children and transitions. The theoretical framework presented can be useful for understanding transitions related to children's diversity and inclusion as well as understanding what teachers perceive as obstacles related to children's needs in different educational transitions. Some of the key concepts discussed regarding children's transitions highlight obstacles in children's learning and development.

4.4   Study Methodology

A qualitative method, with an interpretive approach, was used in the study described in this chapter, to explore the variety and the understanding of teachers' ways of communicating about obstacles and challenges that children can encounter in the transitions between different school forms.

The data collection was carried out through focused thematic interviews (Esaiasson et al. 2012; Kvale et al. 2009) with teachers from three different school forms: preschool (5-year-olds), preschool class (6-year-olds) and primary school (7-year-olds). In Sweden, preschool and preschool classes are voluntary school forms, while primary school is the first part of a 9-year compulsory school system. Six different groups of teachers were included in the study. The six groups consisted of six to eight participants, with two representatives from each stage in each group. A total of 36 teachers took part in the study during the first three meetings. Each group met a total of five times, from fall 2011 to spring 2012. The aim was to include teachers of varying experiences in children's transitions between the different stages.

The participants were informed that they had the right to withdraw from the study at any time. Their participation would be kept anonymous, and the material collected was confidential and could not be traced back to them by anyone other than the researchers themselves. Thus, ethical issues concerning informed consent, confidentiality and management of data have been carefully considered, applying the rules and guidelines from the regulations for research specified by the Swedish Research Council (2015).

A total of 27 thematic interviews were held, each lasting 2 hours. The conversation leaders at these thematic interviews were university researchers. The discussions in the groups were based on three overarching questions: What difficulties do children face in an educational setting and what are the educational implications of these? What are the teachers' expectations regarding transitions? In what ways do the steering school documents influence educational practice? The interviews were recorded and transcribed. Subsequently, these data were processed and analysed using content analysis (Graneheim and Lundman 2004). In the analysis, a modified ecological model was used. Several components, on different levels, were taken into consideration according to an ecological model. The tools used for the analysis were activity, observability, effect and steering (policy) documents (see Fig. 4.1).

All of these components contribute to an understanding of teachers' experiences, with regard to obstacles and challenges in educational transitions. 'Observability' refers to the ways in which the obstacles are identified by teachers in assessments, tests, observations and discussions. 'Activities' are analysed from different angles, according to their focus. In activities with a relationship-oriented focus, special attention is paid to social interaction and play. In activities with a task-oriented focus, such as reading or mathematics, the focus of the analysis is on the intellectual aspects of these tasks. The component 'effect' refers to the implications of certain obstacles, partly on a more organisational level, where the inclusion and exclusion processes are in focus for different measures and can also partly be related to identity-building processes. Under the component 'steering (policy) documents',

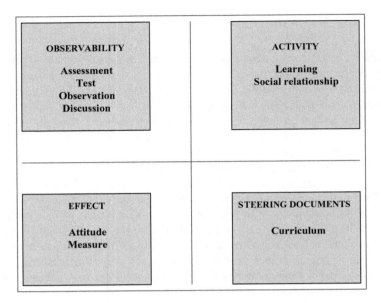

Fig 4.1 The analysis tool: the four components of the ecological model

input from a societal perspective, on a macro level, is considered. Obstacles are related to all of these components. The choice of the components was inspired by Hacking's (1998) use of ecological theory, but in this case, used slightly differently and with a somewhat different choice of components. The obstacles and challenges that teachers highlight are found in the different components of the model used and in different transitions. This knowledge contributes to a deeper understanding about how children are perceived and understood in different transitions.

4.5 The Transition to Preschool, Preschool Class and First Grade in Primary School: Teachers' Perspectives

The discussions of transitions to preschool, preschool class and the first grade in primary school are based on teachers' experiences of these events. The focus is the changes involved in each of these transitions, as experienced by teachers. Teachers' perceptions of the various obstacles for children in the different transitions are also considered.

4.5.1 Social Interaction and Relationships

During the transition from a home environment to preschool, children experience becoming part of a new group community in which they will form new relationships, both with other children and with adults. The child is met with expectations and demands to function in a group. This involves showing respect for others, learning to wait for their turn, listening to others, picking up after themselves and so on. These practices are all part of the process of learning and socialising: 'Many children want an immediate reaction from adults, but they often have to wait a minute' (Teacher a2). Obstacles can be linked to the child's learning and socialisation processes, in which new activities and social interactions are essential. These obstacles can occur in different situations, such as when a child is demonstrating challenging behaviour, when there are cultural clashes among the children, when there is a lack of communication or when there is a case of misunderstanding due to language barriers.

In preschool, the focus is on giving children good experiences from engaging in activities; therefore, the focus should be on playfulness and joy rather than the difficulty level of the activity. There seems to be a link between the teacher's role in letting the child influence the choice of activity and the child's level of motivation. By letting children in preschool play among themselves and not forcing them to engage in arranged activities, children have the opportunity to engage in peer learning and to experience natural social interactions as well as conflicts:

> And then I had two boys, both typical troublemakers but they had a great time together when they played on the ice. They spent hours playing together without there being any fighting, teasing or nagging at each other but … well, it was just great. (Teacher a4)

At the preschool level, social interactions are of paramount importance for giving children opportunities to form relationships. When children have different backgrounds, clashes can occur, due to a child being unfamiliar with the specific rules of a game or being unsure as to what social rules apply in a particular situation.

4.5.2 To Reflect upon Oneself Through Comparisons

The transition to preschool class marks a new stage and can be seen primarily as a collective transition that many children do simultaneously. There is no difference in their ages and they are moulded into a new group in a relatively short time, before the next transition to primary school. This implies that the child will become a member of a new community, but the difference from preschool is that the children do not have the same experience of having to adapt and fit into an already existing group of children. Children as individuals also compare themselves with other children in the group and this can affect their perceptions of themselves:

> If you don't understand the reading code, it can lead to a sense of failure and lack of self-esteem if you are suddenly seen as someone who cannot, like the others. (Teacher b1)

During the transition to preschool class, the focus changes to emphasise children's abilities in a new way. Preschool children compare themselves to their peers, based on their abilities. In the same way as in preschool and in the preschool class, it is important to pay attention to obstacles in social relationships and communication. Social interactions, as part of children's learning processes, may require attention. A recurring problem mentioned by teachers in conversations about children's difficulties in learning activities was children not being able to keep up with the pace in the preschool class and not having enough time to complete their tasks. Obstacles in the preschool class can be related to both individual characteristics and to conditions in the environment.

4.5.3 The 'Span' Between the Children and Conquering New Skills

The transition to the first grade of primary school implies that another dimension appears in connection with the assessment of the child's individual abilities, based on current learning objectives that now become relevant. The obstacles highlighted here are 'span'; children have various capabilities and experiences. The focus is now on evaluating how well pupils are succeeding at reaching their goals, in terms of skills and knowledge. Time is now emphasised more, with the children, as individuals, being exposed to more challenges such as completing certain tasks or amounts of work within a given period. The child's identity shifts from that of a preschool child to that of a student. As part of this change, further expectations are placed on the children, such as taking responsibility, being on time for class, remaining seated throughout class, listening respectfully to instructions and being able to understand them. Children are expected to acquire many new skills, such as learning how to read, write and count, as well as how to function in a group and collaborate with others. Curriculum governance is evident in teachers' conversations about children's learning and development:

> Many children are in a grey area. It is my duty to help them achieve goals even if they do not have the most ideal prerequisites. And then there is the middle group who are slightly more advanced and who need more challenges. For the pupils in this group it is required that they all achieve the goals and then I will be held accountable for making sure all students attain the goals. (Teacher c3)

4.6 A Model to Deepen Understanding

The findings of this research project are presented here through the components of the ecological model: observability, activity, effect and steering documents. Obstacles that appear in the environments of all three types of school forms are considered via each of the components respectively.

4.6.1 Observability: Assessment

In preschool, it is often possible to observe processes. Social functions are often observable behaviours in various activities and what appear are collective expectations of the individual in the group. The obstacles present in preschool, such as social interaction, are identified and assessed through observations and conversations.

The 'educational eye', as one teacher mentions, is used to observe and identify children at risk or who may need support.

In the preschool class, there is a change from the preschool's special focus on social development to include aspects of individualisation. Children's conditions are assessed on the basis of tests as part of the preparations for the transition to the first grade of primary school. In the preschool class, the capacity of the individual becomes a more important factor with regard to what are perceived as obstacles. The teacher expects the individual to perform certain school-like activities. This can have an effect on the individual level, when the children compare themselves with their peers, based on what they can and cannot do. Performance anxiety is mentioned by several teachers. Their attitudes now change, to some extent, to include educational individualisation.

In the first grade of primary school, the assessment process, through examinations and tests, increases and is directly linked to measurable results based on the student's ability to meet learning objectives. The obstacles highlighted are about 'span'; that is, the children are under different conditions, and these are related to difficulties in meeting the new expectations in the first grade. Identification of pupils' capabilities also implies the need to provide them with appropriate educational assistance and, in some cases, group them according to ability. A dilemma emerges around teachers' views on the way diversity should be addressed.

4.6.2 Activity Involving Relationship and Tasks

In preschool learning, social interaction with others is essential. Language difficulties may create obstacles in the child's interaction within the group. Activities present opportunities for children to develop and learn and for teachers to identify certain problems. Successful strategies to support children with diverse abilities include involving them in a range of activities, commending them and showing patience. Obstacles can also be a consequence of activities and tasks that are not perceived to be pleasurable, with the consequence that the child chooses not to participate in them. The starting points for the activities in preschool, according to the curriculum, are the children's interests. The tension between individualisation ideas and group community emerges. In the preschool class, there is a shift towards task-oriented activities. Teachers emphasised that it is the school-like activities, such as reading and listening, which may cause difficulties. It is about 'being capable to perform' associated with more task-oriented activities and in comparison with peers.

Activities in the preschool class demonstrate a shift towards more school-like tasks, such as developing skills in literacy and mathematics. Although similar activities have been available in the preschool, in the preschool class they become part of the preparation for the next transition. In the first class of primary school, a significant number of the obstacles mentioned by teachers were related to task-oriented activities, for example, 'they take too much time' and 'they have unfinished work all the time' (Teacher c5). The various activities are now becoming more time dependent and can lead to children losing the urge, stamina and motivation to learn. Teachers also expressed the dilemma related to children's different capabilities and needs. The span is problematised from the basis that learning demands, according to the curriculum, are the same for everyone. As a consequence, some children will 'fail'. Children could be grouped according to ability, but this would perhaps run counter to the idea of an inclusive school.

In primary school, children need instruction even if the activities are perceived as boring, unlike the preschool situation where the pleasure principle is an important starting point for activities. Children's differences in motivation become more obvious at this stage. This places demands on teachers' skills to understand and address problems and is described as a pedagogical challenge. The ability to cope with the challenges of the learning objectives may be crucial for the child's continued learning journey.

4.6.3 Steering Document: Curriculum

In preschool, the children themselves often choose their activities and they can also stop them when they want to. It is a form of 'freedom' that does not exist in the same way in the preschool class. The curriculum emphasises play and social interaction as key areas, with the principal aim being to engage the children in a social community. According to the curriculum, the task of the children is to 'seek and develop knowledge through play and social interaction' (The National Agency for Education 2010, p. 6). Any inability to interact socially is important for teachers to address. This is also consistent with what the preschool curriculum points out as important for the learning process. Obstacles at this stage are often related to relationships and group processes. The intentions of the curriculum may be seen as the voice of the society; lack of ability to interact socially should be addressed in preschool.

The teachers in the preschool class do not relate to the curriculum in their daily work. Indeed, there are passages in the curriculum that state, 'schools should encourage each pupil to form and grow with their tasks' (The National Agency for Education 2011, p. 10):

> I was thinking like this, when the new curriculum came. It is written nicely on the front side but the preschool class is barely mentioned. (Teacher b5)

This comment reflects the understanding expressed by teachers of the preschool class, namely, that the curriculum is indistinctly written. This may be a reason for not often referring to it in the interviews. In the first grade of primary school, the curriculum states that certain learning objectives should be achieved, and more tests are carried out. The curriculum can be regarded as a rule of the learning goals, since the teachers refer to them as important in everyday life in school. The activities mentioned show a clear relationship to the learning objectives that the curriculum highlights as important for children's learning and development:

And then we started talking about the new curriculum ... we understood that we're not working so much with social studies. So we wanted to go into it pretty quickly to see how we need to change our approach. Then we discussed it and looked at what we are already doing, what it says and what we need to do and how to get to it. (Teacher c2)

Based on this quote, it is obvious that the curriculum is included as a guiding tool for the activities that the first grade teachers plan.

4.6.4   Effects of Obstacles and Challenges Regarding the Diversity of Children

Different educational strategies are described in the various educational settings. Teachers in this study highlighted various measures related to children's different needs. Two conflicting approaches emerged from teachers in preschool regarding the pedagogical effects of children's needs and capabilities: children's own will, based on desire and interest, as opposed to the ambition to teach the children to follow the rules of a group. Already in preschool classes, a need to track children according to ability emerges, depending on their ability to read. This can be a consequence of the child's performance becoming more of a focus. Such strategies may be perceived as exclusionary, based on the child's lack of certain abilities.

There is also a shift from the preschool's perception of children's differences as assets to the primary school's perception of children's differences as the basis for special educational measurements. Diversity is thus related both to an inclusive and an exclusive approach. Children's different capabilities are linked to the way they are perceived and understood from teachers' perspectives. Different pedagogical strategies are thus apparent as effects of diversity in the educational settings.

In primary school, both inclusionary and exclusionary processes are linked to the individualisation and socialisation processes, as well as to children's knowledge development. Based on these processes, children's diversity contributes to different effects as challenges or obstacles. On a more individual level, effects can include a feeling of exclusion, such as when a child in the preschool class does not carry out the planned activities. Attitudes in the environment can also contribute to the way children perceive themselves. Perceptions of identity can also be influenced by both organisational conditions and individual efforts on different levels.

4.7   Discussion

The aim of the study that has been discussed in this chapter was to deepen understanding of the way children, with their unique capabilities and experiences, are perceived and understood by teachers in the different school forms, with special reference to obstacles and challenges. An ecological model has been used to contribute to this understanding of the obstacles highlighted by teachers in preschool, in preschool class and in the first grade of compulsory school.

The results showed that the three transitions presented implied changes for the child and constituted dynamic processes in which factors and conditions at different levels interacted. This indicates a connection with the ecological point of departure (Hacking 1998). The results also showed the interactions between obstacles and activities, current assessment tools, policy documents and contextual circumstances, with these four components contributing towards an understanding of the obstacles and challenges presented. The results also demonstrated that obstacles in children's encounters with different school forms varied across the school forms.

Teachers' discussions about their work have been highlighted in several studies as being important for acquiring knowledge of the content and meaning of transitions and thereby obtaining the in-depth picture needed to understand the role of children in these (Lago 2014; Markström 2005; Simonsson and Thorell 2010). In several studies, discussions of the contents of transitions are in the focus (Ackesjö 2014). These studies have highlighted a number of issues that can be linked to the current study.

The teachers in preschool described deficient social relationships and social interaction as obstacles to children's learning. Social relationships and relationship-creating processes have been highlighted in several studies of transitions (Shevlin et al. 2008). In this study, the transition to preschool implies entering into a group community, where processes of interaction become important (Corsaro and Molinari 2000). According to Rimm-Kaufman et al. (2000), the transition to preschool implies new situations and new relationship-creating activities. When children start preschool, they meet an already established community of which they are to be a part (Ackesjö 2014; Bjervås 2011; Dockett and Perry 2009). In preschool, a culture of norms is created by the children who are already there (Simonsson and Thorell 2010). For some children, it can take some time to get a feeling of belonging to this culture. Attention to such reactions is required, as the experiences that children have in the early stages of their learning journey have significance for their continued development (Corsaro and Molinari 2008).

Relationship-creating processes were found to be worthy of attention in this current study, particularly the concept of belonging. The sense of belonging is an important part of the socialisation process; it is a question of acquiring a role identity in the group (Leggett and Ford 2015). This current study found there were different identity-creating events that could have a negative effect on the child's well-being if they created a feeling of exclusion. Aspects of identity, as well as aspects of inclusion, can be understood through such occurrences, as has been highlighted in several studies (Renshaw et al. 2014). Bulkeley and Fabian (2006) regard belonging, as well as social and emotional well-being, as important in educational transitions. These can be compared with the problematisation of children's vulnerability, based on the way differences are perceived and understood (Ackesjö 2014; Haug 2014; Lago 2014). The obstacles that are prominent in preschool are primarily connected to activities and the current curriculum (Hellblom-Thibblin 2004). Thus, the planning of transitions is also important (Rimm-Kaufman et al. 2000). Knowledge of children's differences can contribute to an understanding of how the needs of the various children can be met (Harwood and Allen 2014; Hellblom-

Thibblin 2004), thereby creating the prerequisites for a positive learning journey. Contextual circumstances, such as how the child is prepared for different transitions, also contribute to this.

4.8   Conclusion

The results of the study described in this chapter can be summarised in a few main points. Based on the ecological model used in the analysis, it was clear that the four source components – activity, observability, effect and steering documents (curriculum) – contributed to an understanding of what may create barriers in children's learning and development.

The results indicated a relationship between obstacles presented and the activities provided. What is also clear is a shift, over time, from a focus on play and social development in the preschool community, where children's different circumstances are presented as unproblematic, to the view later in the process that different circumstances are more of a challenge than an asset. This span implies that different approaches to children's learning emerge and influence the actions taken. The way different children experience the encounter with preschool, preschool class and the first grade of primary school implies diverse conditions for their learning journeys.

The different educational environments that children and young people are offered are important for their learning journeys. This can be seen as a dynamic process in which factors and conditions at different levels contribute to the process (Bronfenbrenner 1999; Bronfenbrenner and Morris 2006; Hacking 1998). The ecological model used in the analysis of this study showed that the four components can contribute to the way diversity, as it is viewed in this chapter, can be understood in the context of educational transitions. Each of the components may help to highlight the way children's learning journeys are affected by conditions in their environment, for example, the way different children can meet in an inclusive learning community. The model can also highlight the way diversity can be assessed as the basis for pedagogical efforts. What teachers perceive as obstacles and challenges related to a child's various educational transitions can contribute valuable knowledge for constructing an inclusive educational practice to satisfy all children.

References

Ackesjö, H. (2014). *Barns övergångar till och från förskoleklass. Gränser, identiteter och (dis) kontinuiteter* [Children's transitions to and from preschool class. Borders, identities and (dis-) continuities- Akademisk avhandling för filosofie doktorsexamen i pedagogik vid Institutionen för pedagogik. Kalmar: Linnéuniversitetet.

Bines, H., & Lei, P. (2011). Disability and education: The longest road to inclusion. *International Journal of Educational Development, 31*, 419–424.

Bjervås, L. L. (2011). *Samtal om barn och pedagogisk dokumentation som bedömningspraktik i förskolan: en diskursanalys* [Teachers' views of preschool children in relation to pedagogical documentation – A discourse analysis]. Avhandling. Göteborg: Göteborgs universitet.

Bronfenbrenner, U. (1999). Environments in developmental perspective: Theoretical and operational models. In S. L. Friedman & T. D. Wachs (Eds.), *Measuring environment across the life span: Emerging methods and concepts* (pp. 3–28). Washington, DC: American Psychological Association.

Bronfenbrenner, U., & Morris, P. (2006). The bioecological model of human development. In W. Damon & R. M. Lerner (Eds.), *Handbook of child psychology Vol 1. Theoretical models of human development* (6th ed., pp. 793–828). Hoboken: Wiley.

Bulkeley, J., & Fabian, H. (2006). Well-being and belonging during early educational transitions. *International Journal of Transitions in Childhood, 2,* 18–30.

Clark, C., Dyson, A., & Millward, A. (1998). *Theorising special education.* New York: Routledge.

Corsaro, W. A., & Molinari, L. (2000). Priming events and Italian children's transition from preschool to elementary school: Representations and action. *Social Psychology Quarterly, 63*(1), 16–33.

Corsaro, W. A., & Molinari, L. (2006). *I Compagni: Understanding children's transition from preschool to elementary school.* New York: Teachers' College Press.

Corsaro, W. A., & Molinari, L. (2008). Policy and practice in Italian children's transition from preschool to elementary School. *Research in Comparative and International Education, 3*(3), 250–265.

Dockett, S., & Perry, B. (2004). What makes a successful transition to school? Views of Australian parents and teachers. *International Journal of Early Years Education, 12*(3), 217–230.

Dockett, S., & Perry, B. (2009). Readiness for school: A relational construct. *Australasian Journal of Early Childhood, 34*(1), 20–27.

Dockett, S., Perry, B., & Kearney, E. (2011). Starting school with special needs: Issues for families with complex support needs as their children start school. *Exceptionality Education International, 21*(2), 45–61.

Esaiasson, P., Gilljam, M., Oscarsson, H., Wägnerud, L. (2012). *Metodpraktikan. Konsten att studera samhälle individ och marknad* [Methods manual – The art of studying society, the individual and the market]. Stockholm: Norstedt förlag. AB.

Fabian, H., & Dunlop, A.-W. (2006). *Outcomes of good practice in transition processes for children entering primary school.* Paris: UNESCO.

Garpelin, A. (2011). *Borderlands, bridges and rites of passage: Understanding children's learning journeys from preschool into school.* Application for Project Research Grant. Swedish Research Council. Västerås: Mälardalen University.

Garpelin, A. (2014). Transition to school – A rite of passage in life. In B. Perry, S. Dockett, & A. Petriwskyj (Eds.), *Transitions to school: International research, policy and practice.* Dordrecht: Springer.

Garpelin, A., Kallberg, P., Ekström, K., & Sandberg, G. (2010). How to organize transitions between units in preschool. *International Journal of Transitions in Childhood, 4*(1), 4–11.

Graneheim, U. H., & Lundman, B. (2004). Qualitative content analysis in nursing. *Education Today, 24*(2), 105–111.

Göransson, K., Nilholm, C., & Karlsson, K. (2011). Inclusive education in Sweden? A critical analysis. *International Journal of Inclusive Education, 15*(5), 541–555.

Hacking, I. (1998). *Mad travelers. Reflections on the reality of transient mental illness.* Cambridge, MA: Harvard University Press.

Hacking, I. (1999). *Social construction of what.* Cambridge, MA: Harvard University Press.

Harwood, V., & Allen, J. (2014). *Psychopathology at school. Theorizing mental disorders in education.* New York: Routledge.

Haug, P. (2014). Emotional and behavioural difficulties: The practices of dealing with children with special needs in school. *Emotional and Behavioural Difficulties, 19*(3), 296–310.

Heimdahl Mattson, E., & Malmgren Hansen, A. (2009). Inclusive and exclusive education in Sweden: Principals' opinions and experiences. *European Journal of Special Needs Education, 24*(4), 465–472.

Hellblom-Thibblin, C. (2004). *Kategorisering av barns "problem" i skolans värld: en undersökning av skolhälsovårdsrapporter läsåren 1944/45-1988/89* [Categorization of children's problems in school. A study of health care reports]. Doctoral thesis, Uppsala University, Acta Universitatis Upsaliensis. Uppsala Studies in Education, 106.

Hellblom-Thibblin, T., Klang, N., & Åman, K. (2012). Biopsychosocial model and the ICF-CY in inservice training: General educators' reflections. *International Journal of Developmental Disabilities, 58*(1), 12–19.

Hjörne, E., & Säljö, R. (2014). Representing diversity in education: Student identities in con-texts of learning and instruction. *International Journal of Educational Research, 63*, 1–4.

Kvale, S., Brinkmann, S., & Torhell, S. E. (2009). *Den kvalitativa forskningsintervjun* [The qualitative research interview]. Lund: Studentlitteratur.

Lago, L. (2014). *"Mellanklass kan man kalla det". Om tid och meningsskapande vid över-gången från förskoleklass till årskurs ett* ["You could say in-between class": Time and meaning-making in the transition from preschool class to first grade]. Doctoral thesis. Linköping: Linköping universitet.

Leggett, N., & Ford, M. (2015). Group time experiences: Belonging, being and becoming through active participation within early childhood communities. *Early Childhood Education Journal.* doi:10.1007/s10643-015-0702-9.

Margetts, K. (2002). Transition to school: Complexity and diversity. *European Early Childhood Education Research Journal, 10*(2), 103–114.

Markström, A. M. (2005). *Förskolan som normaliseringspraktik: en etnografisk studie* [Pre-school as a normalizing practice – An ethnographic study]. Doctoral thesis, Linköpings universitet, Linköping.

Moen, T. (2008). Inclusive educational practice: Results of an empirical study. *Scandinavian Journal of Educational Research, 52*(1), 59–75.

Mowat, G. J. (2014). 'Inclusion – that word!' Examining some of the tensions in supporting pupils experiencing social, emotional and behavioural difficulties/needs. *Emotional and Behavioural Difficulties.* doi:10.1080/13632752.2014.927965.

Nilholm, C., & Alm, B. (2009). An inclusive classroom? A case study of inclusiveness, teacher strategies, and children's experiences. *European Journal of Special Needs Education, 25*(3), 239–252.

Peters, S. (2010). Shifting the lens: Re-framing the view of learners and learning during the transition from early childhood education to school in New Zealand. In D. Jindal-Snape (Ed.), *Educational transitions: Moving stories from around the world* (pp. 68–84). New York: Routledge.

Petriwskyj, A., Thorpe, K., & Tayler, C. (2014). Towards inclusion: Provision for diversity in the transition to school. *International Journal of Early Years Education, 22*(4), 359–379.

Renshaw, P., Choo, J., & Emerald, C. (2014). Diverse disability identities: The accomplishment of 'Child with a disability' in everyday interaction between parents and teachers. *International Journal of Educational Research, 63*, 47–58.

Rimm-Kaufman, S. E., Pianta, R., & Cox, M. J. (2000). Teachers' judgements of problems in the transition to kindergarten. *Early Childhood Research Quarterly, 15*(2), 147–166.

Sandberg, G. (2012). *På väg in i skolan. Om villkor för olika barns delaktighet och skriftspråkslärande* [On their way into school. About conditions for participation and learning]. (Studia Didactica Upsaliensia 6). Uppsala: Acta Universitatis Upsaliensis.

Shevlin, M., Kenny, M., & Loxley, A. (2008). A time of transition: Exploring special educa-tional provision in the Republic of Ireland. *Journal of Research in Special Educational Needs, 8*, 141–152.

Simonsson, M., & Thorell, M. (2010). Att börja på förskolan. Exemplet på barns sociala samspel under inskolningen [To begin at the preschool. The example on children's social interaction during induction]. *Educare, 1,* 53–73.

The National Agency for Education. (2010). *Lpfö98. Läroplan för förskolan* [Curriculum for the preschool]. Stockholm: The National Agency for Education.

The National Agency for Education. (2011). *Lgr11. Läroplan för grundskolan, förskoleklassen och fritidshemmet* [Curriculum for compulsory school, preschool class and recreation centre]. Stockholm: The National Agency for Education.

The Swedish Research Council. (2015). CODEX, rules and guidelines for research. http://www. codex.vr.se. Accessed 29 Mar 2015.

United Nations Educational, Scientific and Cultural Organization (UNESCO). (1994). *The Salamanca statement and framework for action on special needs education.* Paris: UNESCO.

Chapter 5
Collaboration in Transitions from Preschool: Young Children with Intellectual Disabilities

Jenny Wilder and Anne Lillvist

Diversity can be defined as the qualities of having variety and catering for a wide range of different people. The concept of diversity is often thought of as the integration and inclusion of all ethnic/cultural groups, genders and ages in the community. Children with disabilities are part of the variety of society and disabilities can be considered as a diversity category alongside others. This chapter explores the educational transitions of young children with intellectual disabilities, especially focusing on collaboration between educational settings. The chapter describes an ongoing research project on the educational transitions of young children with intellectual disabilities in Sweden and its preliminary results. It also aims to widen the appraisal of diversity and inclusion in the discourses and practice of professionals who work with children in times of educational transition.

5.1 Introduction

Our research aimed to deepen our understanding of ways to meet diversity, from an inclusive perspective, with consideration for individual differences. This chapter explores educational transitions of young children with intellectual disabilities, especially focusing on collaboration between educational settings. The chapter will contribute to widening the appraisals of disabilities, diversity and inclusion in the

J. Wilder (✉)
Mälardalen University, Västerås, Sweden

Stockholm University, Stockholm, Sweden
e-mail: jenny.wilder@mdh.se

A. Lillvist
Mälardalen University, Västerås, Sweden

© Springer International Publishing Switzerland 2017
N. Ballam et al. (eds.), *Pedagogies of Educational Transitions*, International
Perspectives on Early Childhood Education and Development 16,
DOI 10.1007/978-3-319-43118-5_5

discourses and practices of professionals who work with children in times of educational transitions. In this chapter, 'young children' refers to children aged up to 7 years.

5.2 Disabilities, Diversity and Inclusion

The process of development can be viewed as a transactional process, influenced by the interactions between the child and the environment over time (Wachs 2000). A point of departure for young people's growth and development is also the way children and young people, with their individual experiences, approach different challenges. Young children with intellectual disabilities display considerable variability in the ways they function in everyday life (Guralnick 2011). They may have special educational needs, although in varying degrees. Intellectual disabilities shows great heterogeneity; for example, people can have different levels of intellectual disabilities even though they have the same diagnosis. This is also reflected in the prevailing definition of intellectual disabilities, which has shifted in recent years to focus on functioning and fulfilment for quality of life (Schalock et al. 2010). Intellectual disabilities can range from mild to moderate to severe to profound (Schalock et al. 2010). People with intellectual disabilities may also have complementary disabilities such as vision, auditory or motor impairments and may have complex communication needs. To compensate, augmentative and alternative communication (AAC) can be used to support their communication and learning. For people with complex communication needs, AAC can have important benefits. AAC includes the use of gestures, sign language, picture symbols and speech-generating devices to augment communication and speech (Beukelman and Mirenda 2005).

Burkhardt (2014) stated that 'a group impacted by the attitudes and beliefs of the majority in the society around them' (p. 35) can be identified as belonging to a diversity category. On a societal level, disabilities is an identified diversity category. For example, as one of its prioritised agendas, the United Nations aims to promote equality and access to all aspects of society to persons with disabilities through the *Convention of the Rights of Persons with Disabilities* (United Nations 2006). Although international standards for the inclusion of children with disabilities were set by UNESCO in the 1994 Salamanca Declaration, issues around diversity and education have usually focused on the confluence of race, class and culture (Milner 2009). It is only in recent years that identifications of disabilities have been positioned alongside other markers of diversity in the area of education (Collins 2013). On an individual level, diversity is related to disabilities when considering students with special educational needs and the way schools meet their needs.

The goal of special education is to give students with disabilities the chance to achieve at levels similar to peers without disabilities and, in achieving this, the accommodations within the environment that support students with disabilities are of paramount importance (Burkhardt 2014). According to Burkhardt (2014), special education can be viewed through the lenses of primary, secondary and tertiary prevention levels. These are terms that map out the range of interventions available to professionals; at each level, the interventions become more intense and specific for individual differences and type and degree of disabilities. At the primary prevention level, all efforts are made to prevent disabilities through, for example, prenatal care, parent education and preschool programmes. At the secondary prevention level, efforts to promote functioning for students with disabilities can be found – for example, identification of disabilities and eligibility and educational programmes. The tertiary prevention level can be associated with many traditional views of special education, such as special schools or intensive special services for children with severe disabilities.

Young children with special educational needs are not always formally identified according to traditional categorisations, which can affect the actual support they are given in educational settings (Lillvist 2010; Wilder 2015). As diversity is always defined in the eyes of the beholder, descriptions of what defines a diversity category also define the norm. In inclusive transition research, this was theoretically problematised by Petriwskyj (2014), who highlighted critical theorists' ways of approaching diversity. Applying a critical theory approach to special education focuses on critical reflection of normative assumptions on child development and underlying cultural frames for curriculum and pedagogy, as well as teacher practice. In accordance with a critical approach, Burkhardt (2014) argued that a starting point in a diversity perspective is to consider a person's functionality instead of their impairments or differences. She stated, 'Special education is ideally considered a means to achieving functionality for students with disabilities rather than an end in and of itself' (p. 39).

A recent tendency in many countries has been to develop educational policy towards inclusion of students with special educational needs (Hotulaineñ and Takala 2014; Lim et al. 2014). Internationally, most countries require schools to be inclusive of children with disabilities. Apart from special schools, physical integration and/or separate facilities or classes within a regular school are common ways of organising education for students with intellectual disabilities. The students may then be given opportunities to participate in the mainstream setting to an extent decided for each individual. Special education facilities may have a separate principal and teaching staff. In some countries, there is a consistent trend towards integrating children with disabilities in mainstream programmes. For example, in Australia, Forlin (2006) reported that, following legislation in the early 1990s, the number of children with special educational needs enrolled in regular schools increased. In Western Australia, of the 10,108 students identified with intellectual disabilities in 2004, only 4.7 % were enrolled in a special school, while 36 % were in a mainstream setting (this also included those in a separate class). The remaining students were enrolled in educational support centres on the sites of regular schools. Although policies include all children, in many countries children with disabilities are still enrolled in special schools. For example, in Ireland a trend has developed whereby an increasing number of students with mild general learning disabilities[1]

---

[1] The concept 'learning disabilities' is used primarily in the UK and has the same meaning as 'intellectual disabilities' (Scanlon 2013; Schalock 2013).

(MGLD) are leaving mainstream primary and post-primary schools and transferring to special schools for students with MGLD (Kerins 2014). Another example is Singapore; although current policies mandate the school system to become more inclusive, the country's education system is structured in dual track, including mainstream schools and special schools, and few children with disabilities are in inclusive educational settings (Lim et al. 2014).

5.3   The Swedish School System

In Sweden, children from birth up to 5 years of age attend preschool and 95 % of all Swedish 5-year-olds attend preschool (National Agency of Education 2014). The Swedish preschool is inclusive in kind; that is, formally diagnosed children and children in need of special support who are not formally identified attend regular preschool, together with typically developing children. Support systems exist for preschool staff working with children who, for some reason, are in need of special provision. Preschool staff can receive assistance from municipal support teams for an individual child or for the whole class, although supports given are most often based on the formally identified needs of children – that is, a child's diagnosis (Lillvist 2010; Wilder 2015).

Since 1998, municipalities in Sweden have been obliged to provide a place for all children in the preschool class from the autumn term of the academic year when the child turns six. The intention of the preschool class reform was to bridge the transitions children make from informal systems (family/preschool) to more formal systems (school). The difference between a preschool class and compulsory school is that, while compulsory school has goals to be attained, the preschool class only has goals to strive for. The intentions of the preschool class reform were also to promote a fusion of preschool and school education and to lay the foundation for continued education for children by encouraging learning and development (National Agency of Education 2012). Statistics show that 96 % of all 6-year-olds attend this voluntary form of schooling (National Agency of Education 2014). Children with intellectual disabilities are entitled to attend the preschool class and, while most of them do, some of them skip the preschool class and instead go to compulsory school for students with intellectual disabilities (CSSID) at the age of 6.

At age 7, school attendance is compulsory. Sweden has two parallel school types: compulsory school and CSSID. CSSID is provided for children with diagnosed intellectual disabilities who are anticipated to be unable to reach the educational goals of compulsory school. The aim of the CSSID is to offer educational practices based on the need of individual children. There are 667 CSSIDs in 280 Swedish municipalities. The CSSID can be organised in different ways: either as separate schools in a community or by having separate facilities or classes physically integrated within a regular school. Children can be enrolled in these schools at different ages. The decision to start CSSID lies with the parents and is often made in collaboration with education and care professionals. Before enrolment, educational, social,

Table 5.1 Number of students with intellectual disabilities in different types of schools (2012–2013) (National Agency of Education 2014)

Type of school	Number of students %
CSSID	5995
	55 %
Training school (part of CSSID, open to students with severe disabilities)	3661
	33 %
Inclusive education in compulsory school	1275
	12 %
Total	10,931
	100 %

psychological and medical investigation of the child is made by professionals, and it is a requirement for the child to have a diagnosed intellectual disabilities to be enrolled in the CSSID. One type of CSSID is the 'training school'. Children attending training school have moderate to severe intellectual disabilities and often additional disabilities. A training school does not offer academic subjects. Rather, it has subjects that relate to daily living. Statistics show that 1 % of all Swedish students are enrolled in CSSID. The number of enrolments in CSSID increases for each grade and peaks in the 6th grade. Thereafter, the admission rate remains constant. Children who are 6–7 years old when they start CSSID often have more severe than mild intellectual disabilities.

Although inclusion of children with disabilities is the prevailing practice in preschool, actual inclusion of students with intellectual disabilities in regular compulsory schooling is not very common. Most students who are included in compulsory schools are taught and study according to the CSSID curriculum. Table 5.1 (2012–2013 figures) illustrates that most students with intellectual disabilities (55 %) were enrolled in CSSID, while about a third (33 %) were enrolled in training school. Only 1275 (12 %) of students with diagnosed intellectual disabilities who were studying the CSSID curriculum were in inclusive educational settings.

In Sweden, cooperation and collaboration with the home and other professionals are prioritised as an important area of school development and school responsibility in both the national curriculum for the compulsory school and preschool class (National Agency of Education 2011a) and in the specific national curriculum for CSSID (National Agency of Education 2011b).

5.4 Collaboration

Educational transitions involve bridging knowledge through collaboration. For children with intellectual disabilities, positive early educational transitions are characterised by well-functioning collaboration between microenvironments such as the home, the preschool and the school. Transitions for children with special needs and their families have been linked to children's future outcomes (McIntyre et al. 2007). Transitions for children with special needs tend to involve a range of professionals, increasing the complexity of the process and sometimes making these necessary changes difficult for both parents and children (Bailey 2011). For all children and their families, transition requires the processes of planning, implementing, evaluating and balancing parents' lives and responsibilities with the needs of their children to achieve the best outcomes for the whole family (Ankeny et al. 2009; Stoner et al. 2007). This is particularly the case for children with special needs and their families.

According to Danermark and Germundsson (2011), collaboration processes exist within three frames: regulation, organisation and different viewpoints or approaches of stakeholders. Regulation is determined by guidelines and stated aims, such as in national curricula or national guidelines. The frame of organisation is the way collaboration processes are supported and how the work is locally organised, such as by the principal of the school or in staff teams. The third frame is signified by the different viewpoints and approaches of the stakeholders within the organisation. The approaches of the stakeholders in collaborating educational settings affect what actual collaborative activities are performed and how they are performed. The involved parties' social representations of one another play significant roles in collaborative processes. Stakeholders in the microenvironments of children with intellectual disabilities are the parents or guardians and the teachers (or assistants) in preschool and in CSSID. In collaborative educational transition processes, there is a risk of power imbalance (Petriwskyj 2014). Parents of young children are often novices when it comes to school routines, practices and school regulations. At the same time, they are experts on their children. Parents often depend on teachers and principals to provide information and initiate transition activities. Promoting teachers' awareness of power in transition processes, combined with efforts to balance power, can be a strategy to facilitate the range of different stakeholders' perspectives being considered in collaboration (Petriwskyj 2014). Wilder et al. (2015) showed that teachers and parents sharing their learning about communication and interaction for children with intellectual disabilities can be promoted through distance learning networks. This neutral type of meeting place was experienced as rewarding by the participants and the shared learning also shaped their views of each other in a positive direction.

Parents of children with disabilities desire to work closely with teachers, although there may be challenges to reciprocal relationships, such as when teachers hold deficit views of parents or there are cultural differences or issues of trust. Dobbins and Abbot's (2010) review of the field of collaborative processes regarding education and young children with intellectual disabilities shows a research focus on teachers' and parents' expectations and viewpoints of each other, cultural differences and the role of principals. They studied parents' views of the home–school relationship in special schools and found that parents appreciated the schools as having an important supportive function in their everyday lives. At the same time, there was also some dissatisfaction. This study reported that parents in special schools in Northern Ireland wished to know much more about, and work closer with, their child's school and those professionally involved within it. When investigating the collaboration between parents and teachers in special schools, Dobbins (2006) found that teachers sometimes viewed parents as inherently problematic, in the sense that they were perceived to be unreliable and less effective implementers of the school agenda. As such, the teachers saw their own views as superior to those of the parents. In her research about children with severe disabilities in special schools in Austria, Pickl (2011) reported that different cultural views about the school and home responsibilities of parents and teachers, as well as the multilingual backgrounds of the children, were great obstacles and challenges for collaboration between home and school. In a qualitative study investigating the perspectives of mothers of children with disabilities, Shelden et al. (2010) found that not only was the trust from teachers valued by parents but also the trust as it was established by, and with, principals. From the mothers' perspectives, the trust of the principals was shown and realised through the personal and professional attributes of principals. These included their accessibility and knowledge about disabilities, as well as their actions, such as attending parental meetings and interactions with the children. Meaningful and productive relationships between parents and teachers are underpinned by respect, trust, open communication and honesty (Keen 2007).

In research concerning collaboration between parents and school professionals in phases of early educational transition, such as into preschool or from preschool to school entry, parents generally have expressed that they lacked information about the planned transitions (Bailey 2011). Bailey's study revealed a systemic lack of information provided to families by early childhood professionals at entry to preschool. Families were not aware that transition was not just a one-time event, but a continuous process that occurred over time. Further, families were unclear about what types of activities should occur, and when, during the transition process. Janus et al. (2008) studied the pre- and post-transition experiences of parents of children with disabilities at school entry. Post-transition parents reported less average disabilities impact on their family and generally lower perceptions of quality of care than pre-transition parents and long waiting periods for school-based support (e.g. in the form of educational assistants/paraprofessionals/teacher assistants). Walker et al. (2012) showed similar findings, with both teachers and parents noting a lack of accommodation in the physical environment of school for children with developmental disabilities after their transition to school. Results from this study also showed that although parents were satisfied with the teachers' helpfulness and respect, more than one-third of the 56 parents thought that the transition had been difficult and this was associated with the school being unprepared through lack of knowledge about the child.

5.5 Transfer of Knowledge

In transition activities, Peters (2010) emphasised the meaning of 'bridging' between different stages of education to support learning. This bridging depends on the connections that are made between teachers in different educational settings, as well as with parents. Peters referred to developing a borderland, a shared space of understanding. She formulated the way the children's learning processes through transitions from preschool to school can be understood in terms of the concept 'learning journeys'. For children with special needs and their families, transitions can be the cause of stress as new situations and education settings are introduced (Ankeny et al. 2009). What knowledge should be shared to ensure a smooth transition for young children with intellectual disabilities? Educational practices for children with intellectual disabilities are not only focused on learning but also on communication and interaction, everyday functioning and type and degree of everyday care needs of the children. Apart from pedagogical descriptions, knowledge transfer must also include these aspects to enable and enhance continuity of learning. Learning journeys for young children with intellectual disabilities can thus be more complex than those of young children without disabilities.

Parents or guardians, preschool teachers, school teachers and special school teachers and assistants in preschool and school are the holders of knowledge for young children with intellectual disabilities who are making educational transitions from preschool. The stakeholders who have worked closely with specific children have unique knowledge and also unique practices for working with the children. Parents of children with disabilities are often considered experts on their children's communication and interaction (Marshall and Goldbart 2008; Wilder and Granlund 2014). For children with severe disabilities, parents are usually the ones who know the most about their children's daily medical and care needs (Ölund 2012). Parents can provide information regarding routines, activities, abilities, relationships and other familial events that may affect children's development and learning. Parents of children with disabilities often have a key role in teaching others about their own child, but they may feel that they are not being listened to by professionals (White and Hastings 2004).

The holders of child knowledge at preschool are the preschool teachers or assistants who have worked closely with the child. They may have practical as well as theoretical knowledge about the child's functioning and care needs. In Sweden, preschool is focused on play and on learning basic skills in reading, writing and counting. It is mandatory for teachers to document children's development and to plan how the preschool can support the child's development. Preschool teachers have meetings with parents about the children's social, emotional and academic progress. These preschool teachers build up comprehensive knowledge about the preschool child (Sheridan and Pramling Samuelsson 2013). It is common that preschool teachers of children with diagnosed intellectual disabilities participate in the educational investigation of the child in preparation for their transition. This educational investigation is written down as a pedagogical description of the child and is one of the documents necessary for the application for CSSID.

School teachers who are to receive children making educational transitions are stakeholders of another kind. Being on the receiving side puts demands on preparation and welcoming activities. The receiving stakeholders have a critical role in relation to how the transition works out and are the ones who will have a child's social, cultural and transition capital as a point of departure, as they will stay with the same children for several years (O'Kane 2007). Teachers' perspectives, attitudes and expectations colour collaboration processes. For example, they affect the kind of knowledge that teachers seek when they are to receive a child with intellectual disabilities. A positive development in the knowledge and attitudes towards learning and children with more severe disabilities is spreading across the world. For example, in the UK, teachers' attitudes have shifted from a medical and care philosophy to the contemporary appreciation of disabilities in accordance with the social model of disabilities (Jones 2006). Examples of this are found in research that elaborates the knowledge about communication and interaction as a basis for learning. Jones (2006) showed how teachers of students with severe disabilities embraced positive views of their students as learners, such as in regarding every subtle communication component as a possibility with which to work.

5.6   Swedish Research Example

This ongoing research project was designed to deepen the understanding about the transitions of young children with intellectual disabilities and the educational practices they encounter during their time in transition from preschool into the first year of CSSID. The research was designed in two parts: a quantitative survey study for teachers, called special teachers, in CSSID and case studies of eight children's transitions. The specific aims of the research project were (1) to explore the transition that children with intellectual disabilities make from preschool into CSSID; (2) to explore the way collaboration between home, preschool and CSSID is carried out; and (3) to explore how transitions of knowledge about pedagogical profiles of learning, the children's communication and interaction, everyday functioning and type and degree of everyday care needs of children with disabilities are treated in these practices. The research project was approved by the regional ethics committee, Uppsala, Dnr 2013/512. This chapter presents the preliminary survey results.

Parts of the questionnaire that was developed by the researchers were inspired by a Norwegian questionnaire about collaboration between preschool and regular school (Hogsnes and Moser 2014). Our questionnaire was set in a Swedish context and included collaboration aspects regarding children with disabilities. The latter was based on considerations of earlier research about the special needs of children with intellectual disabilities. A preliminary version of the survey was tested in a pilot study with 22 special teacher students. Following the pilot study, more background items were included and some modifications of language were made. The final version of the questionnaire included background questions about each teacher's gender, age and current working place, teacher education and characteristics of the children with intellectual disabilities who were received into their school. The core questionnaire was structured and focused on pre- and post-transition organisation, transition activities and teacher attitudes. The items were to be answered on five-point Likert scales and ranged from 'I totally disagree' to 'I totally agree'. The core questionnaire included 51 items concerning routines pre-/during transitions, collaborative activities in receiving children, type of information passed on between stakeholders, teacher attitudes, knowledge about policies and practice and time management.

Participants in the study were teachers who worked in CSSID (called special teachers) and had experience of receiving young children with intellectual disabilities into their classes. Information about the study and a call for interest was posted on Internet networks for special teachers working in CSSID, and information was sent to principals in a wide range of Swedish CSSIDs. Through convenience sampling, data were collected from autumn 2013 until spring 2015. The questionnaire was sent to a wide range of CSSIDs, both in the largest cities of Sweden and in more rural parts of Sweden. Further, all Swedish universities that hosted special teacher programmes, in which working special teachers can study a postgraduate programme to receive formal recognition as special teachers, were visited and engaged in the recruitment of participants. So far, 685 questionnaires have been distributed and 230 have been returned. Nine questionnaires were excluded due to being incomplete. For this chapter, the preliminary findings from 221 participants are presented. The response rate can be explained by the difficulty in locating those special teachers who had experience of receiving children aged 6–7 into CSSIDs. In the data analyses, frequency analyses of responses to the Likert scales were undertaken and correlations between teachers' views and performed collaboration activities were calculated using Spearman's rank correlation test.

5.7   Results

This section examines the special teachers' appraisals of certain aspects of collaboration processes when children aged six or seven with intellectual disabilities started Swedish CSSID. Specifically, we present findings about child characteristics, the contents and pathways of knowledge transfer between different stakeholders in children's transitions and the relationships between the collaboration activities that were considered important versus the collaboration activities that were performed in transitions. The results are presented at an aggregated level.

To gather more information about the characteristics of the young children who started CSSID, the questionnaire asked the special teachers to select the type of disabilities the children most often had, from the following categories: only intellectual disabilities, intellectual disabilities in combination with complex communication needs, physical disabilities, medical difficulties or a combination of several of the disabilities categories above. More than half (57 %) of the special teachers reported that children who started CSSID had intellectual disabilities in combination with several of the other disabilities categories presented; just 10 % reported that children had intellectual disabilities only. Further, 31 % pinpointed that the children had complex communication needs in combination with intellectual disabilities.

5.7.1   Contents and Pathways of Knowledge Transfer

The special teachers were asked to estimate to what degree they thought it was important to gain knowledge from stakeholders about the child's learning, everyday functioning, communication, pedagogical description and health-care needs. The ranking of importance was made on a scale from 'not important', 'small importance', 'somewhat important', 'quite important' and 'very important'. As can be expected, most respondents indicated that it was very important to gain knowledge about the child in all areas. Most (85 %) indicated that gaining knowledge about the child's communication and health-care needs was very important.

Concerning pathways of knowledge transfer between different stakeholders, the special teachers answered questions about who primarily gave them information about the child's learning, everyday functioning, communication, pedagogical description and health-care needs. The respondents were asked to select only one category as the primary person who gave information about each aspect. Despite the instructions, some respondents marked several categories; therefore, Table 5.2 contains a row labelled 'Several of the above'. The results showed a significant skew to preschool teachers giving the information in all areas (see Table 5.2).

Information about the children's learning, everyday functioning, communication and pedagogical descriptions were predominantly given to special teachers by teachers in the children's previous educational setting. Parents were reported as being involved in knowledge transfer in these areas to a much lesser degree. Information about the pedagogical descriptions of children was given by several stakeholders, including the special educator (25 %) and principal (12 %). All other stakeholders were involved in that knowledge transition to a greater degree than parents; only 5 % of special teachers reported that parents were involved. On the other hand, parents were involved to a large extent in transferring knowledge about their children's health-care needs. In this knowledge area, special teachers gained information especially from parents and to a very low degree from other stakeholders.

Table 5.2 Pathways of knowledge transfer: degree to which special teachers ($n=221$) received information from stakeholders about knowledge areas in transitions

Stakeholders	Learning (%)	Everyday functioning (%)	Communi-cation (%)	Pedagogical descriptions (%)	Health-care needs (%)
Preschool teacher	73	53	57	42	15
Parent	7	26	13	5	66
Special educator	7	1	5	25	1
Principal	0	0	0	12	1
Several of the above	13	20	25	16	17

5.7.2 Special Teachers' Views of Important Versus Actually Performed Collaboration Activities

To explore the features of collaboration processes further, the special teachers were asked about specific activities, to estimate how important these were and how often they were performed. We then analysed the statistical relationships between the estimates of importance versus performance to examine patterns of the actual approach to collaboration activities. To test the relationships, Spearman's rank correlation test was used with the p value set to $p < 0.05$.

Table 5.3 presents the participants' perspectives of six collaboration activities, how often they were performed and how important they were considered to be. The results in the middle column show that the items *CSSID held a parents' meeting before school starts*, *Special teacher met the parents and child together for a meeting* and *Special teacher met preschool teacher to talk about what the child has learnt and experienced in preschool* were considered important. In contrast, the right-hand column in Table 5.3 shows that the items *CSSID and preschool organise common parents' meetings before school starts*, *Special teacher visits the child at home* and *Special teacher and preschool teacher have meetings about what the child will learn and experience in CSSID* were not considered important by the special teachers and were not performed. It should be noted that no negative correlations were found in the data analyses. That means that there were no suggested collaborative activities that were performed but considered to be of no importance and there were no suggested activities that were considered important but not performed.

Table 5.3 Correlations between important versus actually performed collaboration activities

Collaboration activities	Important and performed	Not important and not performed
CSSID holds a parents' meeting for all parents before child starts school	0.705**	
Special teacher meets parents and child together for a meeting before school start	0.597**	
Special teacher and preschool teacher meet to talk about what the child has learnt and experienced in preschool	0.480**	
Special teacher and preschool teacher meet to talk about what the child will learn and experience in CSSID		0.624**
CSSID and preschool have common parents' meetings before school starts		0.509**
Special teacher visits the child at home		0.509**

5.8 Discussion

In this chapter we have considered aspects of disabilities, diversity and inclusion in the discourses and practices of different stakeholders in times of children's educational transitions. To illustrate these issues, an ongoing research project and its preliminary findings about educational transitions of young children with intellectual disabilities in Sweden have been presented.

Our conclusion from the preliminary analysis of these data is that inclusion of children with intellectual disabilities is not facilitated by the parallel school types that exist in Sweden – the compulsory school and the CSSID. Approximately 13 % of all students diagnosed with intellectual disabilities are in inclusive education and the rest go to CSSIDs, either as separate schools in a community or separate facilities or classes physically integrated within a regular school. In considering these figures, it is important to note that the eligibility criterion of an intellectual disabilities diagnosis means that students with other kinds of disabilities only, such as ADHD, autism spectrum disorder, visual or hearing impairments or physical disabilities, are not eligible to attend CSSID. Instead, they attend mainstream compulsory school. How this is organised within schools is another matter that cannot be disentangled here. Quantitative results from our survey show that from the perspectives of special teachers, children aged 6–7 years most often exhibit combinations of disabilities when they start CSSID. This is reflected in the category of intellectual disabilities, especially in combination with complex communication needs. Only 10 % of responding teachers reported that children had only intellectual disabilities. Having complementary disabilities to intellectual disabilities holds extra challenges for children's learning. Complex communication needs and visual and hearing impairment all demand specially adjusted and adapted learning environments and teaching skills. Well-functioning collaboration among all the stakeholders in the child's life is of vital importance to ensure that receiving schools and teachers can be properly prepared.

The special teachers in this study thought it was important to gain knowledge about children's learning, everyday functioning, communication, pedagogical description and health-care needs. Knowledge about communication and health-care needs was reported as very important. The special teachers gained knowledge about children primarily from preschool teachers; generally, parents were only involved in transferring knowledge about their children's health-care needs. In transferring their knowledge in the other areas, parents were reported to share their knowledge about communication (13 %) and learning (7 %) infrequently. This result can be considered rather serious, as many researchers emphasise the importance of parents' expert knowledge about their own children, especially their knowledge about their children's communication (Marshall and Goldbart 2008; Wilder and Granlund 2014) in promoting positive educational environments. Parents know their child in all aspects of everyday life and can provide information about how the child acts, reacts and communicates in routines and in new activities. They have a lifetime of knowledge about their child, which would certainly add to the knowledge of other stakeholders.

Further, the results may reflect that special teachers hold an academic view about learning. The results indicated that the special teachers' attitudes about the differences between a child's learning in preschool and at home, as well as the preschool teachers' knowledge about a child's learning and communication, was more similar to that of CSSID teachers than parents' knowledge. Moreover, the results also revealed special teachers' attitudes about a common understanding of learning that is tied to the teaching profession and to the preschool's role as being preparation for school.

The collaboration activities with the home and preschool reported so far in our study have indicated that CSSIDs focus on traditional ways of collaborating, such as having overall parents' meetings as well as separate meetings with the parents and child together before school starts and meetings with the preschool to talk about what the child has learnt and experienced in preschool. The CSSID was not reported to involve the preschool or the home in more elaborate ways; for example, the special teachers did not visit the child's home nor think it was important to do so. Additionally, the CSSID and preschool teachers did not hold parents' meetings together, even though the experiences and knowledge of professionals in a child's previous pedagogical microenvironment can be built on in the new setting. It can be anticipated that preschool teachers, with their unique knowledge about specific children and their unique practices with the children, can contribute with knowledge and planning of, for example, how to best motivate and teach the children. When preschool teachers are not involved further, the stakeholders' knowledge about a child's social, cultural and transitions capital is not utilised.

In viewing our results, we question whether or not a shared space of understanding, as proposed by Peters (2010), can be achieved for the learning journeys that young children with intellectual disabilities make in transition from preschool to CSSID. The range of perspectives that exist in children's lives (Petriwskyj 2014) cannot be seen to be considered in collaboration. These results are significant, considering that children with intellectual disabilities starting CSSID at the age of 6 or 7 often have multiple disabilities. For them to experience continuity of learning, great efforts should be taken to ensure that all knowledge about a child's strengths have been transferred between stakeholders. To start with, parents' knowledge about their children in all areas should always be sought. There is always a risk of discontinuity in children's learning in educational transitions, but for these children, the risk is that the learning journey stops and then has to start over again completely. To eliminate that risk for fragile children, collaboration in educational transitions needs to be multifaceted and based on stakeholders acknowledging each other's expertise.

References

Ankneny, E., Wilkins, J., & Spain, J. (2009). Mothers' experiences of transition planning for their children with disabilities. *Teaching Exceptional Children, 41*(6), 28–36.

Bailey, H. N. (2011). *Transitions in early childhood: a look at parents' perspectives.* Doctoral thesis, Faculty of the Graduate School, University of North Carolina at Greensboro. North Carolina, USA.

Beukelman, D., & Mirenda, P. (2005). *Augmentative and alternative communication* (3rd ed.). Baltimore: Paul H. Brookes Publishing.

Burkhardt, S. (2014). Diversity and disability. *Advances in Special Education, 27*, 33–52.

Collins, K. (2013). A disability studies response to JTE's themed issue on diversity and disability in teacher education. *Journal of Teacher Education, 64*(3), 283–287. doi:10.1177/0022487112473155.

Danermark, B., & Germundsson, P. (2011). Social representations and power. In M. Chaib, B. Danermark, & S. Selander (Eds.), *Education, professionalization and social representations: On the transformation of social knowledge* (pp. 33–44). New York: Routledge.

Dobbins, M. (2006). *Creating enabling environments for students with severe learning difficulties in a special school setting*. Doctoral thesis, University of Ulster, Belfast, Northern Ireland.

Dobbins, M., & Abbot, L. (2010). Developing partnership with parents in special schools: Parental perspectives from Northern Ireland. *Journal of Research in Special Educational Needs, 10*(1), 23–30.

Forlin, C. (2006). Inclusive education in Australia. *European Journal of Psychology of Education, 20*(1), 265–277.

Guralnick, M. J. (2011). Why early intervention works: A systems perspective. *Infants & Young Children, 24*, 6–28.

Hogsnes, H. D., & Moser, T. (2014). Forståelser av gode overganger og opplevelse av sammenheng mellom barnehage, skole og skolfritidsordning [Understandings of positive transitions and experiences between preschool and school]. *Nordic Early Childhood Education Research Journal, 7*(6), 1–24.

Hotulainen, R., & Takala, M. (2014). Parents' views on the success of integration of students with special education needs. *International Journal of Inclusive Education, 18*(2), 140–154.

Janus, M., Kopenchanski, L., Cameron, R., & Hughes, D. (2008). In transition: Experiences of parents of children with special needs at school entry. *Early Childhood Education Journal, 35*, 479–485.

Jones, P. (2006). Teachers' views of their pupils with profound and multiple learning difficulties. *European Journal of Special Needs Education, 20*(4), 375–385.

Keen, D. (2007). Parents, families, and partnerships: Issues and considerations. *International Journal of Disability, Development and Education, 54*(3), 339–349.

Kerins, P. (2014). Dilemmas of difference and educational provision for students with mild general learning disabilities in the Republic of Ireland. *European Journal of Special Needs Education, 29*(1), 47–58.

Lillvist, A. (2010). *The applicability of a functional approach to social competence in preschool children in need of special support*. Doctoral thesis, Örebro studies in Psychology, Örebro, Sweden.

Lim, S. M.-Y., Wonga, M. E., & Tanb, D. (2014). Allied educators (learning and behavioural support) in Singapore's mainstream schools: First steps towards inclusivity? *International Journal of Inclusive Education, 18*(2), 123–139.

Marshall, J., & Goldbart, J. (2008). 'Communication is everything I think'. Parenting a child who needs augmentative and alternative communication (AAC). *International Journal of Language & Communication Disorders, 43*(1), 77–98.

McIntyre, L. L., Eckert, T. L., Fiese, B. H., DiGennaro, F. D., & Wildenger, L. K. (2007). Transition to kindergarten: Family experiences and involvement. *Early Childhood Education Journal, 35*(1), 83–88.

Milner, R. (2009). *Diversity and education: Teachers, teaching, and teacher education (e-book version)*. Springfield: Charles C. Thomas, Publishing.

National Agency of Education. (2011a). *Läroplan för det obligatoriska skolväsendet, förskoleklassen och fritidshemmet* [Curriculum for the compulsory school, preschool class and the recreation centre]. Stockholm: Skolverket.

National Agency of Education. (2011b). *Läroplan för grundsärskolan* [Curriculum for the compulsory school for learning disabilities]. Stockholm: Skolverket.

National Agency of Education. (2012). *Förskoleklassen är till för ditt barn. En broschyr om förskoleklassen* [The preschool class is for your child. A brochure about the pre-school class]. Stockholm: Skolverket.

National Agency of Education. (2014). *Beskrivande data 2013. Förskola, skola och vuxenutbildning. Rapport Nr. 399* [Descriptive statistics 2013. Preschool, school and adult education. Report Nr. 399]. Stockholm: Skolverket.

O'Kane, M. (2007). *Building bridges: The transition from preschool to primary school for children in Ireland.* Doctoral thesis, Dublin Institute of Technology, Dublin, Ireland.

Ölund, A- K. (2012). *Medicinsk omvårdnad vid svåra flerfunktionshinder* [Medical care for severe multiple disabilities]. Stockholm: Gothia förlag.

Peters, S. (2010). Shifting the lens: Re-framing the view of learners and learning during the transition from early childhood education to school in New Zealand. In D. Jindal-Snape (Ed.), *Educational transitions: Moving stories from around the world* (pp. 68–84). New York: Routledge.

Petriwskyj, A. (2014). Critical theory and inclusive transitions to school. In B. Perry, S. Dockett, & A. Petriwskyj (Eds.), *Transition to school: International research, policy and practice* (pp. 201–215). Dordrecht: Springer.

Pickl, G. (2011). Communication intervention in children with severe disabilities and multi-lingual backgrounds: Perceptions of pedagogues and parents. *Augmentative and Alternative Communication, 27*(4), 229–244.

Scanlon, D. (2013). Specific learning disability and its newest definition: Which is comprehensive and which is insufficient? *Journal of Learning Disabilities, 46*(1), 26–33.

Schalock, R. (2013). Introduction to the intellectual disability construct. In M. Wehmeyer (Ed.), *The story of intellectual disability: An evolution of meaning, understanding and public perception* (pp. 1–18). Sydney: Brookes Publishing.

Schalock, R., Borthwick-Duffy, S., Bradley, V., Buntinx, W., Coulter, D., Craig, E., & Yeager, M. (2010). *Intellectual disability: Definition, classification, and systems of supports* (11th ed.). Washington, DC: American Association on Intellectual and Developmental Disabilities.

Shelden, D. L., Angell, M. E., Stoner, J. B., & Roseland, B. D. (2010). School principals' influence on trust: Perspectives of mothers of children with disabilities. *The Journal of Educational Research, 103*, 159–170.

Sheridan, S., & Pramling Samuelsson, I. (2013). Preschool a source for young children's learning and well-being. *International Journal of Early Years Education, 21*(2–3), 207–222.

Stoner, J. B., Angell, M. E., House, J. J., & Bock, S. J. (2007). Transitions: Perspectives from parents of young children with autism spectrum disorder (ASD). *Journal of Developmental & Physical Disabilities, 19*, 23–39.

United Nations. (2006). Convention on the rights of persons with disabilities. http://www.un.org/disabilities/convention/conventionfull.shtml. Accessed 10 Feb 2015.

Wachs, T. (2000). *Necessary but not sufficient.* Washington, DC: American Psychological Association.

Walker, S., Dunbar, S., Meldrum, K., Whiteford, C., Carrington, S., Hand, K., et al. (2012). The transition to school of children with developmental disabilities: Views of parents and teachers. *Australasian Journal of Early Childhood, 37*(3), 22–29.

White, N., & Hastings, R. P. (2004). Social and professional support for parents of adolescents with severe intellectual disabilities. *Journal of Applied Research in Intellectual Disabilities, 17*(3), 181–190.

Wilder, J. (2015). Access and delivery of formal support to young children with developmental delay in Sweden. *Research and Practice in Intellectual Developmental Disabilities, 2*(2), 136–147.

Wilder, J., & Granlund, M. (2014). Stability and change in sustainability of daily routines and social networks of families of children with PIMD. *Journal of Applied Research in Intellectual Disabilities.* doi:10.1111/jar.12111.

Wilder, J., Magnusson, L., & Hanson, E. (2015). Parents' and professionals' shared learning about communication and augmentative, alternative communication in blended learning networks. *European Journal of Special Needs Education.* doi:10.1080/08856257.2015.1023002.

Part II
Transition to School for Indigenous Children

Chapter 6
Transition to School for Indigenous Children

Margie Hohepa and Leonie McIntosh

This chapter considers current research literature on educational transitions from early childhood to primary school for Indigenous children, their families and communities. While there is a relatively small corpus of research on educational transitions pertaining to Indigenous peoples, there is an increasing policy focus across a number of countries and continents. Policy directions are examined with regard to the implications for Indigenous educational transitions in the Pedagogies of Educational Transitions (POET) countries of Aotearoa New Zealand and Australia. This chapter sets the scene for the following two chapters, which consider Indigenous educational transition as it has been researched in recent projects in these two countries. The current state of research linked to Indigenous educational transition in the respective countries is also explored. The emergence of Indigenous research approaches is discussed in terms of the implications these have for research into pedagogies of educational transition.

6.1 Introduction

Historically, early childhood education and schooling have played a strong role in the assimilation and integration of Indigenous, minoritised peoples (Hickling-Hudson and Ahlquist 2003; Prochner 2004; Ritchie and Skerrett 2014). This has left a legacy of mistrust on formal education amongst many Indigenous peoples (Hare and Anderson 2010). More recently, early childhood education has become a focal point

M. Hohepa (✉)
University of Waikato, Hamilton, New Zealand
e-mail: mkhohepa@waikato.ac.nz

L. McIntosh
Charles Sturt University, Albury, NSW, Australia

© Springer International Publishing Switzerland 2017
N. Ballam et al. (eds.), *Pedagogies of Educational Transitions*, International
Perspectives on Early Childhood Education and Development 16,
DOI 10.1007/978-3-319-43118-5_6

of Indigenous-driven efforts to retain and regenerate Indigenous languages and cultures across the world, including Aotearoa New Zealand (Hohepa et al. 1992), Australia (Martin 2007), Canada (Maracle et al. 2011) and Hawaii (Iokepa-Guerrero and France 2007). However, there are few published studies on the impact of such programmes (Prochner 2004). There is also relatively little international research that focuses on either Indigenous educational transitions in early childhood (Hare and Anderson 2010) or transitions from early childhood education to schooling (Peters 2010).

While the development of a robust corpus of research is still in progress, educational transition for Indigenous learners is a focus in policy directions and key reforms across a number of countries and continents. This chapter examines current policy directions in Aotearoa New Zealand and Australia as they pertain to Indigenous education, identifying the relative importance given to transition. It also considers the current state of research linked to Indigenous educational transition in the respective countries.

Educational policy in both Aotearoa New Zealand and Australia includes specific and targeted policies aimed at making a positive difference for Indigenous learners, although policy directions may differ in terms of focus. In Aotearoa New Zealand, the focus is on 'realising Māori potential' via 'Māori learners enjoying and achieving educational success as Māori' (Ministry of Education 2013, pp. 6–7). In Australia, the focus is on addressing outcome gaps between Indigenous and non-Indigenous Australians by increasing access to education (Council of Australian Governments [COAG] 2011). Both countries, however, share an explicit focus on strengthening educational transitions during early childhood as a means to help achieve their respective goals.

Available research evidence from both countries highlights the significance of relationships and culture in enhancing transitions for Indigenous children and their families. In Australia, developing strength-based approaches emerges as a strong theme in educational transition research, while in Aotearoa New Zealand, the existence of Māori medium and English medium education pathways are generating increased transition research activity.

This chapter also overviews and advocates for Indigenous research approaches emanating out of Indigenous knowledge systems that challenge colonising theories and methodologies. The significance of the respective approaches for researching Indigenous educational transitions is examined. This chapter helps set the scene for the following two chapters, which consider Indigenous educational transitions as they have been recently researched in the two POET alliance countries.

6.2 Transition to School for Māori Children in Aotearoa New Zealand

In Aotearoa New Zealand, there is an explicit policy and practice focus on improving Indigenous children's educational transitions, reflected in two consecutive Māori education strategies. *Ka Hikitia Managing for Success: The Māori Education*

Strategy 2008–2012 (Ministry of Education 2008) is focused on 'building strong foundations for learning early in the system and at key transition points as a prerequisite for further education and qualifications' (p. 2). Similarly, a key focus in *Ka Hikitia Accelerating Success: The Māori Education Strategy 2013–2017* is 'supporting successful transitions across the educational journey of Māori students' (Ministry of Education 2013, p. 24). These strategies reflect a shift in policy from a 'closing the gaps' (Te Puni Kōkiri 1998) approach to a 'Māori potential' approach. The Māori potential approach reduces the focus on identifying and remedying deficits and promotes investing in strengths, opportunities and potential.

Both strategies acknowledge that effective transitions are important throughout the educational journey. The 'foundation years', identified as early childhood education and the first years of schooling, were emphasised as a focus area in the 2008–2012 strategy. Priorities that were proposed for action to improve Māori children's transition to school included provision of transition resources and information programmes to Māori families and their children, professional development and transition toolkits for early childhood education and school teachers to work with Māori families, evaluative reviews of the effectiveness of transition to school for Māori children as a priority in 2008–2009 and 2009–2010 and using best evidence about effective teaching and learning in early childhood education settings to influence quality teaching in the first years of school (Ministry of Education 2008, p. 30). The strategy also emphasised the importance of effective transitions for academic achievement and the development of conventional academic skills, namely, literacy and numeracy.

In contrast, the 2013–2017 strategy sets out actions to support successful transitions across and within five focus areas: Māori language in education, early learning, primary and secondary education, tertiary education and organisational success (Ministry of Education 2013). While this strategy emphasises conventional academic outcomes and qualifications, it also calls attention to the importance of developing 'a strong sense of belonging' and the importance of supporting identity, language and culture for successful education transitions (p. 24). Goals identified for early childhood and primary schooling under the early learning focus include Māori parents and families accessing their choice of high-quality early childhood education (English and Māori medium education).

The key actions set out for achieving the goals have implications for Māori children's transitions within and across English and Māori medium education. These implications include increasing the supply and quality of early childhood education and early learning in both English and Māori medium education, removing barriers to access and promoting the benefits of participation in quality early childhood education along with the benefits of Māori language in education (Ministry of Education 2013, p. 34).

The 2013–2017 strategy makes the observation:

> Transitions can be challenging for Māori students. Māori students place strong importance on relationships with education professionals and their peers. Tailored solutions are required for Māori students transitioning between Māori medium and English medium education. (Ministry of Education 2013, p. 23)

Māori medium education statistics for early childhood and primary schooling may assist in the tailoring of solutions, as they can show the extent to which Māori children are able to experience effective continuity of learning in either Māori or English medium and/or the extent to which they can transition to 'unlike' schooling pathways (i.e. English medium to Māori medium, Māori medium to English medium) (Bright et al. 2013). For example, in July 2012, 22 % of preschool Māori children were enrolled in full immersion *kōhanga reo* (Māori immersion preschool language nests), and 24 % of school-aged Māori learners were learning in immersion (81–100 % immersion) or bilingual (51–80 % immersion) settings. It is unclear, however, what percentage of *kōhanga reo* children carry on to Māori medium schooling or how many children enter Māori medium schooling from English medium early childhood programmes.

Transition is also a consideration in review processes used to evaluate the quality of early childhood services and schools in Aotearoa New Zealand. The Education Review Office (ERO) evaluates services and schools and reports on the quality of education practice. The ERO has an explicit focus on Māori children in its review processes for early childhood education services and *kōhanga reo* (ERO n.d.). Evaluation indicators also focus on movements to or within early childhood education and to school. The criteria or indicators for transition include the extent to which children's sense of belonging is nurtured, the degree to which transition practices honour Māori cultural uniqueness and nurture their sense of belonging and the extent to which transitions are supported by effective partnerships between families, services and schools (ERO 2013, p. 6).

ERO (2015) evaluated how well 376 English medium early childhood services and 100 English medium schools supported children's transitions to school. ERO found that while practice in many of the centres supported successful transition, and Māori children were 'disproportionately represented in the least supportive services' (p. 27). They also found that few of the centres 'nurtured and maintained children's connections to their language, culture and identity as they approached transition to school' (p. 24) and noted that this was likely to impact significantly on Māori (and Pacific) children.

In 2013 and 2014, two projects were carried out under the auspices of the Continuity of Early Learning (CoEL) workstream of the *Ministerial cross-sector forum on raising student achievement* (Ministry of Education 2014). The projects focused on raising the achievement of priority learners, which included Māori learners. These projects highlighted challenges relating to early childhood education and school cross sector understanding of curriculum frameworks and assessment practices (Ministry of Education n.d.). Of significance to educational transitions was the identification of the implementation of curriculum frameworks as a key area for focus, as well as connecting teaching practice across early learning services and school settings for children from birth up to 8 years.

At the end of 2014, the Minister of Education established an advisory group on early learning. The group's function is to help ensure that all children have consistent teaching and learning from birth to 8 years. Its main objective is to provide advice to the minister on how to strengthen the implementation of the early childhood curriculum, *Te Whāriki* (Ministry of Education 1996), along with practical ways to align curriculum planning, implementation and evaluation across early learning services and the early years of English medium and Māori medium schooling. The rationale for the advisory group is that there are indications that children's development is enhanced if they experience consistent teaching and learning that is responsive to their needs and that students who have fallen behind their peers in the initial years of schooling tend to stay behind.

The main foci of the advisory group include explicit attention to transition, including strengthening relationships and communication about progress and next learning steps with children, families and whānau, particularly at key transition points; examining practical ways to align curriculum planning, implementation and evaluation across early childhood education and the early years of school in English and Māori medium programmes; and developing a plan for improving the implementation of *Te Whāriki* and aligning teaching practice across early learning services and the early years of Māori and English medium schooling (Ministry of Education 2014).

Despite the emphasis on Māori children's educational transitions in both *Ka Hikitia* documents (Ministry of Education 2008, 2013), education review processes and education workstreams, Māori voices and experiences are still noticeably absent from much of Aotearoa New Zealand's research literature on transitions.

6.3 Research Relating to Māori Educational Transition

While internationally there has been a lot of interest in the transition to school, a literature review carried out for the New Zealand Ministry of Education (Peters 2010) noted that there was little research on the transition experiences of Māori children, let alone their families.

Peters (2010) found transition studies prior to 2010 that included Māori children tended to focus on literacy (e.g. Rubie-Davies et al. 2006; Tamarua 2006). Rubie-Davies et al.'s (2006) study also touched on assessment, identifying issues of lower teacher expectation and judgement of Māori students' reading achievement that did not reflect actual performance. More recent work on assessment in the context of early childhood Māori medium education (Rameka 2011) has led to the development of *kaupapa Māori* approaches to assessment, which encompass physical, emotional and spiritual aspects alongside intellectual growth. Māori medium schools have begun to explore the application of these processes in their assessment practices, signalling the potential applicability of Māori medium early childhood assessment approaches to the early years of Māori medium schooling.

Peters' (2010) review did identify themes that relate to educational transitions of Māori children, including the extent to which the school context welcomed their culture, the nature of their relationships with teachers and others, the nature of the teachers' expectations for their success and whether a sense of belonging was fostered (p. 26). A major theme cutting across the review was the importance of teacher knowledge and respect for other cultures and the ability to recognise and foster children's culture through pedagogies and approaches in the classroom (p. 15). Educators' levels of knowledge pertaining to Māori culture impact on the degree to which the other identified themes might be addressed. This highlights the imperative for cultural awareness and competence and for (particularly but not only[1]) non-Māori teachers to actively increase their knowledge about Māori cultural values and preferences.

Tātaiako: Cultural competencies for teachers of Māori students (Ministry of Education 2011) has since emerged as a resource to support teachers' relationships with Māori learners, their families and communities, particularly in personalising learning for, and with, Māori learners. The document focuses on the levels of cultural competency that teachers are expected to exhibit at different stages of their careers. Cultural locatedness is emphasised, which involves teachers understanding their own cultural identity, the importance of culture in education 'and developing an understanding and openness to Māori knowledge and expertise' (p. 4). The document spans teaching in early childhood and school settings, ensuring shared knowledge and understandings across the sectors that can be drawn on to support transition across the two settings.

6.3.1 Transition in Māori Medium Education

Peters' (2010) literature review identified only two research studies that included a specific focus on transitions involving Māori medium education settings – Ka'ai (1990) and Cooper et al. (2004). While Cooper and colleagues set out to examine transition experiences from *kōhanga* to *kura* (Māori immersion schools), no publicly available report exists. Ka'ai's (1990) small-scale study of children's transitions from *kōhanga* to *kura* compared pedagogical patterns she observed in a *kōhanga reo* with those in Māori bilingual and English medium new entrant classrooms. She found that children who move from *kōhanga* into bilingual schooling experienced greater continuity and coherency between the settings than those who moved from *kōhanga* to English medium classrooms. From this, she advocated for the development of Māori medium schooling pathways.

In Aotearoa New Zealand, culture is a significant part of early childhood education, reflected in the existence of a bicultural, bilingual early childhood curriculum and programmes operating through English, Māori and Pacific Island languages and indexed by their respective cultures. There is some evidence supporting Ka'ai's (1990) findings that transitions are likely to be more effective and positive when children have received early childhood education based on their language and cul-

---

[1] Māori are not a homogenous people, and Māori teachers, learners and families may have vastly different experiences of what it means to be Māori. Therefore, Māori teachers also have to learn to understand Māori learners as culturally located individuals.

ture, and this continues into their first years of schooling (Podmore et al. 2001; Yeboah 2002).

Both Peters and Paki's *Learning Journeys* and Hohepa's *Riarikina ō Rongo Hirikapo* projects (see Chap. 7) sought to address the relative lack of research-based evidence about Māori children's transitions from early childhood education to schooling. Peters and Paki's study included the transition experiences of a number of Māori children and the Māori perspectives of families and teachers with regard to their aspirations for their children's learning, how they might view successful transitions for children and how these notions of success might be supported. However, these perspectives on Māori transition were only part of a larger project. While the project included transition from both English and Māori medium early childhood settings, it focused only on transition to English medium schooling. Hohepa's collaborative study with a *kōhanga reo* and *kura* (see Chap. 7) explores children's, parents' and teachers' views of successful transition within Māori medium education and the way shared approaches to curriculum delivery might be developed across the two settings to further strengthen transitions.

Although the current literature base is small, there is increasing interest in transitions involving Māori medium education (Bright et al. 2013, 2015; Hohepa and Paki, see Chap. 7; Skerrett 2010). Bright et al. (2013, 2015) investigated Māori language in families during key educational transitions and how best to support continuity of language development. Their findings included identification of critical decision-making points for Māori families who have chosen to participate in Māori language education when assessing the viability of learning pathways for supporting their aspirations for Māori language and education. Early childhood critical decision-making points involve, in particular, choosing either Māori medium or English medium learning environments. Bright and her associates noted that transition from Māori medium early childhood education to schooling can be strengthened when Māori language and practices are included. They noted that the degree to which early childhood education programmes and schools recognise and support bilingualism also impacts on children and families' Māori language learning journeys.

The findings of Bright et al. (2013, 2015) resonate with those of Skerrett (2010), whose study encompassed all levels of Māori educational transitions from early childhood to tertiary education, including transitions between Māori medium and English medium. Skerrett (2010) found that transition across culturally and linguistically congruent education settings is critical for Māori learners. Her findings clustered around themes of partnerships, relationships and knowledge sharing; identity, language and culture; and policies, procedures and practices. A rubric of helpful strategies was developed to outline successful transitions for learners, teachers and families. Strategies that related directly to development and implementation of pedagogies of educational transitions included showing respect for, and use of, Māori language, involvement in cultural practices such as *pōwhiri* and *poroporoaki* (welcome and farewell ceremonies), creating well-planned and resourced initiation programmes, liaison with Māori communities and recognising and drawing on children's and communities' funds of knowledge.

A common thread across recent and current studies of Māori education transition is the utilisation of *kaupapa Māori* (Māori principles/philosophy) theoretical and methodological approaches.

6.4 Transition Research by and with Māori

Kaupapa Māori research approaches have developed, in part, as responses to what research has and has not delivered for Māori (Pihama 2010; Smith 1991). Negative feelings that Māori and other Indigenous peoples have about research are well documented. These include critiques of research processes, outcomes and its complicity in undermining Indigenous cultural integrity and viability, not to mention alienation of physical and environmental resources. The development of *kaupapa Māori* research approaches has included movement away from intense dislike and distrust of research to considering how research and theory may be useful for Māori.

Māori knowledge as valid and legitimate in today's society is one of the fundamental elements underpinning *kaupapa Māori* research (Smith 1997). That is, the value of Māori knowledge is not only located in the 'traditional' or 'historic'; rather, it can be utilised in today's world. *Kaupapa Māori* research is grounded in Māori knowledge, language and cultural practices (Pihama 2010) – the Māori worldview is embedded in the language. The notions of autonomy and self-determination are fundamental elements in *kaupapa Māori* research approaches, which express clear and explicit political intent regarding the rights and abilities of Māori to shape their own research agendas and their own research processes.

Kaupapa Māori research encompasses distinctively Māori conceptualisations of 'relationship', which extend beyond developing respectful and productive relationships between living individuals. Culturally conceptualised relationships between living and dead, between human and environment and between genealogically located individuals – male and female, younger and older (Nepe 1991) – are of critical importance in any research enterprise.

Bishop (2005) has identified key research concerns that need to guide the initiation, development and undertaking of *kaupapa Māori* research. These concerns need to be located in Māori conceptualisations of relationship – *whanaungatanga* – rather than approached as a checklist to ensure culturally safe research. These are now being drawn on to guide research focused on Māori educational transitions, as illustrated in Hohepa and Paki's discussion in Chap. 7.

6.5 Transition to School for Aboriginal and Torres Strait Islander Children in Australia

In this section of the chapter, current tensions, challenges and issues facing many Aboriginal and Torres Strait Islander people in relation to education and transition to school are highlighted. An Aboriginal perspective is offered around appropriate research methodologies and their elements in relation to education and transition to school.

In Australia, not all children have equal access to education, including early childhood education (Harrison et al. 2012). While gains have been achieved in Aboriginal and Torres Strait Islander education over recent years, the gap between Indigenous and non-Indigenous outcomes is still wide (Australian Bureau of Statistics 2011). COAG (2011) recognised this via key reforms to address issues of access, including *Closing the Gap on Indigenous Disadvantage.*

Addressing the outcome gap between Indigenous and non-Indigenous Australians requires a sustained focus on appropriate Indigenous programmes (Sims 2011). As part of efforts to address and close the gap on Indigenous disadvantage, especially around education, COAG (2011, 2013) has focused on promoting universal access to early childhood education, including access in remote communities.

To support this work, the Ministerial Council for Education, Early Childhood Development and Youth Affairs (MCEECDYA) (2011) *Aboriginal and Torres Strait Islander Education Action Plan (2010–2014)* recognises that:

> … participation in culturally inclusive, high quality early childhood programmes and care can assist Aboriginal and Torres Strait Islander children to get the best start in life. These programmes build upon the rich cultural, linguistic and conceptual skills that Aboriginal and Torres Strait Islander children bring to early childhood education. (p. 9)

In Australia, the Early Years Learning Framework (EYLF) is the first national early years curriculum (Department of Education, Employment and Workplace Relations (DEEWR) 2009). This framework acts as a guide for education from birth to 5 years, including the transition to school. For Aboriginal and Torres Strait Islander children, this framework offers many opportunities to engage, develop and grow within a supportive and culturally appropriate environment. However, to achieve such an environment, educators need to reach out and form trusting and lasting relationships with Aboriginal and Torres Strait Islander children, families and communities.

6.6 Relationships and Transition

Trusting and lasting relationships can only be formed when teachers have a strong background and understanding of Indigenous history and perspectives. Teacher education is one area where such understanding needs to be developed, especially when children and teachers come from different cultural backgrounds (Howard and Perry 2001). Hickling-Hudson and Ahlquist (2003, p. 88) have suggested 'to prepare teachers to implement authentic and powerful pedagogies for Indigenous students, they need to be provided with a different kind of teacher education'. This extends to early childhood education, where a culturally strong childcare programme incorporates cultural values (Guifoyle et al. 2010). This view is reflected in the EYLF, which states that 'educators who are culturally competent respect multiple cultural ways of knowing, seeing and living, celebrate the benefits of diversity and have an ability to understand and honour differences' (DEEWR 2009, p. 16). For educators to provide a culturally strong and culturally appropriate service, they need to form trusting, respectful partnerships with children, families and communities (Hunt 2013). This includes valuing knowledge that Indigenous families and communities bring when building such trusting relationships (Herbert 2012). Mason-White (2012, p. 38) suggests that 'positive partnerships are founded on respect, non-discrimination and valuing families' knowledge'.

Understanding that partnerships need to be formed also assists in identifying appropriate strategies that promote cultural safety. According to Bin-Sallik (2003, p. 7) 'cultural safety is an outcome that enables safe service to be defined by those who receive the service'. Issues of access not only relate to availability of services, whether they are Indigenous-specific or mainstream, but also to whether they are 'safe, comfortable and culturally appropriate for Indigenous families and children (Sims 2011, p. 7). To define what cultural safety means for each service, educators need to form positive, trusting partnerships and relationships with all those involved, including communities. The EYLF supports these statements and provides a positive guide for educators (DEEWR 2009). Despite this, there still remain a number of tensions and challenges for Aboriginal and Torres Strait Islander children, families and communities.

Some of the tensions around the early years and transition-to-school programmes stem from a long history of past exclusionary policies and practices aimed at Aboriginal and Torres Strait Islander people (Malin and Maidment 2003). Past educational practices in Australia not only excluded generations of Aboriginal and Torres Strait Islander peoples from accessing education but also excluded the dominant mainstream society from learning about Aboriginal and Torres Strait Islander peoples and their culture. This exclusion has resulted in a long-lasting legacy of mistrust. As a consequence, low levels of participation and success in schooling and tertiary education persist, despite targeted education policies and programmes (Malin and Maidment 2003). Low levels of engagement also extend to the early childhood years: 'Given the research and policy emphasis on the importance of early childhood education, it is concerning that Indigenous Australian families have low levels of engagement' (Trudgett and Grace 2011, p. 16).

6.7   Strengths-Based Approaches in Indigenous Transition

As well as tensions in relation to education in Australia for Aboriginal and Torres Strait Islander people, there are also tensions in relation to research: 'In some science disciplines we are over-researched, and this has generated mistrust, animosity and resistance from many Aboriginal people' (Martin 2003, p. 203). To address this mistrust, animosity and resistance, especially when exploring Aboriginal and Torres Strait Islander education and transition to school, conceptual frameworks, research methodologies and methods of data collection need to build from a strengths base. A framework that is based on the perspective of belonging to an Indigenous group, rather than on deficit views or mainstream views of school readiness, may present challenges but also brings many strengths, and this is a way forward (Saleebey 2008).

The assets that Aboriginal children and families bring to an educational setting may be missed by the dominant mainstream society (Dockett and Perry 2007; McIntosh 2012). For example, in a community living in Wiradjuri country in Australia, knowing their culture was considered the most important asset for a child starting school. However, that aspect of the child's life was not considered an asset by the schools within the community. Having writing, reading and counting skills and being able to follow classroom rules were considered much more important (McIntosh 2012). Dealtry, Perry and Dockett (see Chap. 8) provide another example of the complexities involved in recognising the strengths and needs that Aboriginal children bring to school.

Many people face challenges in their lives. Within communities there are many natural resources that an individual, child, family or group can call upon for comfort, guidance and direction in times of need (Saleebey 2008). Children do not exist in isolation; they grow and develop as members of families and communities (Dockett and Perry 2013). When Aboriginal children transition to formal education, their families and communities are also there to provide support and to make this transition with them. Aboriginal children, families and communities have much strength, and understanding the strengths in relation to educational settings can assist educators to form positive relationships, have meaningful interactions and move forward together to meet the challenges and take hold of the opportunities that may be present during times of transition.

While a strengths-based perspective is often applied in the field of health (Saleebey 2008), its use within education is still quite new. However, 'recent research in this area has identified a need to develop resources and provide professional learning opportunities to support schools in identifying the knowledge, skills, attributes and experiences that Aboriginal and Torres Strait Islander children bring with them' (Armstrong et al. 2012, p. 32). Using a strengths-based perspective helps researchers to explore transitions, including the challenges and opportunities presented during transition, without a negative or deficit starting point, by believing all participants bring assets, strengths, values and resources.

Schools and communities both have responsibility to ensure children transition successfully to school (Dockett and Perry 2013). Early transition experiences can provide challenges and present opportunities (Dockett et al. 2002), and how Aboriginal children, families and communities navigate their way through this time deserves a respectful, culturally appropriate, strengths-based design that highlights this experience in a positive way (Saleebey 2008).

Transition-to-school programmes that have strong community input, support and ownership can offer Aboriginal children, families and communities a positive start to formal education. To ensure this success, Aboriginal children, families and communities need to be consulted, to feel valued and to feel that their ideas around education are supported. The EYLF also supports Aboriginal children's, families' and communities' input and engagement in developing a culturally appropriate curriculum (DEEWR 2009). The challenge now lies with further advancements around closing the gap in educational outcomes between Indigenous and non-Indigenous Australians. This challenge can be met with further research that aligns more closely with Aboriginal ways of knowing, being and doing.

Thus, another essential step in forming positive relationships is exploring research that complements Aboriginal ways of knowing, being and doing (Martin 2003). Research in Aboriginal communities must have a strong focus on relationships, giving back to community and being respectful. Western research traditions have come under the scrutiny of Aboriginal and Torres Strait Islander academics, thinkers and researchers (Martin 2003). Having Aboriginal and Torres Strait Islander researchers working alongside communities can have powerful benefits in formulating particular ways of conducting research in respectful ways. In Australia, research that includes both Indigenous and non-Indigenous researchers and is formed around respectful relationships and partnerships has been quite successful (Farmer and Fasoli 2010; Perry et al. 2007). At the basis of this success is the ability of all concerned to form strong relationships as well as utilise methodologies that recognise, validate and draw on Aboriginal ways of conducting oneself.

6.8   A Critical Indigenous Research Approach to Indigenous Transitions

Forming respectful research relationships requires all parties to be aware of self, others and context; to have an input; and to feel that their voices are being portrayed respectfully. A Critical Indigenous Research Methodology (CIRM) offers the researcher opportunities for community-driven ideas to be shared in a positive, culturally appropriate and respectful way. CIRM is 'rooted in Indigenous knowledge systems, is anticolonial and is distinctly focused on the needs of communities' (Brayboy et al. 2011, p. 423). It was designed to serve the needs of the community, and several critical elements have been identified as essential to achieving this. CIRM can be utilised to explore and investigate transitions in the early years for Aboriginal children, families and communities through the following elements:

- *Relationality*. The researcher needs to establish relationships with Aboriginal communities as well as educators. These relationships need to be maintained, based on mutual respect, and are of critical importance to the overall success of the research.
- *Responsibility*. The researcher is responsible to the relationships that are constructed. These responsibilities go beyond the physical world and into the Aboriginal spiritual world. The researcher needs to maintain and respect all relationships and remember that the link between relationships and responsibilities is critical.
- *Respect*. Respecting all those involved in the research and respecting the Aboriginal lands and all contained in those lands, including the spiritual world, need to be held in high regard and at the forefront of the research process.
- *Reciprocity*. Whatever is received makes its way back to others. Community consultation will direct the researcher at all times. Reciprocity also takes into account the needs of the Aboriginal community and the needs of the academic community in a respectful and transparent way.

- *Accountability*. The researcher needs to be accountable to all involved at all times. This means that the researcher needs to be accountable to the local ways of the communities, recognise that these ways may change from time to time, conduct community consultation from the beginning all the way through the research process and ensure that researchers are also accountable to cultural ways when conducting themselves on Aboriginal lands. Accountability is important and recognises the value of the relationships formed.

The elements contained in the CIRM highlight the importance of relationships. Forming mutually respectful relationships provides for genuine results, allowing Aboriginal children, families and communities a voice that can provide an important platform to create change.

6.9   Concluding Comments

Two general and broad approaches, although not necessarily mutually exclusive, can be identified in current research literature that provides some insight into Indigenous educational transitions in Australia and in Aotearoa New Zealand. One approach gives attention to education and Indigenous children and families that centres on addressing issues of access and participation, with the goal of increasing equitable outcomes across Indigenous and non-Indigenous groups of students. From this vantage point, transition is often approached in terms of how it might be strengthened to raise Indigenous student achievement. Relationships, cultural continuity, cultural safety and cultural responsiveness are amongst the factors highlighted as significant in relation to transition in the relatively small pool of available literature.

Another approach relates to efforts to develop Indigenous educational pathways. These efforts are often located in struggles for Indigenous people's self-determination over their own lives and greater control over the education of their children (Hohepa 2015; McCarty 2002; Penetito 2010). While a focus on raising achievement is often present, the development of such pathways is often driven by concern for linguistic and cultural survival, maintenance and continuity. Literature on the establishment of Indigenous education can also provide insights into the role that transition can play in supporting and strengthening the development of ongoing Indigenous schooling pathways for Indigenous children and their families. Relationships within and between settings that are predicated on Indigenous knowledge, values and practices are critical elements in Indigenous education journeys across these pathways.

Relationships emerge as fundamentally important in both approaches to Indigenous education. Strong, trusting relationships are significant for transitions, whether they span Indigenous and non-Indigenous children, families and educators or whether they involve Indigenous individuals only. Respect for and a strengths-based view of cultural ways of knowing and cultural difference are key in the development of healthy and effective relationships between Indigenous and non-Indigenous in the education arena.

The importance of relationships extends to the consideration of appropriate ways of researching Indigenous educational transition. 'Indigenous research' encompasses research by Indigenous peoples and research with Indigenous peoples. In Australia, research has begun to provide space for the development of cross-cultural as well as intercultural research relationships based on mutual trust, respect and reciprocal responsibilities. Critical Indigenous Research Methodology respects multiple cultural ways of knowing and has potential for the investigation and strengthening of early transitions for Aboriginal children, families and communities. In Aotearoa New Zealand, *kaupapa Māori* approaches feature strongly in recent and current Māori education transition research, reflecting a culturally centred position on research relationships in which Māori proactively participate as both researchers and the researched.

References

Armstrong, S., Buckley, S., Lonsdale, M., Milgate, G., Kneebone, L. B., Cook, L., & Skelton, F. (2012). *Starting school: A strengths-based approach towards Aboriginal and Torres Strait Islander children.* http://research.acer.edu.au/indigenous_education/27. Accessed 27 Mar 2015.

Australian Bureau of Statistics. (2011). *Australian social trends March 2011: Education and Indigenous wellbeing* (ABS catalogue no. 4102.0). Commonwealth of Australia.

Bin-Sallik, M. (2003). Cultural safety: Let's name it. *Australian Journal of Indigenous Education, 32,* 21–28.

Bishop, R. (2005). Freeing ourselves from neo-colonial domination in research. A kaupapa Māori approach to creating knowledge. In N. K. Denzin & Y. S. Lincoln (Eds.), *The Sage handbook of qualitative research* (3rd ed., pp. 109–138). London: Sage.

Brayboy, B., Gough, H. R., Leonard, B., Roehl, R. F., II, & Solyom, J. A. (2011). Reclaiming scholarship: Critical indigenous research methodologies. In S. D. Lapan, M. T. Quartaroli, & F. J. Riemer (Eds.), *Qualitative research: An introduction to methods and designs* (pp. 423–450). Hoboken, NJ: Wiley.

Bright, N., Barnes, A., & Hutchings, J. (2013). *Ka whānau mai te reo: Honouring whānau: Upholding reo Māori.* Wellington: New Zealand Council for Educational Research.

Bright, N., Barnes, A., & Hutchings, J. (2015). *Ka whānau mai te reo kia rite! Getting ready to move: Te Reo Māori and transitions.* Wellington: New Zealand Council for Educational Research.

Cooper, G., Arago -Kemp, V., Wylie, C., & Hodgen, E. (2004). *Te rerenga ā te pīrere: A longitudinal study of kōhanga reo and kura kaupapa Māori students—Phase I Report.* Wellington: New Zealand Council for Educational Research.

Council of Australian Governments. (2011). *COAG reform agenda.* http://www.coagreformcouncil.gov.au/agenda. Accessed 23 Mar 2015.

Council of Australian Governments. (2013). *Indigenous reform 2011–12: Comparing performance across Australia.* http://www.naccho.org.au/download/aboriginal-health/COAG%20 reform%20Council%20Indigemous%20reform%202011-2012.pdf. Accessed 19 Nov 2015.

Department of Education Employment and Workplace Relations (DEEWR). (2009). *Belonging, being and becoming: The early years learning framework for Australia.* Department of Education Employment and Workplace Relations. https://docs.education.gov.au/system/files/ doc/other/belonging_being_and_becoming_the_early_years_learning_framework_for_australia.pdf. Accessed 26 Nov 2015.

Dockett, S., & Perry, B. (2007). *Transitions to school: Perceptions, experiences and expectations.* Sydney: University of New South Wales Press.

Dockett, S., & Perry, B. (2013). Trends and tensions: Australian and international research about starting school. *International Journal of Early Years Education.* http://dx.doi.org/10.1080/096 69760.206.832943. Accessed 21 Nov 2015.

Dockett, S., Perry, B., Howard, P., Whitton, D., & Cusack, M. (2002). Australian children starting school. *Childhood Education, 78*(6), 349–353.

Education Review Office. (2013). *He Pou Tātaki: How ERO reviews early childhood services.* Wellington: Author.

Education Review Office. (2015). *Continuity of learning: Transitions from early childhood services to schools.* Wellington: Author.

Education Review Office. (n.d.). *Review process.* http://www.ero.govt.nz/Review-Process. Accessed 17 Feb 2015.

Farmer, R., & Fasoli, L. (2010). *You're in new country: Advice for non-Indigenous early childhood mentors, trainers and teachers.* Canberra: Commonwealth of Australia.

Guilfoyle, A., Saggers, S., Sims, M., & Hutchins, T. (2010). Culturally strong childcare programs for Indigenous children, families and communities. *Australasian Journal of Early Childhood, 35*(3), 68–76.

Hare, J., & Anderson, J. (2010). Transitions to early childhood education and care for indigenous children and families in Canada: Historical and social realities. *Australasian Journal of Early Childhood, 35*(2), 19–27.

Harrison, L. J., Goldfeld, S., Metcalfe, E., & Moore, T. (2012). *Early learning programs that promote children's developmental and educational outcomes* (Resource sheet no. 15). Canberra: Australian Institute of Health and Welfare & Melbourne: Australian Institute of Family Studies. http://www.aihw.gov.au/uploadedFiles/ClosingTheGap/Content/Publications/2012/ctgc-rs15. pdf. Accessed 21 Nov 2015.

Herbert, J. (2012). Ceaselessly circling the centre: Historical contextualization of Indigenous education within Australia. *History of Education Review, 41*(2), 91–103.

Hickling-Hudson, A., & Ahlquist, R. (2003). Contesting the curriculum in the schooling of indigenous children in Australia and the United States: From Eurocentrism to culturally powerful pedagogies. *Comparative Education Review*, Special Issue on Black Populations, *47*(1), 64–89.

Hohepa, M. (2015). Te reo Māori – He reo kura? Māori language – A school language? In C. Volker & F. Anderson (Eds.), *Education in languages of lesser power: Asia-Pacific perspectives* (pp. 244–260). Amsterdam: John Benjamins.

Hohepa, M., Smith, G., Smith, L., & McNaughton, S. (1992). Te Kōhanga Reo hei tikanga ako i te reo Māori: Te Kōhanga Reo as a context for language learning. *Educational Psychology, 12*(3–4), 333–346.

Howard, P., & Perry, B. (2001). *Learning mathematics: The voices of Aboriginal Children.* http://www.merga.net.au/documents/RR_Howard&Perry.pdf. Accessed 17 Oct 2015.

Hunt, J. (2013). *Engagement with Indigenous communities in key sectors. Resource sheet no. 23.* Canberra: Australian Institute of Health and Welfare & Melbourne: Australian Institute of Family Studies.

Iokepa-Guerrero, N., & France, C. (2007). Nest of voices: Early childcare and education in Hawaii. *Canadian Journal of Native Education, 30*(1), 41–47.

Ka'ai, T. (1990). *Te hiringa taketake: Mai i te kōhanga reo ki te kura: Māori pedagogy: Te kōhanga reo and the transition to school.* Unpublished Masters thesis. University of Auckland, Auckland, New Zealand.

Malin, M., & Maidment, D. (2003). Education, indigenous survival and well-being: Emerging ideas and programs. *The Australian Journal of Indigenous Education, 32*, 85–100.

Maracle, I., Hill, K., Maracle, T., & Brown, K. (2011). Rebuilding our language foundation through the next generation. In M. E. Romero Little, S. J. Ortiz, T. L. McCarty, & R. Chen (Eds.), *Indigenous languages across the generations: Strengthening families and communities* (pp. 83–93). Tempe, Arizona: Arizona State University Center for Indian Education.

Martin, K. (2007). Ma(r)king tracks and reconceptualising Aboriginal early childhood education: An Aboriginal Australian perspective. *Childrenz Issues, 11*(1), 15–20.

Martin, K. (Booran Mirraboopa). (2003). Ways of knowing, being and doing: A theoretical framework and methods for indigenous and indigenist research. *Journal of Australian Studies, 27*(76), 203–214.

Mason-White, H. (2012). *Learning from good practice: Implementing the early years learning framework for Aboriginal and Torres Strait Islander children*. North Fitzroy: Secretariat of National Aboriginal and Islander Child Care (SNAICC).

McCarty, T. L. (2002). *A place to be Navajo: Rough rock and the struggle for self-determination in Indigenous schooling*. Mahwah, NJ: Lawrence Erlbaum.

McIntosh, L. (2012). *Assets indigenous children bring to school*. Unpublished Honours thesis, University of Western Sydney.

Ministerial Council for Education, Early Childhood Development and Youth Affairs (MCEECDYA). (2011). *Aboriginal and torres strait Islander education action plan 2010–2014*. Carlton South Victoria: Author. http://www.mceecdya.edu.au. Accessed 21 Nov 2015.

Ministry of Education. (1996). *Te whāriki. He whāriki mātauranga mō ngā mokopuna o Aotearoa: Early Childhood Curriculum*. Wellington: Learning Media.

Ministry of Education. (2008). *Ka hikitia managing for success: The Māori education strategy 2008–2012*. Wellington: Author.

Ministry of Education. (2011). *Tātaiako: Cultural competencies for teachers of Māori students*. Wellington: Author.

Ministry of Education. (2013). *Ka hikitia accelerating success: The Māori education strategy 2013–2017*. Wellington: Author.

Ministry of Education. (2014). *Terms of reference – Advisory group on early learning*. http://www.education.govt.nz/assets/Documents/Early-Childhood/News/TORAdvisoryGroupOnEarlyLearning.pdf. Accessed 24 Feb 2015.

Ministry of Education. (n.d.). *Leadership in early childhood education for '5 out of 5' children*. http://www.education.govt.nz/early-childhood/teaching-and-learning/educational-leadership/5-out-of-5/. Accessed 24 Feb 2015.

Nepe, T. (1991). *E hao nei e tēnei reanga: Te Toi Huarewa Tipuna–Kaupapa Māori, an educational intervention*. Unpublished Masters thesis. University of Auckland, Auckland, New Zealand.

Penetito, W. T. (2010). *What's Māori about Māori education? The struggle for a meaningful context*. Wellington: Victoria University Press.

Perry, B., Dockett, S., Mason, T., & Simpson, T. (2007). Successful transitions from prior-to-school to school for Aboriginal and Torres Strait Islander children. *International Journal for Equity and Innovation in Early Childhood, 5*(1), 102–111.

Peters, S. (2010). *Literature review: Transition from early childhood education to school. Report commissioned by the Ministry of Education*. Wellington: Ministry of Education.

Pihama, L. (2010). Kaupapa Māori theory: Transforming theory in Aotearoa. *He Pukenga Kōrero: A Journal of Māori Studies, 9*(2), 5–14.

Podmore, V., Sauvao, L., & Mapa, L. (2001). Transition to school: Current issues and Pacific Islands early childhood contexts. *New Zealand Annual Review of Education, 10*, 71–88.

Prochner, L. (2004). Early childhood education programs for Indigenous children in Canada, Australia and New Zealand: An historical review. *Australian Journal of Early Childhood, 29*(4), 7–16.

Rameka, L. (2011). Being Māori: Culturally relevant assessment in early childhood education. *Early Years: An International Research Journal, 31*(3), 245–256.

Ritchie, J., & Skerrett, M. (2014). *Early childhood education in Aotearoa New Zealand: History, pedagogy, and liberation*. New York: Palgrave Macmillan.

Rubie-Davies, C., Hattie, J., & Hamilton, R. (2006). Expecting the best for students: Teacher expectations and academic outcomes. *British Journal of Educational Psychology, 76*, 429–444.

Saleebey, D. (2008). Commentary on the strengths perspective and potential applications in school counselling. *Professional School Counselling, 12*(2), 68–75.

Sims, M. (2011). *Early childhood and education services for Indigenous children prior to starting school.* Canberra: Australian Institute of Health and Welfare and Melbourne: Australian Institute of Family Studies.

Skerrett, M. (2010). *Ngā Whakawhitinga! The transitions of Māori learners project - Milestone 3.* Christchurch: University of Canterbury.

Smith, L. T. (1991). Te Rapunga Ki Te Ao Marama, searching for the world of light'. In J. Morss & T. Linzey (Eds.), *Growing up: The politics of human learning* (pp. 46–55). Auckland: Longman Paul.

Smith, G. H. (1997). *The development of Kaupapa Māori: Theory and praxis.* Unpublished doctoral thesis. University of Auckland, Auckland, New Zealand.

Tamarua, L. (2006). *Pathways to literacy and transitions to school: Enabling incorporation and developing awareness of literacy.* Unpublished doctoral thesis. University of Auckland, Auckland, New Zealand.

Te Puni Kōkiri. (1998). *Progress towards closing social and economic gaps between Māori and non-Māori: A report to the Minister of Māori affairs.* Wellington: Author.

Trudgett, M., & Grace, R. (2011). Engaging with early childhood education and care services: The perspectives of indigenous Australian mothers and their children. *Kulumun Indigenous Online Journal, 1,* 15–36. https://novaojs.newcastle.edu.au/ojs/index.php/kulumun/article/view/54/43

Yeboah, D. A. (2002). Enhancing transition from early childhood phase to primary education: Evidence from the research literature. *Early Years: An International Research Journal, 22*(1), 51–68. doi:10.1080/09575140120111517.

Chapter 7
Māori Medium Education and Transition to School

Margie Hohepa and Vanessa Paki

Little research exists on educational transition experiences of Māori, the Indigenous people of Aotearoa New Zealand. In line with the primary aim of the Pedagogies of Educational Transitions (POET) project, to expand knowledge and understanding of educational transitions internationally, this chapter focuses on transitions involving children from Māori medium early childhood educational[1] settings to school. Children and families in these programmes may either continue their Māori medium educational journey or transition to English medium schooling. In this chapter we begin with a historical overview of the emergence and development of Māori medium education. Drawing on two Teaching and Learning Research Initiatives (TLRI), we then identify and discuss the opportunities, challenges and implications that different journeys of transition from Māori medium early childhood education offer. We focus particularly on the significance of Māori values, practices and 'culturally constructed' lived experiences in those transition journeys for understanding and responding to educational transitions.

7.1 Introduction

Although the current Māori education strategy *Ka Hikitia: Accelerating Success* (Ministry of Education 2013a) includes a focus on transitions, there is relatively little research on the educational transition experiences of Māori. Despite high

---

[1] Māori medium education is defined as early childhood education and schooling immersion settings in which teaching occurs in and through Māori language for 51–100 % of the time (Ministry of Education 2013b).

M. Hohepa (✉) • V. Paki
University of Waikato, Hamilton, New Zealand
e-mail: mkhohepa@waikato.ac.nz

© Springer International Publishing Switzerland 2017
N. Ballam et al. (eds.), *Pedagogies of Educational Transitions*, International Perspectives on Early Childhood Education and Development 16, DOI 10.1007/978-3-319-43118-5_7

international and national interest in transitions, a recent literature review on transitions to school noted the paucity of studies on transition experiences of Māori *tamariki* (children) (McNatty and Roa 2002)[2] and their *whānau* (families) (Peters 2010).

This chapter focuses on educational transitions involving Māori medium early childhood educational programmes. *Tamariki* (children) and *whānau* (families) may either continue their Māori medium educational journeys or transition over to English medium schools. First, an overview of the historical landscape from which Māori medium education emerged is provided, followed by identification and discussion of the opportunities, challenges and implications that different journeys of transition from Māori medium early childhood education offer, with a particular focus on Māori values and culturally constructed experiences.

Two recent Teaching and Learning Research Initiatives (TLRI) have explored transitions from Māori medium early childhood to compulsory school settings. We have deliberately focused first on transitions within Māori medium education as a normalising act. That is, we wish to locate transition from Māori medium early childhood education to Māori medium schooling as the normal, expected journey that *tamariki* (children) and *whānau* (families) in Māori medium education may take. In doing so, we acknowledge that realising both the potential of schooling as a supportive context for Indigenous language regeneration and beneficial outcomes of bilingualism requires continuity of learning in the target language (Baker 2011; May et al. 2006; Ratima and Papesch 2014). Drawing on the more recent TLRI, we discuss cultural values and practices as inherent and fundamental to transition experiences in Māori medium education.

We also recognise that many *tamariki* (children) and *whānau* (families) do not experience continuous Māori medium educational journeys. Families who choose to participate in Māori medium early childhood education may transition their children to English medium schooling for a range of reasons, including accessibility, presence of family members, school reputation and parent language fluency (Bright et al. 2013). We therefore turn to the earlier TLRI project to examine cultural values underpinning a Māori medium early childhood centre and their implications for children's transitions into English medium school settings.

7.2   Historical Landscape

Māori medium education has emerged out of a historical landscape of colonial education. The landscape is one in which struggles for power and control have underpinned a collision of cultures (G. Smith 1992, L. Smith 1992). The Māori language and culture were positioned as obstacles to educational progress and denied space in the education system (McMurchy-Pilkington 2001; L. Smith 1992). In 1900,

---

[2] For ease of reading, we have provided concise English translations for Māori terms at their first usage in a paragraph. We acknowledge issues of translation; please note that concise translations are not able to reflect the fullest meanings of these terms.

after more than 30 years of schooling through the English language, over 90 % of Māori new school entrants still spoke Māori as their first language (Ritchie and Rau 2009). By 1960, the hardening of assimilationist policies and practices resulted in only 26 % of young Māori children speaking their native language fluently (Walker 2004).

In the latter part of the twentieth century, Māori education took a new direction in the creation of *Te Kōhanga Reo*, total immersion Māori language settings for preschool children. *Te Kōhanga Reo* introduced an educational approach that repositioned Indigenous Māori culture and language as legitimate in provisions now called Māori medium education. *Te Kōhanga Reo* also had a fundamental impact on the development of *Te Whāriki* (Ministry of Education 1996), New Zealand's early childhood curriculum. *Te Whāriki* is arguably the world's first, if not only, bilingual and bicultural early childhood curriculum. Its development 'is a clear example where theorising in education from an Indigenous worldview has had a tangible impact on the educational theory and practice of people from a dominant majority culture' (Macfarlane et al. 2008, p. 108).

A literal translation of *Te Kōhanga Reo*[3] is 'The Language Nest'. *Kōhanga* became a vehicle for self-determining efforts to live as Māori (Hohepa 1990; Irwin 1990; Ka'ai 1990; Reedy 1995). Emerging within wider ethnic revitalisation movements of the 1970s and 1980s, alongside rising Māori political consciousness long oppressed by assimilationist agendas and hegemonic ideology, it is grounded in the belief that language and culture are critical components in Māori educational enhancement (Bishop and Glynn 1999; Smith 1997). *Kōhanga* advocates for Māori language immersion *whānau* (family) programmes for *tamariki* (children), from birth to 6 years old (Royal Tangaere 1997a; Te Kōhanga Reo National Trust 1995). The emphasis on children developing Māori language reflects the premise that without language there is no culture or identity (Walker 2004). While *kōhanga* is often described as an early childhood education provision, it is much more than that. With children and parents as its focal point, its raison d'être is strengthening *whānau* learning and development to sustain and advance *te reo Māori* (Māori language), *tikanga* (customs) and *āhuatanga Māori* (Māori tradition) (Royal Tangaere 1997a).

Kōhanga aspirations and the strength and speed of its development led to independent, self-funded total immersion schools. As *tamariki* (children) reached school age, *kōhanga whānau* (communities) set about developing these schools, which later became known as '*Kura Kaupapa Māori*' (schools based on Māori principles). While only six were operating as independent schools when *Kura Kaupapa Māori* was recognised and funded as a state school provision in 1989, there are now 72 (Ministry of Education 2014). A further 210 schools provide Māori medium educational programmes, including 21 'special designated character' schools, many of which affiliate to an *iwi* (tribe) (Ministry of Education 2013b). As an educational movement, *Kura Kaupapa Māori*[4] was the first to provide schooling within Māori cultural and philosophical frameworks (Smith 1997). A significant ingredient in its

---

[3] From here, referred to as '*kōhanga*'.
[4] From here, referred to as '*kura*'.

development has been the philosophy statement *Te Aho Matua*, described later in this chapter (see Sect. 7.3.1), which has guided the provision of schooling in which Māori knowledge, values and practices are integral (Nepe 1991).

Kōhanga and *kura* were catalysts for the development of *Kaupapa Māori* theory, which underpins this chapter (Bishop 2005; Smith 1997, 1999). As a theory that challenges unequal power relations and advocates transformative praxis, *Kaupapa Māori* draws on critical theory, in particular that of the Frankfurt School (Gibson 1986; Pihama 2010; Smith 1997). *Kaupapa Māori* theory is grounded in Māori cultural frameworks and epistemologies, and it 'is an assertion of the right for Māori to be Māori on our own terms and to draw from our own base to provide understandings and explanations of the world' (Pihama 2010, p. 11). Key elements include *tino rangatiratanga* (self-determination) and the validation and normalisation of Māori language, knowledge and culture – that is, a Māori worldview (Durie 1998; Pihama 2010; Smith 1997, 1999).

Kōhanga has helped pave the way for other Māori medium early childhood education provisions. *Kōhanga* is by far the largest Māori medium early childhood education provider, with nearly 10,000 *tamariki* (children) across 463 centres (Ministry of Education 2013b). *Puna reo* (language springs) are also full immersion preschool centres and *Puna kōhungahunga* (infant springs) are either full immersion or bilingual centres (Ministry of Education n.d.). Twenty-six *puna* cater for 278 *tamariki*.

Kōhanga reconnects to Māori language as a vehicle for socialisation and to traditional practices by which Māori passed culture and heritage through generations (Mead 2003). Theoretical perspectives on socialisation acknowledge that children must develop within the cultural context to understand and internalise their culture (Vygotsky 1978), which itself undergoes development and change (Rogoff 2003). *Kōhanga* reignites intergenerational language and culture transmission processes and enables *whānau* (family) to pass Māori language on to their *tamariki* (children) through culturally preferred socialisation practices, even when parents are not fluent speakers (Hohepa et al. 1992; Ka'ai 1990; Reedy 1995; Royal Tangaere 1997b). *Kōhanga* as a collective space acts as a change agent for *tamariki* and *whānau* in which values such as *whanaungatanga* (shared family responsibilities), *aroha* (love) and *manaakitanga* (support) are enacted. This helps to create a learning environment in which *te reo Māori* (the Māori language) is the medium of communication and cultural practices, values and beliefs become both pedagogical framework and tools for cultural knowledge transmission.

If this is the essence of *kōhanga* and *puna*, then successful transition for a child moving from Māori medium early childhood educational settings to school settings is measured by the child's ability to maintain connections to their cultural history into the future. We now turn to two research studies in which transitions have been enhanced through close connections with home and between educational institutions, with continuity of language and culture being fundamental to these connections.

7.3 Mai i te Kōhanga ki te Kura: From the Kōhanga to the Kura

In this section we consider the articulation of Māori knowledge, values and understandings in the movement of *tamariki* (children) between a *kōhanga* and a *kura*. While the respective contexts have particular and unique characteristics, they also reflect knowledge, values and understandings present in Māori medium educational settings more generally (Royal Tangaere 1997a; Smith 1995, 1997).

Riariakina ō rongo hirikapo: From kōhanga to kura was a 2-year TLRI project (2014–2015). The project involved teacher-researchers in Te Kōhanga Reo o Ngā Kuaka and Tōku Māpihi Maurea Kura Kaupapa Māori, along with university-based researchers at the University of Waikato. It aimed to provide new insights into enhancing transitions from Māori medium early childhood education to Māori medium classrooms. The overarching research question was: *Pēhea rā te āhuatanga me te kounga o ngā whakawhitinga mai i te kōhanga ki te kura mō ngā tamariki, whānau, kaiako me te hapori? –* What do effective transitions from *kōhanga* to *kura* look like, feel like, and sound like, for children, families, teachers and the community? In line with the project's *Kaupapa Māori* methodology, it was initiated by members of *kōhanga* and *kura whānau* (community) members, who also collaborated in identifying research questions and designing and implementing the research.

7.3.1 Kei ā tātou anō te ara tika[5]: The Answers Are Within Us

In 1989, fuelled by their desire to educate their *tamariki* (children) within *te reo Māori* (the Māori language) and *te ao Māori* (the Māori world), *whānau* (families) established Te Kōhanga Reo o Ngā Kuaka (Ministry of Education 2009b). Establishment *whānau* included University of Waikato staff and students, and the *kōhanga* derived its name from a Māori student group called 'Ngā Kuaka Marangaranga' – the arising godwits. The name was deemed appropriate because like the *kuaka* (godwits), migrating birds that come together to feed for their epic journeys between Aotearoa New Zealand and Alaska, 'tamariki come to kōhanga, feed and grow on the knowledge within and then continue on their journey. Like the kuaka, they keep returning, bringing with them their *teina, akuanei pea, ā rātou mokopuna* [italics added]'[6] (Ministry of Education 2009b, p. 37). From its small beginnings in a parent's home, Ngā Kuaka now covers three adjacent suburban houses and has a roll of more than 60.

Tōku Māpihi Maurea Kura Kaupapa Māori was established in 1993 by three *kōhanga*, including *Ngā Kuaka*, so that *tamariki* (children) could continue learning

---

[5] This saying is attributed to the Kōhanga Reo National Trust Board.

[6] *teina, akuanei pea, ā rātou mokopuna* – younger relatives and perhaps their grandchildren.

through Māori language. The *kura* (school) takes its name from a *whakataukī* (proverb) reflecting the importance of Māori language to Māori identity – '*Tōku reo tōku ohooho, tōku reo tōku māpihi maurea, tōku reo tōku whakakai mārihi*' (my language is my precious gift, my object of affection and my prized ornament). Initially run as an independent school in a leased building, the *kura* received government recognition and funding as a state school in 1995 and shifted to its current site adjacent to Ngā Kuaka. It has a roll of around 100 *tamariki* aged 5–13 years.

Tōku Māpihi Maurea adheres to *Te Aho Matua*. Written in Māori by founding leaders of the *Kura Kaupapa Māori* movement, it sets out guiding principles and provides a philosophical base for teaching and learning, curriculum planning and design. It supports diversity across different *kura* 'while maintaining an integral unity' (New Zealand Gazette 2008, p. 740). *Te Aho Matua* has six parts, briefly described below:

- *Te Ira Tangata* (human element) refers to the importance of an education that nurtures the entire child, including physical and spiritual aspects.
- *Te Reo* (language) identifies *te reo Māori* as the primary language of teaching and learning and expectations for bilingual competencies.
- *Ngā Iwi* (peoples) emphasises the importance of genealogical links, knowledge of and interaction with one's cultural heritage and learning about and acknowledging other cultures.
- *Te Ao* (the world) recognises the importance of Māori knowledge of the world as an integral part of learning and how aspects of the world impact on learning.
- *Āhuatanga Ako* (teaching aspects) covers principles of teaching practice fundamental to *Kura Kaupapa Māori*.
- *Te Tino Uaratanga* (the key desire) describes desired graduating outcomes for the child, emphasising the realisation of individual talents alongside spiritual, social and emotional development.

7.3.2   Transition as 'Staying on the Kaupapa'[7]

Transition is often considered with regard to children, families and teachers, along with educational settings. Transition takes on a particular significance to *kōhanga* and *kura*, as they are not only educational settings but also sites of transformative praxis and comprise a cultural-political movement (Pihama 2010; Smith 1997). *Kōhanga* and *kura* settings have unique characteristics located within aspirations for Māori language and culture.

As the first *kura* developed out of *kōhanga* desires for ongoing education through Māori language, *kura* and *kōhanga whānau* (communities) are often one and the same; at the very least, there is a shared *kaupapa* (purpose) and vision. Rather than conceptualising the journey of *tamariki* (children) and *whānau* (families) from

---

[7] Plan, agenda, purpose.

kōhanga to *kura* as 'transition', it might be better understood as the ongoing evolution, growth and development of the shared *kaupapa*. However, since the early development of *kōhanga* and *kura*, there have been changes that have impacted on the extent to which they are able to maintain that shared *kaupapa*. These include the development of distinct curricula in the form of *Te Whāriki*, the early childhood curriculum (Ministry of Education 1996), and *Te Marautanga o Aotearoa* (Ministry of Education 2008), the curriculum for Māori medium school settings.[8]

Ngā Kuaka and Tōku Māpihi Maurea have sought to maintain the integrity of the shared *kaupapa* (purpose) from which they emerged while navigating developments and changes taking place in the wider education landscape. Commitment to Māori knowledge, values and understandings is evidenced in practices supporting movements between the *kōhanga* and the *kura* sites. Both also maintain a strong tribal identity, recognising and affirming the *mana whenua* (tribal authority) of the Waikato tribe. The following section draws on parents' voices to illustrate the centrality of values and practices to 'transition', focusing on the examples of *whanaungatanga* (sense of family) and *pōwhiri* (welcome ceremonies).

7.3.3   Tikanga[9] in Transition: A Journey of Māori Values and Practices

7.3.3.1   Whanaungatanga

Whanaungatanga refers to kinship, sense of family and belonging. While its meanings are generated in contexts of enactment, 'it always involves value processes that are interrelated' (McNatty and Roa 2002, p. 91) and encompass spiritual, social and relational dimensions. *Whanaungatanga* includes relationships developed through socially shared experiences of working together, undertaking duties, roles and responsibilities (Bishop et al. 2014; Smith 1995).

Whanaungatanga is evident in long-standing relationships and involvement across the *kōhanga* and *kura*. One parent related how his long relationship with the *kura* supported moving from *kōhanga* to *kura* as a normal expectation:

> I've had a long relationship with Tōku Māpihi since about 1996 [before becoming a parent]. I helped out in the classes and ran sports programmes. My kids in particular are involved in a lot of sports; the younger ones get to go to those sports days and practices and get to engage with those kids from the school quite often, so there's a huge amount of familiarity between the *kura* kids and my kids who are in *kōhanga*. [Daughter] would say, "When am I going to the *kura*?" It was normal to her to transition over to the *kura*. (Father, Dec 2014)

---

[8] A third Māori medium curriculum document, *Te Marautanga o Te Aho Matua*, was launched in March 2015 for *kura* that adhere to *Te Aho Matua*.

[9] Customs, conventions, protocols.

Whanaungatanga carries expectations that the relationships, roles and responsibilities that the parents undertake do not disappear when their *tamariki* (children) move from one setting to another.

> I'm still involved with *kōhanga* stuff, still on the committee for the 25-year birthday …'Cos I implemented the Matariki event at *kōhanga*, which still happens every year, we still will probably be involved in the *kōhanga*. (Mother, Dec 2014)

Parents described maintaining *whanaungatanga* links to *kōhanga* after *tamariki* have moved to *kura* by attending *kōhanga* events and celebrations as well as taking their *tamariki* to visit *kōhanga*.

Rangatiratanga (leadership/self-determination) is a critical element in *kōhanga reo* and *kura* developments (Smith 1992a; Pihama 2010). *Rangatiratanga* in the sense of leadership is a key dimension of *whanaungatanga* (McNatty and Roa 2002). *Whanaungatanga* ensures that parents will exercise leadership, such as identifying and taking on roles or tasks to ensure that *whānau* (family) needs relating to *tamariki* (children) moving from *kōhanga* to *kura* are addressed. This helps all *kōhanga* and *kura* members experience a sense of belonging.

> I definitely think some parents are too scared, some parents don't have the [Māori] language skills to approach them [teachers] or feel as though you have to speak in Māori to approach them and talk about your kids. I certainly don't think that everybody has that … I know some parents just don't, and sometimes I'll advocate on their behalf. … I sometimes talk to the *kaiako* [teachers] about particular issues that have come up and frame it that, frame it in such a way that it comes from me. (Father Dec 2014)

7.3.3.2   Pōwhiri

Pōwhiri are welcome ceremonies and rituals of encounter. These rituals highlight the inextricable connectedness of spiritual and physical domains, dead and living, and roles and responsibilities of those who are welcoming and those who are being welcomed (Barlow 1991; Mead 2003). *Pōwhiri* are essential for building new and reinforcing existing relationships across and between groups of people (Bishop et al. 2014).

Pōwhiri are an integral part of moving from Ngā Kuaka to Tōku Māpihi Maurea. *Tamariki* (children) and their *whānau* (family) experience *pōwhiri* to the *kura* before visits to the new entrants' classroom begin. *Kōhanga kaiako* (teachers) and peers accompany those who are transitioning and pass them over as treasures to the care of the *kura*. Some *whānau* may experience multiple *pōwhiri*, depending on the number of *tamariki*. Parents view *pōwhiri* as invaluable for their *tamariki* and *whānau*.

> Yes, I went to their *whakatau* [formal welcome akin to *pōwhiri*] which is a really good thing to do because all the kids see who's about to come over … and it's a good way to *whakanui* [celebrate] the kids from the school's behalf. So it's not the run of the mill, "Oh here comes another kid", but "here's a *taonga* [treasure] from the *kōhanga* that's supported by the *kōhanga* and this *taonga* is coming into this school". I mean, that's the impression I always get and during that *whakatau* the school will say some words and the *tuakana* [senior peers]

of the school will get up and run some of the process too. So that *pōwhiri* approach is, I think, ... one of those invaluable and yet intangible things that are hard to quantify. (Father, Dec 2014)

Pōwhiri provide a cultural assurance that a child will be safe, loved, nurtured and developed when they move to the *kura*. They also provide rich opportunities for cultural learning in a real-life, meaningful context. For those who come from other tribal regions, *pōwhiri* also provide assurances that the local Waikato tribe will care for their child:

Kāre au i tino whai wā ki te hokihoki ki te kāinga. Ko te pōwhiri he mea āhua tauhou ki a rātou, nā reira, i tae atu ki te pōwhiri kātahi ka rongo i te karanga, ka kī a [tama], kua mate tētahi? (laughter) I mōhio ai i te tangihanga ēngari kāre anō kia waia ki ērā atu momo. Nā reira koinā tētahi o ngā āhua pai o te pōwhiri, kia waia ngā tamariki ki ērā whakatau. Tētahi atu i āhei au ki te tono atu ki te whānau kia haramai ahakoa kāre taku whānau i kōnei, kāre au i tono ēngari pai kia mōhio kia tāea te pērā, rawe! Ka pai. Me te mea hoki kia tae mai te kōhanga hei tautoko, rawe!	I don't get a lot of opportunity to return home. The *pōwhiri* was somewhat unfamiliar to them, so when we arrived at the *pōwhiri* and heard the call of welcome, [son] asked, "Has someone died?" He knew about bereavement *pōwhiri* but he wasn't yet familiar with other kinds of *pōwhiri*. So, you know, that's one of the positive aspects of *pōwhiri*, to familiarise children with those kinds of welcomes. Another thing is that I was able to ask other family members to come. Although I don't have family living here, that was good to know. So it was great that the *kōhanga* came as support! (Mother, Dec 2014)

This section has focused on transition from early childhood to school within Māori medium education. What might the transition from Māori medium early childhood settings to English medium school settings look like? The following section draws on a 3-year (2010–2013) TLRI project *Learning Journeys from Early Childhood to School*. The project investigated children's learning journeys from early childhood centre to school and involved three early childhood settings (two English medium and one Māori medium) and two English medium schools, with at least 12 teacher-researchers. The section draws on findings for one of the research questions – What does a successful transition look like for Māori children?

7.4 Transitioning from Māori Medium to English Medium

Successful transitions are identified as being important to children's long-term learning (Education Review Office 2015; Ministry of Education 2009a), but what do successful transitions look like for Māori children transitioning from Māori medium settings to English medium settings? We consider some implications from interviews with teachers and parents from Apakura Te Kākano, a Māori medium early childhood centre involved in the *Learning Journeys* TLRI project.

Both expressed concern about the lack of a Māori medium schooling equivalent for their *tamariki* (children) on leaving Apakura, as shared by this mother:

Table 7.1 *Ngā uara* – values underpinning Te Wānanga o Aotearoa and Apakura Te Kākano

Te Whakapono	The basis of our beliefs and the confidence that what we are doing is right
Ngā Ture	The knowledge that our actions are morally and ethically right and that we are acting in an honourable manner
Te Aroha	Having regard for one another and those for whom we are responsible and to whom we are accountable
Kotahitanga	Unity among iwi and other ethnicities standing as one

> At Apakura there's nothing like language and culture at school. That's what's hard because it's not *kōhanga* and *kōhanga* has its equivalent, mainstream has its equivalent, but there's no equivalent of what Apakura is at school.

We argue that a deeper understanding of traditional cultural values and knowledge can aid in the design and adaption of support for children transitioning from a Māori medium setting to an English medium school.

7.4.1 Tūrangawaewae: 'A Place to Stand'

Tūrangawaewae is a powerful Māori concept – 'a place to stand'; its literal meaning is 'a standing place for feet'. It symbolises a place with a sense of belonging, empowerment and connection. Importance of place resonates with the establishment of Te Wānanga o Aotearoa (TWOA) as a Māori training and education provider for those whose needs and aspirations are not being met by the mainstream education system. TWOA was recognised as a tertiary education institution in 1987 and given statutory recognition alongside universities and polytechnics in 1993. Today, TWOA is one of the largest tertiary institutions in Aotearoa New Zealand, offering certificate- and degree-level qualifications to approximately 35,000 students at over 100 sites across the country. TWOA is the overall service provider and governance body for five early learning centres, including Apakura te Kākano.

7.4.2 Ngā Uara: The Values

Underpinning both TWOA and Apakura Te Kākano are *ngā uara* – the values, described in Table 7.1. These are cultural values drawn from traditional Māori knowledge systems (Buck 1987; Papakura 1986).

These values resonate with *Te Whāriki* (Ministry of Education 1996), the early childhood curriculum in Aotearoa New Zealand. The curriculum recognises that diversity in early childhood education is encapsulated in different programmes, philosophies, structures, physical environments and resources. Pedagogy is also diverse, influenced by cultural, political and social values and images of children and childhood underpinned by distinctive theoretical and philosophical perspectives. *Tamariki* (children) transitioning from Apakura te Kākano embody and reflect the centre's philosophy, pedagogy and values. Their identity, shaped within their *whakapapa* (genealogy), develops in interaction with their experiences of cultural values, teaching and learning, dispositions and orientations towards themselves, towards others and towards learning (Ritchie and Rau 2010). The connection with *ngā uara* sits as a guiding principle developed within a Māori cultural framework, founded on ancient roots that are as valid today as they were when first created (Hemara 2000). The connection also identifies the importance of quality learning and teaching being viewed from their cultural and social context (Macfarlane and Macfarlane 2012). Below, one of the teacher-researchers discusses how these values are enacted and explained:

> We have *Ngā Uara* up on our walls, in the *rūma kaimahi* [staff room] and on our main planning wall. *Ngā Uara* are embedded in what we do and how we do it. Working with *tamariki* [children] and their *whānau* [family] is based upon relationships and *Ngā Uara* are deeply embedded within those relationships. We have faith that what we are doing is right, that we are following the rules and regulations, that we are working with *whānau* and their *tamariki* to achieve their goals and aspirations, that we build positive relationships with each other, that we work together to achieve the best outcomes and environments for the *tamariki*. Those are some of the broad ways we can see *Ngā Uara* working within our environment.

7.4.3 Te Whakapono: Truth

Te Whakapono refers to one's beliefs and the confidence that what one is doing is right. *Whaka* is a prefix 'to do' and *pono* means truth. It is in the knowing of being Māori that *whakapono* is grounded, in the intergenerational knowledge valued through culture and language. To be '*pono*' – 'true' – is a significant part of being Māori (Mead 2003; Nepe 1991; Smith 1997). This cultural value of *Te Whakapono* binds intergenerational relationships as a method of knowledge transmission defined as treasures from our ancestors and as 'central Māori epistemological constructs' (Bishop and Glynn 1999, p. 171). It legitimates Māori ways of knowing, being and doing within our educational settings (Ritchie 2002). A teacher at Apakura te Kākano discusses the importance of *Te Whakapono*, showing links between people, places and things:

> … creating an environment where *kaiako* [teacher], *tamariki* [children] and *whānau* [family] feel safe to be Māori, where *te ao Māori* [Māori world] is not only acknowledged, but also encouraged. We are providing an environment that is empowering to *tangata whenua* [people of the land]. By underpinning our curriculum with the principles in *Te Whāriki*, we are basing our curriculum in a Māori framework.

7.5 Ngā Ture: To Be Morally and Ethically Right

Creating a place for *Te Whakapono* (doing what is right) to exist is supported by the second value, *Ngā Ture*, which advocates for one's actions to be morally and ethically right and undertaken in an honourable manner. It is about actions and behaviours that are not only right for the self but also right towards other people.

One of the teachers of Apakura te Kākano described approaching the notion of 'right' from a place of responsibility and obligation. She explains:

> For our pedagogy to be responsive and culturally effective we must ensure that the approach is determined by the child and family and the benefits are directly aligned to the needs and interests of the child and family. I believe also that when this is realised, the learning and teaching is meaningful.

In research, working together involves responsibility and commitment that creates a framework in which researchers can work alongside the participants rather than working as individual agents or observers. In this project we were very much interested in being guided within the cultural practices derived from and appropriate for Māori. For the teacher, applying this value through transitional pedagogies draws on previous generations' funds of knowledge and understandings of the world in critical engagement with the language, activities, significant customs, practices, expectations and cultural nuances (Sullivan 2001).

7.5.1   Te Aroha: Love

The third value, *Te Aroha*, refers to 'having regard for one another and those for whom we are responsible and to whom we are accountable' (TWOA 2015). A teacher describes the many ways this value is enacted, particularly in the daily running of the programme:

> The *whānau* [family] and *tamariki* [children] are welcomed into the centre and become part of our *whānau*. The *tamariki* in our care are treated with respect and love and we value them for who they are. ... We teach the *tamariki* through role modelling, demonstrating and through our daily interactions about empathy, *manaakitanga* [support], caring, sharing, being together and being part of a bigger, wider family. We have *karakia* [prayer], where we share *pānui* [messages, news] together. This helps to set the day up in a positive way. We have a *karakia* at the end of the day as well. This helps to again create a feeling of sharing and respect – a coming together. Our *whānau* and community are invited to attend the tamariki graduation ...

According to Pere (1991), learning and development should be based around *aroha* (love) so that the child's essence is protected and nurtured. In Māori belief, if decisions create any negative force, these would affect the child indirectly or directly (Royal Tangaere 1997b). The same holds true for the relationships and enactment of *aroha* at Apakura te Kākano. A parent explains the importance of trust when forming strong relationships:

> It's all based around trust, it's a relationship thing, and it can only come from a relationship thing first. Not a managerial or whatever; it's got to come from a relationship where you gain trust first, because when you trust people and you're made to feel welcome then, yeah, *kei te pai* – all good.

7.5.2 *Kotahitanga: Unity*

> Through our interactions with the kids we are actually making them think of not only them-
> selves, but the environment around them, as well as their peers, as well as that their actions
> have consequences. *Would you have any examples of that Whaea?* Mmm. One of the kids
> accidently knocked one of the other children with the shovel. Straight away he said, "I'm
> sorry, I didn't mean it. I not see you there". Straight away he knew that what he'd done
> wasn't right – but at the same time he explained that he didn't mean it, [he] just didn't see
> the child. This comes under *aroha* [love], which also comes under *whakapono*, [truth]
> which also comes under *kotahitanga* [unity]. (Apakura te Kākano teacher)

Kotahitanga refers to unity. For TWOA and Apakura te Kākano, the value of
unity is the foundation among *iwi* (tribes) to stand as one. It draws from a commitment to work towards transformation, in their families and in community development. Within the context of education, *Te Whāriki*, the early childhood curriculum,
draws on one of the four principles of *kotahitanga* to reflect, '… the holistic way
children learn and grow' (Ministry of Education 1996, p. 7), woven within a curriculum that should provide children with opportunities 'to grow up competent and
confident learners and communicators, healthy in mind, body, and spirit, secure in
their sense of belonging and in the knowledge that they make a valued contribution
to society' (p. 9). We suggest that transitional pedagogies should nurture and surround the child through their funds of knowledge and view a child's transition as a
'whole' rather than in 'pieces'. If we consider that *kotahitanga* speaks about the
concept of wholeness, then we have a responsibility to view the holistic nature of
each child as the lens through which we will guide our decisions. A teacher explains:

> *Kotahitanga* symbolises the unity we have together and the way we provide a safe and sup-
> portive environment for Māori to be Māori, and for other ethnicities to be who they are. A
> sense of well-being and belonging is fostered through *Kotahitanga*.

This study identified the essence of culture through imprinted traditions as a
knowledge base. Through *Kaupapa Māori*, notions of Māori cultural capital (Smith
1997) and self-determination provide fundamental components as constructs to the
relevance of culture and language. The research was an ever-changing adaption of
what was happening as a place of action and reflection. Throughout the project there
were opportunities for people to question their own thinking in a way that led to
positive discursive shifts (Paki and Peters 2015).

7.6 Final Comments

An overarching aim of POET is to expand knowledge and understanding of the
significance of educational transitions for young children, their families and communities in national and international contexts. In this chapter we have considered
the urgency of addressing culture and identity and the need to consider cultural
values and culturally lived experiences as a place for understanding and responding
to educational transitions.

In our increasingly globalised world, where knowledge is evermore internationalised, there are calls to support and maintain local knowledge, values and practices. Many Indigenous peoples are devoting significant energy to ensuring cultural continuity, cultural regeneration and, in some cases, sheer cultural survival. Formal education has been co-opted as a supportive site by many Indigenous peoples focused on such endeavours. A case in point is the development of Māori medium education pathways that place Māori language, knowledge, values and practices at the centre.

Our position is that transitions within Māori medium pathways are best understood as a normal journey predicated on language and cultural survival and regeneration. Understanding and enhancing this journey can best be achieved by centring Māori knowledge, values and practices. Positioning cultural values and practices as fundamental to successful transition in Māori medium education, and in Indigenous language education pathways more generally, also means the relevance of transition research and theory is interrogated from within a culturally centred pedagogy.

The world is also more of an interconnected whole today than ever before. It is increasingly difficult to claim an understanding of one's own culture without realising the need to understand other ways of thinking and other cultural traditions. Inasmuch as research serves as a repository of, and a window into, cultural histories, intercultural understanding of transitions is indispensable. Cultural values provide and support culturally responsive transitions. A cultural pedagogy of relationships founded on respect and responsibility suggests that a successful transition for a child from a Māori medium early childhood setting to an English medium school requires a deep engagement with the values and practices of the child's particular cultural context in an endeavour to develop mutual connections when transitioning to a mainstream school. We also believe this is part of the process of normalising the role of culture and understanding and adapting practices and views to connect with the child, their family and wider contexts. As children transition to school as 'individuals', they also represent knowledge frameworks, values and beliefs belonging to their culture.

Finally, our practice and research around transitional pedagogies for Indigenous education pathways are arguably best guided by the cultural worldview and its accompanying values that have been drawn on to construct those Indigenous educational settings.

Acknowledgement We thank the Teaching and Learning Research Initiative (TLRI) for their funding and support and acknowledge children, families and teachers who participated in the projects. He mihi ki a koutou katoa, thank you all.

References

Baker, C. (2011). *Foundations of bilingual education and bilingualism* (4th ed.). Bristol: Multilingual Matters.

Barlow, C. (1991). *Tikanga whakaaro: Key concepts in Māori culture*. Auckland: Oxford University Press.

Bishop, R. (2005). Freeing ourselves from neo-colonial domination in research. A kaupapa Māori approach to creating knowledge. In N. K. Denzin & Y. S. Lincoln (Eds.), *The Sage handbook of qualitative research* (3rd ed., pp. 109–138). London: Sage.

Bishop, R., & Glynn, T. (1999). *Culture counts. Changing power relation in education*. Palmerston North: Dunmore Press.

Bishop, R., Ladwig, J., & Berryman, M. (2014). The centrality of relationships for pedagogy: The whanaungatanga thesis. *American Educational Research Journal, 51*(1), 184–214. doi:10.3102/0002831213510019.

Bright, N., Barnes, A., & Hutchings, J. (2013). *Ka whānau mai te reo: Honouring whānau: Upholding reo Māori*. Wellington: New Zealand Council for Educational Research.

Buck, P. (1987). *The coming of the Māori*. Wellington: Whitcombe & Tombs.

Durie, M. (1998). *Te mana, te kawanatanga: The politics of Māori self-determination*. Auckland: Oxford University Press.

Education Review Office. (2015). *Continuity of learning: Transitions from early childhood services to schools*. Wellington: Author.

Gibson, R. (1986). *Critical theory and education*. London: Hodder & Stoughton.

Hemara, W. (2000). *Māori pedagogies: A view from the literature*. Wellington: NZCER.

Hohepa, M. (1990). *Te Kōhanga Reo hei tikanga ako i te reo Māori: Te Kōhanga Reo as a context for language learning*. Masters thesis, Education Department, University of Auckland.

Hohepa, M., Smith, G., Smith, L., & McNaughton, S. (1992). Te Kōhanga Reo hei tikanga ako i te reo Māori: Te Kōhanga Reo as a context for language learning. *Educational Psychology, 12*(3–4), 333–346.

Irwin, K. (1990). The politics of Kōhanga Reo. In S. Middleton, J. Codd, & A. Jones (Eds.), *New Zealand education policy today: Critical perspectives*. Wellington: Allen & Urwin.

Ka'ai, T. (1990). *Te hiringa taketake: Mai i te kōhanga reo ki te kura: Māori pedagogy: Te kōhanga reo and the transition to school*. Unpublished Master of Philosophy thesis, University of Auckland, Auckland.

Macfarlane, S., & Macfarlane, A. (2012). Diversity and inclusion in early childhood education: A bicultural approach to engaging Māori potential. In D. Gordon-Burns, A. Gunn, K. Purdue, & N. Surtees (Eds.), *Te Aotūroa Tātaki: Inclusive early childhood education: Perspectives on inclusion, social justice and equity from Aotearoa New Zealand* (pp. 21–38). Wellington: NZCER Press.

Macfarlane, A., Glynn, T., Grace, W., Penetito, W., & Bateman, S. (2008). Indigenous epistemology in a national curriculum framework? *Ethnicities, 8*(1), 102–127.

May, S., Hill, R., & Tiakiwai, S. (2006). *Key findings from bilingual/immersion education: Indicators of good practice*. Wellington: Ministry of Education.

McMurchy-Pilkington, C. M. (2001). Māori education: Rejection, resistance, renaissance. In V. Carpenter, H. Dixon, E. Rata, & C. Rawlinson (Eds.), *Theory in practice for educators* (pp. 161–187). Palmerston: Dunmore Press.

McNatty, W., & Roa, T. (2002). Whanaungatanga: An illustration of the importance of cultural context. *He Puna Kōrero: Journal of Māori and Pacific Development, 3*(1), 88–96.

Mead, H. M. M. (2003). *Tikanga Māori: Living by Māori values*. Wellington: Huia Publications.

Ministry of Education. (1996). *Te whāriki: He whāriki mātauranga mō ngā mokopuna o Aotearoa: Early childhood curriculum*. Wellington: Learning Media.

Ministry of Education. (2008). *Te marautanga o Aotearoa*. Wellington: Learning Media.

Ministry of Education. (2009a). *Ka hikitia: Managing for success: The Māori education strategy 2008–2012*. Wellington: Group Māori.

Ministry of Education. (2009b). *Te whatu pōkeka: Kaupapa Māori assessment for learning early childhood exemplars*. Wellington: Learning Media.

Ministry of Education. (2013a). *Ka hikitia: Accelerating success: The Māori education strategy 2003–2017*. Wellington: Group Māori.

Ministry of Education. (2013b). *Tau mai te reo: The Māori language in education strategy.* Wellington: Author.

Ministry of Education. (2014). Number of schools by kura type and school type 2000–2014. https://www.educationcounts.govt.nz/statistics/maori-education/maori-in-schooling/6040. Accessed 20 Jan 2015.

Ministry of Education. (n.d.). *Establishing a certificated kura kōhungahunga* (Māori language playgroup). http://www.lead.ece.govt.nz/~/media/Educate/Files/Reference%20Downloads/Lead/Files/Establishing/EstablishingACertifiedPuna.pdf. Accessed 10 Feb 2015.

Nepe, T. (1991). *Te toi huarewa tipuna.* Master of Arts thesis, University of Auckland, Auckland, New Zealand.

New Zealand Gazette. (2008). *Official version of Te Aho Matua o ngā Kura Kaupapa Māori and an explanation in English.* http://www.dia.govt.nz//pubforms.nsf/NZGZT/Supplement_TeAho32Feb08.pdf/$file/Supplement_TeAho32Feb08.pdf. Accessed 13 July 2014.

Paki, V., & Peters, S. (2015). Exploring Whakapapa (genealogy) as a cultural concept to mapping transition journeys, understanding what is happening and discovering new insights. *Waikato Education Journal, 20*(2), 49–60.

Papakura, M. (1986). *Makereti: The old time Māori.* Auckland: New Women's Press.

Pere, R. (1991). *Te wheke: A celebration of infinite wisdom.* Gisborne: Ao Ako Global Learning.

Peters, S. (2010). *Literature review: Transition from early childhood education to school. Report commissioned by the Ministry of Education.* Wellington: Ministry of Education. http://www.educationcounts.govt.nz/publications/ece/78823. Accessed 11 Feb 2015.

Pihama, L. (2010). Kaupapa Māori theory: Transforming theory in Aotearoa. *He Pukenga Kōrero: A Journal of Māori Studies, 9*(2), 5–14.

Ratima, M. T., & Papesch, T. R. (2014). Te Rita Papesch: Case study of an exemplary learner of Māori as an additional language. *International Journal of Bilingual Education and Bilingualism, 17*(4), 379–393. doi:10.1080/13670050.2013.806431.

Reedy, T. (1995). *Knowledge and power set me free.* Paper presented at the sixth early childhood convention, Tamaki Makaurau-Auckland, New Zealand.

Ritchie, J. (2002). *"It's becoming part of their knowing": A study of bicultural development in an early childhood teacher education setting in Aotearoa/New Zealand.* Unpublished PhD thesis, University of Waikato, Hamilton.

Ritchie, J., & Rau, C. (2009). Ma wai ngā hua? 'Participation' in early childhood Aotearoa/New Zealand. *International Critical Childhood Policy Studies, 2*(1), 93–108.

Ritchie, J., & Rau, C. (2010). Poipoia te Tamaiti kia tū tangata. The first years: Ngā tau tuatahi. *New Zealand Journal of Infant and Toddler Education, 12*(1), 16–22.

Rogoff, B. (2003). *The cultural nature of development.* Oxford: Oxford University Press.

Royal Tangaere, A. (1997a). Te kōhanga reo: More than a language nest. *Early Childhood Folio, 3*, 41–47.

Royal Tangaere, A. (1997b). *Te puawaitanga o te reo Māori: Ka hua te hā o te potiki i roto i te whānau: Ko tēnei te tāhuhu o te kōhanga reo. Learning Māori together: Kōhanga reo and home.* Wellington: New Zealand Council for Education Research.

Smith, G. H. (1992a). *Tane-nui-a-Rangi's legacy ... Propping up the sky: Kaupapa Māori as resistance and intervention.* In: NZARE/AARE Joint conference, Deakin University of Australia and University of Auckland, New Zealand.

Smith, L.T. (1992b). Te rapunga i te ao Marama. Māori perspectives on research in education. In J. Moss & J. Linzey (Eds.). *Growing up: The politics of human learning.* Auckland, New Zealand: Longman Paul.

Smith, G. H. (1995). Whakaoho whānau: New formations of whānau as an innovative intervention into Māori cultural and educational crises. *He Pukenga Kōrero, 1*(1), 18–36.

Smith, G. H. (1997). *The development of Kaupapa Māori: Theory and praxis.* Doctoral thesis, University of Auckland, Auckland, New Zealand.

Smith, L. (1999). *Decolonizing methodologies: Research and indigenous peoples.* London: Zed Books.

Sullivan, A. (2001). Cultural capital and educational attainment. *Sociology, 35*, 893–912.
Te Kohanga Reo National Trust. (1995). *Te Korowai*. Wellington: Author.
Te Wānanga o Aotearoa (TWOA). (2015). *Ngā Uara – Our values*. http://www.twoa.ac.nz/Te-Whare/Nga-Uara.aspx. Accessed 14 Feb 2015.
Vygotsky, L. S. (1978). *Mind in society: The development of higher mental processes*. Cambridge, MA: Harvard University Press.
Walker, R. (2004). *Ka whawhai tonu matou. Struggle without end* (Rev. ed.). Auckland: Penguin.

Chapter 8
A Social Justice View of Educators' Conceptions of Aboriginal Children Starting School

Lysa Dealtry, Bob Perry, and Sue Dockett

This chapter addresses pedagogies of educational transitions by offering a critical exploration of the ways in which Aboriginal children are positioned by educators' pedagogical beliefs in the context of their transition to primary school settings in urban communities. The chapter explores the pedagogical principles that educators draw on when they consider Aboriginal children's strengths and needs during their transition from prior-to-school to school settings. These principles are examined for the ways in which they might construct and reconstruct Aboriginal[1] children in educational settings. Particular pedagogical stances are interpreted through a social justice lens that views social justice as multifaceted, contingent and relational. Specific notions of all children as individuals with diverse needs and strengths are discussed as problematic in two ways: first, as they shape what educators can 'know' about Aboriginal children and second, for the rationale they provide for educators to engage (or not) in practices and programmes that support transition to school for Aboriginal children and families.

---

[1] Indigenous/Aboriginal: The word Indigenous has been used to refer to people of either Aboriginal or Torres Strait Islander background, and when used, it reflects the use of the word Indigenous in the source literature. References to Aboriginal children, families and community will be used for the research participants to reflect local preferences in the research site and the protocol established in the *Report of the Review of Aboriginal Education* (New South Wales Aboriginal Education Consultative Group Inc. & New South Wales Department of Education and Training [NSW AECG/ NSW DET] 2004, p. 11). Accordingly, the term Aboriginal is inclusive of both Aboriginal and Torres Strait Islander people living in New South Wales.

L. Dealtry (✉) • S. Dockett
Charles Sturt University, Albury, NSW, Australia
e-mail: ldealtry@csu.edu.au

B. Perry
Research Institue for Professional Practice, Learning and Education (RIPPLE),
Charles Sturt University, Albury, NSW, Australia

© Springer International Publishing Switzerland 2017
N. Ballam et al. (eds.), *Pedagogies of Educational Transitions*, International
Perspectives on Early Childhood Education and Development 16,
DOI 10.1007/978-3-319-43118-5_8

8.1   Introduction

A critical approach to social justice underpins this chapter, with particular attention
to Indigenous Australian voices. Indigenous voices can provide a critical and culturally sensitive lens and make visible the ways a 'Western order of things' (Nakata
2007) might inform the positioning of Aboriginal students and families in school
settings. Consideration is given to the way developmentally oriented views of transitioning children can lead to a narrow focus on the child as a learner and reduce
pedagogical thought and action to remedial and academic programmes of support
that draw attention to what children cannot do. This narrow focus is troubled, tip-
ping the social justice scales towards an emphasis on social and economic redistribution and away from recognition of the cultural and relational dimensions of social
justice.

The chapter begins by briefly describing (1) the relevant conceptual and research
field, specifically attending to the literature that informs our understanding of successful transition to school for Aboriginal children, and (2) the broader research
programme from which the findings reported in this chapter derive.

The chapter concludes by attending to what is possible when taken-for-granted
redistributive discourses are displaced. An expanded, relational view of Aboriginal
children as multipositioned is offered to consider how a focus on building relations
between and amongst home, school, prior-to-school, local and wider community
can better inform approaches to transition for Aboriginal children and families.

8.2   Social Justice and Education

In the context of reform that promotes equitable participation and outcomes for all,
educational settings are increasingly being reconstructed as spaces for contributing
to more socially just societies (Educational Transitions and Change [ETC] Research
Group 2011; Thomson et al. 2012; Vandenbroeck 2007). However, the term 'social
justice' has been described as an ill-defined (Perry 2014) and 'amorphous' concept,
lacking a metanarrative to guide practice (Vincent 2003). The lack of a theoretical
and practical basis for framing socially just education and the increasing heterogeneity of communities have led to tensions and uncertainty as educators grapple with
how best to move forward in the name of social justice (Keddie 2012).

Definitions of social justice have tended to operate within two distinct ideologies. One of these posits that social justice is 'a matter of redistributing goods and
resources to improve the situations of the disadvantaged' (Bankston 2010, p. 165).
The other places equal emphasis on economic and cultural injustices, depicting the
attainment of social justice as also requiring identity recognition (Fraser 1997):
'This approach is not about recognising group identity simply on the basis of mar-
ginality or privilege, but rather on dismantling the concrete arrangements that
impede parity' (Keddie 2012, p. 266). More recently, a political imperative has been

articulated that portrays social justice at an intersection of redistributive, recognitive and representative and participatory practices. These practices aim to displace injustices that 'silence or misrepresent marginalised students' (Keddie 2012, p. 266). This chapter is concerned with the relationship between educators' pedagogical principles and the possibilities that they present for redistributive, recognitive and representative and participatory practices during the transition to school.

Scholars promoting social justice work in education have drawn on many standpoints, particularly critical, post-colonial and decolonising scholarship, to argue for a rereading of the pedagogical landscape that redresses the marginalisation of minority groups and decentres taken-for-granted assumptions in educational philosophy and practice (Freire 2005; McLaren 2007; Trifonas 2003). This work is inherently political and envisions educators striving for reflexive practice that recognises multiple perspectives and their cultural locations, as well as acknowledging the effect of their location (Bristol 2012; Thomson et al. 2012). In post-colonial terms, this requires recognition that images of Aboriginality as homogenous and problematic are colonial constructions (Fforde et al. 2013). To interrogate constructions of Aboriginality in their professional lives effectively, educators are charged with the task of developing 'a critical cultural consciousness that allows the teacher to interrogate the meanings of images and concepts represented within the shared linguistic turns of the culture of teaching' (Bristol 2012, p. 20). Conceptions of social justice from this perspective become relational and contingent on positions such as race, gender, class and age (Vincent 2003). In practice, this conception of social justice denotes a shift away from 'one-size-fits-all' approaches to recognising and acknowledging heterogeneity.

8.3   Educational Transitions Through Critical and Social Justice Lenses

Several Australian authors have employed critical lenses to interrogate normative assumptions about the transition needs of groups of children (Dockett 2014) and the understandings that have come to be taken-for-granted knowledge about transition (Petriwskyj 2014; Petriwskyj and Grieshaber 2011). Extending on these writings, and to counter normative images of transition to school for Australian Indigenous children, strengths-based readings of children's attributes recognise the assets and resources that Indigenous children hold as school entrants (Armstrong et al. 2012; Dockett et al. 2010). Internationally, participation and recognition issues have been described for minority children in mainstream educational settings (Brooker 2002). However, Perry (2014, p. 184) cautions 'there is still much to be done to ensure that for all stakeholders in transition to school, social justice is paramount'.

8.3.1   Educational Transitions and Social Justice

Positive early school experiences support the transition to school, laying the foundation for children and families to construct positive identities as competent, capable and connected in their present and future educational contexts (Brooker and Woodhead 2008; ETC Research Group 2011). Successful entry points into educational settings for children from marginalised groups are recognised as important precursors to breaking patterns of disadvantage and providing improved life chances for these children (Smart et al. 2008; Taylor and Nelms 2006). Positive early educational experiences are viewed as a gateway to equal opportunity and outcomes (ETC Research Group 2011).

8.3.2   Social Justice Dimensions of Education for Australian Aboriginal Peoples

In Australia, the pursuit of social justice by and for Australia's first peoples is a highly complex issue. Over many years, successive governments have fallen far short of their commitments. Aboriginal scholars remind us that much of the transformation required to realise change is outside of the purview of the current discourses operating in recent educational reforms (Pearson 2011; West 2000). The Australian Government's Closing the Gap discourse locates Aboriginal peoples in a structurally and culturally (not historically) determined position of disadvantage, and its policy emphasis is to combat this disadvantage. Phillips (2012) argues that this discourse positions Aboriginal inequality as 'matters of economy' and deflects consideration of what actually happens in educational settings as making a difference for Aboriginal children.

Emphasis on the recognition of identity calls for the work of education for social justice outcomes to be bicultural – both in its origins and in its implementation and delivery – to ensure not only social and economic but also cultural and relational prosperity for Aboriginal peoples (Pearson 2011; Sarra 2011). This takes education for social justice beyond matters of social and economic redistribution, towards the realisation of cultural and relational dimensions of social justice (Vincent 2003). Greater recognition of the importance of cultural prosperity mirrors Aboriginal peoples' aspirations for their children to be successful participants in mainstream systems of education, as well as their local and community cultural contexts (Mason-White and Secretariat of National Aboriginal and Islander Child Care [SNAICC] 2013; Pearson 2011).

8.3.3 Transitions to School for Aboriginal Children

Educational settings play a central role in promoting a positive transition to school for Aboriginal children when they acknowledge and value children's culture (Dockett et al. 2010; Dockett et al. 2008). Indeed, Aboriginal peoples' aspirations for their children to be successful in 'two-worlds' (Mason-White and SNAICC 2013) are unlikely to be realised without such recognition and affirmation of children's cultural worlds. To this end, Australia's national curriculum framework for early childhood guides the implementation of culturally responsive approaches to education (Department of Education, Employment and Workplace Relations [DEEWR] 2009), and various documents have been developed to support educational transitions for Aboriginal children (Armstrong et al. 2012; Dockett et al. 2008; Mason-White and SNAICC 2013).

8.4 The *Gudaga Goes to School* Study and Sense of Self

The *Gudaga goes to school* study, which includes the doctoral study considering Aboriginal children's sense of self as they start school conducted by the first author of this chapter, builds on a long history of community/researcher involvement and partnership developed in a number of studies conducted in suburban Sydney (Comino et al. 2010; Knight et al. 2009). The Gudaga study sought to identify and map the health and well-being issues that needed to be addressed to support mothers and their young children in the local Aboriginal community. Recruitment over a period of 18 months from 2005 to 2007 at a suburban Sydney maternity hospital resulted in 150 mothers and their Aboriginal children participating in the study. This was the first research project to employ a longitudinal research design with an urban Aboriginal birth cohort in the eastern states of Australia (Comino et al. 2010). The Gudaga study and its subsequent extensions were conducted under a strict set of principles and protocols that were developed jointly by the community and the researchers. The study was approved by the relevant university, health and education sector ethics review committees.

In 2011, as the oldest of the Gudaga children were approaching their start to school, the study was expanded to include exploration of the children's experiences of school. This component of the study was titled *Gudaga goes to school: Understanding the health, development, and early education experiences of Aboriginal children in an urban environment*. The *Gudaga goes to school* (Gudaga-GtS) project team brings together Indigenous and non-Indigenous researchers from health and education backgrounds to build on the important work and relationships established within the Gudaga study to explore transition to school and the early years of school. The formal aims of the Gudaga-GtS are:

1. To describe the transition and early education experiences for a cohort of urban Aboriginal children up until the end of year 2, from the perspectives of children, family members and educators
2. To examine potential relationships between school achievement for urban Aboriginal children and early childhood health, development and service participation
3. To understand what constitutes successful school transition for urban Aboriginal children by exploring child, teacher, family and community views
4. To explore the aspirations and expectations for urban Aboriginal children held by key stakeholders and examine the relationships between these variables and school performance and engagement (Kemp et al. 2011, p. 5)

Within Gudaga-GtS, an independent doctoral study was conducted by the first author of this chapter, exploring the following research questions:

- How do urban Aboriginal children and parents express a positive sense of self and belonging in relation to school?
- What enables and contributes to a positive sense of self for urban Aboriginal children and families?

It is from this doctoral study that the data discussed in this chapter are drawn. In particular, these data arise from surveys and interviews conducted as part of the main study. Surveys were completed by 21 early childhood educators (ECEs) working in prior-to-school settings such as preschools and long day care centres. As part of the doctoral study and collected by the first author of this chapter, data from interviews conducted in 2013 with seven primary school principals and five educators employed by schools to facilitate Aboriginal education programmes have also been included. Interviews and surveys with ECEs were conducted at the end of 2010 and 2011. The interviews with primary school educators drawn from the main study were conducted in 2012. The primary school educator responses examined in this chapter were all contributed by non-Aboriginal educators working in schools with enrolments of Aboriginal children that were less than 10 % of total enrolments. Data about the cultural identity of the ECEs were not collected.

8.5 The Findings: Redistributive and Diversity-Oriented Discourses in ECE Settings

The majority of early childhood educators (ECEs) responded in very similar ways to the survey question: *Do Aboriginal children and families have particular strengths and needs in school transition?* Responses typical of those offered by 12 of the 21 educators interviewed were:

1. All children and families, to various degrees, have strengths and needs in school transition.

2. Every child and their families have their own individual strengths and needs.
3. All our children are special and they all have their needs.
4. All children are individuals who have needs and strengths. Aboriginal children are no different.

These 12 ECEs' responses drew on a commonly prescribed principle for a developmental curriculum; that is, 'each child is an individual and should be respected as such' (Siraj-Blatchford and Clarke 2000, p. viii). Most of these survey responses were quite brief statements, suggesting that this was a widely held, and seemingly self-explanatory, 'principle' amongst these educators. A more detailed understanding of why this was such a common reference point for the educators was not offered in the survey responses. However, of interest is the preponderance of the principle and what it might suggest about how Aboriginal children are positioned and how their strengths and needs are identified and catered for during the transition to school.

Filtered through a socially just education lens, several interpretations of the above expressions from ECEs are possible. Each has implications for how Aboriginal children and their transition to school are considered. It is possible that ECEs:

- View Aboriginal children as being as diverse as the general population. In this view, children start school with the same range of strengths and needs as all other children – that is, their strengths and needs are a reflection of their membership of the general community, rather than their Aboriginality
- Are reluctant to essentialise, draw binaries or homogenise experiences, preferring to recognise diversity and complexity and not to make normative assumptions about the transition strengths and needs of individuals or groups of children
- Are reluctant and/or unprepared to draw on ethnic/racial[2] or political discourses in relation to Aboriginality

When educators draw on this principle of every child as an individual, there is no recognition of group identity, uniqueness or difference or any articulation of the historical, social and cultural factors that can shape a different experience of the world for Aboriginal children (Nakata 2007).

It would appear that by evoking this principle, many educators were indicating the belief that Aboriginal children or families do not have particular strengths or needs in school transition. A level of sameness or universality is implied. That is, Aboriginal children are positioned as not having any notable uniqueness or difference from other children.

Many writers have problematised constructions of the child, childhood and child development in mainstream settings formulated from a Western orientation (Fleer 2003; Martin 2012). Using Western lenses, educators will 'rarely capture the range

---

[2] The use of ethnic/racial acknowledges that racial categories based on physical characteristics, while being social constructions, do continue to impact everyday realities. The cultural diversity that derives from groupings that have their basis in shared beliefs, values, identities, heritage and ancestry is better understood through the construct of ethnicity.

of contexts, abilities, and strengths that an Aboriginal child has' (Martin 2012, p. 37). Recognition of children as members of 'culturally defined groups or communities of value' (Fraser 1997, p. 2) would appear to be ignored through such a filter. Moreover, it is unlikely that Aboriginal children and families are considered as having any common family history and/or life experiences that could impact their experience of transition to school.

In contrast to this principle, nine of the 21 ECE respondents indicated that some Aboriginal families may have particular needs that can impact on the transition to school. Several of these ECEs first expressed the majority sentiment about the individual nature of strengths and needs but then expanded on their responses to state considerations in relation to Aboriginal parents and children. These fell into three broad themes:

1. Negative experiences of school: Educators suggested that Aboriginal parents may themselves have had negative experiences of school and expected this to have implications for the way they engaged with educational settings.
2. Greater support needs: Aboriginal children were described as having greater need for additional support for their adjustment to structural and social aspects of school and for their literacy and numeracy.
3. Cultural experiences: Educators referred to the role of schools in the provision of cultural activities and groups.

While parental negative experience of school was identified as a particular need by one educator, she also pointed out that such experiences can serve to heighten the value that parents place on education for their children as they may 'feel that it is more important to complete schooling in order to have a different life'.

These ECE's responses were largely silent on the sociohistorical context that has produced particular family histories and/or life experiences for Aboriginal peoples. In the absence of any recognition of why these circumstances may exist for families, there is a danger that the particular needs that are being identified will be perceived as culturally determined deficits (Moreton-Robinson 2000). Even though the question asked about both needs and strengths, the responses reflected the perception that Aboriginal children had needs rather than strengths at school transition.

Two ECEs gave responses that were exceptions to those listed above. Their responses are reproduced below. They highlighted the way strong family and community relationships formed a foundation for a successful transition to school for Aboriginal children. In her written response, one of these ECEs elaborated on her response, using a series of dot points to detail the conditions at school that were required to support Aboriginal children and families during the transition.

ECE 1 – Response in Interview

Interviewer: Do Aboriginal children and families have particular strengths and needs in school transition?

ECE: Yes, I do believe that Aboriginal children and families have both strengths and needs in school transitions. In this instance, focus child A and family have a very strong community connection and are confident in enrolling children in school.

ECE 2 – Written Response to Survey Question

Question: Do Aboriginal children and families have particular strengths and needs in school transition?

ECE: Yes. The focus child B was proud of her identity.

If the classroom is 'Aboriginal friendly' with posters, books, flags, etc. that depict the ATSI [Aboriginal and Torres Strait Islander] culture it helps the child feel comfortable, makes the environment feel familiar and accepting of their culture and identity.

Family is important to Aboriginal children, so teachers that get to know families, talk to the child about their family, can help to settle and ease children into Kindergarten as the child still holds that attachment until the child feels comfortable and then the teacher becomes their secondary attachment.

Helping children to feel comfortable and welcomed is important. Also making the parents feel welcomed and comfortable is important. Inviting parents into the room and listening to their concerns if any. Regular transition visits to Kindergarten classrooms, playground, etc. prior to starting is important for school transition.

These expressions recognise aspects of children's cultural worlds and their potential to influence transition to school in positive ways. The second response offers recognition of the child's Aboriginal identity as a strength and notes that educational settings play an important role as co-constructors of this when it is recognised, valued and affirmed.

There appears to be some recognition by the second ECE that educational settings may not represent a consistently positive environment for all Aboriginal families and that educators need to act as a buffer against barriers that may exist (Grace and Trudgett 2012; Hayes et al. 2009). This recognition could be seen as working towards a relational form of social justice, whereby educators acknowledge the marginalising potential of educational settings and act to redress past and present practices that are complicit in the exclusion of marginalised groups from education (Schoorman 2011). However, the cultural and political imperatives of a social justice-oriented approach would advocate for more in this educator's response, calling for the recognition of the collective cultural and political aspirations of Aboriginal peoples and the historical relations in which these aspirations have been embedded. This aligns with appeals from Indigenous scholars for recognition of the agency that has existed, and continues to exist, in Aboriginal lifeworlds and of the ongoing presence and impact of Western and colonialist discourses in educational settings (Martin 2007; Nakata 2007; West 2000).

8.5.1 Redistributive Discourses in School Settings

8.5.1.1 Redistributive Principles Located in Diversity-Oriented Approaches

Interviews with primary school principals sought information about their expectations of Aboriginal children as they started school. An excerpt from one interview is reproduced below:

Interviewer:	So thinking about starting school, do you have any expectations around how children might present at that time, in terms of arriving at school, any expectations?
School Principal 1:	No. We have exactly the same expectation of every child that walks through the door.
Interviewer:	In terms of the notion of school readiness?
School Principal 1:	In terms of our Aboriginal students?
Interviewer:	All students, and then does it differ for the Aboriginal students?
School Principal 1:	No, I don't think it does. Look, in terms of all students we get the absolute gamut of kids here so we've got kids that fall in the IM [Mild Intellectual Impairment] and the IO [Moderate Intellectual Impairment] range. Usually the IO ones are identified before they come to school so we've organised funding support and all that type of stuff that you do. And we've got a number of children that would fall into the gifted and talented range as well. So I guess our expectation is that everything is going to walk through the door [laughs] … And we've also got kids that are on the autism spectrum and stuff like that so it's just all happening. So that is our expectation – whatever … we don't actually do anything different for our Aboriginal students. Everybody walks through the door and it's a totally level playing field and our Aboriginal students perform at all levels.

This school principal also filtered her response through the pedagogical principle that assumes the individual and diverse nature of children's attributes and abilities. This established an expectation that each year, the children starting school would present with a wide range of strengths and needs. It is apparent from this principal's expectations for all children that the 'needs' that are being assumed are learning needs, and transition support is seen as a matter of organising and allocating resources and services to counter learner disadvantage. This suggests that one of the school-based priorities at the time of transition is to assess learning support needs and the ways they will be met.

As with ECEs, there appears to be a reluctance and/or unpreparedness from this principal to draw on ethnic/racial or political discourses in relation to Aboriginality. On the one hand, this could be seen as honouring diversity and reflecting the redistributive social justice notion that all children are equal and all should have access to the goods and resources they require to achieve equitable educational outcomes. On the other hand, such an approach does not provide the basis of transformative pedagogy, nor does it promote the realisation of social justice outcomes based on principles of recognition. Without ethnic/racial or political discourses to draw on, children making the transition to school are framed solely within discourses of education and resource distribution (transition support), according to their learning abilities. Assumptions of diversity as they relate to each child as a learner exist within this framing, but not recognition of the unequal playing field in education that derives from a collective Aboriginal experience of a long history of inequitable education policies and practices in Australia.

In the principal's response earlier, Aboriginality is not recognised as a cultural, social or racial category that may signify particular experiences, strengths and needs during the transition to school. Here all transitioning children are positioned primarily as the 'academic child' – that is, they are categorised according to who they are, or are known to be, as learners. Aboriginality as a cultural identity or community of value is again imperceptible, and thinking about the transition for Aboriginal children becomes subsumed into the discourse of special or additional learning needs.

It is important not to assume that all Aboriginal children arrive at school with a particular set of social, cultural or historical experiences and/or circumstances. Indeed, to state this takes up the very pedagogical principle that we are calling into question but hopefully repackages it with both a disclaimer and a prompt for educators to interrogate their 'view' of children's needs and strengths through critical and social justice lenses. Reliance on this diversity-oriented approach has the potential to mask the inequalities children may experience because of their membership of a particular identity category and the positioning of that category. Critical lenses can provide a means to trouble this. So, while it may be reasonable that expectations of children do not differ, it is important to recognise difference in terms of life experiences and worldviews and their influence on children's experiences of transition to school. Treating all children equally might equate with the premise that 'all children have equal life-chances, regardless of their social and cultural background and identity [which has] not been borne out by research evidence to date' (Brooker 2006, p. 118).

8.5.1.2 Redistributive Principles and Tensions Operating in Recognition Discourses

In asserting that expectations were the same for all children, another principal reasoned that Aboriginal children enrolled in the school did not see themselves as different from anyone else and neither did the educators:

Interviewer: So, thinking to the start of school when the children are arriving, do you have any expectations around that time?

School Principal 2:   I guess our expectations are the same for Aboriginal stu-
                             dents as they are for all our students. While we have a [sepa-
                             rate Aboriginal group/programme], the normal school day
                             doesn't change for them. I guess for us, we're in the suburbs
                             of Sydney, the outer suburbs of Sydney. So our students are
                             basically born in the suburbs. I don't think they see them-
                             selves as necessarily being different from the rest of the
                             population …

**School Learning
Support Officer[3]:**   No, I don't think so either.

School Principal 2:   … and yeah, our expectations are exactly the same. Our
                             expectations are that we do run a transition programme for
                             all our students. We would give the same support to them
                             starting school as any other child and if achild had a diffi-
                             culty of transitioning, regardless of where they camefrom,
                             their identity, or national background, we would still sup-
                             port them.

This view suggests that any child can present with support needs during the transition to school and that a child's Aboriginality would not prompt differential support. Expectations and practice relating to transitioning children would appear to
operate under an ethos of 'we're all equal and same'. However, the school does
practise a differentiated distribution of resources for Aboriginal children in the form
of Personal Learning Plans (PLPs), a separate Aboriginal group/programme that
children attend weekly, and School Learning Support Officer (SLSO) assistance for
Aboriginal children in their classroom. In the context of the principal and SLSO's
account of 'sameness', these everyday practices have seemingly become normalised
differential treatment of Aboriginal children. Siraj-Blatchford and Clarke (2000)
argue that these everyday inequalities do matter to children's identity formation. At
the very least, a question is raised about the contradiction between ethos and practice. This is an interesting tension, as a form of recognition is played out in a redistributive practice – with many Aboriginal children encountering different educative
resources and services from their non-Aboriginal peers. Some of this is based on
assumptions about what Aboriginal children need to be successful in school and
life. Assumptions are being made about children based on recognition of their identity through an academic lens. This can have the effect of positioning this facet of
children's self-identity (Aboriginality) as 'in need' and, by virtue, 'in deficit'. While
not wanting to undermine the importance of resource provision, an arbitrary, culturally determined allocation of resources risks reinforcing images of Aboriginal

---

[3] School Learning Support Officers (SLSOs) are employed to assist teachers in the classroom with
general class activities and to attend to the needs of students with additional needs. SLSOs can be
employed in assigned roles to support the needs of particular groups of students, including
Aboriginal students. The SLSO in this interview was employed to work with Aboriginal students
in the school. These positions can be designated for Aboriginal persons only or can be open to all
applicants (New South Wales Department of Education and Communities n.d).

underachievement and locating social justice as a set of practices designed to close literacy and numeracy gaps between Aboriginal and non-Aboriginal children.

The tension apparent in this scenario suggests that there is a need for the balancing and interrogation of the kinds of recognition that underpin social justice work. Here is where the language and perspectives of Indigenous and non-Indigenous critical, post-colonial and strengths-based approaches can reveal unintentional perpetuations of marginalising and inequitable practices. These perspectives also position educators as active participants in achieving social justice, capable of engaging in reflexive practice that connects them with the personal, cultural, historical and structural dimensions of injustice and inequity (Freire 2005).

8.5.1.3 Redistributive Principles and Tensions Operating in Recognition Discourses: Authenticity and Entitlement

A further tension exists in the complex ties between the perceived 'authenticity' of Aboriginal identity (by a White educator) and the assumed greater necessity for, or entitlement to, resources:

School Educator[4]   There's a lot of Aboriginal kids in this school that don't really have a lot of strong Aboriginal links outside of school, but those that do have a lot of strong Aboriginal links outside of school, I don't – still don't see them as Aboriginal, like, because – I mean they just behave and act and say and do all the things that all of their other friends do. So sometimes I wonder whether we need to put such an emphasis on, "You're Aboriginal", because how do we want – we want them to maintain their knowledge of heritage and their culture, but whether it's really the role of the school to push it as heavily as we should or not, I'm not sure. But I know that to give them a hand in these early stages of re-establishing that, yes we can, but how long we maintain that for, I don't know.

Partly, this educator appears to be questioning the role of schools in assigning particular identities and 'needs' to Aboriginal children, especially when they do not behave in an overtly Aboriginal way (seemingly determined through behavioural characteristics that somehow differ to those of 'other children'). When educators make comparisons using stereotypical imagery of the 'authentic' Aboriginal, such as through references to 'being born in the suburbs' or 'being no different to the rest of the population', they risk reproducing discourses that reflect a powerful assimilationist narrative that has its legacy in Australia's colonial past (Fforde et al. 2013). Here, Aboriginal people who are born, living and acting like their non-Aboriginal peers are positioned at the cultural centre of White mainstream society, and cultural

---

[4]This generalist classroom teacher initiated and ran a cultural programme for the Aboriginal children enrolled at the school. The programme was attended once each week during school hours by all Aboriginal children from kindergarten to Grade 6.

identity is narrowly understood through emphasis on 'the "doing" of culture, rather than its "beingness"' (Phillips 2012, p. 20). At one level, the educator's expressions might be perceived as disrupting processes of racial categorisation (Goodyer and Okitikpi 2007). At another, they may also reflect a colonialist narrative that deflects from and constrains the way social justice outcomes (both redistributive and recognitive) can be realised for Aboriginal children by disavowing the heterogeneity of Aboriginal identities (Nakata 2012).

8.6   Conclusion

Many early childhood educators in this study referred to notions of individuation and diversity, both of which reflect traditional early childhood educational philosophy (Fleer 2003). Children making the transition to school were positioned as individuals with strengths and needs located in their particular individual equation. As they made the transition to school, they were depicted as a diverse cohort of learners. However, this view of children has the potential to conflate and subsume difference that has arisen in, and is perpetuated by, unjust historical and contemporary conditions. In this respect, an individuation and diversity-oriented view generated a homogenic, rather than heterogenic, view of transitioning children. The principle that children should be treated as individuals, as taken up by educators in this investigation, appeared to deflect their thought and action from cultural and political dimensions of social justice. While these results cannot identify the particular ideologies about social justice that the educators held, they may point to a need for initial and in-service teacher education that focuses specifically on building awareness of the cultural-political implications of the principles that guide their work.

As school entrants, Aboriginal children were positioned in relation to the particular pedagogical principles and priorities that school educators, particularly principals, held about transitioning children. Some principals in this study were predisposed to seeing children as diverse – but solely in reference to their diversity as learners. This positioned children along a continuum of ability that is narrowly defined by performance on academic skills. This is a construction of children (Petriwskyj and Grieshaber 2011) and a focus of what educators want to know about children (Hopps 2014) that has previously been identified in transition research. Arguably, conceptualising children in this way could limit educators' attention to practices identified as contributing to successful transitions such as:

- Connecting with funds of knowledge (Moll et al. 1992) that children bring to school
- Culturally responsive teaching (Armstrong et al. 2012; Martin 2007)
- Learning about children and their families (Peters 2010)
- A holistic approach to addressing the specific health, development and well-being needs of Aboriginal children in the context of strengthening the capacity of families and communities to meet those needs (Dockett et al. 2007)

- Strength-based approaches and cultural competence (Mason-White and SNAICC 2013)

Notions of diversity and respect for the child as an individual are important, but '[f]or justice to be genuinely "social justice", benefits need to accrue beyond the individual level' (Perry 2014, p. 176). Yet, based on the findings in this study, current educational thinking that frames the child as an individual would appear to be delimiting in this respect, particularly when the individual is positioned as ahistorical and acultural. A combination of critical and relational approaches to the transition to school for Aboriginal children could facilitate more nuanced understanding of how individual and collective needs and strengths intersect to create both challenges and opportunities at this time.

It would appear that the social justice interests and aspirations of Aboriginal peoples as a culturally marginalised collective may be addressed through a balance of redistributive, recognitive and representative practices. This will require educators to engage in critical reflection and to highlight, rather than 'suture over' (Jipson 1995; Nakata 2007), issues of diversity and complexity. From this, alternatives to universalising and 'amnesia-ridden' (Tejeda et al. 2003) representations of Aboriginal children that do not facilitate recognition of their, or their community's, strengths and interests in their transition to school may be established. This requires a pedagogical stance that critically evaluates pedagogies of educational transitions, including the principles that underpin them. Educators might also consider their own definitions of, and aspirations for, social justice through critical and culturally sensitive lenses to ensure they reflect the strengths, needs and interests of all stakeholders. Such reflexivity will equip educators to reread discourses of individuation and diversity for their potential to continue or dismantle patterns of inequality.

References

Armstrong, S., Buckley, S., Lonsdale, M., Milgate, G., Bennetts Kneebone, L., Cook, L., & Skelton, F. (2012). *Starting school: A strengths-based approach towards Aboriginal and Torres Strait Islander children*. Canberra: Australian Council of Educational Research (ACER) & Department of Families, Housing, Community Services and Indigenous Affairs (FaHCSIA).

Bankston, C. L., III. (2010). Social justice: Cultural origins of a perspective and a theory. *Independent Review, 15*(2), 165–178.

Bristol, L. (2012). Postcolonial thought: A theoretical and methodological means for thinking through culturally ethical research. In J. Lavia & S. Mahlomaholo (Eds.), *Culture, education, and community: Expressions of postcolonial imagination* (pp. 15–32). New York: Palgrave Macmillan.

Brooker, L. (2002). *Starting school – Young children learning cultures*. Buckingham: Open University Press.

Brooker, L. (2006). From home to the home corner: Observing children's identity-maintenance in early childhood settings. *Children & Society, 20*(2), 116–127. doi:10.1111/j.1099-0860.2006.00019.x.

Brooker, L., & Woodhead, M. (2008). *Developing positive identities. Early childhood in focus 3: Diversity and young children*. Buckingham: The Open University.

Comino, E., Craig, P., Harris, E., McDermott, D., Harris, M., Henry, R., et al. (2010). The Gudaga Study: Establishing an Aboriginal birth cohort in an urban community. *Australian and New Zealand Journal of Public Health, 34*(S1), 9–17.

Department of Education Employment and Workplace Relations [DEEWR]. (2009). *Belonging, being and becoming: The early years learning framework for Australia.* Canberra: DEEWR. http://docs.education.gov.au/system/files/doc/other/belonging_being_and_becoming_the_early_years_learning_framework_for_australia.pdf. Accessed 27 Feb 2015.

Dockett, S. (2014). Transition to school: Normative or relative? In B. Perry, S. Dockett, & A. Petriwskyj (Eds.), *Transition to school: International research, policy and practice* (pp. 187–200). Dordrecht: Springer.

Dockett, S., Perry, B., Mason, T., & Simpson, T. (2007). Successful transitions from prior-to-school to school for Aboriginal and Torres-Strait Islander children. *International Journal for Equity and Innovation in Early Childhood, 5*(1), 102–111.

Dockett, S., Perry, B., Mason, T., Simpson, T., Howard, P., & Whitton, D., et al. (2008). *Getting it together: Successful transition programs from prior-to-school to school for Aboriginal and Torres Strait Islander children.* Canberra: MCEETYA. http://www.curriculum.edu.au/verve/_resources/ATSI_Successful_Transition_programs_Report_Dec_2007.pdf. Accessed 6 Oct 2015.

Dockett, S., Perry, B., & Kearney, E. (2010). *School readiness: What does it mean for Indigenous children, families, schools and communities?* Issues Paper no. 2 produced for the Closing the Gap Clearinghouse. Canberra: Australian Institute of Health and Welfare and Australian Institute of Family Studies.

Educational Transitions and Change [ETC] Research Group. (2011). *Transition to school: Position statement.* http://www.csu.edu.au/faculty/educat/edu/transitions/publications/Position-Statement.pdf. Accessed 16 Aug 2015.

Fforde, C., Bamblett, L., Lovett, R., Gorringe, S., & Fogarty, B. (2013). Discourse, deficit and identity: Aboriginality, the race paradigm and the language of representation in contemporary Australia. *Media International Australia, 149*, 162–173.

Fleer, M. (2003). Post-Vygotskian lenses on Western early childhood education: Moving the debate forward. *European Early Childhood Education Research Journal, 11*(1), 55–67.

Fraser, N. (1997). *Justice interruptus: Critical reflections on the 'postsocialist' condition.* New York: Routledge.

Freire, P. (2005). *Teachers as cultural workers: Letters to those who dare to teach.* Boulder, CO: Westview Press.

Goodyer, A., & Okitikpi, T. (2007). "… But…but I am brown". The ascribed categories of identity: Children and young people of mixed parentage. *Child Care in Practice, 13*(2), 83–94. doi:10.1080/13575270701201169.

Grace, R., & Trudgett, M. (2012). It's not rocket science: The perspectives of indigenous early childhood workers on supporting the engagement of Indigenous families in early childhood settings. *Australasian Journal of Early Childhood, 37*(2), 10–18.

Hayes, D., Johnston, K., Morris, K., Power, K., & Roberts, D. (2009). Difficult dialogue: Conversations with Aboriginal parents and caregivers. *Australian Journal of Indigenous Education, 38*, 55–64.

Hopps, K. (2014). *Intersetting communication and transition to school.* Unpublished doctoral thesis, Charles Sturt University, Albury, NSW.

Jipson, J. A. (1995). The stealing of wonderful ideas: The politics of imposition and representation in research in early childhood. In L. Diaz Soto (Ed.), *The politics of early childhood education* (Vol. 10, pp. 166–177). New York: Peter Lang.

Keddie, A. (2012). Schooling and social justice through the lenses of Nancy Fraser. *Critical Studies in Education, 53*(3), 263–279.

Kemp, L., Dockett, S., Grace, R., Perry, B., Comino, E., Jackson-Pulver, L., & Haswell, M. (2011). *Australian Research Council: Discovery – Projects: Proposal for funding commencing in 2012.* Sydney: The University of New South Wales.

Knight, J., Comino, E., Harris, E., & Jackson-Pulver, L. (2009). Indigenous research: A commitment to walking the talk. The Gudaga study – An Australian case study. *Bioethical Inquiry, 6*, 467–476. doi:10.1007/s11673-009-9186-x.

Martin, K. (2007). Ma(r)king tracks and reconceptualising Aboriginal early childhood education: An Aboriginal Australian perspective. *Childrenz Issues, 11*(1), 15–20.

Martin, K. (2012). Aboriginal early childhood: Past, present and future. In J. Phillips & J. Lampert (Eds.), *Introductory indigenous studies in education: Reflection and the importance of knowing* (pp. 26–39). Frenchs Forest: Pearson.

Mason-White, H., & Secretariat of National Aboriginal and Islander Child Care (SNAICC). (2013). *Supporting transition to school for Aboriginal and Torres Strait Islander children: What it means and what works?* Melbourne: Secretariat of National Aboriginal and Islander Child Care.

McLaren, P. (2007). *Life in schools: An introduction to critical pedagogy in the foundations of education* (5th ed.). Boston: Pearson.

Moll, L., Amanti, C., Neff, D., & Gonzalez, N. (1992). Funds of knowledge: Using a qualitative approach to connect homes and classrooms. *Theory Into Practice, 31*(2), 132–141.

Moreton-Robinson, A. (2000). *Talkin' up to the white woman: Indigenous women and feminism.* St Lucia: University of Queensland Press.

Nakata, M. (2007). *Disciplining the savages: Savaging the disciplines.* Canberra: Aboriginal Studies Press.

Nakata, M. (2012). Indigenous memory, forgetting and the archives. *Archives and Manuscripts, 40*(2), 98–105. doi:10.1080/01576895.2012.687129.

New South Wales Aboriginal Education Consultative Group Inc., & New South Wales Department of Education and Training [NSW AECG/NSW DET]. (2004). *The report of the review of Aboriginal education: Yanigurra Muya: Ganggurrinyma Yaarri Guurulaw Yirringin.gurray Freeing the spirit: Dreaming an equal future.* Sydney: New South Wales Department of Education and Training, https://www.det.nsw.edu.au/media/downloads/reviews/aboriginaledu/report/aer2003_04.pdf. Accessed 14 Dec 2015.

New South Wales Department of Education and Communities. (n.d.). *Employing Aboriginal peoples.* http://www.dec.nsw.gov.au/about-us/careers-centre/employing-aboriginal-peoples. Accessed 14 Dec 2015.

Pearson, N. (2011). *Radical hope: Education and equality in Australia.* Collingwood: Black Inc.

Perry, B. (2014). Social justice dimensions of starting school. In B. Perry, S. Dockett, & A. Petriwskyj (Eds.), *Transitions to school: International research, policy and practice* (pp. 175–186). Dordrecht: Springer.

Peters, S. (2010). *Literature review: Transition from early childhood education to school. Report to the Ministry of Education.* Wellington: Ministry of Education.

Petriwskyj, A. (2014). Critical theory and inclusive transitions to school. In B. Perry, S. Dockett, & A. Petriwskyj (Eds.), *Transition to school: International research, policy and practice* (pp. 201–215). Dordrecht: Springer.

Petriwskyj, A., & Grieshaber, S. (2011). Critical perspectives on the transition to school. In D. Laverick & M. Jalongo (Eds.), *Transitions to early care and education* (pp. 75–86). New York: Springer.

Phillips, J. (2012). Indigenous knowledge perspectives: Making space in the Australian centre. In J. Phillips & J. Lampert (Eds.), *Introductory Indigenous studies in education: Reflection and the importance of knowing* (2nd ed., pp. 9–25). Frenchs Forest: Pearson.

Sarra, C. (2011). *Strong and smart: Towards a pedagogy for emancipation: Education for first peoples.* New York: Routledge.

Schoorman, D. (2011). Reconceptualising teacher education as a social justice undertaking: Underscoring the urgency for critical multiculturalism in early childhood education. *Childhood Education, 87*(5), 341–344.

Siraj-Blatchford, I., & Clarke, P. (2000). *Supporting identity, diversity and language in the early years.* Buckingham: Open University Press.

Smart, D., Sanson, A., Baxter, B., Edwards, B., & Hayes, A. (2008). *Home-to-school transitions for financially disadvantaged children: Summary report.* Sydney: The Smith Family and Australian Institute of Family Studies.

Taylor, J., & Nelms, L. (2006). *School engagement and life chances: 15 year olds in transition* (Life chances study stage 7). Melbourne: Brotherhood of St. Laurence.

Tejeda, C., Espinoza, M., & Gutierrez, K. D. (2003). Towards a decolonizing pedagogy: Social justice reconsidered. In P. P. Trifonas (Ed.), *Pedagogies of difference: Rethinking education for social change* (pp. 10–40). New York: RoutledgeFalmer.

Thomson, P., Lingard, B., & Wrigley, T. (2012). Ideas for changing educational systems, educational policy and schools. *Critical Studies in Education, 53*(1), 1–7. doi:10.1080/17508487.2011.636451.

Trifonas, P. P. (Ed.). (2003). *Pedagogies of difference: Rethinking education for social change.* New York: RoutledgeFalmer.

Vandenbroeck, M. (2007). Promoting social inclusion and respect for diversity in young children's environments. *Early Childhood Matters, 106,* 5–6. http://www.bernardvanleer.org/English/Home/Publications/Browse_by_topic.html?ps_page=3&ps_count=0&getTopic=38

Vincent, C. (2003). Introduction. In C. Vincent (Ed.), *Social justice, education and identity* (pp. 1–13). London: RoutledgeFalmer.

West, E. G. (2000). *An alternative to existing Australian research and teaching models: The Japanangka teaching and research paradigm, an Australian Aboriginal model.* Unpublished doctoral thesis, Southern Cross University, Lismore, NSW. http://epubs.scu.edu.au/cgi/viewcontent.cgi?article=1015&context=theses. Accessed 27 Nov 2015.

Part III
Continuity and Change as Children Start School

Chapter 9
Continuity and Change as Children Start School

Sue Dockett and Jóhanna Einarsdóttir

While there has been much discussion – theoretically, conceptually and practically – about addressing discontinuity and promoting continuity at times of educational transition, less attention has been given to examining what is meant by continuity and the rationale for its promotion. One of the implications of the focus on continuity has been less attention to the notions of change in transitions and the importance of balancing both continuity and change for those involved. In this chapter, we consider current positions and debates around continuity and change in educational transitions, particularly the transition to primary school. We draw on a range of theoretical and conceptual perspectives to explore these.

9.1 Introduction

Continuity is not a new term within early childhood education. Soon after establishing the first kindergarten, Fröbel (1887/2005) emphasised the importance of continuity – unity – between home and kindergarten, and Dewey (1938) argued that the basis for educational activities was continuity with the everyday lives of children in the home and the community. This sense of continuity, in which experiences and learning build on what has gone before, is at the heart of statements such as 'Connections and continuity between learning experiences … make learning more meaningful' (Department of Education, Employment and Workplace Relations

S. Dockett (✉)
Charles Sturt University, Albury, NSW, Australia
e-mail: sdockett@csu.edu.au

J. Einarsdóttir
University of Iceland, Reykjavik, Iceland

© Springer International Publishing Switzerland 2017
N. Ballam et al. (eds.), *Pedagogies of Educational Transitions*, International
Perspectives on Early Childhood Education and Development 16,
DOI 10.1007/978-3-319-43118-5_9

133

[DEEWR] 2009, p. 32) and 'Learning begets learning' (Organisation for Economic Cooperation and Development [OECD] 2006, p. 37).

The principle of continuity holds a central place in theories of child development, particularly stage-based theories, in which the achievements of one stage are regarded as integral to the achievements in those that follow. For example, theorists such as Piaget (1973) proposed that continuity – continuous development – was promoted by the alignment of learning environments and developmental stages, and Erikson (1950/1993) described developmental continuity, the resolution of conflict in one stage of psychosocial development, as the basis for later achievements. The influence of stage theories of development tends to have lessened in recent decades as variation and diversity in children's learning have been highlighted. However, the emphasis on developmental continuity remains in the promotion of lifelong learning agendas (OECD 2006).

While developmental continuity has featured strongly in approaches to early childhood education, so too has discontinuity. Through much of its history, the field of early childhood education has been characterised by discontinuity: discontinuities between services focused on care and education, between preschool and school education, different curricula and pedagogies employed in different settings and between home and school education. In a similar vein, discontinuities have been evident in the histories, goals and purposes of preschool and school education, as well as the demands and expectations of these settings (Bennett 2013; OECD 2006). Recognising these many discontinuities, there is often talk of a gap between preschool settings and primary schools and of the need to bridge this gap to promote continuity (Dunlop and Fabian 2007; Huser et al. 2015; OECD 2006).

Transitions have also been characterised as times of change. Indeed, several of the same developmental theorists who have noted the importance of continuity have also proposed that transitions are prompted by change: both inner change, as individuals are required to manage times of crisis (Erikson 1950/1993) or disequilibrium (Piaget 1973), and physical changes that accompany movement from one location to another. Drawing on sociocultural theory, Zittoun (2008, p. 165) defines transitions as 'the processes that follow ruptures', with ruptures in turn defined as 'disruption[s] to the usual processes' (p. 165), when 'taken-for-granted meanings cease to be taken for granted' (Zittoun et al. 2003, p. 415).

Transition points, such as between home and preschool or school and between early childhood education and school, are focal points for discussions of continuity and discontinuity, whether they be discussions about developmental and learning continuity for children or a lack of systemic continuity regarding philosophy, administration or pedagogy. Transitions are spaces where different contexts, systems and approaches intersect, and those making the transition are charged with adapting to new environments. Transition points, such as the transition to school, can be considered impediments to continuous development, reflected in a dip in learning or loss of confidence in learning (Broström 2003). They can also serve as prompts for new learning, as individuals cross new boundaries and enter new spaces or systems (Bronfenbrenner and Morris 2006; Vygotsky 1978). In this latter sense, transitions are characterised:

… not as a moment of change but as the experience of changing … of living the discontinuities between the different contexts … Transitions arise from the individual's need to live, cope and participate in different contexts, to face different challenges, to take profit from the advantages of the new situation …. (Gorgorió et al. 2002, p. 24)

While recognising the changes made by individuals during transitions, policymakers in developed nations have focused on promoting systemic continuity between preschool and school. For example, guidelines issued by the Council of Europe in 1981 supported integrated curricula across the early childhood years and argued for combined professional development for preschool and school educators (Lazzari and Balduzzi 2013). These guidelines are built on earlier calls for greater continuity between early childhood education and school as a means of promoting equality of educational outcomes (Vrinioti et al. 2010).

An older example comes from the US National Society for the Scientific Study of Education, which in 1908, produced a series of reports aimed to 'further the effort to establish the kindergarten more firmly as a part of the public-school system by bridging the chasm which lies between it and the primary grades' (Gregory et al. 1908/2013, p. 7). In describing continuity between kindergarten and elementary school, school superintendent Benjamin Gregory noted:

In passing from the kindergarten to the primary school there is a break. Do what you will to soften the change, to modify the break, it still remains a break. Three general methods of dealing with the difficulty have been employed: (1) To provide a connecting class to take the child out of his [sic] kindergarten habits and introduce him to those of the primary school; in the words of some teachers, "To make him over." (2) To modify the kindergarten to make it more nearly resemble the primary school. (3) To modify the primary school to make it more nearly resemble the kindergarten. To these might be added a fourth: To do a little of each. (1908/2013, p. 22)

Gregory's four methods for promoting continuity resonate in current debates. In more than 100 years since this was written, a number of education systems have implemented the first of these methods, introducing a kindergarten or reception year into the school system. While these years started as transition years, in countries like Australia, they have now become part of the formal school curriculum (Dockett and Perry 2014b). The second strategy has been labelled schoolification, where 'early education is assimilated, both conceptually and administratively, to a traditional primary school model' (Bennett 2013, p. 58). Schoolification tends to be resisted strongly by early childhood sectors around the world. Just as contentious for school educators and systems is the third approach, which would result in schools becoming more like prior-to-school settings.

Variations of the fourth option have been implemented in several contexts. For example, the Swedish preschool class is positioned as a place where 'the two institutions of preschool and school should meet, forming a third institution with the purpose of creating a practice built upon the best from 'both worlds'' (Ackesjö 2013, p. 389). However, concerns about the place and role of the preschool class have been raised, with Garpelin (2014, p. 123) also invoking the metaphor of a bridge and asking:

Does the preschool class have a role as a 'bridge' between the worlds of the preschool and
the school? … the aim to make the transition as 'smooth' as possible [has] contributed to an
uncertainty for everyone …

While the intention of the Swedish preschool class has been to create a new
space by combining the attributes of both preschool and school, the success or oth-
erwise of this approach will depend largely on the nature of relationships that are
forged between the different institutions and those who operate within them.

9.2   Professional Relationships and Continuity

Several different forms of relationships between early childhood education and
school have been described. These range from one-way functional linkages (Boyle
and Petriwskyj 2014), where the focus is on early childhood settings preparing children for school, to transformative relationships that have the potential to revolutionise each setting (Moss 2013b).

Four forms of professional relationships, and the linkages they generate, have
been outlined by Boyle and Petriwskyj (2014): functional linkages, systemic linkages, partnership interactions and dialogic interactions. Using this typology, Boyle
and Petriwskyj nominate characteristics of the various relationships, their theoretical bases and the forms of continuity promoted. While they are not an exact match,
these four forms of professional relationship are similar to those described by Moss
(2013a): readying for school, a strong and equal partnership and a meeting place.

The first form of relationship in both descriptions is characterised by school
readiness discourse that reduces the function of early childhood education to preparing children for school. As one example of an increasing worldwide focus on
school readiness (OECD 2006), Gulløv (2012, p. 101) reflected on the changes of
the role of kindergartens in Denmark, and the influence of neoliberal governance.
She argued that kindergartens have become 'the first step in the educational career,
and the programmes should therefore prepare the child for the cognitive demands of
school as well as the demands of the labour markets'.

This form of relationship – a functional linkage, using Boyle and Petriwskyj's
term – assumes that continuity is achieved by making children 'ready' for school.
Drawing on developmental theory (Moss 2013a), functional linkages position continuity as progression and preparation for school as a process of distributing information about the nature and expectations of school in order that children can be
prepared to meet these (Dockett and Perry 2002). One consequence is the schoolification of early childhood education, where school structures, curriculum and expectations are introduced in efforts to make young children 'school ready'.

The predominance of academically oriented curriculum in early childhood is
regarded as problematic, both in terms of the reduced focus on social development
and play-based programmes (Gulløv 2012) and in terms of increased expectations
that all children will start school with similar levels of preparation. The latter

expectation has implications for the capability of schools to respond to children's diverse abilities and experiences (Vandenbroeck et al. 2013).

Rather than resisting it totally, Kagan (2013, p. 138) argues that, under some conditions, 'schoolification might not be so bad'. Conceding that conditions such as the alignment of early childhood and school education are not yet in evidence, Kagan contends that much could be gained by aligning early childhood education with schools which have an established and supported role in the public conscience.

The notion of a strong and equal partnership between early childhood education and school education has been advocated by the OECD (2001, p. 129), on the basis that such partnerships 'provide the opportunity to bring together the diverse perspectives and methods of both ECEC and schools, focusing on the strengths of both approaches'. While the notion of partnership is well accepted, the nature of that partnership, particularly the equality of partners, is more contentious, with early childhood education often perceived as the junior or less expert partner in any exchange (Moss 2013a).

The potential for strong and equal partnerships is reflected in Boyle and Petriwskyj's (2014) conceptualisation of systemic linkages and partnership interactions. Systemic linkages reflect bioecological theory (Bronfenbrenner and Morris 2006), emphasising efforts to promote the importance of sustained contact between settings and stakeholders in the transition to school. Drawing on bioecological theory, continuity is conceptualised as the smooth intersection of different systems. Transition approaches focus on interactions between and across systems, such as home, preschool setting and school. Priming events (Corsaro and Molinari 2000), such as reciprocal visits by preschool and schoolchildren, may be planned (Einarsdóttir 2011, 2013b) to encourage familiarisation with the new environment, with the aim of generating seamless transitions.

Partnership interactions are characterised by collaboration between a range of stakeholders involved in the transition; at the least, including children, families and educators. Partnership interactions recognise transitions as a time of changing roles, identities and status (Griebel and Niesel 2009). Continuity of relationships for children, families and educators is promoted through interactions such as educator and/ or professional networks, peer programmes and family engagement in transition programmes. These acknowledge diversity of experiences and perspectives among participants.

Dialogic interactions – the fourth form of relationship envisaged by Boyle and Petriwskyj (2014) – are the basis for creating a 'meeting place' (Moss 2013a, p. 19), with educators from different settings working to create a shared vision in which they can explore 'the pedagogical possibilities and risks involved in an integration of the two school forms' (Moss 2013a, p. 20). The meeting place described by Moss echoes Dahlberg and Lenz-Taguchi's (1994) exploration of the ways in which school and preschool can experience cultural encounters. The meeting place is conceptualised as a location for reflection, analysis and critique, promoting the construction of shared meanings, as the knowledge, culture and traditions of the different sectors are valued and respected, and new pedagogical practice is generated.

Relationships that occur at the meeting place are transformative (Moss 2013b), bringing together both sectors with a focus on deconstructing what has been taken for granted and generating new ways of approaching pedagogy in each setting. The continuity generated through dialogic interaction goes beyond mutual respect, aiming instead for a shared philosophical vision that incorporates elements from the traditions of both early childhood education and school.

While it may be tempting to regard these different professional relationships as a ladder, moving from the least complex (functional linkages, readying children for school) to the most complex (dialogic interactions, the meeting place), this would be an oversimplification. The different forms of relationships reflect different contexts, participants and intentions. While we might aim for the ideal of dialogic interactions occurring with a meeting place, elements of the other forms of relationship may be valuable and/or appropriate at some time. For example, early childhood educators have described the importance of receiving information about school expectations and approaches (Dockett and Perry 2007b) and conceptualised one of their roles during the transition as preparing the children for school in some way (Dockett et al. 2012). While such relationships may be a useful starting point, professional relationships that do not move beyond these can be frustrating and challenging for those involved. This is particularly for early childhood educators, who may interpret the focus on preparing children for school as a lack of professional regard for their own role (Barblett et al. 2011; Hopps 2014).

Strong and equal partnerships that promote smooth transitions are important in many contexts. For example, educators working with families and children who have special education needs have described the importance of a smooth transition between services and across contexts and have outlined the ways this can be facilitated by creating a bridge between the different settings and systems. Such connections can generate strategies to maintain access to specialist support for children and families as they move from an early childhood setting to school – something emphasised as a key to promoting a smooth transition (Dockett et al. 2011a). Where such links are not maintained, consistent professional relationships may be lost, families may need to reapply for support and children will often face new assessment or new criteria for support. These situations exacerbate any challenges, with the result that the transition may be anything but smooth.

Partnerships can be promoted by professional networks and collaboration. Networks, for example, can provide the forum for dialogic interactions, provided they create a safe, supportive and challenging space to raise issues, question assumptions and explore alternative ways of being and doing (Dockett and Perry 2014a). Keys to achieving genuine collaboration include the availability of time to meet, discuss, engage and reflect, and the willingness of participants to engage in the thinking that takes them out of their comfort zone.

As one example of a meeting place, Carr (2013) described the ways in which New Zealand educators have taken up opportunities afforded by the development of a revised school curriculum and its alignment of key competencies with the early childhood curriculum, *Te Whāriki* (Ministry of Education 1996). Dialogue across sectors has been supported by a context of recognition and respect for *Te Whāriki* and those who enact it, as well as a focus on children's developing competencies and the contribution of these to specific areas of learning (Peters et al. 2009). Further, the notion of meeting space has been expanded to include cultural communities and contributions they make to transforming education.

Professional relationships set the scene for continuity, particularly during the transition to school. These relationships occur in, and are influenced by, social, cultural and political contexts. Despite the potential for partnerships and critical dialogue in a transformative meeting place, the trend towards relationships focused on school readiness described by the OECD in 2006 has continued, with increasing pressure on early childhood educators to measure, assess and redress children's readiness for school (Dockett and Perry 2013a). One consequence of school readiness discourse has been the promotion of measures of continuity that are couched in terms of children's readiness for school or children's readiness for learning (Swanson 1991).

9.3 Continuity in Educational Transitions

The content, as well as the context, of professional relationships contribute to understandings and perspectives of continuity. Promoting continuity at times of educational transitions has the potential to involve many stakeholders, diverse perspectives and multiple strategies. Mayfield (2003) identified several types of continuity that may be addressed, as connections between early childhood settings and contexts are forged. While these different approaches to continuity were listed as discrete entities, they often overlap and intersect. Professional relationships can be forged around any of these efforts to generate continuity. All these approaches to continuity lend themselves to critique, analysis and reflection, and all can be subject to transformation as a result of these processes.

9.3.1 Developmental Continuity

The emphasis on developmental continuity in children's education is evident in the work of John Dewey, who maintained that genuine education occurred when teachers built upon children's experiences. Dewey (1938, p. 35) introduced the 'the principle of continuity of experience', which argued that every experience takes up something from what has happened before and modifies it in some way. Dewey's approach supported a balance between continuity and change in education: continuity as children's experiences provided the base for further learning and change as learning in one context was challenged and extended. His work also flagged some ongoing debates about continuity, notably about the role/s of preschool education and the nature of curriculum as children moved to school. When considering the connection between different school levels, Dewey questioned the assumption that each level served as preparation for that which followed. He argued that preparation achieved only controlling ends, with the potentialities of the present sacrificed for an unknowable future.

Developmental continuity is supported when educators consider individual children and the ways in which learning builds on their previous knowledge and experience. Positive acknowledgement of developmental continuity requires recognition of the strengths and understandings that children bring with them to a specific context, as well as consistency of responses from adults. A regard for developmental continuity may be seen in individual transition strategies, rather than a 'one-size-fits-all' approach. However, an uncritical focus on developmental continuity can be used to make decisions about children's school readiness, emphasising what children can do or have already achieved, rather than their developmental potential.

9.3.2   Philosophical Continuity

Clear differences between early childhood settings and schools contribute to philosophical discontinuities. These reflect different histories, goals and purposes and may be evident in different conceptualisations of children and childhood, different pedagogies and focus on different educational outcomes (Bennett 2013). Philosophical continuity can be achieved when those involved in different settings work to develop shared understandings and approaches. Dialogic interactions can provide the context for critically reflexive praxis (Moss 2013b), affording opportunities to build some common ground between and among educators in different settings. Dahlberg and Lenz-Taguchi (1994) proposed that this common ground should be based on similar visions of children, school levels and practices that involve perceiving children as constructors of knowledge, identity and culture.

9.3.3   Curriculum Continuity

Curriculum continuity can occur across services and across stages of education. Some curricula span both school and early childhood settings; many do not. There can be considerable resistance to curriculum continuity if it is perceived as a strategy to subsume one stage of education into another. References to the schoolification (Moss 2013a) of early childhood settings highlight concerns that academically oriented school curriculum may be imposed in these settings under the guise of curriculum continuity. Despite this, curriculum continuity need not mean that settings lose their identity and focus (Einarsdóttir 2013a). Achieving connections across settings that address issues of curriculum fragmentation, promote educational coherence and acknowledge the unique contributions of different educational contexts (Wood 2004) requires a commitment to collaboration and critical reflection from all involved.

In some contexts, continuity has been considered in terms of curriculum alignment or curriculum coherence (Bogard and Takanishi 2005). In a different approach, a number of countries have introduced integrated curricula that span both early childhood and compulsory school years. As one example, the recent revision of the Icelandic national curricula used the same six fundamental pillars to underpin all curriculum guidelines, from preschool to upper secondary school, and to form the essence of educational policy (Ministry of Education, Science and Culture 2011). These pillars – literacy, sustainability, health and welfare, democracy and human rights, equality, and creativity – provide the basis for the working methods, content and learning environment at every school level, including preschool. The pillars are intended to support continuity throughout the Icelandic educational system. To be effective, these efforts to create continuity at the policy level need to be supported by relationships between and among educators.

Neuman (2007) cautioned that curriculum continuity and pedagogical continuity are not necessarily the same. She argued that pedagogical continuity is achieved when there is consistency of approaches across sectors, positive teacher–child interactions that build on previous experiences and commitment to working with children as unique individuals. Pedagogical continuity may be promoted by curriculum continuity, but the two do not necessarily go hand in hand.

9.3.4 Physical Continuity

Children often highlight the physical discontinuity and continuity across settings, noting the differences in the size of buildings, extent of the playground, available resources and layout of classrooms (Dockett and Perry 2007a; Einarsdóttir 2010). Physical continuity may be promoted by the incorporation of similar resources and materials in settings and by the co-location of services. However, proximity and co-location are not sufficient to generate continuity (Dockett and Perry 2007b).

9.3.5 Organisational Continuity

Organisational discontinuities and continuities relate to issues such as the length of the school or preschool day, teacher-child ratios, the nature of regulations that govern different settings and the employment conditions and expectations of educators. Discontinuities can be experienced in moves between settings, such as when requirements for access to specialist support differ or change (Dockett et al. 2011b).

9.3.6   Administrative Continuity

Continuity may be supported when educational services are administered by the same organisation or department, or where settings are governed by similar policies, regulations and expectations. The history of early childhood education provides many examples of administrative discontinuity, as different government departments or agencies have been responsible for the provision of childcare and education services and different policy approaches have been reflected in each. Bringing care and education services together under the one auspicing agency can provide one approach to promoting administrative continuity (Moss 2013a). However, administrative continuity may not be sufficient to create other forms of continuity. This has been noted in some of the Nordic countries, where preschools have been under the administration of the Ministry of Education for decades (Broström et al. in press).

While each of these types of continuity is important, attention to one aspect alone is unlikely to promote continuity of experiences and expectations for children, families and educators. To achieve the latter, cross-sectoral professional relationships are necessary (Boyle and Petriwskyj 2014; Moss 2013a). That is, personal and sometimes individual relationships among professionals in the different settings are critical to promoting continuity. These may build on, contribute to or even initiate structural changes, such as those discussed above.

9.4   Discontinuity

There are clear instances where discontinuity creates problems and would be best avoided. These include discontinuity in service access or provision for children with special education needs (Dockett et al. 2012), the lack of communication between educators and/or professionals in different settings (Hopps 2014) and discontinuities in supportive relationships (Neuman 2007).

However, Peters (2000) argued that not all forms of discontinuity in transition are detrimental. Discontinuity sets up challenges for those involved in transition, particularly children making the transition to school. Rather than trying to avoid discontinuity, Peters has noted the importance of appropriate support and scaffolding to help children manage discontinuity. While recognising that discontinuity has the potential to cause some distress, she also recorded the pleasure of children as they encountered new environments and experiences, and as they learned new things. Reporting similar results, White and Sharp (2007) noted children's pleasure at encountering new experiences and overcoming challenges as they made the transition to Year 1.

While not wishing to argue that educators should intentionally make transition experiences difficult or challenging, these results remind us that the transition to school is a time for both continuity and change. Indeed, it is argued that continuity provides the basis for managing change:

> ... with continuity, young children and their families are able to form meaningful relationships with teachers, caregivers, and other service providers and learn to anticipate the rules and expectations of an unfamiliar setting. When a transition is necessary, continuity between settings balances new experiences with familiar ones. (Mangione and Speth 1998, p. 384)

Transitions can support continuity by recognising and building on what has gone before; they can also facilitate change by providing scaffolding. Early childhood and school educators are well placed to provide this scaffolding, particularly when they are prepared to articulate, question and reflect upon their own practice. Recognising that many children look forward to the transition to school and feel a sense of mastery and achievement when they manage this, Bennett (2007, p. 60) has urged educators to 'use the transition in children's lives far more positively, with greater insight into their potential, rather than seeing transition as problematic for every child'. Regarding transition as an opportunity, (Educational Transitions and Change [ETC] Research Group, 2011) opens up many possibilities to explore the place of both continuity and change.

9.5   Change in Educational Transitions

Change is an integral part of any transition. Transition to school involves the move from known and familiar contexts, such as home and early childhood settings, to the less familiar context of school. Beach (1999) described the educational transition from prior-to-school to school as a lateral transition, in which participation in one sphere is replaced by participation in another. At the same time, children starting school make a collateral transition (Beach 1999), as they participate simultaneously in activities across two arenas – home and school – and move back and forth between these. Both lateral and collateral transitions can generate change for the individuals involved. Moving from prior-to-school to a school setting can involve changes 'in the form of knowledge construction; the adaptation of old skills or the incorporation of new ones; change in identities; and/or changes in social position' (Crafter and Maunder 2012, p. 12). Negotiating movements between home and school also requires change, particularly as children develop strategies to please both parents and teachers (Crafter and de Abreu 2010).

The system of supports, relationships and expectations across contexts can differ markedly. Shifts in identity and agency are required as children and families negotiate the new contexts and become school students or parents of school students. Educators, too, experience change in status and agency as they become kindergarten or preschool teachers or school teachers. Looking at transition in this way suggests that transition is itself a process of change, whereby those involved change identity, status and role (Crafter and Maunder 2012; Zittoun 2008).

9.5.1 Individual Change

A great deal of recent research has highlighted the potentially negative aspects of change as children start school. In particular, challenges have been highlighted for children and families who are considered disadvantaged in some way. For example, one Australian report concluded that:

> … the transition to school is likely to be more challenging for children from financially disadvantaged families, Indigenous families, families with children who have a disability, and culturally and linguistically diverse (CALD) families. Children from these backgrounds are also less likely to attend early childhood education and care services before they start school. (Rosier and McDonald 2011, p. 1)

The focus on the negative aspects of change often leads to the development of strategies to minimise change, overcome obstacles or remove barriers. However, studies of organisational change examine the positive dynamics of change and the ways in which people make sense of and respond to change, as well as how they can contribute to it in positive ways (Douglass 2014). Refocusing attention to the positive impact of change during the transition to school can help to highlight the ways in which children themselves are active agents in their own transition, adopting a range of strategies and approaches as they navigate their new status, environments, interactions and expectations.

Not only the children making the transition but also peers, siblings and friends contribute to collaborative interactions and build shared understandings (Corsaro and Molinari 2000; Dockett and Perry 2013b). In many countries, children start school as a cohort, if not all on the same day, around about the same time. This cohort group can be a very effective support for individual children, as they develop a collective resilience – 'the collective capacity to thrive or flourish under adverse conditions' (Douglass 2014, p. 2). While the notion of collective resilience is drawn from organisational theory, and has been applied to situations involving trauma or major disruption, and we do not want to suggest that starting school involves either of these, it nevertheless reminds us that children are active participants in their own transition and that they make that transition as part of a social network, be it a family, community or peer network. As individuals within that network, they both draw upon and provide support for others. In other words, they develop collective, as well as individual, strategies for managing change. The child who notices another who is sad and sets about 'helping her make friends' not only demonstrates her own strategy for managing change but also contributes to a collective sense that change can be managed positively. Focusing only on the challenges of transition 'fails to capture the ways that people handle change in positive, agentic, or adaptive ways' (Douglass 2014, p. 3). This holds not only for children but for all involved in the transition process.

Three levels of change have been identified for children, families and educators during the transition to school (Griebel and Niesel 2009): change at the individual level, the relationships level and the contextual level. Changes for children at the individual level include becoming a member of a large class group, changes in expectations and patterns of behaviour, as well as changes in routine. At this individual level, changes in identity, knowledge and sense-making have been described as integral to transitions (Zittoun 2008). When starting school, children enter a new and different social environment, requiring a change in identity as they encounter new expectations, goals or possibilities. Entering the new environment – school – also requires changed knowledge and skills, including prescribed academic knowledge and the skills of negotiating with the classroom environment. Further, starting school requires individuals to 'make sense' of the new environment, building understanding of the symbolic environment of school, as well as their role and place within it (Bruner 1990).

At the relationships level, children are required to form new relationships with adults and children at school, while at the same time losing some relationships from prior-to-school settings. Building new relationships requires a change, or reorientation of identity (Zittoun 2006), as children become 'school students'. The way children see themselves in relation to others, including the social and academic comparisons they make, contribute to these changes in identity (Crafter and Maunder 2012). Changes in family relationships are also likely at this time, as children seek to exercise the autonomy that is associated with becoming a school student and as parents adjust their parenting style and practices in response. Changes at the contextual level are required as children adjust to the timing and routines of school and how these impact on their leisure time. When children attend school-age care, at the beginning or end of the school day, they are required to manage this change in contexts as well. Families and educators experience similar changes as their individual circumstances, roles and identities change – some relationships are lost and others need to be built – and as they seek to manage their involvement in different contexts.

9.5.2 Systems-Level Changes

Systems-level changes, including attention to quality agendas, teaching and learning standards and standardised curricula, feature in many countries, supporting efforts to promote quality and accountability (Douglass 2014). Partly, such changes can be attributed to increased recognition of the role of early childhood education in contributing to educational success. This concept emerged around the same time as national and international comparisons of educational outcomes revealed that some groups of children had lower levels of educational attainment than others (Rizvi and Lingard 2010). International research emphasising the significance of early brain development and the economic imperative of investing in early childhood education have resulted in increased government attention to this field (Shonkoff and Phillips 2000). This, in turn, has prompted changes in governance, regulation, curriculum, pedagogy and assessment (Wood 2004). In many ways, these changes have contributed to discourses of school readiness and professional relationships focused on promoting readiness (Gulløv 2012; Lazzari and Balduzzi 2013).

While it is important to recognise the increased stress and tension that systems-level changes can generate, much is to be gained from exploring approaches that 'implement change in ways that strengthen, rather than deplete' (Douglass 2014, p. 2) the work of early childhood educators. Key strategies to achieve this include recognising the strengths and commitments of people involved in the change process, enhancing leadership capacity, generating opportunities for relationship building within and across organisations and ensuring regular communication (Douglass 2014; Hopps 2014). Each of these strategies has an important role in managing the changes involved as children and their families make the transition to school.

Systems-level changes are reflected in much of the administrative, organisational and curriculum change that has occurred in recent years throughout the world. Administratively, early childhood services and schools have been brought together under the same organisational umbrella in several countries. At least part of the rationale for this change relates to the potential to enhance continuity within a common organisational framework. However, tensions can also be generated as those within the different sectors feel pressure to adopt similar approaches, pedagogies or curricula. Early childhood educators cite these tensions when describing pressure to adopt academically oriented curriculum (Moss 2013a).

Changes to the curricula that govern early childhood and school education have provided opportunities to consider the transition to school as either the pivot between two different curricula approaches or as a bridge between the two (Huser et al. 2015). Within this context, transition to school has acquired an increased profile, influencing policy development. Many organisations now have policies to guide the transition to school and provide access to resources and professional support to facilitate the process.

9.6   Continuity and Change as Children Start School

The dual processes of continuity and change are integral to educational transitions. Continuity is often cited as the rationale for specific approaches to transition that seek to 'smooth over' differences between prior-to-school settings and school environments. However, a focus on continuity alone ignores the importance of change, the agency of those involved in the processes of change and the significance of achievement that can accompany the sense of mastery that goes with meeting and overcoming challenges (Peters 2000; Zittoun 2008).

While there are many types of continuity, the extent to which these are achieved depends largely on the professional relationships that underpin efforts to generate continuity. Strong and respectful cross-sector relationships generate the space for educators to share their expertise and to negotiate critical understandings of effective and appropriate educational practice across the transition to school. Those operating in this space – the meeting place (Moss 2013b) – recognise the history and traditions of the different sectors, the varying administrative and curriculum contexts and the experiences of all involved in the transition, while at the same time exploring possibilities for transformational change. The meeting space is where pedagogies of educational transition are likely to be devised, implemented and evaluated.

Recognition of the integral role of both continuity and change prompts a re-examination of approaches to the transition to school. It requires reconceptualisation of transition as a time of opportunity, rather than a time of adversity; a time to recognise, build upon and maintain the strengths of those involved, rather than to expect problems; and a time to acknowledge diversity, rather than a time to paper over differences.

References

Ackesjö, H. (2013). Children crossing borders: School visits as initial incorporation rites in transition to preschool class. *International Journal of Early Childhood, 45*(3), 387–410.

Barblett, L., Barratt-Pugh, C., Kilgallon, P., & Maloney, C. (2011). Transition from long day care to kindergarten: Continuity or not? *Australasian Journal of Early Childhood, 36*(2), 42–49.

Beach, K. (1999). Consequential transitions: A sociocultural expedition beyond transfer in education. *Review of Research in Education, 24*, 101–139.

Bennett, J. (2007). Achieving successful transitions. In M. Woodhead & P. Moss (Eds.), *Transitions in the lives of young children* (Early childhood in focus, 2, p. 60). The Hague: Bernard van Leer.

Bennett, J. (2013). A response from the co-author of 'a strong and equal partnership'. In P. Moss (Ed.), *Early childhood and compulsory education: Reconceptualising the relationship* (pp. 52–71). London: Routledge.

Bogard, K., & Takanishi, R. (2005). PK-3: An aligned and coordinated approach to education for children 3 to 8 years old. *SRCD Social Policy Report, 19*(3), 1–23.

Boyle, T., & Petriwskyj, A. (2014). Transitions to school: Reframing professional relationships. *Early Years, 34*(4), 392–404. doi:10.1080/09575146.2014.953042.

Bronfenbrenner, U., & Morris, P. A. (2006). The bioecological model of human development. In W. Damon & R. M. Lerner (Eds.), *Handbook of child psychology, Vol. 1: Theoretical models of human development* (6th ed., pp. 793–828). New York: Wiley.

Broström, S. (2003). Problems and barriers in children's learning when they transit from kindergarten to kindergarten class in school. *European Early Childhood Education Re-search Journal Monograph Series, 1*, 51–66.

Broström, S., Einarsdóttir, J., & Pramling Samuelson, I. (in press). The Nordic perspective on early childhood education and care. In M. Fleer & B. van Oers (Eds.), *International handbook on early childhood education and development*. Dordrecht: Springer.

Bruner, J. (1990). *The culture of education*. Cambridge, MA: Harvard.

Carr, M. (2013). Making a borderland of contested spaces into a meeting place. In P. Moss (Ed.), *Early childhood and compulsory education. Reconceptualising the relationship* (pp. 92–111). London: Routledge.

Corsaro, W., & Molinari, L. (2000). Priming events and Italian children's transition from preschool to elementary school: Representation and action. *Social Psychology Quarterly, 63*(1), 16–33.

Crafter, S., & de Abreu, G. (2010). Constructing identities in multicultural learning contexts. *Mind, Culture, and Activity, 17*(2), 1–17.

Crafter, S., & Maunder, R. (2012). Understanding transitions using a sociocultural framework. *Educational and Child Psychology, 29*(1), 10–18.

Dahlberg, G., & Lenz-Taguchi, H. (1994). *Förskola och skola: om två skilda traditioner och om visionen om en mötesplats* [Preschool and school: Two different traditions and the vision of a meeting place]. Stockholm: HLS Förlag.

Department of Education, Employment, and Workforce Relations (DEEWR). (2009). *Belonging, being and becoming: The early years learning framework for Australia*. http://docs.education. gov.au/system/files/doc/other/belonging_being_and_becoming_the_early_years_learning_ framework_for_australia.pdf. Accessed 6 Feb 2015.

Dewey, J. (1938). *Experience and education*. New York: Macmillan.

Dockett, S., & Perry, B. (2002). Who's ready for. what? Young children starting school. *Contemporary Issues in Early Childhood, 3*(1), 67–89.

Dockett, S., & Perry, B. (2007a). Children's transition to school: Changing expectations. In A.-W. Dunlop & H. Fabian (Eds.), *Informing transition: Building research policy and practice* (pp. 92–104). London: Open University Press.

Dockett, S., & Perry, B. (2007b). *Starting school: Perceptions, expectations and experiences*. Sydney: UNSW Press.

Dockett, S., & Perry, B. (2013a). Trends and tensions: Australian and international research about starting school. *International Journal of Early Years Education., 21*(2–3), 163–177. doi:10.10 80/09669760.2013.832943.

Dockett, S., & Perry, B. (2013b). Siblings and buddies: Providing expert advice about starting school. *International Journal of Early Years Education, 21*(4), 348–361.

Dockett, S., & Perry, B. (2014a). *Continuity of learning: A resource to support effective transition to school and school age care*. Canberra: Australian Government Department of Education. http://www.csu.edu.au/__data/assets/pdf_file/0015/1101093/continuity.pdf. Accessed 3 Feb 2015.

Dockett, S., & Perry, B. (2014b). Universal access to preschool education – Approaches to integrating preschool with school in rural and remote communities. *Early Years, 34*,420–435. http://dx.doi.org/10.1080/09575146.2014.968100

Dockett, S., Perry, B., & Kearney, E. (2011a). Starting school with special needs: Issues for families with complex support needs as their children start school. *Exceptionality Education International, 21*(2), 45–61.

Dockett, S., Perry, B., Kearney, E., Hampshire, A., Mason, J., & Schmied, V. (2011b). *Facilitating children's transition to school from families with complex support needs*. Albury: Research Institute for Professional Practice, Learning and Education, Charles Sturt University. http://www.csu.edu.au/__data/assets/pdf_file/0009/154899/Facilitating-Childrens-Trans-School. pdf. Accessed 21 Dec 2014.

Dockett, S., Perry, B., & Kearney, E. (2012). Family transitions as children start school. *Family Matters, 90*, 57–67.

Douglass, A. (2014). Resilience in change: Positive perspectives on the dynamics of change in early childhood systems. *Journal of Early Childhood Research*. doi:10.1177/14767 18X14555704.

Dunlop, A.-W., & Fabian, H. (Eds.). (2007). *Informing transitions in the early years*. Maidenhead: Open University Press.

Educational Transitions and Change (ETC) Research Group. (2011). *Transition to school: Position statement*. http://www.csu.edu.au/faculty/educat/edu/transitions/publications/Position-Statement.pdf. Accessed 12 Nov 2014.

Einarsdóttir, J. (2010). Children experience of the first year of primary school. *European Early Childhood Education Research Journal, 18*(2), 163–180.

Einarsdóttir, J. (2011). Icelandic children's early education transition experiences. *Early Education and Development, 22*(5), 737–756.

Einarsdóttir, J. (2013a). Leikskóli og grunnskóli á sömu leið [Preschool and primary school on the same path]. In J. Einarsdóttir & B. Garðarsdóttir (Eds.). *Á sömu leið* [On the same path] (pp. 11–24). Reykjavík: Háskólaútgáfan, RannUng.

Einarsdóttir, J. (2013b). Transition from preschool to primary school in Iceland from the perspectives of children. In K. Margetts & A. Kienig (Eds.), *International perspectives on transition to school: Reconceptualising beliefs, policy and practice* (pp. 69–78). New York: Routledge.

Erikson, E. (1950/1993). *Childhood and society*. New York: Norton.

Fröbel, F. (1887/2005). *The education of man.* (Translated and annotated by W.N. Hailmann. Original published by D. Appleton & Co, New York). Mineola: Dover

Garpelin, A. (2014). Transition to school: A rite of passage in life. In B. Perry, S. Dockett, & A. Petriwskyj (Eds.), *Transitions to school: International research, policy and practice* (pp. 117–128). Dordrecht: Springer.

Gorgorió, N., Planas, N., & Vilella, X. (2002). Immigrant children learning mathematics in mainstream schools. In G. de Abreu, A. Bishop, & N. Presmeg (Eds.), *Transitions between contexts of mathematical practice* (pp. 23–52). Dordrecht: Kluwer.

Gregory, B. (1908/2013). The necessity of continuity between the kindergarten and the elementary school. The present status illogical and unFroebelian. In B. Gregory, J. Merrill, B. Payne, & M. Giddings (Eds.), *The co-ordination of the kindergarten and the elementary school, Supplement to Sixth Yearbook* (Vol. 2, pp. 22–23). London: Forgotten Books. (Original work published 1908, University of Chicago Press). http://www.forgottenbooks.com/readbook_text/ The_Co-Ordination_of_the_Kindergarten_and_the_Elementary_School_v2_1000268283/23. Accessed 7 Feb 2015.

Gregory, B., Merrill, J., Payne, B., Giddings, M. (1908/2013). *The co-ordination of the kindergarten and the elementary school, Supplement to Sixth Yearbook* (Vol. 2). London: Forgotten Books. (Original work published 1908, University of Chicago Press). http://www.forgottenbooks.com/readbook_text/The_Co-Ordination_of_the_Kindergarten_and_the_Elementary_School_v2_1000268283/23. Accessed 7 Feb 2015.

Griebel, W., & Niesel, R. (2009). A developmental psychology perspective in Germany: Co-construction of transitions between family and education system by the child, parents and pedagogues. *Early Years, 29*(1), 59–68.

Gulløv, E. (2012). Kindergartens in Denmark – Reflections on continuity and change. In A.-T. Kjørholt & J. Qvortrup (Eds.), *The modern child and the flexible labour market: Early childhood education and care* (pp. 90–107). Basingstoke: Palgrave Macmillan.

Hopps, K. (2014). Prior-to-school + school + communication = what for educator relationships? *Early Years.* doi:10.1080/09575146.2014.963032.

Huser, C., Dockett, S., & Perry, B. (2015). Transition to school: Revisiting the bridge metaphor. *European Early Childhood Education Research Journal.* doi:10.1080/1350293X.2015.1102414.

Kagan, S. (2013). David, Goliath and the ephemeral parachute: The relationship from a United States perspective. In P. Moss (Ed.), *Early childhood and compulsory education. Reconceptualising the relationship* (pp. 130–148). London: Routledge.

Lazzari, A., & Balduzzi, L. (2013). Bruno Ciari and 'educational continuity'. In P. Moss (Ed.), *Early childhood and compulsory education. Reconceptualising the relationship* (pp. 149–173). London: Routledge.

Mangione, P., & Speth, T. (1998). The transition to elementary school: A framework or creating early childhood continuity through home, school, and community partnerships. *The Elementary School Journal, 98*(4), 381–397.

Mayfield, M. (2003). Teaching strategies: Continuity among early childhood programs. *Childhood Education, 79*(4), 239–241. doi:10.1080/00094056.2003.10521201.

Ministry of Education. (1996). *Te Whāriki.* Wellington: Learning Media.

Ministry of Education, Science and Culture. (2011). *The Icelandic national curriculum guide for preschools.* Reykjavík: Ministry of Education, Science and Culture. http://www.menntama-laraduneyti.is/utgefid-efni/namskrar/nr/3952. Accessed 13 Apr 2015.

Moss, P. (2013a). The relationship between early childhood and compulsory education: A proper political question. In P. Moss (Ed.), *Early childhood and compulsory education: Reconceptualising the relationship* (pp. 2–49). London: Routledge.

Moss, P. (2013b). Citizens should expect more! In P. Moss (Ed.), *Early childhood and compulsory education. Reconceptualising the relationship* (pp. 194–205). London: Routledge.

Neuman, M. (2007). Pedagogical continuity. In M. Woodhead & P. Moss (Eds.), *Transitions in the lives of young children* (Early childhood in focus, 2, p. 50). The Hague: Bernard van Leer.

Organisation for Economic Co-operation and Development (OECD). (2001). *Starting strong: Early childhood education and care*. Paris: Author.

Organisation for Economic Co-operation and Development (OECD). (2006). *Starting strong II: Early childhood education and care*. Executive summary. Paris: OECD. https://www.oecd.org/newsroom/37425999.pdf. Accessed 19 Feb 2015.

Peters, S. (2000). *Multiple perspectives on continuity in early learning and the transition to school.* Paper presented at the European Early Childhood Education Research Association Conference, London. ED447916.

Peters, S., Hartley, C., Rogers, P., Smith, J., & Carr, M. (2009). Early childhood portfolios as a tool for enhancing learning during the transition to school. *International Journal of Transitions in Childhood, 3*, 4–15.

Piaget, J. (1973). *Psychology of intelligence*. Totowa: Littlefield, Adams.

Rizvi, F., & Lingard, B. (2010). *Globalizing education policy*. Abingdon: Routledge.

Rosier, K., & McDonald, M. (2011). *Promoting positive education and care transitions for children*. Communities and Families Clearinghouse Resource Sheet. http://www.aifs.gov.au/cafca/pubs/sheets/rs/rs5.html. Accessed 12 Dec 2014.

Shonkoff, J., & Phillips, D. (Eds.). (2000). *From neurons to neighbourhoods: The science of early childhood development*. Washington, DC: National Academy Press.

Swanson, B. (1991). *An overview of the six national education goals*. ERIC Digest. ED334714. http://www.ericdigests.org/pre-9220/six.htm. Accessed 9 May 2015.

Vandenbroeck, M., de Stercke, N., & Gobeyn, H. (2013). What if the rich child has poor parents? The relationship from a Flemish perspective. In P. Moss (Ed.), *Early childhood and compulsory education. Reconceptualising the relationship* (pp. 174–191). London: Routledge.

Vrinioti, K., Einarsdóttir, J., & Broström, S. (2010). *Transition from preschool to primary school.* Early Years Transition Programme (EASE). www.ease-eu.com/documents/compendium/chapter02.pdf. Accessed 27 May 2015.

Vygotsky, L. (1978). *Mind in society*. Cambridge: Harvard University Press.

White, G., & Sharp, C. (2007). 'It's different…because you're getting older and growing up'. How children make sense of the transition to Year 1. *European Early Childhood Education Research Journal, 15*(1), 87–102.

Wood, E. (2004). A new paradigm war? The impact of national curriculum policies on early childhood teachers' thinking and classroom practice. *Teaching and Teacher Education, 20*, 361–374. doi:10.1016/j.tate.2004.02.014.

Zittoun, T. (2006). *Transitions: Development through symbolic resources*. Greenwich: Information Age.

Zittoun, T. (2008). Learning through transitions: The role of institutions. *European Journal of Psychology of Education, 23*(2), 165–181.

Zittoun, T., Deveen, G., Gillespie, A., Ivinson, G., & Psaltis, C. (2003). The use of symbolic resources in developmental transitions. *Culture and Psychology, 9*(4), 415–448.

Chapter 10
Educators' Views on Transition: Influence on Daily Practice and Children's Well-Being in Preschool

Bryndís Garðarsdóttir and Sara Margrét Ólafsdóttir

This chapter reports on a study in which two researchers worked collaboratively with a group of educators in one preschool setting to implement a new learning area in the *Icelandic National Curriculum Guide for Preschool* (Ministry of Education, Science and Culture 2011), focusing on children's well-being. This action research approach was used to reflect on practice and the way this influenced the children's well-being. The findings indicated that the educators experienced a dilemma between being in control of children's activities and learning and supporting their autonomy. Educators argued that it was important to prepare children for the transition between preschool settings and primary school, and to achieve this, they tended to use controlling approaches. During the project, the educators' views towards the children changed; they realised that the children were more competent and diverse than they, the educators, had assumed. In that way, the educators saw the transition to school more as a continuing process.

10.1 Introduction

Well-being and participation are important aspects of early childhood education. Factors that influence well-being are children's competencies, interests, identities and sense of belonging, amongst others (Carr 2001; Laevers 1994). However, there is a tendency to judge children on their 'school readiness', which emphasises skills such as concentrating, sitting still and literacy knowledge (Dunlop 2013; Óskarsdóttir 2012). The educators who participated in this research reflected on their views on

B. Garðarsdóttir (✉) • S.M. Ólafsdóttir
University of Iceland, Reykjavik, Iceland
e-mail: bryngar@hi.is

© Springer International Publishing Switzerland 2017
N. Ballam et al. (eds.), *Pedagogies of Educational Transitions*, International Perspectives on Early Childhood Education and Development 16, DOI 10.1007/978-3-319-43118-5_10

transition and on how these influenced the daily schedule at the preschool setting, as well as children's well-being and participation.

This chapter is based on a collaborative action research project, in which two researchers worked with a group of educators in one preschool setting. The main focus of the study was to implement the learning area, Health and Well-being, from the *Icelandic National Curriculum Guide for Preschool* (Ministry of Education, Science and Culture 2011). Data were gathered through interviews, participant observations and reflection meetings.

10.2   Children's Well-Being and Participation

Children's health and well-being are important topics in education and form one of the six fundamental pillars in the Icelandic National Curriculum Guide for all school levels (Ministry of Education, Science and Culture 2013). The embedding of these pillars in pedagogy aims to encourage increased continuity in children's learning and support their growth and well-being. According to the curriculum, educators should create an environment that fosters the factors that influence well-being, such as children's competence, interests, communication, identity and decision making (Ministry of Education, Science and Culture 2011). 'Health and Well-being' is also one of four learning areas in the curriculum for preschools.

Children's identities are shaped in connection to their sense of belonging to their peer group and their relationships with educators. Respectful relationships help children develop confidence and build positive identities. Children's identities, and consequently their well-being, can therefore be promoted by educators showing them respect, listening to their opinions and beliefs and responding to their interests. Additionally, it is critical for children to adjust to their peer group in a positive way, to strengthen their social status and their sense of belonging as active participants in the preschool setting (Katz 1996; Roberts 1998; Waters 2009).

In preschools, promoting children's well-being includes providing opportunities for them to be active participants in daily activities. Children's active participation has been identified as having a say in matters that affect them in any way (Einarsdóttir 2008). Handley (2005) suggests that children's right to participate does not mean that they can make all decisions by themselves, regardless of their age and competence. However, it is important that educators support children's participation by recognising their differences, needs and interests.

Well-being and participation are important aspects of early childhood education that indicate the quality of preschool practice. Children need care, attention and social recognition in order to feel good, secure and happy (Laevers 1994). According to Carr (2001), in the preschool, well-being is connected to children's identity, confidence and how they deal with challenges, for instance, whether children seek to improve their knowledge and competence by themselves or seek out the opinions of educators or other children regarding their own performance. Children's well-being is also related to the way they show interest in certain activities. Csikszentmihalyi

(1990) developed a theory connected to well-being in which the main concept is 'flow'. Flow is defined as children being absorbed in their activities to such an extent that nothing else matters, and the experience in itself is so enjoyable that they want to keep on with it. In order to experience this condition, it is critical to have a choice, be motivated, feel good and be presented with appropriately challenging activities. Flow can be seen on a daily basis in children's play when they are involved in activities that interest them, are focused and are responding to and continuing the activity (Laevers 1994). Flow can be related to the concept of learning disposition, which refers to the way children participate and show interest in certain activities or situations and the way they respond to these.

Children's participation can be gauged by considering the way they respond to difficulties or insecurity, communicate their ideas and feelings and respond to different situations (Carr 2001). This means that children's well-being can be promoted when they are involved in choosing and when this choice is supported by educators.

10.2.1 Daily Routines in Preschool Settings

In Iceland, preschool practice can be organised in several different ways. In many preschools, educators use schedules as a kind of framework for their practice, outlining a timetable from the time the school opens in the morning until the end of the day. In such a schedule, the daily routine is divided into certain activities, for example, group work, circle time, outdoor activities and mealtimes, each of which starts and ends at a certain time.

The *Icelandic National Curriculum Guide for Preschool* (Ministry of Education, Science and Culture 2011) suggests that play is the ideal approach for children to learn and should be at the centre of each preschool curriculum. The educator's role is therefore to stimulate children's play by creating varied and flexible environments and by giving children's activities adequate time and space. In that way, they support children's spontaneous activities and interests. Further, their role is to organise different places where children can play and learn from each other and have quiet time, as well as space for diverse movements or exercise. As a consequence, educators are encouraged to facilitate children's movement from one place to another and to encourage them to use diverse materials that are accessible and appealing to different ages and interests.

It has been argued that children should have access to play with materials and playmates of their choosing, which creates opportunities for expression and communication and allows them to create and find solutions in ways that suit them (Van Hoorn et al. 2011). Incorporating these factors into the organisation of children's activities can promote a positive and friendly atmosphere. In addition, Pramling Samuelsson and Asplund Carlsson (2008) emphasised the importance of organising children's activities in such a way that they have many opportunities to communicate with other children and adults.

Research conducted in Icelandic preschools by Einarsdóttir (2008) suggested that educators' views of children are a critical factor influencing the organisation of the daily routine and curriculum. If educators believe in children as powerful members of their preschool communities and emphasise their strengths and capabilities, children become active participants in creating their own culture and knowledge (Einarsdóttir 2008; Garðarsdóttir and Karlsdóttir 2012). A range of views amongst educators has been reported in Icelandic preschools. For example, research has documented contrasting views amongst educators regarding the question of how much preschool practice should be planned (Sigurðardóttir 2012). On one hand, some educators want to give children ample time for play, but on the other hand, they want to keep certain aspects of the daily routine, such as group work, circle time and outdoor activities. Educators, therefore, need to be aware of the views they hold when organising children's daily routines.

A study on the effect of a detailed schedule on children's self-control in preschool (Lewin-Benham 2011) revealed that children had few opportunities to be in control of their daily activities, since the schedule determined what to do and when. The rapid changes of the daily routine, from one activity to another, disturbed the children's concentration, and this affected their learning. Further, there was evidence that active children became more active under such circumstances, while the more quiet children became inactive. Additionally, the children were quiet at the beginning of the day, but at the end of the day, they became restless and irritated.

The findings of Lewin-Benham (2011) can be related to a study undertaken by Bjarnadóttir (2004), who suggested that a rigid schedule and adult control can prevent children from creating their own culture in the preschool. Therefore, it is important to create flexible routines that offer children sufficient time and space for play. However, a flexible routine can be more challenging for educators than a detailed one that indicates what to do and when. In Icelandic preschools, there is a lack of qualified teachers and frequent changes in the staff group. In such conditions, it can be difficult to deviate from the routine (Hreinsdóttir and Einarsdóttir 2011). Nonetheless, the important aspects of preschool children's well-being, such as their needs, interests and views, need to be prioritised when educators organise their daily routines (Van Hoorn et al. 2011). Thus, educators are encouraged to explore and use these aspects to plan and develop the preschool day, organising the environment and being present as they support children's play and activities.

10.2.2 Transition from Preschool to Primary School

The successful transition of children from one school level to another is critical for their well-being and performance in school. Transition refers to a child's movement from one setting to another or from one subject or age group to another in a certain time. Continuity means that there is a normal flow in children's education instead of sudden changes, such as in the requirements of children when moving from preschool to primary school (Einarsdóttir 2004). Transition between preschool and primary school involves educators building on and using children's experiences and activities from preschool to deal with new activities and subjects in primary school (Einarsdóttir 2007). This means that children will not be dealing with the same activities in primary school as they did in the preschool.

Questions have been asked regarding whether there are differences between the pedagogies of preschool and primary school (Dockett and Perry 2014). Einarsdóttir (2007) conducted a study of two preschools and two primary schools in Iceland and found that the pedagogies of these two school levels were quite different. The main difference was that the preschool educators emphasised supporting children's identities, interactions, collaboration, care and play and gave the children opportunities to have a choice about their own activities. The primary school teachers emphasised teaching subjects, such as literacy and mathematics, and children's activities were organised beforehand, requiring that all children often did the same activities at the same time. Óskarsdóttir (2012) studied continuity in children's learning in Icelandic preschools and primary schools and suggested that even though the pedagogy was different in these school levels, the day schedule, practices and use of classroom space were similar. Einarsdóttir (2013a) indicated that the schedule and subjects of primary schools were spreading into preschools, reducing the latter's emphasis on important aspects of early childhood education, such as play, with implications for children's interactions and social competence.

In many preschools, play has been emphasised as the main approach to children's learning. The rationale for this has noted the inappropriateness of formal teaching methods and concern that academic pressure on children too early can have a negative effect on their learning habits later, when they need to work independently and take responsibility for their own learning (Marcon 2002). Informal teaching methods, such as play, have been considered more appropriate than formal approaches in supporting young children's learning.

Children's time for play reduces as they grow older. Óskarsdóttir (2012) argued that while the main emphasis should be on play when children start preschool, as they grow older, the time for play is reduced as other activities are added to their schedule. By the time children start primary school, only a short amount of the school day is dedicated for children's play or free activities.

Dunlop (2013) suggested that many curricula are based on learning outcomes, with messages about what children should know and be able to do when starting school. Therefore, children are often judged on their 'school readiness', that is, on skills such as writing, fastening clothing and relating to others. Primary school teachers in Iceland have discussed different skills that they think children need and what they should be able to do when starting primary school. These skills include sitting still, concentrating and listening to others (Óskarsdóttir 2012). When the emphasis in children's early education is on promoting these skills, opportunities for play and freely chosen activities decrease.

When children start primary school, they have different backgrounds, diverse experiences and knowledge sets, suggesting that each individual child can experience transition differently. Children with positive identities and good social skills tend to deal more easily with the transition to school (Dockett and Perry 2007;

Einarsdóttir 2007). Transition to school is considered successful when the children enjoy school and show a continuous improvement in learning. Negative transitions are usually related to anxiety, avoiding school, negative attitudes towards school and having difficulty adjusting (Monkeviciene et al. 2006).

In Iceland, children start primary school the year they turn six. To ease children's transitions between the school levels, preschool and primary school teachers collaborate by sharing information about the children and visiting between the schools (Einarsdóttir 2007). Discussions about the pedagogies of each school level have not been emphasised as much (Einarsdóttir 2007; Óskarsdóttir 2012). Preschool and primary school educators in Australia who took part in a study conducted by Dockett and Perry (2014) suggested that it was critical to have discussions about their different views on children's learning and share information about the children because it was 'important to know where the children come from, so what they do is seen as a natural follow up – continuity' (p. 80). Einarsdóttir (2013a) suggested that when continuity is understood as preparation for the future and becomes a primary aim in school practice, the here and now are sacrificed for an imaginary future. As Dewey (1938/2000) pointed out, this means that children's needs for 'today' could be overlooked in favour of the possible needs of the 'future'.

Research on transition in Australia and Iceland indicates that educators do want to see continuity in curricula and pedagogies between preschool and primary schools. However, it is always the 'other' school level that needs to make changes or adapt in order to achieve this continuity (Dockett and Perry 2006). Einarsdóttir (2007) suggested that it is the educator's responsibility to make sure that children's activities in primary school are built on their former experiences where requirements are reasonable. In addition, they need to furnish new ideas and promote children's interests and desire to learn.

10.3 Method and Participants

This study was a part of a collaborative action research project, Playing, Learning and Living, which was carried out in five preschools in Iceland. In this project, educators and researchers from the University of Iceland worked together, reflecting on the preschool practices, each in one of the learning areas of the *National Curriculum Guide for Preschool* (Ministry of Education, Science and Culture 2011). This collaboration contributed to both preschool and teacher education practices (Einarsdóttir 2013b).

The aims of the current study were to support the educators in one preschool setting as they developed practice in line with the new emphasis in the learning area of 'Health and Well-being' and to promote their professional development (Koshy 2005). The purpose was to view and review preschool practice in relation to transition and children's health and well-being. The experience and knowledge gained was used to make changes (McNiff 2010); that is, the educators examined what they were doing and why and how they could improve their own practices. They were given time and opportunities to discuss and reflect on their own practices and make decisions about the issues they wanted to address.

Participants in this part of the study, as is reported here, were five educators and 24 children, aged 3–5 years, in one preschool setting. In addition, the preschool principal and the special educator participated. The preschool applied for participation in the project. The participants were informed about the research, expectations and confidentiality. However, confidentiality was limited, as the educators subsequently chose to take part in presenting the project in conferences and other forums. In all written reports, identifying information, including the names of the participants and the preschool, was not mentioned.

Educators generated data about their own practice, which was used to reflect on and reorganise their practice (Guðjónsson 2008). The emphasis was on viewing practice from different perspectives, which meant that multiple data sources were used (Guðjónsdóttir 2011). The methods used were:

- *Interviews:* At the start and at the end of the research process, the educators were interviewed. The purpose of the interviews was to invite the educators to reflect on their ideas about their practices, their views on the children and their roles as educators. The children also had opportunities to discuss their views about their activities and daily schedules.
- *Research journals:* The educators were encouraged to document their views and reflections in a research journal, noting what worked well each day and how they resolved problems that arose. The purpose of the journal writing was to be able to reflect on their daily work.
- *Participant observations:* The aim of these was to observe daily practice, to analyse the children's participation and interaction with educators and to follow up on the changes that were made.
- *Video recordings:* The purpose of the recordings was for educators to see themselves in action and reflect on their own practices.
- *Reflection meetings:* The educators and the researchers met regularly at meetings in which they reflected on their views and practices, challenges they encountered, changes they wanted to implement and how these resolved themselves. These meetings were important to consider and discuss the changes that were made in the process, as well as to reflect on different data, such as the observations and the video recordings. The meetings were audio-recorded, transcribed and analysed throughout the period, as well as at the end of the project. Thematic analysis was used to identify categories that could answer the research question:

How do educators' ideas about transition influence the daily schedule and children's well-being and participation?

10.4 Findings

10.4.1 Children's Health and Well-Being in Preschool

In the beginning, the educators' views on health and well-being were focused mainly on the physical aspects of this concept, that is, nutrition, resting, hygiene and physical exercise. In the research process, the definition developed to include another aspect – children's emotional well-being. In a discussion of this concept, educators defined children's well-being in regard to the way they saw it appear in daily practice. The educators suggested that well-being was about children feeling safe, relaxed and trusting of the educators. In addition, they thought the children's well-being was exhibited when the children enjoyed coming to preschool in the mornings and sometimes wanted to stay longer in the afternoons. The educators also wondered if children having opportunities to influence what they were doing in the preschool, making choices and playing with their friends contributed to their well-being.

When reflecting on their practices, the educators worried that the children were restless at certain times of the day. For that reason, they thought it was important to reorganise the daily routine. One idea was that the children needed more time to play because preschool practice was not supposed to be organised with a main emphasis on group work and preplanned lessons. They decided that the children needed more opportunities for free play. Therefore, it was suggested that it was critical to reflect on the schedule and examine the daily routine, to increase children's play opportunities for the benefit of their well-being.

10.4.2 Emphases in the Preschool Daily Routine in the Beginning

At the beginning of the research process, the daily routine in the preschool setting was detailed, and the children regularly shifted from one activity to another. For example, they moved from eating breakfast to participating in circle time and then to 'choosing time' (a setup for children's play) until group work started. Each activity – what to do, when and where – was organised beforehand. Three periods per day were nominated as 'choosing times'. The classroom was divided into five areas with predetermined play materials, and there was a rule concerning how many children were allowed to choose each area at a time. The main rules were that the children needed to be at least 30 min in the area they chose and that they were not allowed to move materials from one area to another. The choosing options were of the same number as the children, that is, 24 children with 24 options. The subjects available were, for example, role play, Lego blocks, beads, puzzles, unit blocks, water play and arts. Children took turns being the first to choose, meaning that the child who made the first choice one day was the last to choose the next day. For that reason, the child who was the last to choose did not really have any choice because there was only one space in one area left.

The educators saw opportunities in giving children's play more time and space in the schedule. One of them said: 'We can give children's play higher priority, in a way that the children get uninterrupted time for play.'

10.4.3 The Educators' Views on the Daily Practice

In one of the meetings, the educators discussed the way the children's time for play was arranged. One of the educators wondered if children's play in the preschool could be called 'free play' when it was organised as it was and when the last child each day did not really have a choice. In addition, she pointed out that the children had different needs and levels of resilience: 'Some of the children can sit and paint in the art area for an hour, really enjoying it, while other children can hardly finish painting one picture.' The educators also noticed that the setup of the choosing time limited the children's opportunities to play with their friends. One of them said: 'Sometimes I am wondering about the relation between children's well-being and playing with friends. Children like to be with their friends, but many times they cannot, because the area their friends have chosen is occupied.' She added to this that the choosing times were too connected to the educators' purposes and children seldom had the chance to be the first to choose: 'In a group of 24 children, how often can each child be the first one?' Also, she argued that most of the time, the children could not decide where to play or with whom: '... there are not many opportunities to choose to play with a friend.'

During the discussion of the setup of the choosing time, the educators also noticed that the children were inactive because they needed to wait for the time to switch from one activity to another. That is, they had to sit still for a long time when arriving in the morning. After considering these issues, the educators decided to make changes in the schedule from the time the children arrived in the morning until the group work started at 10 o'clock. They wanted to dedicate more time and space to play by dropping both the circle and choosing times. The daily routine changed from being organised by the educators to the children having more initiative and opportunity to decide what material to play with, where and with whom. Also, the children could stay for as long or short a time as they wanted in each area; that is, the time frame was no longer a rule.

As the children became used to the changes, they were asked how they liked them. One of the boys said: 'I really like it, because I do not like standing in a row waiting. Then I get really tired in my legs, if I just stand.' Another boy pointed out that it was uncomfortable to stand in line, and he felt that he was never the first in line. The third boy said that he liked the fact that he could change activities when he wanted. One of the girls added this question: 'Why can we not choose either to play inside or outside?'

10.4.4 How the Changes Influenced the Children and Preschool Practice

The educators talked about how their communication with the children changed from being prescriptive to being more of a dialogue. The educators observed that they had conversations with the children more often than previously. As one of them pointed out: 'They [the children] more often come and talk to me and tell me something, instead of always asking: Can I change place?' Another added that she used to be telling the children all the time what to do or not to do: 'No, you cannot do that; no, you are supposed to stay there. I am not arguing anymore and I feel more pleased than before the changes.' She also thought she was more aware of children's well-being; they were pleased and more confident.

The educators suggested that the setting was much quieter than before and felt that the children were more confident and independent than before. Also, after the changes, they noticed that conflicts between the children had decreased. As one of them explained:

> It was in a way that a child chose an area and was supposed to be there for a certain time even though he/she did not like the play material, or did not have his/her friend to play with, and did not really want to play with the children who were there. Now the children can just go somewhere else if they feel uncomfortable. For that reason, they are not having as many conflicts as before.

The educators also considered that they had more trust in the children and the preschool practice was more equitable.

During the research process, the educators became more flexible than before, when the children wanted to move the play materials between areas. They suggested that the children found solutions themselves when they decided where to play and proposed that the children were more competent and confident than before: 'Now they choose the material they want to play with and take it to an area they find suitable; if they want to play with the cars, they find out themselves where the best place is.' The educators suggested that the atmosphere in the setting was more relaxed, the children were pleased and they were not as disturbed in their play as before. In addition, the educators thought it was critical for the children to have a say about what to do and with whom to play. The educators also mentioned that with this kind of 'freedom', the children learned to be more responsible. For instance, the educators counted on the children to clean up before they went over to another area.

10.4.5 The Educators' Ideas About Continuity and Transition

The educators discussed their views and ideas about continuity in children's education. One of them suggested that the preschool practices consisted of continuous levels of advancements between entrance at age two and the time that they transferred to primary school at age six. She said:

... we have reviewed what we are doing in literacy with the youngest children, and then what we do with children aged three to four years. In the setting with the oldest children, five to six years, the emphasis is more on formal literacy.

One of the educators suggested that in preschools, the emphasis should be more on children's well-being, but the tendency was more often to focus on formal teaching. She said: 'The preschool is recognised as the first school level, but sometimes I feel that we forget children's well-being.'

One of the educators suggested that the children were different and each child had his or her own needs:

We should not compare the children all the time ... each child should get an opportunity to deal with challenges according to their maturity ... we cannot stop them if they need more challenges and we need to meet them from where they are.

She suggested that children's interests were important and that educators needed to be aware that some children were able to read when they were 5 years old and others when they were seven and that later on this would level out. Another educator added that maybe the child who could not read was able to ride a bike but the child who could read was not. In addition, it was pointed out that these two children most likely would have different social skills.

The educators discussed pressure from parents who wanted their children to be able to learn certain things before starting primary school. They argued that some parents thought it was critical that their child should be able to sit still and do some challenging tasks, usually school related. The educators discussed whether it was important for all 3- to 4-year-old children to be able to sit still for a long time. The educators concluded that because they were different, some children could sit for a long time, while others could not. They discussed a boy who did not sit still in circle time or when educators were reading a book out loud. Even though he could not sit still, he usually participated in the discussion related to the story being told.

In one meeting, the educators discussed the schedule or the clock and how much it had affected and controlled their practice. One of them said that she wanted to change this, but had not worked out how to do it. Another argued that everything in daily life is controlled by the clock: the working hours and children's school hours. She said: 'When children start primary school, certainly the clock determines what to do and when. This is something we cannot change.' A third educator added that even though primary school hours are controlled by the clock, this was not necessary in preschools; the children could learn that later.

In the beginning of the research study, the educators believed it was valuable for the children to follow a routine, being aware of what comes next, and that all children participated in the same activities, usually at the same time. In addition, the educators thought it was convenient for them and for the children to know their routine, to know what to do next. But at the same time, they found this quite stressful to implement: 'When all the children need to do the same things at the same time, it sometimes is like an assembly line.' They started to see more value in children having a chance to deal with different challenges at different times and also considering children's interests. However, they thought it was critical that all children had the same opportunities.

The educators discussed at what point the preschool and primary school curricula should meet: that is, what should children be able to do when they finish preschool? What are the requirements? They mentioned that this discussion had occurred repeatedly and suggested that children are more capable today, when starting primary school, than before. One of the reasons for this is that, today, almost all children attend preschool.

The educators suggested that the collaborative action research had had a great impact on their views and practices. They found it important that the children could have a say in the preschool and that they could make more choices than before. Yet at the same time, they worried that it would be difficult for them to start in another setting with a different day schedule, different rules and more formal learning. One consideration that was discussed in the group was that the changes they had been through in the setting could be important for the children in the future, for their well-being and independence. For that reason, the educators thought it was critical for them to inform educators in other preschool settings about their own learning experiences of listening to children and giving them opportunities to make decisions.

10.5   Discussion

The main focus of the action research reported in this chapter was to reflect on the learning area of 'Health and Well-being' from the *Icelandic National Curriculum Guide for Preschool* (Ministry of Education, Science and Culture 2011) in one preschool setting. In doing so, the educators looked thoughtfully at their own practices and their views on transition and children's education in regard to their well-being and participation. To promote children's well-being, they found that it was critical to make the daily schedule more flexible, so the children could be active participants in preschool practice, emphasising children's opportunities to choose materials and playmates. It was considered more likely that the children would then take part in activities that interested them and in opportunities to play with their friends. These are important aspects that promote children's well-being (Csikszentmihalyi 1990; Laevers 1994).

The changes that were made led to a more positive atmosphere in the preschool, with more equal interactions between children and adults. Previously prescriptive interactions were replaced by more dialogue-based interactions. In addition, the educators suggested that the children were more relaxed, focused and found solutions to problems themselves when the schedule was flexible. This is consistent with Pramling Samuelsson and Asplund Carlsson's (2008) findings, which suggested that children's activities need to be organised in such a way that they have many opportunities to communicate with other children and adults because children learn from each other as well as from adults.

Some of the educators were worried that the flexible schedule they were developing in the preschool differed from the schedule in the primary school, where there is more emphasis on structured lessons and timetables. Einarsdóttir (2007) proposed that continuity means that educators build on and use children's experiences and activities from preschool to deal with new activities and subjects in primary school. For that reason, the practices in these two school levels need to emphasise a normal flow between the requirements in which children's activities are built on their previous experiences, instead of on sudden changes.

In the preschool setting in which this study was conducted, there was a tendency to think of continuity as meaning that children needed to do the same things in the preschool as in the primary school. Consequently, the daily schedule was as determined as the timetable in the primary school, based on the assumption that the children must be prepared for what is to come in the near future, that is, 'school readiness' (Dunlop 2013). However, children have different needs, knowledge and experiences, even though they attend the same preschool. To promote continuity, these differences need to be taken into account, meaning that educators need to build on children's knowledge and experiences. They must also consider children's varied needs (Einarsdóttir 2007) and ground their practice with those differences in mind. When children have opportunities to deal with challenging activities, they become motivated, and when the requirements are suitable, they become active participants. Such participation can influence their well-being (Csikszentmihalyi 1990). These considerations are prioritised when educators emphasise children's well-being and continuity in education.

In a flexible day schedule in which children have opportunities to make choices and learn through play, there are opportunities for them to take part in activities that reflect their interests and to play with their friends. In addition, having fewer interruptions in children's play gives them a better chance to focus on their activities – a critical premise for learning (Csikszentmihalyi 1990; Lewin-Benham 2011). With these conditions in mind, the children will have the opportunity to experience 'flow', which can be related to what Carr (2001) identified as 'learning disposition', referring to the way children show interest in activities or situations and respond to them. These characteristics are important for children when they tackle changes in their lives, such as transitioning to primary school and dealing with different aspects of learning.

The findings from this research are consistent with studies undertaken by Einarsdóttir (2007, 2013a) and Óskarsdóttir (2012), who indicated that there are not many differences between preschool and primary school. In this research, the educators' ideas and views on transition influenced the preschool practice. They emphasised school readiness and found it important to prepare the children for what was to come, including sitting still, concentrating and behaving (Óskarsdóttir 2012). In that way, the emphases of the primary school influenced the preschool practice. However, during the research process, these views developed in regard to the children's well-being and participation, so that the preschool practice came to be planned according to children's needs and active participation.

Children have different needs, knowledge and experiences, which should be taken into account in times of transitions. For instance, some children could be excited to start more formal learning, while others might need time to adjust to the school and its expectations. For that reason, as Dockett and Perry (2014) pointed out, it is critical for preschool and primary school teachers to collaborate by reflecting on and discussing their understandings of the concepts of transition and continuity in children's education, with the aim of supporting children's well-being.

References

Bjarnadóttir, G. (2004). *Jeg er løve som også kunne være lege. Valstund – en ramme rundt barns lek og sosiale prosesser i barnehagen* [I'm a lion who also can be a doctor. Choosing time – A frame for children's play and social learning in preschool]. Hovedfagsoppgave i barnehagepedagogikk. Oslo: Høgskolen i Oslo.
Carr, M. (2001). *Assessment in early childhood settings. Learning stories*. London: Sage.
Csikszentmihalyi, M. (1990). *Flow: The psychology of optimal experience. Steps towards enhancing the quality of life*. New York: Harper Collins Publishers.
Dewey, J. (1938/2000). *Reynsla og menntun > Experience and education@* (G. Ragnarsson, Trans.). Reykjavík: Rannsóknarstofnun Kennaraháskóla Íslands
Dockett, S., & Perry, B. (2006). Continuity and change in early childhood education. *Uppeldi og menntun, 15*(2), 105–110.
Dockett, S., & Perry, B. (2007). *Transition to school: Perceptions expectations, experiences*. Kensington: UNSW Press.
Dockett, S., & Perry, B. (2014). *Continuity of learning: A resource to support effective transition to school and school age care*. Canberra: Australian Government Department of Education.
Dunlop, A.-W. (2013). Curriculum as a tool for change in transitions practices: Transitions practices as a tool for changing curriculum. In K. Margetts & A. Kienig (Eds.), *International perspectives on transition to school: Reconceptualising beliefs, policy and practice* (pp. 135–145). London: Routledge.
Einarsdóttir, J. (2004). Frá leikskóla til grunnskóla: Aðferðir til að tengja saman skólastigin [From preschool to primary school: Approaches to connect the level of education]. *FUM – Tímarit um menntarannsóknir 1*, 208–227.
Einarsdóttir, J. (2007). *Lítil börn með skólatöskur. Tengsl leikskóla og grunnskóla* [Small children with schoolbags. Transition from preschool to primary school]. Reykjavík: Háskólaútgáfan and RannUng.
Einarsdóttir, J. (2008). Þátttaka barna [Children's participation]. In J. Einarsdóttir & B. Garðarsdóttir (Eds.), *Sjónarmið barna og lýðræði í leikskólastarfi* (pp. 115–132). Reykjavík: Háskólaútgáfan and RannUng.
Einarsdóttir, J. (2013a). Leikskóli og grunnskóli á sömu leið. [Preschool and primary school on the same path]. In J. Einarsdóttir & B. Garðarsdóttir (Eds.), *Á sömu leið. Tengsl leikskóla og grunnskóla* (pp. 11–24). Reykjavík: RannUng and Háskólaútgáfan.
Einarsdóttir, J. (2013b). Rannsóknir sem breytingaafl í skólastarfi. [Research as a tool for changing school practice]. In J. Einarsdóttir & B. Garðarsdóttir (Eds.), *Á sömu leið. Tengsl leikskóla og grunnskóla* (pp. 25–35). Reykjavík: RannUng and Háskólaútgáfan.
Garðarsdóttir, B., & Karlsdóttir, K. (2012). Skráning námsgagna. Sjónarhorn barna. [Documenting learning stories. Children's perspectives]. In J. Einarsdóttir & B. Garðarsdóttir (Eds.), *Raddir barna* (pp. 99–118). Reykjavík: RannUng and Háskólaútgáfan.
Guðjónsdóttir, H. (2011). *Rýnt í vinnubrögð starfendarannsókna: Ólíkar leiðir við gagnaöflun* [Action research: Different methods for data collection]. Ráðstefnurit Netlu-Menntavika 2011. http://netla.hi.is/menntakvika2011/010.pdf. Accessed 12 June 2015.
Guðjónsson, H. (2008). *Starfendarannsóknir í Menntaskólanum við Sund* [Action research in Sund College]. Netla-veftímarit um uppeldi og menntun. Menntavísindasvið HÍ. http://netla.khi.is/greinar/2008/002/index.htm. Accessed 12 June 2015.

Handley, G. (2005). Children's rights to participation. In T. Waller (Ed.), *An introduction to early childhood. A multidisciplinary approach* (pp. 1–12). London: Paul Chapman Publishing.

Hreinsdóttir, A. M., & Einarsdóttir, J. (2011). Ólíkar áherslur í leikskólastarfi. Rannsókn á starf-saðferðum fjögurra leikskóla. [The role of preschool curriculum. A study on different approaches in four preschools]. *Uppeldi og menntun, 20*(1), 30–50.

Katz, L. (1996). *How can we strengthen children's self-esteem?* http://www.kidsource.com/kid-source/content2/strengthen_children_self.html. Accessed 20 May 2015.

Koshy, V. (2005). *Action research for improving practice: A practical guide.* London: Sage.

Laevers, F. (1994). The innovative project experiential education and the definition of quality in education. In F. Laevers (Ed.), *Defining and assessing quality in early childhood education* (pp. 159–172). Leuven: Leuven University Press.

Lewin-Benham, A. (2011). *Twelve best practices for early childhood education. Integrating Reggio and other inspired approaches.* New York: Teachers College Press.

Marcon, R. A. (2002). Moving up the grades: Relationships between preschool model and later school success. *Early Childhood Research and Practice, 4*(1). http://ecrp.uiuc.edu/v4n1/marcon.html. Accessed 20 May 2015.

McNiff, J. (2010). *Action research for professional development.* Dorset: September Books.

Ministry of Education, Science and Culture. (2011). *Aðalnámskrá leikskóla* [The Icelandic National Curriculum Guide for Preschool]. Reykjavík: Mennta- og menningarmálaráðuneyti.

Ministry of Education, Science and Culture. (2013). *Aðalnámskrá grunnskóla* [The Icelandic national curriculum guide for compulsory school]. Reykjavík: Mennta- og menningar-málaráðuneytið.

Monkevicencé, O., Mishara, B. L., & Dufour, S. (2006). Effects of the Zippy's Friends pro-gramme on children's coping abilities during the transition from kindergarten to elementary school. *Early Childhood Education Journal, 34*(1), 53–60.

Óskarsdóttir, G. (2012). *Skil skólastiga. Frá leikskóla til grunnskóla og grunnskóla til fram-haldsskóla* [Transitions between school levels. From preschool to primary school and from primary school to upper secondary school]. Reykjavík: Háskólaútgáfan.

Pramling Samuelsson, I., & Asplund Carlsson, M. (2008). The playing learning child: Towards a pedagogy of early childhood. *Scandinavian Journal of Educational Research, 52*(6), 623–641.

Roberts, R. (1998). Thinking about me and them. In I. Siraj-Blatchford (Ed.), *A curriculum devel-opment handbook for early childhood educators.* Stoke on Trent: Trentham Books.

Sigurðardóttir, I. Ó. (2012). *Við getum kennt þeim svo margt í gegnum leik". Hlutverk leikskólak-ennara í leik barna* ["We can teach them so many things through play": The role of three pre-school teachers in children's play]. Netla – veftímarit um uppeldi og menntun. http://netla.hi.is/greinar/2012/ryn/007.pdf. Accessed 25 May 2015.

Van Hoorn, J., Nourot, P. M., Scales, B., & Alward, K. R. (2011). *Play at the centre of the curricu-lum* (5th ed.). Boston: Pearson.

Waters, J. (2009). Well-being. In T. Waller (Ed.), *An introduction to early childhood. A multidisci-plinary approach* (2nd ed., pp. 16–30). London: SAGE Publications.

Chapter 11
Creating Continuity Through Children's Participation: Evidence from Two Preschool Contexts

Kristín Karlsdóttir and Bob Perry

In many countries, there is an ongoing debate about the education of children as they move from preschool to primary school. With the aim of informing this discussion, internationally and nationally, this chapter explores children's participation and learning processes in the year before they start primary school. The study was conducted in two Icelandic preschools with very different early childhood curricular contexts. In both contexts, consideration was given to the way children's participation repertoires can support continuity as children move from preschool to primary school. The findings highlighted the importance of children's opportunities for free play and pedagogies that enable children to have input to their play and learning. Implications for policy decisions related to transition to school pedagogy include a strong claim for child-centred and play-based learning experience. Moreover, the findings suggested that a focus on children's participation repertoires would facilitate continuity as children move between preschool and school.

11.1 Introduction

In Iceland, as elsewhere, there is ongoing debate about children's educational needs across the transition from preschool to primary school. Different stakeholders – parents, teachers and policymakers – advance different views about this, both as groups and as individuals (Dockett et al. 2014; Einarsdóttir 2007b; Peters 2010). Questions such as the following are raised: At what age should children move from preschool

K. Karlsdóttir
University of Iceland, Reykjavik, Iceland

B. Perry (✉)
Research Institue for Professional Practice, Learning and Education (RIPPLE),
Charles Sturt University, Albury, NSW, Australia
e-mail: peridoteducation@outlook.com

© Springer International Publishing Switzerland 2017
N. Ballam et al. (eds.), *Pedagogies of Educational Transitions*, International
Perspectives on Early Childhood Education and Development 16,
DOI 10.1007/978-3-319-43118-5_11

to primary school? How should they be prepared or supported for the move? What should the education of children entail as this move is made?

Children's transition between the two school levels – preschool and primary school – is widely considered a very important change in children's lives (Dockett and Perry 2014; Ministry of Education, Science and Culture 2011). Most parents and children look forward to this transition, but some worry about how they will cope with the process (Dockett and Perry 2007; Kagan and Tarrant 2010). In many situations, transition programmes are planned to 'prepare' children for starting primary school. Many of these programmes tend to focus on traditional skills such as reading and writing, with a focus on individual children (Dockett et al. 2014). However, transition to primary school is not only about individual children but also about groups of children and social experiences within these groups (Petriwskyj 2014). The nature of transition to school depends upon different educational contexts, different characteristics of individual children and the interactions over time between and within contexts and people (Bronfenbrenner and Morris 2006; Wells and Claxton 2002). Such interactions have the potential to build positive relationships among all of the stakeholders in a child's transition to school. Effective transitions will occur when respectful, reciprocal relationships among all involved, including children's families, school communities, teachers and children, are developed (Dockett and Perry 2001, 2014; Hartley et al. 2012; Peters 2014).

While many transition to school programmes and associated research are based around the notion of children's readiness for school (Blair et al. 2007; Lehrer and Bastien 2015), young children continue to demonstrate their strengths and agency, not only in preschools but also in primary schools (Gervasoni and Perry 2015; Laidlaw et al. 2015; Peters 2010, 2014; Smith 2011). Such demonstrations create a sense of continuity in educational transitions as the children are able to show their strengths in the 'new' context, just as they could in the 'old'. Similarly, children's sense of belonging, well-being and identity as learners can be influential in developing continuity in the children's transition processes (Carr 2001; Dockett and Perry 2014). Relationships, recognition and celebration of strengths and identities all seem to be critical aspects of effective transitions to school.

In many countries, the curricular contexts (goals, content, teachers' methods and school environment) in preschools and primary schools tend to be quite different from each other (Bennett 2008; Einarsdóttir 2007b; Peters 2010). Even though the Icelandic preschool and primary school curricula are based upon the same six fundamental pillars of education (Ministry of Education, Science and Culture 2011), studies (Einarsdóttir 2004, 2007a, b) have shown many differences in the practice of the two different levels of schooling, the most profound of which has to do with the acting out of power relations in the two contexts. Additionally, pedagogical approaches differ across these levels of schooling in Iceland (Einarsdóttir 2013). The uniformity of the six pillars has resulted in many similarities across preschool and school in pedagogical planning (Óskarsdóttir 2012); however, it seems that more formal 'primary school' ideologies and pedagogies have been adopted by some preschools, with the purpose of preparing children for primary school (Einarsdóttir 2013; Einarsdóttir and Garðarsdóttir 2013). Advocates who support play-based approaches to young children's learning and their right to play (United Nations 1989) are critical of these changes and seek other strategies to promote greater curricular and pedagogical continuity between the two levels of schooling.

This chapter reports on an observational study in two Icelandic preschools that considered how the children were involved in play and learning situations, how they took part in structuring their own and others' meaning and how they contributed to the preschool community. The purpose of the study was to gain a deeper understanding of the children's learning processes at the time they were preparing to start primary school and to apply this understanding to matters of continuity across this transition.

11.2 Theoretical Views

Early childhood education in both preschools and primary schools is based on a series of views about children, learning, knowledge and equity. These views are often encapsulated into curriculum documents such as the *Icelandic National Curriculum Guides* (Ministry of Education, Science and Culture 2011). In this section, some of these views are explored.

11.2.1 Views About Children and Learning

The underpinning theories of learning and teaching in this study are broadly sociocultural (Rogoff 2003; Wells and Claxton 2002). Children are seen as social beings and active participants in a democratic society; their perspectives are considered an important contribution to their communities and they are treated seriously (Dahlberg et al. 1999). Recognition of children's strengths and rights does not, on its own, result in children's active participation. Traditional adult/child power differentials must be addressed, and this can be difficult for some adults (Dahlberg et al. 1999; Sommer et al. 2010). Woodhead (2005, p. 92) has noted that such recognition of children's agency 'strikes at the heart of conventional authority relationships between children and the adults who regulate their lives'. In Iceland, however, preschool teachers are encouraged to engage with:

> [D]emocratic preschool practices [that] are based on equality, diversity, shared responsibility, solidarity and acceptance of different views. At preschool children are to feel that they are part of a group and a community where justice and respect characterise relations. Children are considered active citizens and participants and everyone gets an opportunity to contribute to and influence the preschool environment. (Ministry of Education, Science and Culture 2011, p. 35)

Such an approach sets the basis for children's learning in Icelandic preschools and for the study reported in this chapter.

11.2.2 Children's Participation Repertoires

Carr (2001, p. 10) defines 'learning dispositions' as 'participation repertoires from which a learner recognises, selects, edits, responds to, resists, searches for and constructs learning opportunities'. Children's learning dispositions reflect a holistic view of what children learn by integrating cognitive, social and emotional factors of learning (Carr 2001).

In this chapter, three constructs are used to analyse the observations of children's participation in activities: involvement, well-being and contribution. Children's involvement with their environment, play and interaction with others is seen in the intensity of the child's interest, exploration and communication in a group (Laevers and Heylen 2003). Children's well-being involves their feelings of 'belonging' (Department of Education, Employment and Workplace Relations [DEEWR] 2009; Ministry of Education 1996). It involves their feeling 'at ease', finding an atmosphere in which they can be spontaneous and meeting their basic needs such as attention, affection, social recognition and a feeling of competence (Laevers 1994). Well-being also appears in children's willingness to attempt challenging tasks and their belief that they can learn through repeated efforts (Smiley and Dweck 1994). Children's contribution concerns how they find ways to influence their contexts and how they communicate with others using various methods. 'Contribution' is related to whether the educational context allows children to have their say and be heard (Carr 2001).

Taken together, teachers' views about children's participation, agency and rights can result in democratic pedagogy in which each individual child can be actively involved in the decision-making process in preschool. However, according to the *Convention on the Rights of the Child* (United Nations 1989), children need to be supported in achieving this aim. Thus, preschool teachers need to work with children so that mutually empowering relationships and opportunities for participation and influence are built (Bae 2009; Rinaldi 2005).

11.2.3 Play in Preschool

Research has confirmed the importance of play in early childhood (Sylva et al. 2004). Several studies have suggested links between play and areas such as socio-emotional competence, literacy and numeracy (Golinkoff et al. 2006; Johnson et al. 2013). It also appears that 'pretend' play facilitates the development of self-regulation (Meyers and Berk 2014).

Children learn from playing (Shonkoff and Phillips 2000), and play can be used as a form of pedagogy (Wood 2014). 'Educational play' is seen by Wood (2014) as having three modes. Two of these – child-initiated play and adult-guided play – are relevant to the current study.

Child-Initiated Play refers to several slightly different forms of play such as free play, role-play or sociodramatic play, in which children use their own ideas and interests to initiate and develop play. Nevertheless, 'free play is always controlled within educational settings because of teachers' beliefs and values' (Wood 2014, p. 149). Even in a relatively democratic preschool context, the preschool teachers usually define what choices are available and what degrees of freedom the children are allowed (Wood 2014).

Adult-Guided Play may be structured, planned, resourced and managed by preschool teachers in ways that promote specific outcomes, but it involves children's free and spontaneous activities and values their contributions to their learning and development. Adult-guided play starts from children's ideas and interests, but teachers are involved in supporting the children's ideas and actions and organising frames within which the children play (Wood 2014).

The notions of 'educational play' and 'playful pedagogies' challenge the idea that play has to be child led, spontaneous, exploratory and voluntary (Brooker 2010). While there is certainly a place for such play in early education, the work of the EPPE project (Siraj-Blatchford and Sylva 2004) shows that play pedagogy also forms part of the pedagogical balance in effective preschools, along with more 'traditional' approaches to instruction, including intentional teaching. More recently, Aydoğan et al. (2015) have shown that a high level of instructional support in preschools is not enough to create an optimal learning environment. 'High instructional support and more positive emotional tone [in the preschool] are both needed' (p. 615).

11.3 The Study

This study draws on data from two preschools that have based their practices on the *Icelandic National Curriculum* (Ministry of Education, Science and Culture 2011). In the Icelandic context, the child centredness found in Nordic tradition has been influential, and child-initiated peer activities and valuing children's own perspectives and interests have been paramount (Einarsdóttir 2006; Kristjánsson 2006).

The two preschools in this study had adopted very different approaches in their day-to-day curriculum and pedagogy. One school worked in the spirit of Reggio Emilia (Malaguzzi 1998), while the other had adopted a relatively new Icelandic curriculum approach, the Hjalli pedagogy (Hjallastefnan 2014b). The main goals of Seaside, the Reggio Emilia preschool, were for children to develop their ideas and hypotheses, to co-construct meaning both individually and in collaboration with others, and for children to be creative when working on projects. The main goals of Lava Ledge, the Hjalli preschool, were to support children in behaving in accordance with rules, engaging in positive thinking and independence and actively cultivating attributes that are typically considered to be strengths in the opposite gender, an aim that was advanced by means of single-sex groups.

Inspired by observational approaches developed in New Zealand (Carr and Lee 2012; Ministry of Education 1996), narrative observations of 24 five-year-old children were undertaken. Data were generated over a period of 3 months in each school, with 11 children from Seaside (five girls and six boys) and 13 children from Lava Ledge (six girls and seven boys). These children were the eldest in the respective preschools, and nearly all were intending to start primary school 1 year later, in the autumn of the year they would turn six.

During the 6-month period of fieldwork, observations of children in the form of written notes, photos and videos were reflected upon and analysed. First, *observations were made with an open mind*, as data were generated and simultaneously analysed, also including both children's and teachers' reflections. Throughout the data generation process, which involved lengthy periods of participation in the two preschools, the researcher tried to be open-minded, avoid being judgemental and remain open to children's multiple meanings by listening to their voices. Next, *narrative observations were linked to participation repertoires*, the observations were sorted and grouped for each child and, after this, narrative observations were written, in a form similar to their New Zealand inspirations, particularly related to participation. For all 24 children, descriptions were written, related to how the child seemed to (1) individually experience well-being and belonging, (2) be involved and communicate in the social context and (3) contribute and take responsibility in the preschool context.

Four main ethical issues were identified and addressed during the study: the confidentiality and anonymity of sensitive data, gaining informed consent, being open and non-judgmental and building trust between the researcher and the children in order to include children's views. The first priority was to reduce the power imbalance between the researcher and the participants (Clark 2005; Dockett 2008). In order to analyse the way the contexts in the two preschools supported children's learning processes, the study engaged with the small details of the children's everyday lives in the social context of the preschools; it focused on engaging with the particularities in each social context and with the emotions of those within them. This concept is referred to as 'minor politics' (Mac Naughton 2005) as it considers the small details of children's everyday lives and involves active ethical practice and a belief in the ethical capacities of individuals and their ability to make judgements. It requires considering many possible views, methods and/or solutions rather than believing in one right answer or method (Dahlberg and Moss 2005).

11.4   Findings and Discussion

In this section of the chapter, the findings from the study are reported and discussed, firstly, in terms of similarities and differences between the two preschools and, secondly, in terms of the nature of children's participation in their play and learning.

11.4.1 Similarities and Differences in the Pedagogies of the Two Preschools

Children in the two preschools experienced quite different structural, environmental, curricula and pedagogical realities, which, in turn, supported the children's learning processes very differently. At Seaside, the Reggio Emilia-inspired preschool, observations by the researcher showed the children to be strong, capable participants in the building of a democratic community. At this preschool, teachers' methods built upon an emergent curriculum within a rich, stimulating environment, and the children were encouraged to express views and ideas as they co-constructed meaning within the group and interacted with their teachers and peers. The Seaside teachers sought a balance of power between adults and children, as shown by their listening to children's perspectives and supporting them in developing their ideas. When working on projects, for instance, the children enjoyed opportunities to influence the process and were simultaneously encouraged to consider others' views and to act on behalf of the group. Not only were children's different understandings, opinions and solutions valued, but their views and solutions were seen as important to their learning and to planning the preschool practice.

At Lava Ledge, the teachers' methods built upon Hjalli pedagogy using transmission approaches in which children are thought to require clear rules and a simple environment, are expected to learn the specific aims of the gendered curriculum and behave accordingly, and are provided with opportunities to be active and independent within a strong framework. The Lava Ledge teachers were clear, in both their actions and words, that adults were supposed to direct the activities in the preschool, that the teachers themselves held the power and that it was their responsibility to clearly state the rules, articulate what was right and wrong and emphasise to children what was allowed and what was not. One example of this was children's introduction to ways of interacting with and being fair to other children. Children were taught not only to do what was seen as good and right by others but also to meet the specific aims of the gender-focused curriculum.

In spite of these major differences between the two preschools, there were also similarities. Firstly, all children were provided with ample time and opportunities to play freely with minimal intervention from teachers. The teachers at both preschools used specific methods to encourage children to express their views, though these methods were built upon highly divergent views and philosophies. The data showed clear similarities regarding the children's opportunities to play. In both preschools, the children's play was highly valued and supported, and the children were provided with the freedom to play, interact and find solutions to problems within their peer groups. Additionally, in both preschools, the children shared experiences, developed a peer culture and attempted to gain control within their groups. They experienced friendship, togetherness and belonging, as well as conflicts, social exclusion and marginalisation. Perhaps there should be no surprise about these similarities between the two preschools as, in spite of their different philosophies and practices, they were both governed by the *Icelandic National Curriculum Guide for Preschools*

(Ministry of Education, Science and Culture 2011) and guided by the child-centred Nordic tradition of early education (Kristjánsson 2006).

11.4.2 Children's Participation

Children's participation within preschool contexts is complex in terms of skills and knowledge, dispositions, understandings displayed (and not displayed), social interactions and co-construction. In this study, observations were made in the two preschools, focusing on the children's participation in the learning processes and social interactions with their peers and teachers. Analysis of these observations was undertaken through the lens of well-being, involvement and contribution.

11.4.2.1 Children's Well-Being

The observed children seemed to experience a sense of 'belonging' and 'well-being' regardless of the preschool attended and used various participatory repertoires to demonstrate these. For example, in most situations, child 1 had imaginative ideas that she expressed through words or actions but was also active in developing and building from open-ended materials such as unit blocks. However, for most of the time, child 2 only used verbal expression to state her views and wishes. Nonetheless, most forms of expression were used by most of the children. In the narratives developed during this study, all of the children's ways of expressing their well-being and belonging were much more similar than different, despite the different contexts. In different situations, children used individual ways to structure their participatory interaction within the social context, which included other children and teachers. Such trends were demonstrated across the groups of children in the study, despite differences between the situations and the participation of other children in the group's activities.

11.4.2.2 Children's Involvement

In both preschools, children were involved with and communicated with others, seemed to understand situations, structured each other's involvement as a means to facilitate engagement in shared efforts and participated in interactive processes involving different social contexts and children's personal factors. These forms of involvement were observed when the children at Seaside were working on a project in which they developed a theme before putting on a play. Each participating child expressed different ideas regarding the theme. These were observed in the children's attempts to accommodate less traditional roles (such as child, alien, dinosaur and mermaid) into an Icelandic folk story that already contained the roles of a boy protagonist, a cow and a female giant. Assisted by a supportive preschool teacher, the children managed to develop the play, reconcile the diverse roles and ultimately include all the ideas. Moreover, during this process, they constructed each other's involvement and facilitated one another's engagement in a shared effort.

Similar involvement and play were observed in the different context of the Hjalli preschool. One of the outcomes of the gender curriculum (Hjallastefnan 2014a) at Lava Ledge was 'daring'. During the data generation period for this study, the girls being observed had been practising 'daring' with their teacher. In the absence of a teacher, they chose to play in a way that seemed to support not only their own 'daring' but each other's 'daring' as well. This was demonstrated as the girls played in the soft cube area, daring each other to jump from the table onto a pile of mattresses. The girls piled up mattresses and soft cubes and practised jumping from the high table to the pile. They helped and encouraged each other: when one girl was reluctant to jump from the same height as the other girls, the rest of the group asked if she wanted them to remove some mattresses from the pile or if they could support her in any other way.

At both preschools, when the opportunities arose, children were able to generate involvement through their own participation and actions. While the amount of time available for such involvement was different in the two sites, there did not seem to be any difference in the intensity of the involvement when it was demonstrated.

11.4.2.3 Children's Contribution

At both preschools, children contributed to their situations and took responsibility for themselves and others. They listened to other children, put their ideas forward and together often found solutions in ways that seemed fair to the others. In the example described above in which the children at Seaside were developing a play for later performance, the children found ways to both develop the theme and include several different, contradictory roles in ways that accommodated different ideas from all of the children. The children were observed to view this challenging task as an opportunity to understand and improve their skills rather than as an opportunity to gain favourable judgements from others about their competence. They took responsibility not only for including everyone's ideas but also for persistently developing the play so it could continue.

At Lava Ledge, the children often seemed to find ways of listening to others and making decisions that were fair to everyone. For example, one girl wanted to join two others inside the playhouse, but they claimed that there was no room for her. Soon after, however, one of the girls inside the house came out and said softly to the 'outside' girl, 'Come to the attic; I will move our cameras'. These two girls prepared 'the attic' so that all three girls could be together in the house. By doing this, one girl not only took responsibility for the situation but also made an effort to be fair to the other girl by helping to prepare a room for her.

11.4.2.4 Summary of Children's Participation Findings

In spite of the clear differences in the values and beliefs extolled in each site in which the observations for this study were made, the results suggest that when given opportunities to be involved in child-initiated and child-led activities, the children in both sites participated in similar ways and with similar intensities.

When the observations of the participant children were considered through the lens of involvement, well-being and contribution, it was concluded that the children:

- Seemed to feel that they 'belonged' in the site, in general, and the activities, in particular.
- Expressed themselves during play activities in a variety of ways including words, gestures and actions.
- Chose similar roles in varying situations: individual children seemed to choose roles as a means of expressing how they preferred to be situated in the group during play.
- Seemed to understand the group dynamics required in play activities, including matters of communication and the structuring of their and others' involvement.
- Listened to other children and often took responsibility for themselves and others.
- Seemed able to use their knowledge, skills and experience to solve problems and overcome difficulties in ways that were acceptable in the particular preschool community.
- Generally acted fairly towards others and seemed able to appreciate other points of view.

The observation of the children at both Seaside and Lava Ledge preschools provided evidence that children can be very able and strong in their interactions with others in genuine play situations. In most situations and with most children, positive learning experiences predominated, although sometimes, some children in some situations encountered challenges that they were not able to handle. In many cases, other children assisted in the resolution of these challenges. Such situations were apparent in each of the preschools in this study.

11.5 Conclusion

In Iceland, as in many other countries, most five-year-old children spend some of their sixth year of life in preschool and the rest in primary school. Both the preschools and the primary schools aim to ensure optimal learning environments for the children, but they often seem to do this in quite different ways (Einarsdóttir 2007b). This is reinforced through many studies across the world that have found that preschools and schools can be quite different (Bennett 2008; Perry et al. 2014;

Peters 2010). From the study reported in this chapter, it is clear that preschools can also be quite different in terms of their approaches to learning and teaching.

There is some evidence that children starting school actually want school to be different from preschool because such differences, and the children's ability to cope with the changes, are indications that the children are growing up (Dockett and Perry 2007; Garpelin 2014). However, they also want some things to display at least some continuity. For example, friendships and relationships remain important (Peters 2010), families and family support continue to be needed (Dockett and Perry 2013; Langford 2010), and the benefits of a sense of 'belonging' continue to be evident (Broström 2003). What does the study reported in this chapter have to say about change and continuity as children start school?

11.5.1 Change as Children Start School

If one reads printed and web-based information about the two preschools in this study, it would not be difficult to conclude that they are very different places; have quite different philosophies about child development, learning and teaching; use different curricula and learning activities; and are pedagogically distinct. However, both preschools have to adhere to the *Icelandic National Curriculum Guide for Preschools* (Ministry of Education, Science and Culture 2011) and its six foundation pillars, and both have the preparation of their children for starting school as part of their aims. That they do these things in quite different ways means that there will be changes as the children start school. Some children will move into schools that resemble their preschool in many ways; others will experience high levels of change. It is known that Icelandic preschools and primary schools can be quite different, as children in some primary schools are provided with strong frameworks and teacher-controlled assignments, while children in many preschools receive play-based opportunities to interact and learn and in general have more power to determine their involvement in activities (Einarsdóttir 2004, 2007b). There was some evidence from the current study that, despite the different structures, rules and expectations apparent in the two preschools, both situations were favourable to the children's participation and well-being. Hence, one way in which 'continuity' or 'discontinuity' could be observed as these children start school is through these constructs.

11.5.2 Continuity as Children Start School

Even though there were distinct differences between the two preschools in this study, many similarities also existed. Some examples of structural and legal similarities have been canvassed in the previous section. However, from the observations of children in the two preschools, it was clear that when children in both sites were given the chance to play, they played in active, creative and stimulating ways, using similar processes of communication, empathy and learning to enact their roles in the democratic situation of child-initiated and child-led play experiences.

As children start school, many aspects of their lives will continue. They will continue to be important members of their families and to gain support from these families. They will continue to have groups of friends, some of whom will be the same people they called friends at preschool and some who will be new friends. They will continue to attend the same cultural venues, to cheer for the same football or handball teams and share leisure of different kinds, and some will continue to attend church events. From the study reported in this chapter, it would seem that another aspect of continuity is the children's participation in different experiences, as well as their abilities and actions that promote feelings of pleasure, sense of 'belonging', challenge and learning from play activities.

What a grand opportunity such continuity of the children's wishes and abilities to play provides schools and school teachers as the children start school. Why would teachers of the first year of school even think of restricting children's play to the breaks in teaching and the playground? Given the evidence from this study and many others (Broadhead et al. 2010; Brooker et al. 2014), play is an integral part of young children's being. This is recognised in the Icelandic curriculum guide (Ministry of Education, Science and Culture 2011) and does not stop when the children start school. As can be seen from the current study, children in preschools use play to learn and, in general, enjoy doing so. It would be a foolish school teacher who did not continue to provide opportunities for their new-start children to play in ways that can activate a sense of belonging in the child, motivate them to find out that school is 'for them' and provide experiences in which the child can be successful, right from the start. All of this can be observed through the lens of children's involvement, well-being and contribution. In these ways, play can provide a very important component of continuity as children start school.

11.5.3   A Methodological Point

The study reported in this chapter used a detailed observational methodology that gave the researcher insight into the 'minor politics' of the two preschool communities, that is, the small details of the everyday lives of the participant children. The data generation in the current study focused on children's play, learning and participation processes. There is also a great deal that could be learned about the social aspects of the children's lives. If similar observations could be undertaken by the preschool and school teachers, even to the extent to which they would be able to do so within their already onerous duties, the insights gained might enable the teachers to understand the children's perspectives better and to use them to develop a more collaborative approach to pedagogy in preschools and schools and pedagogies of educational transitions. In Dahlberg and Moss's (2005) conception, this means looking beyond the general and traditional views towards children and their learning and including the emotions of those involved in these contexts. Discussion among teachers, parents, children and even policymakers about the particularities of what happens when children participate in preschool and school contexts could facilitate the development of practices that value children's rights to be active participants in their social contexts. This could result in children and the adults in their lives seeing their capabilities more clearly. It could also assist in the building of respectful, reciprocal relationships between teachers, parents and children, one of the long-recommended aspects of continuity as children start school (Dockett and Perry 2001; Hartley et al. 2012; Peters 2014). Children might become active participants in both continuity and change.

11.6   Final Words

The demand for 'continuity' as children start school can be easily misunderstood. Transition to school will include both continuity and change. One is reminded of Jean-Baptiste Alphonse Karr's 1849 epigram 'plus ça change, plus c'est la même chose', translated often as 'the more things change, the more they stay the same'. Neither continuity nor change is to be feared. Rather, they can both be used to ensure the optimal transition experiences for all of the stakeholders, particularly the children.

Preschools do not have to look, feel and be like primary schools, and primary schools do not have to look, feel and be like preschools. Clearly, there will be change and this is expected by all involved. As well, there can be continuity, and the study reported in this chapter suggests strongly than one aspect of that continuity could be explored through the lens of children's participatory repertoires. The study may have opened a very fruitful area for future research.

References

Aydoğan, C., Farran, D. C., & Sağsöz, G. (2015). The relationship between kindergarten classroom environment and children's engagement. *European Early Childhood Education Research Journal, 23*(5), 504–618.

Bae, B. (2009). Children's right to participate – Challenges in everyday interactions. *European Early Childhood Education Research Journal, 17*(3), 391–406.

Bennett, J. (2008). Early childhood education and care systems in the OECD countries: The issue of tradition and governance. *Encyclopaedia on Early Childhood Development [online]*. (Vol. 1–5). Montreal, Quebec: Centre of Excellence for Early Childhood Development.

Blair, C., Knipe, H., Cummings, E., Baker, D. P., Gamson, D., Eslinger, P., & Thorne, S. L. (2007). A developmental neuroscience approach to the study of school readiness. In R. C. Pianta, M. J. Cox, & K. L. Snow (Eds.), *School readiness and the transition to kindergarten in the era of accountability* (pp. 140–174). Baltimore: Paul H. Brookes.

Broadhead, P., Howard, J., & Wood, E. (Eds.). (2010). *Play and learning in the early years.* London: Sage.

Bronfenbrenner, U., & Morris, P. (2006). The ecology of human development. In W. Damon & R. M. Lerner (Eds.), *Handbook of child psychology: Theoretical models of human development* (6th ed., Vol. 1, pp. 793–828). New York: Wiley.

Brooker, L. (2010). Learning to play in a cultural context. In P. Broadhead, J. Howard, & E. Wood (Eds.), *Play and learning in the early years* (pp. 27–42). London: Sage.

Brooker, L., Blaise, M., & Edwards, S. (Eds.). (2014). *The SAGE handbook of play and learning in early childhood.* London: Sage.

Broström, S. (2003). Transitions from kindergarten to school in Denmark. In A.-W. Dunlop & H. Fabian (Eds.), *Transitions* (Themed monograph series 1, pp. 5–14). Worcester: EECERA.

Carr, M. (2001). *Assessment in early childhood settings: Learning stories.* London: Paul Chapman.

Carr, M., & Lee, W. (2012). *Learning stories: Constructing learner identities in early education.* London: Sage.

Clark, A. (2005). Ways of seeing: Using the mosaic approach to listen to young children's perspectives. In A. Clark, A. T. Kjorholt, & P. Moss (Eds.), *Beyond listening: Children's perspectives on early childhood services* (pp. 29–50). Bristol: The Policy Press.

Dahlberg, G., & Moss, P. (2005). *Ethics and politics in early childhood education.* London: RoutledgeFalmer.

Dahlberg, G., Moss, P., & Pence, A. (1999). *Beyond quality in early childhood education and care: Postmodern perspectives.* London: Falmer.

Department of Education, Employment and Workplace Relations (DEEWR). (2009). *Belonging, being & becoming: The early years learning framework for Australia.* Canberra: Commonwealth of Australia.

Dockett, S. (2008). Hlustað á raddir barna: Börn og rannsóknir [Listening to children's voices: Children and research]. In J. Einarsdóttir & B. Garðarsdóttir (Eds.), *Sjónarmið barna og lýðræði í leikskólastarfi* (pp. 33–46). Reykjavík: Háskólaútgáfan, Rannsóknarstofa í menntunarfræði ungra barna.

Dockett, S., & Perry, B. (Eds.). (2001). *Beginning school together: Sharing strengths.* Watson: Australian Early Childhood Association.

Dockett, S., & Perry, B. (2007). *Starting school: Perceptions, expectations and experiences.* Sydney: UNSW Press.

Dockett, S., & Perry, B. (2013). Families and the transition to school. In K. Margetts & A. Kienig (Eds.), *International perspectives on transitions to school: Reconceptualising beliefs, policy and practice* (pp. 111–121). London: Routledge.

Dockett, S., & Perry, B. (2014). *Continuity of learning: A resource to support effective transition to school and school age care.* Canberra: Australian Government.

Dockett, S., Petriwskyj, A., & Perry, B. (2014). Theorising transition: Shifts and tensions. In B. Perry, S. Dockett, & A. Petriwskyj (Eds.), *Transitions to school: International research, policy and practice* (pp. 1–18). Dordrecht: Springer.

Einarsdóttir, J. (2004). Frá leikskóla til grunnskóla: aðferðir til að tengja skólastigin [From pre- to primary school: Methods to engage these school levels]. *Tímarit um menntarannsóknir [Journal of Educational Research (Iceland)], 1,* 209–227.

Einarsdóttir, J. (2006). Between two continents, between two traditions: Education and care in Icelandic preschools. In J. Einarsdóttir & J. Wagner (Eds.), *Nordic childhoods and early education: Philosophy, research, policy and practices in Denmark, Finland, Iceland, Norway and Sweden* (pp. 159–182). Greenwich: AGE Pub.

Einarsdóttir, J. (2007a). Children's voices on the transition from preschool to primary school. In A. W. Dunlop & H. Fabian (Eds.), *Informing transitions in the early years: Research, policy and practice* (pp. 74–91). Maidenhead: Open University Press.

Einarsdóttir, J. (2007b). *Lítil börn með skólatösku: Tengsl leikskóla og grunnskóla* [Small children with schoolbags: Transition from preschool to primary school]. Reykjavík: Háskólaútgáfan.

Einarsdóttir, J. (Ed.). (2013). *Leikskóli og grunnskóli á sömu leið* [Pre- and primary school on the same path]. Reykjavík: RannUng & Háskólaútgáfan.

Einarsdóttir, J., & Garðarsdóttir, B. (Eds.). (2013). *Á sömu leið: Tengsl leikskóla og grunnskóla* [On the same path: Transition from preschool to primary school]. Reykjavík: RannUng & Háskólaútgáfan.

Garpelin, A. (2014). Transition to school: A rite of passage in life. In B. Perry, S. Dockett, & A. Petriwskyj (Eds.), *Transitions to school: International research, policy and practice* (pp. 117–128). Dordrecht: Springer.

Gervasoni, A., & Perry, B. (2015). Children's mathematical knowledge prior to starting school and implications for transition. In B. Perry, A. MacDonald, & A. Gervasoni (Eds.), *Mathematics and transition to school: International perspectives* (pp. 47–64). Dordrecht: Springer.

Golinkoff, R. M., Hirsh-Pasek, K., & Singer, D. G. (2006). Why play = learning: A challenge for parents and educators. In D. G. Singer, R. M. Golinkoff, & K. Hirsh-Pasek (Eds.), *Play=learning. How play motivates and enhances children's cognitive and social-emotional growth* (pp. 3–12). Oxford: Oxford University Press.

Hartley, C., Rogers, P., Smith, J., Peters, S., & Carr, M. (2012). *Crossing the border. A community negotiates the transition from early childhood to primary school*. Wellington: NZCER Press.

Hjallastefnan. (2014a). *Gender curriculum*. www-en.hjalli.is/information/ The_Gender_ Curriculum. Accessed 5 Jan 2016.

Hjallastefnan. (2014b). *Principles*. www-en.hjalli.is/information/principles. Accessed 5 Jan 2016.

Johnson, J., Celik, S., & Al-Mansour, M. (2013). Play in early childhood education. In O. Saracho & B. Spodek (Eds.), *Handbook of research on the education of young children* (3rd ed., pp. 265–274). New York: Routledge.

Kagan, S. L., & Tarrant, K. (2010). *Transitions for young children: Creating connections across early childhood systems*. Baltimore: Paul H. Brookes.

Kristjánsson, B. (2006). The making of Nordic childhoods. In J. Einarsdóttir & J. T. Wagner (Eds.), *Nordic childhoods and early education: Philosophy, research, policy and practice in Denmark, Finland, Iceland, Norway, and Sweden* (pp. 13–42). Greenwich: AGE Pub.

Laevers, F. (1994). The innovative project Experiential Education and the definition of quality in education. In F. Laevers (Ed.), *Defining and assessing quality in early childhood education* (pp. 159–172). Leuven: Leuven University Press.

Laevers, F., & Heylen, L. (Eds.). (2003). *Involvement of children and teacher style: Insights from an international study on experiential education*. Leuven: Leuven University Press.

Laidlaw, L., O'Mara, J., & Wong, S. (2015). "Daddy, look at the video I made on my iPad!" Reconceptualizing "readiness" in the digital age. In J. M. Iorio & W. Parnell (Eds.), *Rethinking readiness in early childhood education* (pp. 65–76). New York: Palgrave Macmillan.

Langford, J. (2010). Families and transitions. In S. L. Kagan & K. Tarrant (Eds.), *Transitions for young children: Creating connections across early childhood systems* (pp. 185–209). Baltimore: Paul H Brookes.

Lehrer, J., & Bastien, R. (2015). Ready for school? Lessons from a sociocultural investigation into mechanisms of preparation and classification of children for primary school from 1911 to 1979. In J. M. Iorio & W. Parnell (Eds.), *Rethinking readiness in early childhood education* (pp. 19–32). New York: Palgrave Macmillan.

Mac Naughton, G. (2005). *Doing Foucault in early childhood studies: Applying poststructural ideas*. New York: Routledge.

Malaguzzi, L. (1998). History, ideas, and basic philosophy: An interview with Lella Gandini. In C. Edwards (Ed.), *The hundred languages of children: The Reggio Emilia approach-advanced reflections* (2nd ed., pp. 49–97). London: Ablex.

Meyers, A. B., & Berk, L. E. (2014). Make-believe play and self-regulation. In L. Brooker, M. Blaise, & S. Edwards (Eds.), *The SAGE handbook of play and learning in early childhood* (pp. 43–55). London: Sage.

Ministry of Education. (1996). *Te Whāriki. He Whāriki Mātauranga mō ngā Mokopuna o Aotearoa. Early childhood curriculum*. Wellington: Ministry of Education.

Ministry of Education, Science and Culture. (2011). *Aðalnámskrá leikskóla* [The Icelandic national curriculum guide for preschools]. Reykjavík: Ministry of Education, Science and Culture. http://www.dalvikurbyggd.is/resources/Files/krilakot/adskr_leiksk_ens_2012.pdf. Accessed 5 Jan 2016.

Óskarsdóttir, G. G. (2012). *Skil skólastiga: Frá leikskóla til grunnskóla og grunnskóla til framhaldsskóla* [Across borders: From preschool to primary school and primary school to college] Reykjavík: Háskólaútgáfan & Skóla- og frístundasvið Reykjavíkurborgar.

Perry, B., Dockett, S., & Petriwskyj, A. (Eds.). (2014). *Transitions to school: International research, policy and practice.* Dordrecht: Springer.

Peters, S. (2010). *Literature review: Transition from early childhood education to school.* Report to the Ministry of Education. http://ece.manukau.ac.nz/__data/assets/pdf_file/0008/85841/956_ ECELitReview.pdf. Accessed 3 Aug 2015.

Peters, S. (2014). Chasms, bridges and borderlands: A transitions research 'Across the border' from early childhood education to school in New Zealand. In B. Perry, S. Dockett, & A. Petriwskyj (Eds.), *Transitions to school: International research, policy and practice* (pp. 105–116). Dordrecht: Springer.

Petriwskyj, A. (2014). Critical theory and inclusive transitions. In B. Perry, S. Dockett, & A. Petriwskyj (Eds.), *Transitions to school: International research, policy and practice* (pp. 201–215). Dordrecht: Springer.

Rinaldi, C. (2005). Documentation and assessment: What is the relationship? In A. Clark, A. T. Kjorholt, & P. Moss (Eds.), *Beyond listening: Children's perspectives on early childhood services* (pp. 17–28). Bristol: Policy Press.

Rogoff, B. (2003). *The cultural nature of human development.* Oxford: University Press.

Shonkoff, J., & Phillips, D. (2000). *From neurons to neighborhoods: The science of early childhood development.* Washington, DC: National Academy Press.

Siraj-Blatchford, I., & Sylva, K. (2004). Researching pedagogy in English pre-schools. *British Educational Research Journal, 30*(5), 713–730.

Smiley, P. A., & Dweck, C. (1994). Individual differences in achievement goals among young children. *Child Development, 65,* 1723–1743.

Smith, A. B. (2011). Respecting children's rights and agency. In D. Harcourt, B. Perry, & T. Waller (Eds.), *Researching young children's perspectives* (pp. 11–25). London: Routledge.

Sommer, D., Pramling Samuelsson, I., & Hundeide, K. (2010). *Child perspectives and children's perspectives in theory and practice.* London: Springer.

Sylva, K., Melhuish, E., Sammons, P., Siraj-Blatchford, I., & Taggart, B. (2004). *The effective provision of pre-school education (EPPE) project: Final report.* London: Institute of Education, University of London.

United Nations. (1989). *Convention on the rights of the child.* http://www.ohchr.org/en/professionalinterest/pages/crc.aspx. Accessed 10 Aug 2015.

Wells, G., & Claxton, G. (Eds.). (2002). *Learning for life in the 21st century: Sociocultural perspectives on the future of education.* Oxford: Blackwell.

Wood, E. (2014). The play-pedagogy interface in contemporary debates. In L. Brooker, M. Blaise, & S. Edwards (Eds.), *The SAGE handbook of play and learning in early childhood* (pp. 145–156). London: Sage.

Woodhead, M. (2005). Early childhood development: A question of rights. *International Journal of Early Childhood, 37*(3), 79–98.

Chapter 12
Contexts of Influence: Australian Approaches to Early Years Curriculum

Sue Dockett, Bob Perry, and Jessamy Davies

The study reported in this chapter has generated new knowledge promoting positive transitions to school through analysing the impact of the *Early Years Learning Framework* and the *Australian Curriculum* on transition to school and interrogating current pedagogies of educational transition, to inform the transition to school intentions of the two curricula. The project's significance is its potential to impact on the transition to school experiences of Australian children and families and, through this, to promote a positive start to school. Research outcomes address the development and implementation of pedagogies of transition at the time of school entry and the impact of the national curricula on these. The project used a mixed-method approach to interrogating policy intentions and implementation at the federal, state, systems and practitioner levels. It used a large number of face-to-face and telephone interviews, as well as a large-scale national survey of practitioners, concerning transition to school. The chapter provides a description of the structure of the overall project and an analysis of the federal level of data generation.

12.1 Introduction

Curriculum, pedagogy and assessment have been identified as the three 'message systems' of schooling (Bernstein 1975). These message systems have been described as 'symbiotic ... with change in one affecting the practices of the others' (Lingard

S. Dockett (✉) • J. Davies
Charles Sturt University, Albury, NSW, Australia
e-mail: sdockett@csu.edu.au

B. Perry
Research Institue for Professional Practice, Learning and Education (RIPPLE),
Charles Sturt University, Albury, NSW, Australia

© Springer International Publishing Switzerland 2017
N. Ballam et al. (eds.), *Pedagogies of Educational Transitions*, International
Perspectives on Early Childhood Education and Development 16,
DOI 10.1007/978-3-319-43118-5_12

2009, p. 13). Hence, changes in the curriculum frameworks that inform early childhood and school education influence, and are in turn influenced by, changes in pedagogy and assessment. In this chapter, we consider relationships between curriculum (as policy) and pedagogy, particularly the role of pedagogy in enacting the curriculum and the ways in which pedagogies are shaped through changes in curriculum.

Our focus is directed to the pedagogies of educational transition, specifically, the transition to school. We frame this discussion by providing some historical context to both early childhood and school education in Australia, outlining the path to the two recent curriculum reforms, culminating in Australia's first national Early Years Learning Framework and first national school curriculum. Both of these curriculum documents reflect specific policy directions and are relevant for educators who work with children in the early childhood years (birth to age 8).

Our ongoing analysis of the policy-to-practice context of these documents uses Ball's (1993, 2006) policy trajectory model. In this chapter, we report the first phase of analysis, focusing on the context of influence, and explore the ways in which policy has been initiated and policy discourse constructed. In attending to policy discourses, we recognise the power of such discourses to frame our discussions, expectations and assumptions, as well as the development and enactment of pedagogies to support these.

12.2 Background

12.2.1 Early Childhood Education

Early childhood education and care (ECEC) in Australia has a long and complex history. Preschool provision for 4-year-olds has been available in some locations for well over 100 years. However, it was only during the 1950s and 1960s that families started to embrace the educational function of preschool, particularly in relation to preparing children for school (Elliott 2006). In contrast, from the beginning of the twentieth century, childcare was provided as a welfare service for families living in poverty. Even in this early history, the divide between educational preschool programmes and compensatory childcare was established (Brennan and O'Donnell 1986). Over the last century, this division has variously expanded and contracted, largely dependent on the social, economic and political contexts of the time.

From around the 1970s, the issue of women's workforce participation has been linked to the availability, affordability and accessibility of childcare. As a result, there has been rapid expansion of both public and private childcare provision. However, preschool education has remained the province of states and territories, with access and affordability distributed unequally across the country (Brennan and O'Donnell 1986). Tensions between access to ECEC as an educational entitlement for children and/or providing the means for women to engage in the workforce are long standing. They draw upon a complex set of factors that includes attitudes towards working mothers, economic imperatives, state and federal government responsibilities, the costs and benefits, and social and academic outcomes of ECEC.

Soon after being elected in 2007, the Labor government introduced a raft of reforms predicated on the positioning of ECEC as a key component of a promised 'education revolution'. These reforms were:

> ... an integrated package of early childhood initiatives across health, education, development and care ... pitched as both an equity agenda and productivity reform ... the plan ... was solidly grounded in the international research on brain development and the economic analysis of the benefits of investment in quality early childhood education and care. (Jarvie and Mercer 2014, p. 4)

ECEC was positioned both as an educational good, preparing children for school and helping to ameliorate educational disadvantage, and a means for enhancing productivity by facilitating workforce participation. The commitment to develop the first national early childhood curriculum approach – the Early Years Learning Framework – was envisioned as a platform to 'increase the emphasis on learning and development within Early Learning Centres', with the caution that it would not be 'a school-like curriculum and will not result in early childhood centres becoming schools'. Rather, it was to emphasise age-appropriate learning and 'play as the vehicle through which young children learn' (Rudd et al. 2007, p. 2). A key theme across this policy was the focus on school readiness. Children's involvement in ECEC was identified as setting the 'foundation for success or failure at school and life beyond', with the caution that 'even by school age it may be too late to intervene to influence a child's learning and motivation if bad learning practices habits are already entrenched' (Rudd et al. 2007, p. 10).

12.2.2 School Education

School education in Australia also has a long history. By the end of the ninetieth century, various states had legislation in place that supported free, compulsory and secular education for children from the age of 6 years, while also retaining provision for denominational schools (Shorten 1996). The responsibility for schools has remained a state and territory responsibility, despite the formation of a federal government in 1901.

Differences and discrepancies across the states and territories were almost inevitable and were reflected in different starting school ages, nomenclature and curriculum. In recent years, differences were also noted in the performance of students in national and international testing programmes, often attributed to the different curricula and approaches taken.

Australia has participated in international benchmarking since 1994 (Gable and Lingard 2013). Student performance on international surveys, such as *Programme for International Student Assessment* (PISA) (Organisation for Economic Co-operation and Development [OECD], 2015), *Trends in International*

Mathematics and Science Study (TIMSS) (International Association for the Evaluation of Educational Achievement [IEA], 2015) and *Progress in International Reading Literacy Study* (PIRLS) (IEA 2015), has become a preferred measure of the effectiveness of education systems (Masters 2010) and, through this, a key driver of domestic educational policy (Rizvi and Lingard 2010).

In recent decades, there have been several attempts to develop and implement a national school curriculum in Australia. In the main, these have been unsuccessful because the constitutional responsibility for school education resides with states and territories, and any national curriculum requires agreement across each jurisdiction as well as with the federal government. Despite this, the federal government has utilised several strategies to influence educational policy (Brennan 2011; Reid 2009).

Part of the 'education revolution' involved the development of a national curriculum, facilitated by the Council of Australian Governments (COAG). Starting in 2008, COAG endorsed the staged development of a national curriculum with the first four subject areas – English, mathematics, science and history – launched in 2010. Further areas have followed, but it will be some years before full implementation is achieved. Curriculum for each area has two major components: content and achievement standards. In addition, the Australian curriculum outlines a number of general capabilities that cross subject boundaries and three cross-curriculum priorities (Australian Curriculum, Assessment and Reporting Authority [ACARA] 2012).

12.3   The Policy Documents: Early Years Learning Framework and the Australian Curriculum

Evolving from this context were two curriculum documents: *Belonging, Being and Becoming: The Early Years Learning Framework for Australia* (EYLF) (Department of Education, Employment and Workforce Relations [DEEWR] 2009) and the *Australian Curriculum* (AC) (ACARA 2014). They reflect the first national Australian curriculum approaches for the early childhood and school sectors, respectively.

Both documents were central to the 'education revolution' of the Labor government and, as such, reflected both the human capital and equity focus inherent in identifying desirable outcomes for all. Both are mandated within relevant educational settings across Australia, and both draw upon outcome-based frameworks, albeit in different ways. Despite this, the only explicit connection between the documents is the stated intention of the AC to 'build on the national Early Years Learning Framework and … to accommodate the varied learning experiences that children experience prior to school' (ACARA 2012, p. 10). The suggested pathways for this accommodation align the EYLF's broad learning outcomes with the general capabilities of the AC (Connor 2011).

Differences are evident in the structure and organisation, as well as the content, of the documents. For example, the EYLF is described as a learning framework that 'provides general goals or outcomes for children's learning and how they might be attained' as well as a 'scaffold to assist early childhood settings to develop their own, more detailed curriculum' (DEEWR 2009, p. 46). In contrast, the AC 'is presented as a continuum that makes clear what is to be taught across the years of schooling. It makes clear to students what they should learn and the quality of learning expected of them as they progress through school' (ACARA 2012, p. 10).

The AC is organised around discrete subject areas, whereas the EYLF adopts a holistic approach to curriculum. Both documents describe learning outcomes, yet in quite different ways. The AC outlines achievement standards aligned with each year of schooling and each subject area, whereas the EYLF notes five broad learning outcomes to be promoted for all children across their early childhood years. The role and place of pedagogy within each document also vary. The EYLF (DEEWR 2009, p. 13) defines pedagogy as the 'professional practice of early childhood educators, especially those aspects that involve building and nurturing relationships, curriculum decision making, teaching and learning'. While the AC offers no general definition of pedagogy, each subject document makes some general statements about preferred pedagogy within that domain.

12.4   Transition to School Policy

The concurrent introduction of two new curricula governing the early childhood years has provided a unique opportunity to examine both the policy expectations around transition to school and the practices adopted to implement and support these. The importance of a positive transition to school is well established. Children who make a successful start to school are likely to engage positively with school, and this is reflected in long-term outcomes (Alexander and Entwisle 1998). Recent conceptualisations of transition position it as a dynamic process of continuity and change as children move into the first year of school. Linked to this conceptualisation, the *Transition to School: Position Statement* (Educational Transitions and Change [ETC] Research Group 2011) outlines four pillars of transition: opportunities, expectations, aspirations and entitlements.

In recent years, policy directions around the transition to school have drawn on social and economic agendas, identifying a positive start to, and continued engagement with, school as one way of disrupting cycles of social and economic disadvantage. The underlying assumption has been that 'improved transition to school' leads to 'improved educational employment, health and well-being outcomes' (COAG 2009, p. 4), resulting in the reduction of 'inequalities in outcomes between groups of children' (p. 6).

Despite this, there is limited reference to transition to school in the EYLF and no mention of it in the AC. However, the regulatory framework outlined in the *National Quality Standard* (Australian Children's Education and Care Quality Authority

[ACECQA] 2013), in which the EYLF is embedded, invites prior-to-school educators to consider the question: 'How do we support each child's successful transition to formal schooling?'

As education remains a statutory responsibility for states and territories in Australia, they, too, retain the responsibility for transition to school. While all provide information and advice about starting school to families and educators, only some have developed dedicated policies around transition and produced a range of resources to support these.

12.5 Pedagogies of Educational Transition

Pedagogies – the processes that 'make vital connections between teaching, learning, knowledge, society and politics' based on 'a vision about society, people and knowledge' (Farquhar and White 2014, p. 822) – have the potential to play an integral role in supporting positive transitions. Pedagogies have both relational (de Lissovoy 2010) and instructional elements (Siraj-Blatchford et al. 2002) and are informed and shaped by a range of theories, beliefs, policies and controversies (Alexander 2008).

Research investigating pedagogies of educational transition is relatively new. While there is considerable literature and research around the areas of pedagogy (Alexander 2008; Siraj-Blatchford et al. 2002) and transition to school (Perry et al. 2014), there has been much less attention directed towards pedagogies *of* educational transition.

Transition to school provides a unique context in which to consider pedagogical practices. It is a time when the different contexts, curricula, policies and approaches converge in a common space, both physically and conceptually (ETC Research Group 2011). As the basis for our investigation of pedagogies of educational transition, we draw on established definitions of pedagogy and the *Transition to School: Position Statement*, to define pedagogies of educational transition as:

> … the interactive processes and strategies that enable the development of opportunities, aspirations, expectations and entitlements for children, families, educators, communities and educational systems around transition to school, together with the theories, beliefs, policies and controversies that shape them. (Davies 2014)

Many factors influence pedagogies of educational transition. We start our investigation of these by applying the policy trajectory model.

12.6 Policy Trajectory Model

The policy trajectory model (Ball 1993, 2006) recognises that policies are developed and enacted in three discrete, yet interlinked, contexts: the context of influence (where policy is initiated and policy discourses constructed), the context of production (where policy related to implementation is created) and the context of practice (where policy is interpreted and reinterpreted by educators as it is implemented in practice). In this project, these three contexts are represented, respectively, by the national ECEC reform agenda and the impetus for the AC, state/territory and organisational/systems approaches and guidelines to promote implementation of the curricula and local educational practice as educators implement the new curricula.

In this chapter we explore the context of influence, where key policy discourses and concepts are described, deliberated and decided. The context of influence frames the processes of policy development. It is in this space that national and international trends, as well as local issues, impact on policy directions and intentions. These influences feed into the development of policy documents (texts), which, in turn, influence the implementation of policy. However, it is important to note that this is far from a linear process. There are interconnections between and across all levels, as both top-down and bottom-up processes intertwine in the processes of policy development.

12.7   The Project

Our exploration of the context of policy influence began with a broad-brush focus on the discourses underpinning the development of the EYLF and the AC. Our focus was on understanding the curriculum documents and their development through analysis of:

1. The policy contexts of influence for each of the new curricula
2. References to pedagogies of educational transition within the policy documents

12.8   Method

Our investigation used interpretive methods to seek the views of a wide range of participants who had been involved in, or had influenced, the development of early childhood and/or school policy. We recognise that the recollections of those who may no longer be involved in policy positions have potential limitations, and, as in similar studies (Aubrey and Durmaz 2012), we have attempted to balance these by seeking the views of multiple participants and analysis of policy documents.

12.8.1   Participants

Potential participants were identified through their past and/or present roles in senior management positions within organisations, systems, agencies and committees involved in the development of early childhood and/or school policy. This approach aimed to identify not only leaders of organisations but also those who had 'important social networks, social capital and strategic positions within social structures' (Harvey 2011, p. 433). These people were considered 'policy elites': 'high profile personnel who have had access to specialised knowledge and power and ... [who have the potential to] provide valuable policy information' (Logan et al. 2014).

While interested in policy developments over the past decade, our focal point was the raft of reforms introduced by the federal Labor government after their election in 2007. As this project commenced in 2013, after there had been a further change of government, contacting potential participants presented some challenges. This was particularly the case for those policymakers who had changed role or left the field, as well as those balancing the demands of a new government in their continuing roles.

After approvals to conduct the study had been granted by the University Ethics Committee and relevant organisations and authorities, the research team set about identifying potential participants. Initial contact provided information about the study and ascertained whether or not the potential participant was willing to be involved. In-depth, semi-structured interviews were held with 29 policymakers. Six invitations to participate were declined, citing reasons based on withdrawal from public life, changes in responsibilities, concern that their comments may make it possible to identify them and/or their organisation and potential conflicts with current roles.

Interviews tended to be lengthy, extending to well over an hour in many cases and covering many different areas of policy development. The mode of interview reflected the preferences of interviewees and encompassed face-to-face, telephone, Skype and written responses to interview questions. With participant consent, interviews were audio-recorded and transcribed for analysis. During each interview, a snowballing technique was used to extend the sample, as participants were invited to suggest further contacts.

12.8.2   Results

We report the preliminary results generated from the analysis of data related to two areas from the interviews:

1. Perceptions of policy changes and the key drivers (national and/or international) for these
2. Relevance of policy for the transition to school

We have described the results as preliminary, as the potential to seek, locate and contact policy elites has been extended with each interview. In reporting comments, we have used the general descriptors of early childhood and school policymakers as a strategy to promote anonymity. We have presented data from early childhood and school policymakers separately, before considering connections and exploring the implications for educational transitions.

Across the interviews, a range of discourses has defined ways of thinking and speaking about the policy intentions underlying the two approaches to curriculum. Naming these has drawn upon Foucault's (1972) position that discourse 'constructs the topic … defines and produces the objects of our knowledge … [and] governs the way that a topic can be meaningfully talked about and reasoned about' (Hall 1997, p. 44). It has also allowed us to question the way some discourses are more authoritative than others and how this authority is established and maintained, as other discourses are marginalised.

12.8.2.1 The Early Years Learning Framework

Part of a Larger Whole

In the space of a few years, Australian early childhood policy became a national focus, resulting in the adoption of a National Quality Framework, underpinned by the EYLF and a National Quality Standard (NQS). This paved the way for a national regulatory framework – something that had never been achieved before. Early childhood policymakers noted the scale of policy changes, describing these as *absolutely massive reforms*, requiring a great deal of *commitment, compromise and collaboration*. This was aided by the political situation, where all states and territories were, at the same time, led by the Labor party. In the words of several policymakers, *the stars were aligned*.

A COAG working group was established to pursue the collaboration. This group was *managed at the Commonwealth level, but involve[d] representatives from each state and territory*. Policymakers spoke of the compromise, as well as commitment, required to generate a *much more unifying national frame* for ECEC policy.

While policymakers talked of the *goodwill* involved, they also noted tensions:

… it was certainly clear that relationships were not always happy between the states and territories. They were coming from very different positions.

In addition to the tangible outcomes – such as the NQS and the EYLF – policymakers described *greater cohesion* across the sector, enhanced *professionalism and recognition* of both early childhood education and educators as a result of the reforms. The EYLF, in particular, was regarded as *helping to build the integrity of the field*.

Policymakers involved in the ECEC reforms described the range, extent and timing of these as *phenomenal, astonishing* and *a real achievement*. The EYLF played a major role in this agenda, developed as the first element of a national quality agenda. It was also developed prior to the AC, with the aim to:

… some extent … set some of the parameters for thinking about the Australian Curriculum. So there was a sense that there was some urgency to do that, to help forestall any tendency for a push down from the Australian Curriculum.

Despite the urgency involved, the development of the EYLF before the AC was regarded positively by ECEC policymakers. While some hoped that the AC might *build on* the EYLF, others were concerned that an established AC could have resulted in an *add-on* for early childhood. *I think in a number of places, the [early childhood] profession was ... tired of being told what to do by schools.*

Consistent reference was made to the sense of urgency underpinning the reforms. The election of the Labor government resulted in an *explosion in a number of reforms that were to be* delivered and political pressure to deliver these *fast, very fast.*

International Influences

Several themes underlying the rationale for the major changes in ECEC policy were identified. There was consensus that, internationally, there was *an early childhood turn, our time in the sun.* All early childhood policymakers interviewed referred to the impact of international attention, particularly from OECD reports and overseas research:

> ... there were a lot of global influences. So things like the OECD report, *Starting Strong*, the 2006 report and also the UNICEF report that came out in 2009 ... they were both reflective of worldwide interest in what was happening in early childhood ... that worldwide interest was driven by a strong human capital agenda and investing in the early years ... the brain research and the influential reports from Canada and also from the US ...that was all very salient. And then interest in what was happening in the UK with Sure Start and EPPE [Effective Provision for Pre-school Education] ... there was a lot of global momentum and ... the pretty poor review that Australia was given by the OECD in 2006 and also in the UNICEF report ... we didn't come out of that looking very good.

Overseas Research Was Influential

> There was also all the work that was being done in brain development and ... the Heckman work on economics ... there was an upsurge internationally around providing reasons, good evidence for why we should move into that space.

International research was regarded as more authoritative than its Australian counterpart: *with Heckman, it's not bad for ... politicians to be able to quote a Nobel Prize winner... it helps to win the argument.* Partly this was attributed to a weak Australian research base:

> ... there wasn't much of a research base in Australia ... we were looking at what was occurring overseas ... crucial pieces of evidence ... used as some kind of evidence base for the Australian context.

National, as well as international, factors influenced ECEC policy. Of particular note were the location of ECEC within the human capital agenda, focus on productivity and equity, national consistency (particularly quality), market issues and the enhanced professionalisation of the workforce.

Investing in Human Capital

Framing ECEC with a human capital agenda in Australia did not start with the reforms of the Labor government, but it was highlighted during this time. Several interviewees noted the moves to highlight investment in human capital:

> We had … all the big economic reforms of the 80s and 90s and now it was investment in human capital … to skill up the nation for the 21st century.
> Early childhood had a place in the human capital agenda … a key place in a bigger reform agenda.

Arguments for improving ECEC also drew on issues of productivity and equity:

> [It was important to] link women's work particularly and workforce participation and having childcare available.
> It's about equity … making sure all children … wherever they are … have the opportunity to access high-quality education.

National Consistency

Recent Organisation for Economic Co-operation and Development (OECD) reports (2001, 2006) had described the complexity of ECEC in Australia, noting the multi-layered levels of administration and regulation, as well as quality issues linked to the training, status and conditions of staff. Part of the motivation for reform came through the opportunity to address these concerns:

> [With the change of government] there came a clearly defined policy for education and care around national consistency and quality, which included the national regulation of the whole sector and greater involvement by the Commonwealth, particularly in terms of funding universal access to preschool education for the 15 h in the year prior to school, with … a promise that regardless of where they resided in Australia they would receive that.

Market issues provided another motivation for change. ABC Learning was one the world's largest providers of ECEC. In 2008, the company collapsed, generating *a political nightmare for the Commonwealth Government but … also a driver to do something around the quality agenda.* There was:

> … frustration involved at not really being able to do anything about that … a sense of wanting to get into a position where that couldn't happen again … a sense of wanting to put in place a strong, quality framework, to at least try to mitigate against some of the … things that appeared to be happening with ABC Learning.

The quality framework also had the potential to impact on the professionalisation of the early childhood workforce:

> … it was very much around the professionalisation of the sector, the regulation of the profession in comparison to schools … early childhood teachers felt that they were the poor relations of the school teachers who looked upon them as not being as professional …it was about lifting the status of educators.

ECEC policymakers concurred that the EYLF had been well received by the profession and was an important tool in responding to the policy drivers noted above. The acceptance of the document was attributed to its integral role in the package of reforms and its contribution to enhancing professionalisation. The EYLF has been:

> … more than accepted, really embraced. It has provided a strong foundation for all the quality reform work which is linked to it … it really has worked to lift the status of the field or the self-perception and morale of educators … The built-in flexibility of the document has allowed early childhood professional practice to occur without being prescriptive and able to be customised to the local context and the individual child … it's been quite successful.

12.8.2.2   The Australian Curriculum

The Australian Curriculum, Assessment and Reporting Authority (ACARA) was established in 2012 to lead the development of the AC. To date, national curricula across a number of subject areas have been developed and are currently being implemented.

School education policymakers noted both the achievement and the ongoing challenges involved:

> A decade ago … if I'd been asked if we would ever have anything national in education, I would have doubted that happening … because … of some of the entrenched views within states and territories about their own products and their desire to not be involved in anything at a national level.

The COAG process has been instrumental in pursuing the national curriculum agenda. However, the process has not been without tensions, particularly around the notion that the national curriculum development process has usurped state responsibilities:

> … in previous attempts there was politically and culturally much more emphasis on issues of states' rights. That political principle … has … been replaced by a different level of more localised ownership process.

While the documentation is referred to as national curriculum, several policymakers distinguished between curriculum and standards:

> A key point that distinguishes this from previous efforts is that we now [have] a set of standards, [but these do] not determine how the curriculum is organised and delivered. What we have got as a national curriculum … is a set of content and achievement standards organised by disciplines, with general capabilities and all those other things in mind.

A Long Lead Time

The staged development and introduction of the national curriculum mean that the process has already been going for several years and has several more to come. The issue of timing and the pace of curriculum reform was mentioned by most school education policymakers. Some noted the *bureaucratic and political timelines, which were very tight*; others talked of the need for a *long lead time* and the associated *desire of states and territories not to do anything quickly or that would unsettle what they have.*

One of the major differences between school and ECEC curriculum is that school curricula have been in place in each state and territory for many years. Often, it has taken considerable time to develop and implement these curricula. Change also requires considerable time.

Accountability Through Comparison

Several reasons were advanced by policymakers for the moves towards a national curriculum. These included international influences, such as testing or international research, as well as national policy drivers.

Education sectors are influenced by the need to be more accountable, and the key drivers are those things that can be measured. PISA and TIMSS data, National Assessment Program – Literacy and Numeracy (NAPLAN) results and other common data are used to measure progress within Australia and internationally. References to international research focused on comparisons between and among countries. International benchmarking was of interest, particularly around the level of expectations for students. However, the complexity of comparing different systems and the value of such comparison were also noted. A broader international dimension was also described:

> There's an international dimension to that but isn't directly PISA or TIMSS or anything. It's more about who we are as a nation in a global context.

Learning from Practice

In addition to international comparisons, *existing effective practice* was identified as a policy driver:

> … when we're working in curriculum, we like to draw on what we see or hear about as practice that is making a difference … We're drawn to that from academic papers. We're drawn by the schooling authorities that tell us about who their best practitioners are. And so we draw on what they're doing, what they're reading about, what they're finding. So … you draw on … best practice in the field.

Despite this, one policymaker described a reluctance to support a particular theoretical or philosophical approach because:

> … unlike early childhood, there's been a strong media focus on ideology with schooling to the point where no one is game to actually credit a particular approach for fear that it will be undone by an attack, an exposure in the media as being some either right-wing sort of push or a progressive push. So … people are reluctant, I think, to name their heroes.

Reasons advanced for a national curriculum most often reflected national perspectives. These included increased efficiencies, greater consistency across jurisdictions and support for mobile students.

Increased Efficiencies from National Consistency

The economic argument for a national curriculum rested on the increased efficiency to be gained by having a common curriculum, a broad market for resources and a platform for common professional development:

> [There's] the realisation that education is resource intensive. If you're going to use your [limited] resources well, [you have to ask], where is it best to spend those? Most of the logic says the investment has to happen closest to where the child is … running expensive exercises to develop curriculum, duplicating … across eight different jurisdictions, someone has to ask the question: Is that the best investment of money?

Increased efficiencies were linked to equity arguments:

> [Some] states and territories … are large enough to be able to bring great resources to bear, to set expectations for their young people. Why wouldn't we use that and leverage that to work for the [other states and territories] who don't have the same resource capacity, the same expertise base to do it?

Policymakers emphasised that the interpretation and implementation of curriculum rested with states and territories and, as a consequence, variation remained across the country:

> Every state and territory has its own history and its own complex set of stakeholders to bring with them. So to think that you can write a national curriculum and they would all say at once 'Forget everything we've done up until now, we'll all start together at once' would be naïve.

Support for Mobile Students

Policymakers indicated that this argument resonated with public perceptions of the national curriculum, but did not feature strongly in the rationale for its development. Partly, this was because the state and territory variation of curriculum implementation meant that there was unlikely to be an exact match between the curricula in each context:

> Initially [the national curriculum] was portrayed [as support] because people moved around the country with work and it was helpful if their children had the same basic curriculum wherever they went … [now] there's a view that Australia will be a more effective knowledge base and employment base if there's some common important strands [of] … learning.

12.8.3   Connections Between the Early Years Learning… Framework and Australian Curriculum

Policymakers indicated that there was no specific connection between the two curriculum documents. Indeed, there was consensus that *they're two different frameworks* and *at the policy level they were treated quite separately*. For some, this was evidence of the *divide between early childhood and schools*.

While a collaborative document had been developed linking the outcomes of the EYLF with the general capabilities of the AC (Connor 2011), there was an agreement that:

> ... the best way to articulate them was through the pedagogical practice ... the Australian Curriculum doesn't dictate anything about pedagogy, whereas the Early Years Learning Framework is more focused around pedagogy ... [articulation would happen when] people used the pedagogical practices of the Early Years Learning Framework as they delivered the Australian Curriculum ...

The independent development of the two curriculum documents was cited as evidence that *early childhood ... is a different phase and a different purpose*:

> ... there's a difference there because of the variation across prior-to-school settings and the base from which they were coming. The EYLF is more than a set of standards. It's a stronger pedagogical statement ... in comparison to the AC.

A further difference was noted in the processes for developing the curriculum documents:

> ... in early childhood it was like a clean field so you could work through it but with the Australian curriculum, curriculum approaches in each state and territory were fairly well entrenched and embedded and no one wanted to give way to the way they wanted to approach content ... hopefully, as things bed down around the AC then we can have something that shows more continuity from early childhood into the school space.

While the timing of the development of the EYLF was such that it could have influenced the AC, this had not happened. One explanation offered was that:

> [There was] no overlap across curricula development – I think in terms of the Australian Curriculum ... the voices of early childhood in those discussions and framing were not being heard ... With the Australian Curriculum, people were more worried about the content in the school space ... and the development of the Australian Curriculum was an incredibly political process.

Comments from the early childhood sector about the possible *schoolification* of ECEC with the pushing down of school expectations are also relevant.

12.8.4   Transition to School Policy

Transition to school is mentioned in the EYLF, but not in the AC:

> ... the EYLF ... does talk a little bit about transitions. It probably could have gone a lot further in some ways. But it's very easy to slip into transition as orientation ... and passage of information, rather than all of the kinds of things you need to think about in terms of new experiences or familiar experiences or thinking about it from children's and families' perspectives of helping them to understand different environments and to operate within them.

Discussions of transition raised issues of continuity and recognition of prior learning:

... people in settings ... in the classrooms ... the teachers ... need to be given some advice ... about continuity of learning.

I think there are still people in the school space who say well ... learning still begins at the school door ... We haven't done a good job of selling that to schools.

There was an agreement that greater attention is needed in each of these areas and that this can only be achieved by working across sectors:

... if we really want to get that transition happening smoothly you need people from the other sectors involved in the work. I guess the critical part is to get that balance right. You don't want to have too many from either side pushing the line. And there are always issues about territory ... whose job is it and who knows more about it than someone else. But if you want to get a smooth transition you have to have involvement from both sectors.

Pedagogies of educational transition offer a space for this to occur:

People ask, what does it mean for the children coming from that sector to that sector? ... transition is a good context, a good place for partnership ...

12.9   Discussion

In this chapter, we have drawn on Ball's (1993, 2006) policy trajectory model to explore the context of influence in the development of policy that impacts on transition to school. This is the context where public policy is initiated and policy discourses are constructed and where decisions are made about what is valued and, by omission, what is not valued. As such, it is an integral part of our consideration of pedagogies of educational transition, which were defined earlier in the chapter.

There have been major changes to educational policy in Australia in the past decade. These have occurred within both the ECEC sector and the school sector. While there are some commonalities, there are also differences in the ways these changes have been approached, developed and promulgated.

Both ECEC and school education were positioned within the 'education revolution' of the federal Labor government when it was elected in 2007. Both sectors were the focus of intense debate and collaboration at the highest levels of policy – represented by COAG.

Both sectors were regarded as fundamental elements of the human capital agenda, supported by arguments around the importance of investing in the early years and preparing Australia's children and young people for their participation in the global economy. To this end, policymakers looked to international trends. In the early childhood sector, this involved recognition and acceptance of the evidence from *the brain research* and *Heckman's graph*. In the school education sector, looking to international testing and the comparative performance of Australian children was important.

In general, ECEC policymakers looked to overseas research, arguing that such a research base did not exist in Australia, while school education policymakers looked to practice and subject traditions as the basis for developing the curriculum documents. There was a clear effort on the part of the EYLF working party to develop an approach that would boost the profession. In contrast, school education policymakers seemed to have one eye looking towards international comparisons and the other looking to reinforce perceptions of existing *good practice*. Perhaps the different approaches signify the professional differences across the sectors, with early childhood educators not yet enjoying the status and working conditions of their school-based peers.

Policy development across both sectors aimed for national consistency. The EYLF was the first of many reforms for the sector, as efforts were made to promote equity of access to settings where the focus was on both education and care. Inherent in the reforms were commitments to improving the quality of ECEC provided across the country. While setting national curriculum directions for the first time was an important outcome, so, too, was the accompanying professionalisation of the sector.

In contrast, states and territories had developed school curriculum and engaged in curriculum reform for many years. Across the country, there were many established ways of 'doing' curriculum at the policy level. Much had been invested in the development of resources and support materials and in the professional development of teachers around the existing curriculum. Changing such well-established structures takes time. A long lead-in time also was required to reach consensus about a national curriculum and the time frame for implementation. It is unlikely that the full development, roll-out and implementation of the national curriculum will be achieved within a decade, given that several years have already elapsed.

The early childhood reforms were undertaken in a relatively short time frame – from the announcement of the 'education revolution' to the publication of the EYLF was a period of less than 3 years. Early childhood policymakers both revelled in the chance to have their *turn in the sun* and worked tirelessly to achieve reform while the opportunity lasted.

Neither curriculum document would have been possible without willingness and compromise. This was helped by the political alignment of state, territory and federal governments, generating a political will for reform. Noting that political will is not sufficient for reform, Flottman and Page (2012) argued that the evidence base and social strategy accompanying the ECEC reforms provided the basis for wide-scale change.

A further point of similarity is that neither curriculum document is described as prescriptive. The EYLF was conceived as a curriculum framework, rather than a curriculum. Educators are encouraged to identify and build on the strengths of children and families and to use a range of pedagogies to help children achieve five broad outcomes. The AC does detail content, specifying outcomes, but does not detail any pedagogical approach. This is a task that rests with education systems. Hence, some policymakers have described the AC as a set of national standards, rather than a curriculum.

Despite the development of the two curriculum documents occurring at around the same time, there was little interaction across the sectors. This may well be because they were indeed different documents for different purposes, drawing on different philosophical positions and different histories and traditions. It could even be the case that such separate development was a strategy for each sector to 'protect' itself from the other, that is, to retain its own identify and focus. The comments from ECEC policymakers indicating a desire for the EYLF to be in place before the AC and concerns from some about the potential 'schoolification' of the EYLF suggest that this may have been so.

Nevertheless, children making the transition from ECEC settings to school and their families, as well as educators who work across the different sectors, 'live' the two curriculum approaches. They experience the connections or disconnections and the continuities or discontinuities, associated with moving from one sector to another. Some efforts have been made to align the documents by linking the outcomes of the EYLF with the general capabilities in the AC. However, policymakers have indicated that the real work of generating connections between the policy approaches occurs in practice. Transition provides the space for this to occur.

12.10   Conclusion

We began this chapter by recognising the role of Bernstein's three message systems in education and the interrelationships among curriculum, pedagogy and assessment. In this chapter, we have explored recent changes to curriculum and the drivers for these. According to Bernstein (1975, p. 85), 'curriculum defines what counts as valid knowledge'. Hence, we expect each of the approaches to curriculum to outline what is valued in each context.

The rationales underpinning the EYLF relate to both the development of the profession and moves to national consistency. The EYLF has been part of a larger raft of reforms, supporting the human capital agenda, but also framed in terms of promoting productivity and equity. Early childhood educators are positioned as professionals, capable of determining appropriate content for children and using a range of pedagogies to achieve this. This suggests a valuing of process over content.

Rationales for the development of national school curriculum have addressed issues of accountability, comparison, efficiency and consistency. The nomination of specific content, in the form of national standards, suggests an approach that values and expects consistent learning outcomes for all children and young people. In the case of a school curriculum, building human capital involves ensuring children and young people acquire the skills and knowledge to equip them for participation in the global economy. How this is achieved is not prescribed at the national level; this remains the province of different education systems.

The transition to school generates an interface between these two approaches to curriculum. It is to be expected that educators working to support children's transition to school draw upon what is valued within their own contexts. Their curriculum focus will influence their approaches to pedagogies and assessment. As we explore the other contexts of Ball's (1993, 2006) policy trajectory model – the context of policy text production and the context of practice – we aim to explore these connections in greater detail and to investigate what is possible in this interface.

Acknowledgement We acknowledge the funding provided for this project by the Australian Research Council Discovery Grant DP130104276, over the period 2013–2016. We extend our appreciation to additional members of the research team – Paige Lee, Emma Kearney and Kathryn Hopps – and to all those who shared their experiences and expertise with us.

References

Alexander, R. (2008). Pedagogy, curriculum and culture. In P. Murphy, K. Hall, & J. Soler (Eds.), *Pedagogy and practice: Culture and identities* (pp. 3–27). London: Sage.

Alexander, K., & Entwisle, D. (1998). Facilitating the transition to first grade: The nature of transition and research on factors. *Elementary School Journal, 98*(4), 351–364.

Aubrey, C., & Durmaz, D. (2012). Policy-to-practice contexts for early childhood mathematics in England. *International Journal of Early Years Education, 20*(1), 59–77. doi:10.1080/0966976 0.2012.664475.

Australian Children's Education and Care Quality Authority (ACECQA). (2013). *Guide to the national quality standard.* http://files.acecqa.gov.au/files/National-Quality-Framework-Resources-Kit/NQF03-Guide-to-NQS-130902.pdf. Accessed 26 Feb 2015.

Australian Curriculum, Assessment and Reporting Authority (ACARA). (2012). The shape of the Australian Curriculum, Version 4. http://www.acara.edu.au/verve/_resources/the_shape_of_the_australian_curriculum_v4. pdf. Accessed 26 Feb 2015.

Australian Curriculum, Assessment and Reporting Authority (ACARA). (2014). Australian Curriculum. http://www.australiancurriculum.edu.au/. Accessed 26 Feb 2015.

Ball, S. J. (1993). What is policy? Texts, trajectories and toolboxes. *Discourse, 13*(2), 10–17.

Ball, S. J. (2006). *Education policy and social class.* London: Routledge.

Bernstein, B. (1975). *Towards a theory of educational transmissions* (Vol. 3). London: Routledge & Kegan Paul.

Brennan, M. (2011). National curriculum: A political-educational triangle. *Australian Journal of Education, 55*(3), 259–280. doi:10.1177/000494411105500307.

Brennan, D., & O'Donnell, C. (1986). *Caring for Australia's children.* Sydney: Allen & Unwin.

Connor, J. (2011). *Foundations for learning: Relationships between the early years learning framework and the Australian Curriculum an ECA-ACARA paper.* Canberra: ECA. http://foundationinquirylearning.global2.vic.edu.au/files/2013/06/ECA_ACARA_Foundations_Paper-2cq59mi.pdf. Accessed 26 Feb 2015.

Council of Australian Governments. (2009). *Investing in the early years – A national early childhood development strategy.* https://www.coag.gov.au/sites/default/files/national_ECD_strategy.pdf. Accessed 26 Feb 2015.

Davies. J. (2014). *Pedagogies of educational transitions: Continuity and change as children start school in rural areas.* Unpublished research proposal. Charles Sturt University.

De Lissovoy, N. (2010). Pedagogy in common: Democratic education in the global era. *Educational Philosophy and Theory, 43*(10), 1119–1134.

Department of Education Employment and Workplace Relations (DEEWR). (2009). *Belonging, being and becoming: The early years learning framework for Australia.* Department of Education Employment and Workplace Relations. https://docs.education.gov.au/system/files/doc/other/belonging_being_and_becoming_the_early_years_learning_framework_for_australia.pdf. Accessed 26 Feb 2015.

Educational Transitions and Change (ETC) Research Group. (2011). *Transition to school: Position statement.* Albury: RIPPLE, Charles Sturt University. http://www.csu.edu.au/faculty/educat/edu/transitions/publications/Position-Statement.pdf. Accessed 15 Feb 2015.

Elliott, A. (2006). *Early childhood education: Pathways to quality and equity for all children.* Camberwell: ACER. http://research.acer.edu.au/cgi/viewcontent.cgi?article=1003&context= aer. Accessed 17 Feb 2015.

Farquhar, S., & White, E. J. (2014). Philosophy and pedagogy of early childhood. *Educational Philosophy and Theory, 46*(8), 821–832. doi:10.1080/00131857.2013.783964.

Flottman, R., & Page, J. (2012). Getting early childhood onto the reform agenda: An Australian case study. *International Journal of Child Care and Education Policy, 6*(1), 17–33.

Foucault, M. (1972). *Archaeology of knowledge.* New York: Pantheon.

Gable, A., & Lingard, B. (2013). *NAPLAN and the performance regime in Australian Schooling: A review of the policy context.* St Lucia: The University of Queensland, School of Social Work and Human Services, Social Policy Unit. http://www.uq.edu.au/swahs/Governing%20performance%20NAPLAN%20Policy%20Summary%20for%20upload.pdf. Accessed 13 Feb 2015.

Hall, S. (1997). The work of representation. In S. Hall (Ed.), *Representation: Cultural representations and signifying practices* (pp. 13–64). London: Sage.

Harvey, W. (2011). Strategies for conducting elite interviews. *Qualitative Research, 11*(4), 431–441.

International Association for the Evaluation of Educational Achievement (IEA). (2015). *Progress in international reading literacy study.* http://timssandpirls.bc.edu/. Accessed 14 Nov 2015.

Jarvie, W. & Mercer, T. (2014). *Labor and the coalition: Policy narratives, evidence and ideology in early childhood education and childcare.* Paper presented public policy network conference. Canberra, January. http://www.ppnc.com.au/uploads/1/9/6/2/19623627/wendy_jarvie_and_trish_mercer.pdf Accessed 8 Mar 2015.

Lingard, B. (2009). Testing times: The need for new intelligent account abilities for schooling. *QTU Professional Magazine,* November, 13–19. http://www.qtu.asn.au/files/9113/2780/3358/29-01-2012_1315_170.pdf. Accessed 26 Feb 2015.

Logan, H., Sumsion, J., & Press, F. (2014). Uncovering hidden dimensions of Australian early childhood policy history: Insights from interviews with policy 'elites'. *European Early Childhood Education Research Journal.* doi:10.1098/1350293X.2104.969086.

Masters, G. (2010). NAPLAN and MySchool: Shedding light on a work in progress. *Teacher: The National Education Magazine,* August, 22–25.

Organisation for Economic Co-operation and Development (OECD). (2001). *Starting strong: Early childhood education and care.* Paris: OECD.

Organisation for Economic Co-operation and Development (OECD). (2006). *Starting strong II: Early childhood education and care. Executive summary.* Paris: OECD. www.oecd.org/newsroom/37425999.pdf. Accessed 15 Feb 2015.

Organisation for Economic Co-Operation and Development (OECD). (2015). *Programme for international student assessment (PISA).* http://www.oecd.org/pisa/aboutpisa/pisafaq.htm. Accessed 14 Nov 2015.

Perry, B., Dockett, S., & Petriwskyj, A. (Eds.). (2014). *Transitions to school: International research, policy and practice.* Dordrecht: Springer.

Reid, A. (2009). Is this a revolution? A critical analysis of the Rudd government's national education agenda. *Curriculum Perspectives, 29*(3), 113.

Rizvi, F., & Lingard, B. (2010). *Globalizing education policy.* Abingdon: Routledge.

Rudd, K., Macklin, J., Roxon, N., & Smith, S. (2007). *Labor's plan for early childhood.* http://www.fitkidz.com.au/~fitkidz/images/stories/pdf/early_childhood_policy-alp2007.pdf. Accessed 26 Feb 2015.

Shorten, A. (1996). The legal context of Australian education: An historical exploration. *Australia New Zealand Journal of Law Education, 1*(1), 2–32.

Siraj-Blatchford, I., Sylva, K., Muttock, S., Gilden, R., & Bell, D. (2002). *Researching effective pedagogy in the early years.* London: Department for Education and Skills.

Chapter 13
Mathematics Learning Through Play: Educators' Journeys

Bryndís Garðarsdóttir, Guðbjörg Pálsdóttir, and Johanna Einarsdóttir

This chapter describes a collaborative action research project that was conducted in one preschool and one primary school in Iceland, investigating approaches to pedagogical continuity across the transition from preschool to school. The participants were one teacher from each school level, who collaborated with the researchers. Data were gathered using interviews and notes from meetings. The teachers agreed upon using play with building blocks to create continuity in children's learning. In this chapter, we report on the way the teachers' ideas about mathematics and play evolved during their participation in the research. The implication of this study is that the teachers experienced a dilemma in the tension between the free play and the teaching of mathematical concepts. They were concerned about the ownership of the play and their own involvement as teachers. Further, they needed support to realise the mathematical concepts that they could expect the children to work on. Their participation in this research project empowered the teachers and influenced their practices and ideas around pedagogical continuity.

13.1 Introduction

In most Western countries, the curricular content and pedagogy of preschools and primary schools tend to be quite different. Typically, the pedagogy of preschools is described in terms of children's free play, while the primary school is seen as a place for learning (Einarsdóttir 2007, 2014; Perry et al. 2012; Pramling Samuelsson and Asplund Carlsson 2008). The national curriculum guidelines for preschools and primary schools in Iceland place emphasis on continuity and building on children's

B. Garðarsdóttir (✉) • G. Pálsdóttir • J. Einarsdóttir
University of Iceland, Reykjavík, Iceland
e-mail: bryngar@hi.is

© Springer International Publishing Switzerland 2017
N. Ballam et al. (eds.), *Pedagogies of Educational Transitions*, International
Perspectives on Early Childhood Education and Development 16,
DOI 10.1007/978-3-319-43118-5_13

earlier experience and education (Ministry of Education, Science and Culture 2011, 2013). Therefore, it is considered that the knowledge and tasks in which children participate at preschool should be the basis for the challenges they will meet in primary school.

In Iceland, where the present study was conducted, preschool children have opportunities to choose their activities, and free play is seen as a main motivation and pathway for learning and development. In primary school, direct instruction and content-based teaching are more common, especially in reading and mathematics, while free play is connected to leisure time and is sometimes used as a time-filler. Hence, the concepts of play and learning can have different meanings to teachers at different school levels (Einarsdóttir 2007).

This chapter reports on a collaborative action research study, *On the Same Path*, which was conducted in one preschool and one primary school in Iceland in collaboration with researchers from the University of Iceland. The project was set up as a professional development course for the teachers who made the decision to focus on continuity in children's learning through the integration of play and mathematics. The chapter discusses the way participation in this action research encouraged the teachers to try different pedagogical methods, using play as a gateway to mathematics learning.

13.2 Integrating Play and Learning

Although numerous research studies confirm the value of play in early childhood education, they also reveal complications in linking play and learning in educational settings (Bennett et al. 1997; Grieshaber and McArdle 2010). Even when planning children's learning with play designated as a primary pedagogy, there are differing views regarding the teacher's role. Some see the teacher's role, first and foremost, as constructing an optimal environment and providing conditions for play, without participating or intervening. Others focus on supporting children's learning by observing their play and scaffolding their learning. Still others emphasise the need to direct children's play according to intended learning outcomes (Pramling Samuelsson and Asplund Carlsson 2008; Wood and Attfield 2005). Thus, teachers who intend to support children's learning through play need to create a balance between child- and teacher-initiated activities, in different ways.

The aim of the present study was to create continuity in children's mathematics learning experiences in preschool and primary school. To do this, child-initiated play and teacher-led play were integrated. That is, activities in which the initiative and objectives came from the teacher and activities in which children had opportunities to play and explore, whether alone or collaboratively with other children and adults, were combined. A longitudinal study of quality in preschools in England (Siraj-Blatchford and Sylva 2004) revealed that such a balance offers children choices and freedom of play without predefined learning outcomes. Children can set their own goals and choose whether or not to invite the teacher to participate or to ask for his or her support (Wood 2010; Wood and Attfield 2005).

Teachers' intentions for using play can differ according to the learning goals they hope to attain. The skills that play is considered to promote cannot always be attained through child-initiated play alone (Wood 2014). Relational pedagogy focuses on respecting children's knowledge and the importance of the activity or the play for the child, instead of insisting on specific learning purposes or outcomes (Rogers 2011). In this approach, the teacher's focus is on taking the child's perspective to create common meaning and understanding, with the child's ideas considered equal in value to those of the adults (Jordan 2004). This requires the teacher to involve him- or herself in children's spontaneous play and activity and to support these. In this way, both adults and children participate in developing sustained knowledge and meaning (Pramling Samuelsson and Asplund Carlsson 2008). In a learning environment based on such ideas, children's learning depends on two main factors: the social context and the child's personal factors, where his or her learning dispositions are in focus (Wells and Claxton 2002). One of the aims teachers need to have in mind is to support children who are in the process of adopting new knowledge, skills, understanding and social competence in collaboration with others (Carr 2001; Karlsdóttir and Garðarsdóttir 2008).

The teacher's roles when supporting play-based learning are to frame the play, plan the play environment, ensure there are learning opportunities, encourage children and support their ideas by asking questions, suggesting new features or solutions and providing information in ways that motivate play and learning (Wood 2014). In this way, teachers pay attention to specific elements of children's play and provide encouragement and feedback on children's learning. Thus, play or activity organised according to the teacher's initiatives can be an important source of inspiration and can lead to free play that develops alignment with pedagogical objectives. According to McLachlan et al. (2011), these ideas can also support teachers to build content and the learning of content through play-based approaches in early childhood education.

13.3 Teachers and Mathematics

Children in preschool and primary school explore mathematical concepts every day. During play, they compare sizes, find patterns, explore space and discover ways to solve problems, such as how to balance building blocks or share biscuits. The teacher's role in these explorations, when using play as a source for mathematics learning, is to observe, listen and notice children's mathematical explorations and to create situations that challenge their mathematical thinking and give them opportunities to try different ways of solving problems, as well as discussing their interests and reflecting on their solutions (Reikerås 2008). Through observations, teachers recognise the mathematical ideas that children are developing and determine the type and level of support they need in order to deepen their mathematical understanding and build on their experiences. Such observations also provide opportunities for discussions and further explorations with children. To be able to use these observations, the teacher needs to have not only a positive attitude and a sound knowledge of mathematics but also knowledge about how children go about developing mathematical concepts. The way teachers organise the learning environment and the mathematical content that they find appropriate are also influenced by their beliefs about mathematics and mathematics learning (Doverborg and Pramling 2006).

The National Association for the Education of Young Children (NAEYC) and the National Council of Teachers of Mathematics (NCTM) put forth a joint statement on early childhood mathematics education in 2002 (revised in 2010). The main idea built on the premise that a child learns by creating, talking, reflecting, discussing, investigating, listening, reasoning and drawing conclusions (NAEYC 2010). Research on learning and mathematics education has changed educators' ideas and beliefs about mathematics learning and teaching (Jaworski and Wood 2008). According to Kristjánsdóttir (2008), there are good possibilities for successful mathematics teaching when the teacher investigates problems alongside children, creating learning opportunities and pointing out different views on solutions as opportunities arise. Therefore, teachers need to have a sense of what kinds of mathematical questions to ask and what kinds of answers to expect. Shulman (1987) introduced the concept of pedagogical content knowledge. This concept was grounded in the idea that the development of understanding the main ideas in each subject is special. According to Shulman, teachers must be able to intertwine their subject knowledge and pedagogical knowledge to plan effective teaching and to meet the needs of individual children. Grevholm (2006) noted that successful teachers are those who can discuss and reflect on mathematics education, who know and implement a variety of strategies for creating rich mathematics learning environments and who notice and assess children's mathematics learning.

The aim of mathematics learning is for children to comprehend mathematical ideas and ways of working. They learn to create and solve problems using mathematical concepts, reasoning and symbols in communication (Boaler 2005; Copley 2010).

13.3.1   Mathematics and Play

The NAEYC and the NCTM joint statement (2010) highlighted that children develop their mathematical ideas and learn from their own and their peers' experiences. Construction play provides opportunities to explore and discuss ideas from geometry and other areas of mathematics (Fösker 2012). In construction play, the teacher can observe and document children's creativity, initiative and perseverance. Further, teachers have opportunities to notice whether children know the features of shapes and can assemble pieces to make a whole, whether they possess the social competence required for collaboration and whether they are able to make connections to the environment and daily life. Children need to have space and freedom to build, but the teacher is available to assist them while observing and communicating with them. The main values of construction play are presented as follows in the statement:

> Construction play offers rich opportunities for mathematics education. Children use their experience about how different items can be assembled from separate parts; this understanding creates a foundation for the development of other concepts. In construction play, children build and rebuild objects to make their own creations. They use patterns and symmetry, and they develop a sense of size and shape. With time and repetition in play, children develop their knowledge and understand concepts they can use later. (NAEYC 2010, p. 8)

In this statement, play is regarded as children's primary way of learning. Therefore, the learning environment should provide opportunities to investigate mathematical ideas through active play. In construction play, children work with their ideas about geometry. According to Fösker (2012), the main ideas in geometry are shape, size, location, orientation and movement in the environment. During play, children have opportunities to develop their spatial sense and knowledge about different shapes so they can understand their environment, rearrange objects and imagine changes that could happen. The role of the teacher is to create situations in which children can investigate shapes, change them, draw them and symbolise them in different ways. These skills give them opportunities to explore beyond their own knowledge and experience the main ideas in geometry in concrete ways.

In the national curriculum for preschools in Iceland (Ministry of Education, Science and Culture 2011) and the curriculum for primary (compulsory) school (Ministry of Education, Science and Culture 2013), the main content and learning goals at each school level are presented. In the curriculum for preschool, the concept of mathematics is not used, but mathematical concepts such as classification, counting, logical thinking, reasoning and problem solving, and the use of these in daily life, are highly valued. In the curriculum for the primary level (grades 1 through 4), the same ideas are presented in greater detail. Teachers in compulsory school use textbooks that align with the curriculum, while the preschool does not.

13.3.2 Professional Development

The NAEYC (2010) statement emphasised the importance of teachers' support from their colleagues and administrators to continue their professional development and to improve and enhance their work with children. They need access to activities that allow them to collaborate in developing goals, teaching materials and strategies for accessing mathematics learning. Therefore, in-service education and collaboration with other educators are essential for teachers' continuing professional growth and development.

Darling-Hammond (1998) studied and wrote extensively about initial and continuing professional education for teachers. She claimed that the most effective learning opportunities for teachers involved collaboration with colleagues and reflection on children's play and work. Learning communities, in which teachers deepened their knowledge of education while reflecting on and sharing their understanding of best practices and worked together to design and improve instruction, created worthwhile opportunities for professional development (Hammerness et al. 2005). Research by Doverborg and Pramling (2006) showed that teachers' knowledge, beliefs and support are all critical for the development of children's mathematical ideas. Participation in a learning community gives teachers opportunities to build their knowledge and develop their professional competencies.

13.4   Present Study

Action research is one approach to professional development. It includes not only inquiry but also action and transformation of practices. Kemmis and McTaggart (1988) described action research as an inquiry undertaken by a group of people with the aim of improving and learning from their experiences and making these experiences available to others. Action research in schools aims to improve practices; new methods, developed in part by the teachers themselves, are investigated and implemented. Records are made of the actions that are taken, and data are gathered and analysed throughout the study period (Einarsdóttir 2014; McNiff et al. 2003).

The project *On the Same Path* was a collaborative action research study that involved collaboration between schools and the University of Iceland. The aim of the study was to contribute to changes in school practices and teacher education, as well as changes in educational policy and society. Collaborative action research places an emphasis on social aspects, with people seeing collaboration as an effective way to change and improve school practices. Through collaboration between schools and universities, an attempt is made to reduce the gap between research and school practices (Bruce et al. 2011).

Researchers have emphasised different views and different aims of action research. These can be classified into three groups that, in this study, were considered equally important:

1. One group places the main emphasis on reflection, increased understanding, action and change. Action research in schools is defined as teachers' approaches to reflecting on and analysing their own practices to ensure they are what they want them to be. The teachers undertake actions and collect data to show how their practices have changed and the results of such changes (McNiff et al. 2003; McNiff and Whitehead 2010).
2. Others have stressed that an important aim of action research is to look critically at school practices and to be a vehicle for educational critique (Griffiths 1998; Townsend 2013). According to Kemmis (2006), action research should be critical and transformative; that is, it must investigate reality in order to transform it.
3. Still others place emphasis on the personal side of action research. By participating in action research, the researcher/teacher undergoes change as well. Thus,

the empowerment of teachers is an important aim of action research where the emphasis is on supporting teachers to rethink their practices and make changes (Yelland et al. 2008).

13.4.1 Participants

This study was conducted in a preschool and a primary school located in the same neighbourhood in the city of Reykjavik. The participants were Helga (pseudonyms have been used), a preschool teacher who had been working in preschools for over 25 years, and Kristin, a primary school teacher who had more than 20 years of teaching experience. The data generation took place in a group of 25 preschool children who were of age 5 and a group of 20 primary school children who were 6 years old.

This action research project was devised as a professional development course for the teachers, who worked collaboratively with two researchers from the university and a postgraduate student (hereafter referred to as the research group). The teachers were awarded course credits from the University of Iceland for their participation.

The schools taking part in the study applied for participation in the study, and the teachers were informed about the different roles and aims of participants in a collaborative study. In addition, during the study the participants discussed the importance of confidentiality between those involved. Children's best interests were kept in the forefront, and the parents were informed about the study. The participants formed a learning community through the project, and the teachers were involved in introducing the project at different levels, during meetings and conferences for teachers, policymakers and researchers.

13.4.2 Method

The study was divided into the following four integrated phases: preparation, planning changes, implementation and evaluation and reflection (Einarsdóttir 2010). During the first phase of the study (preparation), which lasted approximately 6 months, the teachers were introduced to the concept of action research. The participants were given time and opportunities to discuss and reflect on their own practices and make decisions about what they wanted to focus on during the study period. The research group met several times during this period. They were also part of a larger group of preschool and primary school teachers participating in the action research project. Other teachers in the group focused on other content areas. Three interviews were conducted with each of the teachers during the process. The interviews and records from the meetings were analysed throughout the data-gathering period as well as at the end of the project. Member checks were used to establish credibility. Informal member checks took place during the course of the study, and more formal checks were made during the final stages when interpretations and conclusions were reviewed with the participants. The teachers whose practices are discussed in this paper decided to concentrate on the integration of play and mathematics. Emphasis was placed on focusing on a well-defined part of their practice that was important to them and that they wanted to revise. Construction play is common in Icelandic preschools but less common in primary schools. However, KAPLA[1] blocks were available in both schools, so the teachers decided to use them and attempt to develop methods that would create continuity in mathematics learning between the school levels.

During the planning phase of the study, the teachers who participated in the action research met twice a month in a workshop. There, they had opportunities to listen to presentations about the nature of action research, play and learning. They also discussed, reported and reflected in the research group.

During the implementation phase, the teachers put their ideas into practice, tried out ideas and developed projects that they worked on with the children. During monthly common meetings, the teachers reported on successful practices that they had tried out and wanted to share with others. Educators who had participated in action research studies also came and gave presentations. The fourth phase of the study involved evaluation and reflection.

13.4.3   Research Questions

In this chapter, the following research questions are addressed:

1. How did the teachers' ideas about their role in children's mathematics learning evolve during the action research period?
2. How did participation in the action research influence the teachers' professional development and their role in contributing to continuity in children's education?

13.5   Findings

The teachers, Helga (preschool teacher) and Kristin (primary school teacher), expressed their beliefs and ideas about learning, mathematics and play in their journals, during interviews and at common meetings. The evolution of the teachers' ideas about their role in children's mathematics learning during the action research project is presented below.

---

[1] Wooden construction blocks, with dimensions in the ratio 1:3:15.

13.5.1 Teachers' Initial Ideas

Both teachers expressed an interest in using the knowledge and experience from each other's school level to create continuity in the children's learning. In discussions about methods, they both considered play to be an important means of learning. Helga, the preschool teacher, argued that play is the child's way to learn. She contended that play can be either free or organised, and the teacher's role is to ensure that all the learning areas are covered. Kristin, the primary school teacher, also thought it was important to use play together with other teaching methods.

When asked about their roles, the teachers described the following responsibilities:

- Encourage children's interest and creative thinking.
- Create a learning environment with diverse play materials built on children's interests.
- Plan for play and activities that support child development.
- Make children's learning visible in their environment, for example, with writing or photographs.

The teachers expressed themselves with similar words, but when asked to elaborate, Helga said that all children should have opportunity to play and work with special play materials, while Kristin stressed that all children should develop an understanding of basic mathematical ideas. In the first interview, the teachers were asked if they found that the children were interested in mathematics. Helga was hesitant, but, after giving it a thought, she said that she could see from the children's play that they were interested in mathematical ideas. She said, for example, "Construction play is of course mathematics; we could also say that 'beading' is mathematics and they count how many are sitting at the table". Kristin gave several examples of mathematical work, such as "working with numbers, arithmetic, even and odd numbers, measurement, classification, patterns and algebra". She emphasised the importance of children becoming familiar with different areas of mathematics and explained her ways of working with children as follows: "Children are interested in counting and classifying, comparing quantities ... and mathematics can be fun, and it is just play". Both teachers emphasised that children should have access to concrete learning materials and they saw their main role as creating opportunities for learning. They were interested in developing their ideas about learning mathematics through play and saw their collaboration in the research group as an opportunity to accomplish this goal. They wanted to start by becoming more familiar with mathematical concepts. With regard to the teacher's role, Helga said, "What is needed is that we [the teachers] are more conscious that we attract the children's attention to the mathematics in their play ... present the activities as play or a problem because they usually are good problem solvers ...".

The teachers indicated that their role was to challenge the children to think about and reflect on mathematics.

13.5.2   Implementation

During the action research project, the research group discussed ways to develop a learning environment in which mathematics and play were in focus. They decided to use KAPLA blocks as the main material. Children in both groups were familiar with the blocks, so the teachers intended to challenge the children to work with them in a more systematic way. The focus was on geometry, in particular, and there were some reading and discussion about the content. The research group planned several similar mathematical activities to try out at both school levels.

Helga was interested in working more systematically to encourage children's mathematics learning through play. She thought that using materials like the KAPLA blocks, as well as making numbers and shapes and writing more visible in the classrooms, would support the children's mathematics learning. Kristin emphasised the importance of the children working with concrete play materials:

> I am pleased if I manage to have concrete activities. They understand better if they can touch and visualise the activities … use different materials to classify and play with, … classify and count, … problem solving and play with blocks.

Kristin was eager to use play more frequently and to increase her knowledge about the value of play in children's learning so she could better argue for its use.

At first, the children played freely with the KAPLA blocks. The teachers observed their play, and it appeared that the children mostly built similar buildings, such as high towers, with which they explored the law of gravity, finding out if or when things fall down. The children often used small plastic animals when playing with the blocks. Therefore, in the second activity, the children were encouraged to build a house for the animals. The teachers observed and supported them by asking questions such as the following:

- Are you planning to have a roof on the house?
- Do you think this is a good size for your animals?
- Do you think the house will be suitable for your animals?

In the third activity, the children were each given 20 blocks and invited to build an animal. They looked at books with animal pictures before they started building. The teachers focused on mathematical concepts by commenting and asking the children about their constructions in order to support them and challenge their mathematical understanding. The questions included:

- What shapes can you see?
- What parts is your animal made from?
- How did you build your animal?
- Is the size of the head larger/smaller than on the real animal?

The teachers took photographs of the buildings, and the children were interested in looking at them and studying their own animals and those of other children. The children found the tasks complicated at first, but as they continued working, they discovered more possibilities.

Fig. 13.1 Peacock in three dimensions

The next activity was to build collaboratively. Two children were challenged to build one animal using 40 blocks. According to the teachers, the children became more creative than before and worked well together. The photographs showed that their constructions now had more details and were built in three dimensions (see Fig. 13.1).

After that, the teachers felt the children had lost interest in the KAPLA blocks. They thought the reason for this was that they did not get enough time for free play. Thus, the teachers encouraged the children to play without giving them any instructions. As a result, they noticed the play coming back, and, at the same time, the buildings evolved and became more mathematically complex (see Fig. 13.2).

The last activity was carried out differently in the preschool and the primary school. The children built houses for their animals in the primary school, where Kristin noted that they had more choices and autonomy than before and that they enjoyed their play and discovered new possibilities. In the preschool, the children were not enthusiastic about the activity, so the teacher and the children went on a field trip in the neighbourhood and viewed the houses they were living in. That sparked their interest again and they started to build their own houses. To accomplish this, they had to cope with complex mathematical problems such as building verandas and roofs. They experimented, collaborated, discussed and tried out new ideas.

The activities with the KAPLA blocks were an attempt to intervene in children's play and learning by giving them tasks to do with the building blocks in their play. The teachers reflected on their roles in children's play during meetings with the research group. They asked questions about the aims and methods of their practice and discussed how they could develop their skills and pedagogical methods and

Fig. 13.2 An island and the ocean presented with KAPLA blocks

contribute to children's mathematics learning through play. They liked the idea of having discussions with the children during and after their play, but at the same time, they were conscious of interrupting children's play. They found that using questions to support and encourage the children seemed to be requisite for their mathematics learning, and, to lead up to this, they explored and tried out new possibilities.

The teachers were often unsure about when and how to support children's play and how to analyse the mathematical ideas the children were working on. They raised questions such as the following:

- How is it possible to connect play and mathematics?
- Is it possible to find a balance between activities and play in which the teacher takes the initiative or is in control and activities and play in which the children have the opportunity to explore and find solutions?
- How do I challenge children's reflection, inquiry and learning?
- Where is the mathematics in these activities?

13.5.3 Teachers' Reflections

When reflecting on the process at the end of the project, the teachers said that their focus and views had changed. In the beginning, they found it important to use the same words between school levels for concepts. Afterwards, they were more conscious of the way they referred to mathematical concepts when talking to children. Both said that they were now more knowledgeable about children's ideas of mathematics and more conscious of listening to children in order to analyse their ideas and support their mathematical thinking. Kristin expressed, "It's like the world around the mathematics has enlarged". Helga said she hadn't realised how much the children were using mathematics. She was now using questions more often while assisting the children and observing their buildings. She said that she had some-times felt that she was going through a difficult process by participating, but now she felt she was even more conscious about play and the opportunities it can offer.

Both teachers experienced that the children got tired of organised activities with the KAPLA blocks. They were not used to the teachers taking part in their play or giving them assignments while they were playing with blocks, since they had only used them in free play. Kristin said, "I, as a teacher, still looked at it as free play, but they didn't". Helga started to doubt herself and became unsure of her involvement in their play. She thought she was controlling the play too much and was worried about spoiling the children's free play. She talked about how she could give them space for free play as well as challenge the children to develop their mathematical ideas. She said, "Perhaps I was too excited. When I thought about it, I found out that I was maybe interrupting too much …".

The research group discussed if and how the construction play with the blocks was influencing the children's play. Kristin thought the reason it did not in the pri-mary school was that the children did not get enough time to play with the blocks. She felt she needed to have more time for play and that she did not provide enough opportunities to use play as a learning strategy. In the preschool, the children drew upon their previous experiences with the KAPLA blocks. Helga talked about a turn-ing point in the process when the children started to use what they had been working on during organised activities in their free play with the blocks (see Fig. 13.2).

The teachers agreed that play could be an effective mode of learning. Kristin said, "If the children get an opportunity to learn through play-based activities, their experiences become stronger and give them more". Both teachers found that reflect-ing on how they could use play more effectively in their teaching was a significant challenge, both for them and for the children. Finding a balance between children's free play with the blocks and supporting and encouraging their problem solving was a particular challenge. The teachers also noted that the children showed greater perseverance in their construction play, used more problem solving, thought about details and were more conscious about mathematics than they had been at the begin-ning of the research process. In addition, Helga thought the children were now more relaxed in their play, working on their own premises.

Both teachers agreed that their participation in the action research project had supported them in their professional development. The teachers kept journals where they wrote their reflections and used photographs to document children's play. They emphasised the value of documenting their reflections, which they found strength-ened their roles as professionals and increased their awareness. Kristin said, "I feel that the diary writing has been an important element in this project … to learn from my own experience, assess myself and reflect on my teaching".

Helga used a camera to document her experience. She used the photographs as a reference and a resource to analyse the process and to reflect on her own role and intervention. The children also reflected on the photographs. Kristin described the main changes she experienced:

> I feel more confident about my teaching methods … how to guide and support the children. This has helped me to see how I can intervene; where and when to push them further … I feel that I can challenge them without taking from them their creativity or the free play.

When reflecting on the process, the teachers admitted that they had often doubted if their participation in the project was worthwhile, but now they were convinced that it was worth the effort and that it had augmented their identity as teachers. For instance, Helga expressed, "It is always difficult to reflect on oneself … but it helped to be critical and dig into one's practice".

13.6 Discussion

The action research project described in this chapter aimed to develop ways to create continuity between preschool and primary school and thus ease the transition between the school levels. A choice was made to use play as a pedagogical method in children's mathematics learning. The teachers who participated in the study believed that children learned through play and wanted to develop ways to support the children's mathematical thinking during construction play. As such, the action research was also an important vehicle for the teachers' professional development.

The environments and practices in the participating schools were different from each other at the beginning of the research. The findings revealed that at the preschool, play was regarded as the primary path for learning and the children were given opportunities to learn through play. The aim and content of the mathematics, however, were vague, and neither was stated in the preschool curriculum nor as part of the preschool discourse. The preschool teacher was also unsure of whether she was teaching mathematics and had difficulties identifying the mathematical concepts that the children used in their play.

In the primary school, by contrast, the content knowledge targeted was clear, but the methods used were inflexible. The teacher was interested in using play more effectively but found that making time and space for such play was difficult. She also wanted to be able to rationalise using play to herself, her fellow teachers and the parents of her children.

During the research period, both teachers wanted to support children's mathematics learning in more systematic ways. Within the research group, the teachers developed their ideas and practices, although they struggled to strike a balance between play and teaching. They observed how the children approached the assigned tasks and tried to create an environment and methods that would support meaning making and understanding (Jordan 2004; Pramling Samuelsson and Asplund Carlsson 2008). The researchers were new to supporting teachers involved in action research. In retrospect, the researchers perhaps took a more active role than they had intended. They provided the teachers with ideas and led discussions with analytic questions. The teachers used those ideas, but as the process progressed, they became more independent, as can be seen in the last assignment, in which Helga changed the approach. Both teachers were working in similar ways with the children and trying out the same ideas at both school levels. Throughout the project, the teachers' journeys were often characterised by uneasiness. The preschool teacher worried about controlling the play too much, especially upon recognising that the children's interest in playing with the blocks had declined. This is consistent with earlier studies (Bennett et al. 1997; Rogers 2011; Wood and Attfield 2005), indicating teachers' difficulties in integrating play and education in a goal-oriented way without compromising children's free play.

During the course of the research, the teachers received support and guidance from the research group. They discussed mathematical concepts and how they were used, which mathematical ideas they could expect the children to develop and how they could support them in extending those ideas. Their understanding and views developed as they became more aware of the importance of mathematical thinking and competencies. They gradually became more confident in their ability to support children's mathematical thinking and reflections with questions and suggestions. They sought ways to encourage and guide each child individually, and when they observed the children playing, they increased their own knowledge of mathematics and, in turn, the potential development of the children's mathematical understanding.

Supporting teachers' professional development involves providing them with opportunities to discuss and reflect with other teachers. The teachers who participated in this study discussed the value of documenting and reflecting on their teaching and found that doing so strengthened them as professionals. In a similar sense, Darling-Hammond (1998) referred to learning communities as an effective way to facilitate teachers' professional development. In this study, the learning community consisted of one preschool teacher, one primary school teacher and two groups of children; two university specialists; and a postgraduate student. In accordance with Hammerness et al.'s (2005) research on collaboration and learning communities, through this collaboration, the teachers expanded their knowledge as mathematics teachers of young children.

The research group was an important platform for discussions about how to integrate play and mathematics and for trying out ideas to improve mathematics learning in construction play. As noted earlier, the preschool teacher was concerned that the increased interference changed and influenced the play too much. Later, the teachers noticed that the children were using their new knowledge in their free play, experimenting and trying out new ideas.

The teachers were ready to use the knowledge and experience of the specialists to develop their own ideas and pedagogical methods. By the end of the project, they reflected on their experiences and expressed that they missed having colleagues from their own schools as participants. Hence, they called for their own learning communities within their respective schools. The teachers agreed that participating in the action research project had empowered them to form their own ideas about mathematics learning and how to use play in goal-oriented ways.

In this action research project, the teachers tried out ideas across school levels and, in collaboration with researchers, developed ideas to work on mathematics learning. The research group found ways to provide mathematics learning opportunities that supported the development of mathematics teaching across those school levels. By working purposefully together, negotiating meaning and drawing on common knowledge, the teachers learned from each other. The primary school teacher became aware of the pedagogical ideas of preschools, and the preschool teacher became more conscious about the content of mathematics learning. Hence, through collaboration and mutual respect, the teachers worked towards continuity and progress in the transition from preschool to primary school.

References

Bennett, N., Wood, L., & Rogers, S. (1997). *Teaching through play: Teachers' thinking and classroom practice*. Buckingham: Open University Press.

Boaler, J. (2005). *Connecting mathematical ideas*. Portsmouth: Heinemann.

Bruce, C. D., Flynn, T., & Stagg-Peterson, S. (2011). Examining what we mean by collaborative action research: A cross-case analysis. *Educational Action Research, 19*(4), 433–452.

Carr, M. (2001). *Assessment in early childhood settings: Learning stories*. London: Paul Chapman.

Copley, J. V. (2010). *The young child and mathematics*. Washington, DC: National Association of the Education of Young Children.

Darling-Hammond, L. (1998). Teacher learning that supports student learning. *Educational Leadership, 55*(5), 6–11.

Doverborg, E., & Pramling, I. (2006). Varför skall barn inte märka att de lär seg matematik? [Why shall children not notice that they are learning Math?]. In G. Emanuelsson & E. Doverborg (Eds.), *Matematik i förskolan, Nämnaren TEMA* (pp. 49–52). Gautaborg: Nationelt Centrum för Matematikutbildning, NCM.

Einarsdóttir, J. (2007). *Lítil börn með skólatöskur. Tengsl leikskóla og grunnskóla* [Small children with schoolbags. Transition from preschool to primary school]. Reykjavík: Háskólaút-gáfan og Rannsóknarstofa í menntunarfræðum ungra barna (RannUng).

Einarsdóttir, J. (2010). Connecting curricula through action research. In H. Müller (Ed.), Transition from pre-school to school: Emphasizing early literacy (pp. 57–62). Köln: EU-Agency, Regional Government of Cologne/Germany. http://www.ease-eu.com/documents/compendium/compendium.pdf. Accessed 30 Sept 2014.

Einarsdóttir, J. (2014). Play and literacy: A collaborative action research in preschool. *Scandinavian Journal of Educational Research, 58*(1), 93–109.

Fösker, L. I. R. (2012). Grip rommet! [Use the space!]. In T. Fosse (Ed.), *Rom for matematikk – i barnehagen*. Bergen: Caspar forlag.

Grevholm, B. (2006). Matematikdidaktikens möjligheter i en forskningsbaserat lärarutbildning. [Mathematics education in a research-based teacher education]. In S. Ongstad (Ed.), *Fag og didaktik i lærerutdanning: kunnskap i grenseland* (pp. 183–206). Oslo: Universitetsforlaget.

Grieshaber, S., & McArdle, F. (2010). *The trouble with play*. Maidenhead: Open University Press.

Griffiths, M. (1998). *Educational research for social justice: Getting off the fence*. Philadelphia: Open University Press.

Hammerness, K., Darling-Hammond, L., & Bransford, J. (2005). How teachers learn and develop. In L. Darling- Hammond & J. Bransford (Eds.), *Preparing teachers for a changing world: What teachers should learn and be able to do* (pp. 358–389). San Francisco: Jossey–Bass.

Jaworski, B., & Wood, T. (Eds.). (2008). *The mathematics teacher educator as a developing professional*. Rotterdam: Sense.

Jordan, B. (2004). Scaffolding learning and co-constructing understandings. In A. Anning, J. Cullen, & M. Fleer (Eds.), *Early childhood education. Society and culture* (pp. 31–42). London: Sage.

Karlsdóttir, K., & Garðarsdóttir, B. (2008). Learning stories: Children's competence and skills. In J. Einarsdóttir & B. Garðarsdóttir (Eds.), *Sjónarmið barna og lýðræði í leikskólastarfi* [Children's views and democracy in preschool] (pp.133–153). Reykjavík: Háskólaútgáfan og Rannsóknarstofa í menntunarfræðum ungra barna (RannUng).

Kemmis, S. (2006). Participatory action research and the public sphere. *Educational Action Research, 14*(4), 459–476.

Kemmis, S., & McTaggart, R. (1988). *The action research planner* (3rd ed.). Geelong: Deakin University Press.

Kristjánsdóttir, A. (2008). Matematikk [Mathematics]. In E. M. Halvorsen (Ed.), *Didaktikk for grunnskolen: Fellestrekk og særdrag i et fagdidaktisk mangfold* (pp. 147–174). Bergen: Fagbokforlaget.

McLachlan, C., Fleer, M., & Edwards, S. (2011). *Early childhood curriculum. Planning, assessment and implementation.* New York: Cambridge University Press.

McNiff, J., & Whitehead, J. (2010). *Action research: Principles and practice.* London: Routledge/Falmer.

McNiff, J., Lomax, P., & Whitehead, J. (2003). *You and your action research project* (2nd ed.). London: Routledge/Falmer.

Ministry of Education, Science and Culture. (2011). *Aðalnámskrá leikskóla* [The Icelandic national curriculum guide for preschool]. Reykjavík: Menntaog menningarmálaráðuneytið.

Ministry of Education, Science and Culture. (2013). *Aðalnámskrá grunnskóla* [The Icelandic national curriculum guide for compulsory school]. Reykjvík: Menntaog menningar-málaráðuneytið.

National Association for the Education of Young Children (NAEYC). (2010). Early childhood mathematics: Promoting good beginnings. A joint statement of the National Association for the Education of Young Children and the National Council of Teachers of Mathematics. Retrieved from: http://www.naeyc.org/positionstatements/mathematics. Accessed 20 Apr 2015.

Perry, B., Dockett, S., & Harley, E. (2012). The Early years learning framework for Australia and the Australian curriculum – Mathematics: Linking educators' practice through pedagogical inquiry questions. In B. Atweh, M. Goos, R. Jorgensen, & D. Siemon (Eds.), Engaging the Australian curriculum Mathematics: Perspectives from the field (pp. 153–174). Adelaide: Mathematics Education Research Group of Australasia. http://www.merga.net.au/onlinebooks. Accessed 20 Apr 2015.

Pramling Samuelsson, I., & Asplund Carlsson, M. (2008). The playing learning child: Towards a pedagogy of early childhood. *Scandinavian Journal of Educational Research, 52*(6), 623–641.

Reikerås, E. (2008). *Temahefte – om antall, rom og form i barnehagen* [Theme – About number, space and form in pre-school]. Oslo: Kunskapsdepartementet.

Rogers, S. (2011). Play and pedagogy: A conflict of interests? In S. Rogers (Ed.), *Rethinking play and pedagogy in early childhood education: Concepts, contexts and culture* (pp. 5–18). London: Routledge.

Shulman, L. S. (1987). Knowledge and teaching: Foundation of the new reform. *Harvard Educational Review, 57,* 1–22.

Siraj-Blatchford, I., & Sylva, K. (2004). Researching pedagogy in English preschools. *British Educational Research Journal, 30*(5), 713–730.

Townsend, A. (2013). Principled challenges for a participatory discipline. *Educational Action Research, 21*(3), 326–342.

Wells, G., & Claxton, G. (2002). *Learning for life in the 21st. century: Sociocultural perspectives on the future of education.* Blackwell: Oxford.

Wood, E. (2010). Developing integrated pedagogical approaches to play and learning. In P. Broadhead, J. Howard, & E. Wood (Eds.), *Play and learning in the early years* (pp. 9–26). London: Sage.

Wood, E. (2014). The play pedagogy interface: Contemporary debates. In L. Brooker, M. Blaise, & S. Edwards (Eds.), *The SAGE handbook of play and learning in early childhood* (pp. 145–156). London: Sage.

Wood, E., & Attfield, J. (2005). *Play, learning and the early childhood curriculum* (2nd ed.). London: Paul Chapman.

Yelland, N., Lee, L., O'Rourke, M., & Harrison, C. (2008). *Rethinking learning in early childhood education*. Maidenhead: Open University Press.

Part IV
Borderlands, Bridges and Rites of Passage

Chapter 14
Borderlands, Bridges and Rites of Passage

Sally Peters and Gunilla Sandberg

This chapter examines transitions by looking closely at the border or threshold to be crossed between different educational contexts. We explore research findings related to borderlands and bridges between the early childhood and school sectors, the ways in which these might be conceptualised in policy and the implications for practice for the professionals involved. The chapter also considers the child's pathway or learning journey traversing these borders, borderlands or bridges and discusses the place of rites of passage in this process.

14.1 Introduction

Exploring the pedagogy of educational transitions offers the opportunity to reflect on the nature of the transitions being navigated as children progress through the education system. This chapter considers some of the wealth of research in this area and draws specifically on work that explores the possibilities of borderlands and bridges when 'trajectories', 'pathways' or 'passages' through the life course (Hörschelmann 2011) encounter borders to be traversed between different educational settings. Such pathways are not necessarily linear, and the transition points may offer both crisis and opportunity in lives that are 'always in a process of becoming' (Hörschelmann 2011, p. 379). We pay particular attention to the transition from early childhood education to school and include our own research findings

S. Peters (✉)
University of Waikato, Hamilton, New Zealand
e-mail: speters@waikato.ac.nz

G. Sandberg
Mälardalen University, Västerås, Sweden

© Springer International Publishing Switzerland 2017   223
N. Ballam et al. (eds.), *Pedagogies of Educational Transitions*, International
Perspectives on Early Childhood Education and Development 16,
DOI 10.1007/978-3-319-43118-5_14

from both Sweden and New Zealand to discuss pedagogical contributions that aim to enhance children's learning journeys and address inequities.

There are many ways of theorising transition experiences. One approach that is relevant in relation to crossing borders draws on the anthropological work of van Gennep (1977) to consider ideas of rites of passage, of liminality and of being on the threshold (or wavering) between two worlds. We are interested in the inner changes that accompany the physical move between settings (in, e.g. identity or learning), which may occur on a threshold and in becoming a full participant in the culture of the new place. Related to this is van Gennep's (1977) discussion of rites of separation, rites of transition and rites of incorporation and the particular acts and ceremonies that may be involved. The relevance of these for educational transitions is explored in detail, while also recognising that the individual's experience is situated within wider social and cultural settings and influenced by the interaction and interdependence of individual and social processes (Crafter and Maunder 2012).

14.2 Borders

Van Gennep (1977) discussed territorial borders and the ways in which these are drawn clearly on maps but may be less well defined in practice. For example, boundaries can be denoted by natural features such as rocks or a river or by constructed markers that have been installed to indicate the division, rather than continuous lines as on a map. Inhabitants and neighbours learn the limits of these territories. This idea of borders and boundaries and the related ideas of borderlands and border crossings are also employed in a metaphoric sense so that they do not inevitably refer to material spaces:

> Boundaries, by definition, constitute lines of separation or contact. This may occur in real or virtual space, horizontally between territories, or vertically between groups and/or individuals. The point of contact or separation usually creates an 'us' and an 'Other' identity. (Newman and Paasi 1998, p. 191)

Borders therefore impact on identities, which can be both shaped by existing borders and help to create and maintain those borders (Ackesjö 2013), as people define themselves in relation to their social groups and in contrast to 'others'. For example, Wenger (1998) described borders that are socially constructed between communities of practice. These borders help to define the communities, each with their own knowledge, rituals and practices that may be specialised and different from those in other communities.

In many countries, it can be argued that early childhood education and school are divided by both kinds of borders described above: a change of physical setting (often marked by fences and gates) and borders between different communities of practices that are 'negotiated and maintained by individuals' (Ackesjö 2014, p. 5). Despite the different curriculum approaches and different ages of school entry across the world (see Taguma et al. 2013 for some examples), these borders between sectors seem to be evident in many countries. This is perhaps because of the differences in history, philosophy, curriculum, policy, pedagogy and practice that help to shape the culture of the communities of practice in early childhood education and at the beginning level of school. Kagan and Neville (1996) provided a detailed discussion of these differences in the US context, much of which would still be relevant today even though, in many countries, there have been some shifts towards more similarities between the two sectors. The 'us' and 'other' identities (Newman and Paasi 1998) can often be seen in the ways teachers describe their own work and the pedagogy of the other sector.

14.3   Crossing Borders

When children attend early childhood education and care (ECEC) services, they, their families and their ECEC teachers are part of the ECEC community of practice. When policy dictates that it is time for the move to school, children and their families encounter the new community of practice across the border at school, and their established ECEC identity has to change to include the identity of the new group. Fabian (2002) and Garpelin (2014) drew attention to the idea of a transition across a border as being on the threshold (limen) between one known context/status/position and a new context/status/position. When a person is on the threshold, in the liminal phase, he/she is 'being, without belonging to any room (status/position/ stage)' (Garpelin 2014, p. 119). Similarly, Ackesjö (2014, citing the work of Bridges 2013) described three phases in transition: emancipation, a neutral phase and then a new beginning where one finds new meaning and control. The neutral phase sits between what was and what is to come as 'a nowhere between two somewheres' (p. 5), a place that can be disorienting and confusing, but also a time of possibilities. Children starting school clearly make the move to the 'somewhere' of a physical location, but it may take some time until they are incorporated into the new role, and hence, until this incorporation is achieved, they can be thought of as liminal or in the 'nowhere' of the neutral phase. Ackesjö (2013, p. 393) explained the passage through the phases as a move from 'being to becoming' and then to a new 'being'. In terms of identity, this may mean a period of 'unbeing' of the previous role, in preparation for incorporation into the new one. Although the notion of limen implies a threshold, given the time taken for incorporation, it can also be thought of as a corridor (Garpelin 2014; Peters 2014; Turner 1977) in which full incorporation into the new community and role can take some time.

Crossing borders therefore often involves meeting difference and unfamiliar territory (Ackesjö 2013). This difference in itself is not necessarily problematic. Mullholland and Wallace (2003) have argued that all fields of human endeavour may be considered subcultural spaces, each with its own habitus, 'into which all learners must cross by way of borders' (p. 7). Crossing from ECEC to school is just one of these transitions. Some discontinuity can be a basis for learning (Peters 2004), and research with children suggests that they expect, and may look forward to, some changes and challenges when they get to school (Brooker 2008; Einarsdóttir 2007). However, difficulties arise when the challenges are so disorienting that they prevent incorporation into the new setting. An extensive review of research literature indicated that 'almost any child is at risk of making a poor or less successful transition if their individual characteristics are incompatible with features of the environment they encounter' (Peters 2010a, p. 2). This confirms the previous argument that:

> ... children do not require homogeneity, or protection from the potentially difficult situations that they encounter in the process of becoming school pupils. However, when the challenges are too great for them to negotiate alone, a focus on support that is empowering is important. (Peters 2004, p. 437)

Key tasks for teachers in the pedagogy of educational transitions are to understand what is happening for the learner and to offer support in ways that address these challenges. In their work on learning science, Mulholland and Wallace (2003) noted, 'if borders were not acknowledged and hazards unidentified, then students had no real access to education' (p. 19).

In Mulholland and Wallace's (2003) study, teachers tried to understand what the hazards were from the learner's point of view rather than their own. In the process, they become border crossers too, and rather than being 'tour guides to the new space', they became 'tourists' in the learner's subculture (p. 20). This is an important point, because it asks teachers to focus on what is of concern to the learners rather than just showing the learners what the teachers would like them to know. As discussed in the next section, borderland spaces may provide possibilities for this kind of engagement.

14.4   Borderlands and Boundary Spaces

Instead of accepting that transition requires border crossing over a sharp divide between two sectors or cultures, there is a possibility for thinking of a borderland space between them. Returning to the notion of physical territories, van Gennep (1977) explained that while many countries now touch each other, in earlier times some countries were surrounded by a strip of neutral ground, divided into sections or marches. Permits called a 'letter of marque' (perhaps coming from the German word 'mark' – borderland) could be given 'to pass from one territory to another through the neutral zone' (van Gennep 1977, p. 18). Applied to conceptual spaces, neutral zones or borderlands are 'those spaces that exist around borders' that do 'not have a sharp divide line where one leaves one way of making sense for an-other' (Clandinin and Rosiek 2007, p. 59).

Britt and Sumsion (2003, p. 133) explored this possibility of a shared space, a borderland with 'connections and intersections between two different places – points of negotiation, of cohabitation, meshing, transforming, combining ... a space not only of existence, but of coexistence', in their investigation of early childhood teachers working in primary schools in Australia. Ackesjö (2013) added to this idea, discussing trans-boundary experiences, which can combine or merge territories and blur the boundaries between spaces. An example of this was the way, after children experienced the new context, initial understandings were deconstructed and the borders redefined.

Continuity of learning has been a focus of recent research in New Zealand with three recent reports focusing on continuity of learning from ECEC to school (Carr et al. 2015; Education Review Office 2015; Mitchell et al. 2015). The notion of a borderland seems to offer great potential for developing this continuity through shared understandings of curriculum, assessment and pedagogy (Peters 2010b). Several studies have looked at ways in which teachers have worked together to develop borderlands between ECEC and school with the aim of supporting continuity of learning and enhancing children's transition between the two sectors.

In New Zealand, a project on learning journeys (Peters et al. 2015) explored a series of action research projects in which teachers from ECEC and school worked together to create borderlands instead of sharp divides. Teachers in the project examined each other's curricula, spent time observing in the other sector and discussed these observations with each other to gain an understanding of what had been seen. Based on these understandings, they explored ways of sharing information and planning. Regular meetings included discussions that highlighted the constraints within each sector, as well as the similarities in personal teacher philosophies about learning and their goals for the children. Where before there had been some tensions regarding different approaches in the other sector, new understandings were developed about why these existed, and the teachers focused on supporting the children's learning journeys collaboratively. A further small-scale study in New Zealand (Hohepa 2014; also see Chap. 7) is currently examining whether something similar is possible between a Māori medium preschool (*kōhanga reo*) and a Māori medium school (*kura*). Schielack and Seeley (2010) made some similar recommendations for developing shared understandings for teachers in elementary and middle schools in the USA.

A concept that can be compared to borderland is that of boundary space, described as the space where 'the resources from different practices are brought together to expand interpretations of multifaceted tasks, and not as barriers between the knowledge and motives that characterise specialist practices' and 'the learning that occurs in these spaces is not a matter of learning how to do the work of others, but involves gaining sufficient insight into purposes and practices of others to enable collaboration' (Edwards 2011, p. 34).

In a Finnish project, Karila and Rantavuori (2014) used the theory of boundary spaces when exploring the way teachers from ECEC and primary school cooperated in their work with developing joint lessons for the children from the two school forms. This study focused on the boundaries where professional zones and cultural scripts meet. Three discursive frames were identified in the teachers' talk: an initiative frame (where professionals suggest, ask and propose and are willing to take the others' ideas into consideration), a consensus frame (clarifying the purpose of the work and checking for understanding) and a collaboration frame (a common and shared perspective where new practices are developed together). The 'initiative frame' and 'consensus frame' were used during the entire school year. The 'collaboration frame' was only heard later in the year and reflected 'the will and intention to collaborate in a democratic way, giving space for various professionals' (p. 389). The findings indicated that sufficient time was important for deepening shared activity and also that for boundary spaces to be productive, they need to be managed and attention paid to addressing the power imbalance between the participants.

The concept of boundary space was also highlighted in another Finnish study, which noted that in the Finnish language, the phrase 'transition period' is expressed more as 'co-operation of the transition period' (Athola et al. 2011, p. 296). This broad conceptualisation of transition may provide a frame for reciprocal exploration of this boundary space between sectors. Athola et al. (2011) explored whether or not the special activities organised by teachers to facilitate the transition between kindergarten and Grade 1 were of importance for children's learning processes in literacy and numeracy. One of the activities that appeared to have the strongest impact on children's learning in Grade 1 was that teachers from the two school forms cooperated on curricula and thus counteracted a 'break' in the learning processes of children. The cooperation involved teachers meeting and discussing their conceptions and aims regarding the children's learning, sharing written information about children's learning and planning for continuity.

Although cooperation in a borderland appears to be a benign and positive possibility, perspectives from literature remind us that borderlands can be oppressive and potentially violent spaces (De Roover 2012). Dictionary definitions of van Gennep's 'letter of marque' describe them as licences given to private citizens to seize the property of another nation, thus linking them with reprisal and privateers, rather than just as permits to travel through the borderland. Although these examples are extreme compared to the borderland between ECEC and school, they draw attention to the work involved in creating and navigating borderlands. It is important not to underestimate the challenges involved in seeking new ways of working that open up these shared conceptual spaces. Even in the successful Finnish example described above, Athola et al. (2011) found that although cooperation on curricula and related activities was the most successful approach (in terms of predicting children's skills), these were the least commonly used practices. To create borderlands for children, teachers are asked to destabilise practices that are being protected by a boundary (Edwards 2011), a boundary that may have helped to shape their professional identity. De Roover (2012) commented that imposing socially constructed boundaries disrupts the individual's sense of identity, just as a physical boundary disrupts the natural landscape. It seems timely to focus more research in this area to explore the experiences of ECEC and school teachers when they try to create new borderland approaches and the impact for children when teachers are able to engage in this way.

14.5 Bridges

While borderlands involve creating new conceptual spaces and new ways of working, the metaphor of bridges accepts the status quo of the cultures on either side of the border and aims to create a connection leading from one pedagogical setting to another. Anzaldúa (2012, p. 1) described bridges as 'thresholds to other realities' and 'pathways, conduits, connectors that connote transitioning, crossing borders and changing perspectives'. She also reminded us that bridging moves us to unfamiliarity and we are not guaranteed safe passage in the process. The illustration on the *Transition to School: Position Statement* (Educational Transitions and Change [ETC] Research Group 2011) captured the variety of ways that such metaphorical bridges may be experienced, from secure structures to those that appear more risky (see Fig. 14.1). It also includes a reminder that some children will fly across without needing a bridge at all.

In New Zealand, Peters et al. (2015) explored bridges as well as borderlands in their study of learning pathways across sectors. Successful bridge building required communication from both sides and a sense of shared purpose. In a previous study, Hartley et al. (2012) looked at many ways to build bridges between sectors. Of particular interest was the initiation of the bridgework; in the beginning, the ECEC setting initiated most of the projects, but over time, the school, families and children began to make suggestions. Ideas for approaches that were mutually interesting were more likely to offer stronger bridges, because support came from both sides. Bridge building may not be limited to teachers. A small-scale study by Noel (2011) described the work of school administrators to provide support for children and families in the transition to school, and a recent Australian resource (Dockett and Perry 2014) is rich with suggestions for building bridges to support transitions to school and school-age care.

Fig. 14.1 Transition to School: Position Statement illustration (Reprinted with permission)

14.6 The Swedish Preschool Class: A Bridge Between ECEC and School?

In Sweden, local municipalities arrange three different school forms for children in early years: preschool for children from the age of 1–5 years; preschool classes for 6-year-olds; and when children turn 7, they start primary school, the first compulsory form of school. The preschool class, introduced in 1998, was intended as a bridge between preschool and school, in which children could experience both preschool and school approaches to learning and 'encounter school at their own pace' (Ackesjö 2013, p. 389). The intention for preschool classes was that they should integrate the approaches from both sectors and support the transition to school (Kaga 2007). Chapter 15 in this volume provides more detailed insights into this approach. Close examination of the concept of a preschool class implies that it could also be a potential borderland, with shared understandings developed to create new collaborative approaches to pedagogy. However, research conducted on the transition from the Swedish preschool class to primary school (Sandberg et al. 2014) reported a clear lack of the pedagogical cooperation addressed in the New Zealand and Finnish studies described earlier. In an interview study with primary school teachers (Sandberg et al. 2015), there was appreciation of the work undertaken in the preschool class, especially the activities aiming to make the children socially prepared and ready for learning. However, the pedagogical cooperation that might be expected to occur within a borderland of shared understanding between the teachers in preschool class and primary school was described as rather weak. While the institution of the preschool class is an example of a strong educational policy approach to creating a bridge or borderland between ECEC and school, without the external and social processes we noted in the introduction (Crafter and Maunder 2012), to support teachers in working together, Sandberg (2012) concluded that a picture of a 'ditch' might emerge. This idea of a ditch, with an associated dip in children's learning, is explained further in the next section relating to literacy learning.

14.7 Bridges and Ditches in Literacy Learning

Research about the transition from preschool to school often highlights social aspects of the learners' experiences. These include the value of relationships (O'Toole et al. 2014; Peters 2010a) and the development of a sense of security and well-being as a ground for future learning (Bulkeley and Fabian 2006). It is important to acknowledge the dynamic interaction between the social and the academic aspects as well. In a study from Finland, Halonen et al. (2006) showed there was a clear relation between children's literacy development in preschool activities for 6-year-olds and their social well-being in Grade 1. Difficulties in the areas of literacy seem to be a risk factor for developing socio-emotional problems later on.

Similar findings were presented in a project in Sweden (Fischbein et al. 2006), where extra support was given to children in preschool class and Grade 1. After the period of intervention, the children showed better academic results than the control group, as well as a high degree of well-being.

In Sweden, where children start school at age 7, several studies have been interested in providing bridges to support continuity in children's literacy learning and development in transitions from one setting to another. For example, Fast (2007) used the theories of Bourdieu to explore the experiences and abilities children bring with them into preschool and school, concluding that the pedagogical settings did not particularly acknowledge the social and cultural capital of children. Further, she concluded that continuity related to activities and instructions for reading and writing was weak among the three pedagogical settings: preschool, preschool class and primary school. Sometimes, it appeared that children faced the same didactic content in the preschool class and in Grade 1, regardless of where they were in their learning process. In another study, Skoog (2012) explored literacy practices in the preschool class and Grade 1. The conclusions drawn were quite similar to those of Fast (2007), in that there seemed to be a flimsy connection between the preschool class and Grade 1 with regard to instructions and activities related to literacy and, hence, the continuity for children's learning journeys. As addressed by Sandberg (2012), this lack of connection could mean that children, although reading fluently from the age of 4 or 5 years, face introductory reading instructions first in the preschool class and then again in Grade 1. Vygotsky (1934/1986) argued that teaching and instruction ideally 'marches ahead of development and leads it' (p. 188). The implication of this is that the teachers have to find the zone of proximal development for every individual child and make it the starting point for didactic activities. As reported in the Swedish studies (Fast 2007; Sandberg 2012; Skoog 2012), the transitions between different school forms may cause a break or a pause in children's learning journeys, generating a ditch instead of a bridge.

When children's abilities are not identified as the starting point for learning, difficulties arise for those who are capable as well as those who experience learning challenges. The transition between two educational settings may mean that children who are at risk of encountering difficulties in their learning are not identified and given appropriate or timely support (Sandberg 2012). This approach may lead to experiences of failure for the individual child which, in turn, can have long-term impacts on learning and well-being (Adams 1990; Snow and Juel 2007). According to Stanovich (1986, 2000), learners who face difficulties increasingly avoid activities related to the subject with which they struggle and thus risk ending up in a negative spiral. With reference to the gospel of Matthew, he described the 'Matthew effect', where the rich become richer while the poor become poorer. Stanovich (1986, 2000) showed how the Matthew effect, which widens the gap between those who are doing well and those who are struggling, impacted within a few months after formal reading instruction began. New pedagogies of transition would hopefully reverse this trend and support the learning of all children. Ideally, this would become part of everyday practice, checking what the hazards are from the learner's point of view (Mulholland and Wallace 2003) and offering support in ways that do not risk the learner being stigmatised by the attention and the additional support (Hagtvet et al. 2015).

14.8   Bridges Between Home and School

Although the focus of our discussion in this chapter so far has been on building bridges and borderlands between ECEC and school, it is important to acknowledge that children are also moving between home and school. While the move from ECEC to school is one way, once the transition phase is completed, children navigate daily crossings between home and school. Large-scale studies in the UK (Siraj and Mayo 2014) and the USA (Cooper et al. 2010) have focused on children from disadvantaged backgrounds and demonstrated the power of home learning environments and parental involvement in education to help children succeed in education. However, recent research in the USA by Miller (2015) found that many low-income families received little assistance to address concerns that they identified with their children's transition. Given the high proportion of children living in low-income families, Miller (2015, p. 220) highlighted how crucial it is to 'consider the views and experiences of families from lower-income backgrounds and explore the investments and needs of families in order to support a positive school start for all children'. Given the wealth of transition-to-school research, it is of concern that with the exception of some strong examples (e.g. Dockett et al. 2011), our own research in this area over time suggests that change has been slow to address the inequities for children in this process. Strategies that are put in place need to be mindful of the perspectives of the children and families involved. Ecclestone et al. (2010) noted that the blurring between children's home and school lives, which is generally deemed to be a positive way for schools to connect with and build on children's funds of knowledge from home, also opens up questions about the boundaries between public and private lives and children's right to keep aspects of their home and school lives separate. This finding reminds us that there are no straightforward answers in the pedagogy of educational transitions. While learning about children's home lives to better support the connections with school, teachers need to be respectful about what children and families want to share and to ensure that what is shared is utilised in ways that benefit the child.

14.9   Rites of Passage

Transitions can be seen as an intrinsic component of existence, with the life of an individual in any society including a series of passages 'from one age to another and from one occupation to another' (van Gennep 1977, p. 3). 'Rites of passage' are events during which the move from one age or occupation to the next is accompanied by 'special acts' or ceremonies that enable an individual to move from one defined position to another (van Gennep 1977, p. 3). These can include 'rites of separation', 'rites of transition' and 'rites of incorporation' (van Gennep 1977).

Although there are critiques of van Gennep's work (Watts 2013), aspects can be usefully applied to consider educational transitions. For example, Fabian (2002) considered the way preliminal rites (rites of separation), liminal rites (rites of transition) and postliminal rites (rites of incorporation) applied to the transition to school. Other writers (Ackesjö 2013; Peters 2004) have also drawn on the work of van Gennep to consider the rites of passage as children make the move from ECEC to school. More recently, Garpelin (2014) provided an in-depth discussion of van Gennep's work in relation to school transitions. Sandberg (2012) has also drawn from her work on literacy to consider whether children's step into written language can be interpreted as a rite of passage, suggesting that children become members in a new kind of community and thus pass a threshold when they understand how the alphabetic system works and how to use it.

Utilising the theoretical framework of 'rites of passage' implies a rather different pedagogical approach to either borderlands or bridges, as it emphasises the move to something new. Rather than blurring the boundaries, the differences are marked and celebrated through particular acts and ceremonies accompanying life transitions. In some cultures, rites of passage in the liminal zone include demanding feats of endurance from those being initiated, implying that any transition is supposed to present some challenges. Rites of passage to school tend not to include these demands; however, activities such as buying uniforms and participating in entrance ceremonies may well constitute one form of rites (Fabian 2002). The notion of rites may be useful in understanding the way children see starting school. Educational transitions are not chosen by children, but are something that adults determine for them. If children see it as a rite of passage to a valued new identity and status, they may be more willing to persist with aspects that they find difficult than those for whom all their valued roles and identities are outside of school (Peters 2004).

Although rites of passage are mentioned in a number of transition-to-school studies, it is an area that could be explored further. Only a few studies document what some of these rites are and the role they play in separation, transition and incorporation. One study that looked at this directly was Ackesjö (2013). She felt that children may not have the same understanding as adults about what these rites might be and recommended greater transparency to make the intentions clear to the children involved.

14.10   Conclusion

This chapter has explored ideas around educational borders and thresholds, with the aim of exploring what happens for both children and teachers at these transition points. Thinking about the moves between roles, identities and cultures that are incurred when borders are crossed led to discussions of borderlands, bridges and rites of passage, all of them have implications for research, policy and pedagogies in educational transitions. Borderlands provide space for new, shared understandings. It seems that while building new shared meanings and approaches is potentially challenging for teachers, this can open new possibilities for transition and allow children's learning journeys to be viewed with empathy and understanding. This might also assist in seeing the situation from the learner's viewpoint and becoming 'tourists' in the learner's subculture (Mulholland and Wallace 2003, p. 20).

The metaphor of bridges also offers great potential for collaboration across sectors, to support children's learning as they move from the familiar to the unknown. However, the Swedish example of the preschool class has illustrated that structural changes need to be accompanied by pedagogical and curricular support. The Swedish preschool class offers unique possibilities as both a borderland and a bridge and yet, in practice, was considered a potential ditch (Fast 2007; Sandberg 2012; Skoog 2012) because the shared understandings and connections between the different sectors were not necessarily happening in practice.

The theoretical framework of rites of passage provides a different lens for exploring the experience of transition from the learner's point of view. It raises questions as to whether or not it might be helpful to mark the change in role and status through 'rites of separation', 'rites of transition' and 'rites of incorporation' (van Gennep 1977). More research is required to fully understand the potential of this approach as applied to early years transitions. For example, it would be interesting to consider whether more rites and rituals would assist the transition, and adults would need to look closely at what meaning and influence these had for children, given Ackesjö's (2013) finding that adults and children may assign different meanings to the rituals and ceremonies that mark separation, transition and incorporation rites.

The borderlands, bridges and rites of passage discussed in this chapter call for somewhat different pedagogies, but all have indicated the value of considering the learner's perspective. Athola et al. (2011) questioned whether transition practices themselves are effective for supporting learning or whether strong transition practices are characteristics of 'well-functioning schools and preschools, which have good leadership, high-quality teachers, and other good practices' (p. 301). Certainly, these contextual issues are important, as are the wider policy and societal factors that shape the work of teachers (Peters 2010a). Therefore, research, policy and practice should pay attention both to supporting transition initiatives and to the wider context in which these initiatives take place.

References

Ackesjö, H. (2013). Children crossing borders: School visits as initial incorporation rites in transition to preschool class. *International Journal of Early Childhood, 4*(3), 387–410.

Ackesjö, H. (2014). Children's transitions to school in a changing educational landscape: Borders, identities and (dis)continuities. *International Journal of Transitions in Childhood, 7*, 3–5.

Adams, M. J. (1990). *Beginning to read: Thinking and learning about print.* Cambridge, MA: The MIT Press.

Anzaldúa, G. (2012). (Un)natural bridges, (un)safe spaces. In G. Anzaldúa & A. L. Keating (Eds.), *This bridge we call home: Radical visions for transformation* (pp. 1–5). New York: Routledge.

Athola, A., Silinskas, G., Poikonen, P.-L., Kontoniemi, M., Niemi, P., & Nurmi, J.-E. (2011). Transition to formal schooling: Do transition practices matter for academic performance? *Early Childhood Research Quarterly, 26,* 295–302.

Britt, C., & Sumsion, J. (2003). Within the borderlands: Beginning early childhood teachers in primary schools. *Contemporary Issues in Early Childhood, 4*(2), 115–136.

Brooker, L. (2008). *Supporting transitions in the early years.* Maidenhead: Open University Press.

Bulkeley, J., & Fabian, H. (2006). Well-being and belonging during early educational transitions. *International Journal of Transitions in Childhood, 2,* 18–30.

Carr, M., Cowie, B., & Davies, K. (2015). *Continuity of early learning: Learning progress and outcomes in the early years. Report on the literature scan,* Report commissioned by Ministry of Education. Wellington: Ministry of Education.

Clandinin, D. J., & Rosiek, J. (2007). Mapping a landscape of narrative inquiry: Borderland spaces and tensions. In D. J. Clandinin (Ed.), *Handbook of narrative inquiry* (pp. 35–75). London: Sage.

Cooper, C. E., Crosnoe, R., Suizzo, M.-A., & Pituch, K. A. (2010). Poverty, race, and parental involvement during the transition to elementary school. *Journal of Family Issues, 31*(7), 859–883.

Crafter, S., & Maunder, R. (2012). Understanding transitions using a sociocultural framework. *Educational & Child Psychology, 29*(1), 10–18.

De Roover, M. (2012). *Internalizing borderlands: The performance of borderlands identity.* Unpublished Masters thesis, The University of Guelph, Canada.

Dockett, S., & Perry, B. (2014). *Continuity of learning: A resource to support effective transition to school and school age care.* Canberra: Australian Government Department of Education.

Dockett, S., Perry, B., Kearney, E., Hampshire, A., Mason, J., & Schmied, V. (2011). *Facilitating children's transition to school from families with complex support needs.* Albury: Research Institute for Professional Practice, Learning and Education, Charles Sturt University.

Ecclestone, K., Biesta, G., & Hughes, M. (2010). *Transitions and learning through the life course.* London/New York: Routledge.

Education Review Office. (2015). *Continuity of learning: Transitions from early childhood services to schools.* Education Evaluation Reports. http://www.ero.govt.nz/publications/continuity-of-learning-transitions-from-early-childhood-services-to-schools/. Accessed 27 Oct 2015.

Educational Transitions and Change (ETC) Research Group. (2011). *Transition to school: Position statement.* Albury: RIPPLE, Charles Sturt University. http://www.csu.edu.au/faculty/educat/edu/transitions/publications/Position-Statement.pdf. Accessed 15 Feb 2015.

Edwards, A. (2011). Building common knowledge at the boundaries between professional practices: Relational agency and relational expertise in system of distributed expertise. *International Journal of Educational Research, 50*(1), 33–39.

Einarsdóttir, J. (2007). Children's voices on the transition from preschool to primary school. In A.-W. Dunlop & H. Fabian (Eds.), *Informing transitions in the early years: Research, policy and practice* (pp. 74–91). Maidenhead: McGraw-Hill.

Fabian, H. (2002). *Children starting school.* London: David Fulton.

Fast, C. (2007). *Sju barn lär sig läsa och skriva: Familjeliv och populärkultur i möte med förskola och skola* [Seven children learning to read and write: Family life and popular culture meet preschool and school]. (Uppsala Studies in Education, 115). Uppsala: Acta Universitatis Upsaliensis.

Fischbein, S., Rydelius, P-A., & Björck-Åkesson, E. (2006). *Tvärvetenskaplig samverkan—kring lärande, delaktighet och hälsa i samspel med den pedagogiska miljön* [Interdisciplinary collaboration on learning, participation and health in harmony with the educational environment].

I Resultatdialog 2006. Forskning inom utbildningsvetenskap (Vetenskapsrådets rap-portserie 15). Stockholm: Vetenskapsrådet.

Garpelin, A. (2014). Transition to school: A rite of passage in life. In B. Perry, S. Dockett, & A. Petriwskyj (Eds.), *Transitions to school: International research, policy and practice* (pp. 117–128). Dordrecht: Springer.

Hagtvet, B., Frost, J., & Refsahl, V. (2015). *Den intensive leseopplæringen: Dialog og mestring når lesingen har låst seg* [The intensive reading instruction: Dialogue and mastering when reading has locked up]. Cappelen Damm Akademisk 2015.

Halonen, A., Aunola, K., Ahonen, T., & Nurmi, J.-E. (2006). The role of learning to read in the development of problem behaviour: A cross-lagged longitudinal study. *British Journal of Educational Psychology, 76*(3), 517–534.

Hartley, C., Rogers, P., Smith, J., Peters, S., & Carr, M. (2012). *Crossing the border: A community negotiates the transition from early childhood to primary school*. Wellington: NZCER.

Hohepa, M. (2014). Riariakina ō rongo hirikapo. Teaching and Learning Research initiative project. http://www.tlri.org.nz/tlri-research/research-progress/cross-sector/riariakina-%C5%8D-rongo-hirikapo. Accessed 27 Mar 2015.

Hörschelmann, K. (2011). Theorising life transitions: Geographical perspectives. *Area, 43*(4), 378–383.

Kaga, Y. (2007). Preschool class for 6-year-olds in Sweden: A bridge between early childhood and compulsory school, UNESCO Policy Brief on Early Childhood, No. 38. http://unesdoc.unesco.org/images/0015/001508/150815e.pdf. Accessed 27 Mar 2015.

Kagan, S. L., & Neville, P. R. (1996). Combining endogenous and exogenous factors in the shift years: The transition to school. In A. J. Sameroff & M. M. Haith (Eds.), *The five to seven year shift: The age of reason and responsibility* (pp. 385–405). Chicago: The University of Chicago Press.

Karila, K., & Rantavuori, L. (2014). Discourses at the boundary spaces: Developing a fluent transition from preschool to school. *Early Years, 34*(4), 377–391.

Miller, K. (2015). The transition to kindergarten: How families from lower-income backgrounds experience the first year. *Early Childhood Education Journal, 43*(3), 213–221.

Mitchell, L., Cowie, B., Clarkin-Phillips, J., Davis, K., Glasgow, A., & Hatherly, A. et al. (2015). *Continuity of early learning: Learning progress and outcomes in the early years. Overview report on data findings*. Report commissioned by Ministry of Education. Wellington: Ministry of Education.

Mulholland, J., & Wallace, J. (2003). Strength, sharing and service: Restorying and the legitimation of research texts. *British Educational Research Journal, 29*(1), 5–23.

Newman, D., & Paasi, A. (1998). Fences and neighbours in the postmodern world: Boundary narratives in political geography. *Progress in Human Geography, 22*, 186–207.

Noel, A. (2011). Easing the transition to school: Administrators' descriptions of transition to school activities. *Australasian Journal of Early Childhood, 36*(4), 44–52.

O'Toole, L., Hayes, N., & Mhic Mhathúna, M. (2014). A bio-ecological perspective on educational transition. *Procedia-Social and Behavioral Sciences, 140*, 121–127.

Peters, S. (2004). *Crossing the border: An interpretive study of children making the transition to school*. Unpublished doctoral thesis, University of Waikato, Hamilton, New Zealand.

Peters, S. (2010a). *Literature review: Transition from early childhood education to school*. Report commissioned by the Ministry of Education. Wellington: Ministry of Education. http://www.educationcounts.govt.nz/publications/ECE/98894/Executive_Summary

Peters, S. (2010b). Shifting the lens: Re-framing the view of learners and learning during the transition from early childhood education to school in New Zealand. In D. Jindal-Snape (Ed.), *Educational transitions: Moving stories from around the world* (pp. 68–84). New York: Routledge.

Peters, S. (2014). Chasms, bridges and borderlands: A transitions research 'across the border' from early childhood education to school in New Zealand. In B. Perry, S. Dockett, & A. Petriwskyj

(Eds.), *Transitions to school: International research, policy and practice* (pp. 105–116). Dordrecht: Springer.

Peters, S., Paki, V. & Davis, K. (2015). *Learning journeys from early childhood into school.* Teaching and Learning Research initiative final report. http://www.tlri.org.nz/sites/default/files/projects/TLRI_%20Peters_Summary%28v2%29%20%281%29.pdf Accessed 27 Aug 2015.

Sandberg, G. (2012). *På väg in i skolan: Om villkor för olika barns delaktighet och skriftspråkslärande* [On their way into school: About conditions for participation and learning]. (Studia Didactica Upsaliensia 6). Uppsala: Acta Universitatis Upsaliensis.

Sandberg, G., Hellblom-Thibblin, T., & Garpelin, A. (2014). Transition to school: A Swedish perspective. *Early Childhood Folio, 18*(2), 15–21.

Sandberg, G., Hellblom-Thibblin, T., & Garpelin, A. (2015). Teacher's perspective on how to promote children's learning in reading and writing. *European Journal of Special Needs Education.* doi:10.1080/08856257.2015.1046738.

Schielack, J., & Seeley, C. L. (2010). Transitions from elementary to middle school math. *Teaching Children Mathematics, 16*(6), 358–362.

Siraj, I., & Mayo, A. (2014). *Social class and educational inequality: The impact of parents and schools.* Cambridge: Cambridge University Press.

Skoog, M. (2012). *Skriftspråkande i förskoleklass och årskurs 1* [Literacy in preschool-class and grade one]. (Örebro Studies in Education 33). Örebro: Örebro universitet.

Snow, C. E., & Juel, C. (2007). Teaching children to read: What do we know about how to do it? In M. J. Snowling & C. Hulme (Eds.), *The science of reading: A handbook* (pp. 521–537). Malden: Blackwell.

Stanovich, K. E. (1986). Matthew effects in reading: Some consequences of individual differences in the acquisition of literacy. *Reading Research Quarterly, 21*, 360–407.

Stanovich, K. E. (2000). *Progress in understanding reading: Scientific foundations and new frontiers.* New York/London: Guilford.

Taguma, M., Litjens, I., & Makowiecki, K. (2013). *Quality matters in early childhood education and care Sweden.* OECD. http://www.oecd.org/edu/school/SWEDEN%20policy%20profile%20-%20published%2005-02-2013.pdf. Accessed 27 Mar 2015.

Turner, V. (1977). Variations on a theme of liminality. In S. F. Moore & B. G. Myerhoff (Eds.), *Secular ritual* (pp. 36–52). Amsterdam: Van Gorcum.

van Gennep, A. (1977). *The rites of passage.* London: Routledge.

Vygotsky, L. (1934/1986). *Thought and language.* (A. Kozulin, Trans. and Ed.) Cambridge, MA: The MIT Press..

Watts, T. E. (2013). Big ideas: 'Les rites de passage' Arnold van Gennep 1909. *Nurse Education Today, 33*, 312–313.

Wenger, E. (1998). *Communities of practice: Learning, meaning, and identity.* Cambridge: Cambridge University Press.

Chapter 15
Educational Practices and Children's Learning Journeys from Preschool to Primary School

Gunilla Sandberg, Kenneth Ekström, Tina Hellblom-Thibblin, Pernilla Kallberg, and Anders Garpelin

Children all around the world pass through a number of transitions in educational systems. These transitions are organised in different ways in different countries. In Sweden, children pass through three school forms in early childhood education: preschool, preschool class and primary school. In a research project funded by the Swedish Research Council, the Swedish POET group conducted case studies in three municipalities, using participant observations, semi-structured interviews and focus group interviews. The aim has been to deepen the understanding of children's learning journeys from preschool into school. A second aim has been to examine the long-term implications of educational practices across the transitions for children's learning and participation. In this chapter, some findings from the research project are presented. The results show how the complex structure of Swedish early childhood education creates challenges for children and their learning journeys.

15.1 Introduction

Educational transitions are organised in different ways in different countries. Children pass through a number of marked transitions, organised on the basis of age group and stages or types of schools. In Sweden, young children pass through three school forms: preschool, preschool class and primary school. During their learning journey, they face different educational cultures in terms of the ways teachers

G. Sandberg (✉) • T. Hellblom-Thibblin • P. Kallberg • A. Garpelin
Mälardalen University, Västerås, Sweden
e-mail: gunilla.sandberg@mdh.se

K. Ekström
Mälardalen University, Västerås, Sweden

Umeå University, Umeå, Sweden

© Springer International Publishing Switzerland 2017
N. Ballam et al. (eds.), *Pedagogies of Educational Transitions*, International
Perspectives on Early Childhood Education and Development 16,
DOI 10.1007/978-3-319-43118-5_15

arrange their pedagogical settings and provide learning opportunities. In this chapter, the aim is to extend the understanding of different children's learning journeys from preschool to primary school in terms of teachers' perspectives. The way teaching and instruction is shaped can provide clues about teachers' pedagogical beliefs and approaches.

In this chapter, we present some of the different pedagogical territories that children encounter during their early years (3–8 years old) through descriptions of the organisation and regulation of the Swedish preschool, preschool class and Grade 1 in primary school. Empirical examples of teaching practices are presented, revealing teachers' pedagogical beliefs and approaches. Finally, challenges and implications for children's transitions and learning in early childhood education are discussed.

15.2 Background

Transitions may relate to individual events for people, such as their first words or first steps, but they can also be understood in a broader sociocultural perspective, such as constructing roles or identities in a community (Fabian 2007; Garpelin 2003; Rogoff 2003). The term transition in an educational context is generally understood as a process of moving from one setting or phase to another. How the transition from one educational setting to another is experienced and the impact of this on well-being and learning opportunities are well documented. Frequently, such discussions refer to children's school readiness and/or the schools' readiness (Lam and Pollard 2006). Research stresses that these transitions are important events in the lives of children, both from the perspective of here and now, and in the longer term. The transitions in which children take part during their years in the educational system might be considered as natural, something everyone has to do, or regarded as critical, with risks to the well-being of the individual. Children of today are more accustomed to changes and transitions than in the past, but that does not mean that their experiences are the same. For children who are in some way more vulnerable than others, the transition between different activities and types of schools may imply special stresses (Bulkeley and Fabian 2006; Dockett and Perry 2007; Garpelin 2003).

This chapter addresses the different cultures and settings children encounter during their learning journeys from preschool to school. Those two educational institutions are based on different historical and epistemological traditions and represent different ways of arranging pedagogical settings (Mackenzie 2014; Peters 2010). As concluded by Einarsdóttir (2006), the emphasis in preschool is placed on care, play and freedom, while the activity in primary school is more directed to school subjects, lessons and controls.

The introduction of the Swedish preschool class was an attempt to meld together the two different pedagogical traditions from preschool and school, to create a new kind of pedagogical setting for 6-year-olds. However, this aim has not necessarily been achieved, with some studies reporting that the preschool class became school-like in terms of formal instructions and work structured by lessons (Karlsson et al. 2006). The picture emerging from our studies (Sandberg 2012; Sandberg et al. 2014) is that while the teachers in preschool class defend their belief in preschool pedagogy, they also add more school-like activities to their teaching. The results from our research can be compared with findings reported from Norway when the last year of preschool was changed to become the first year of school. The new Grade 1 for 6-year-olds was found to be arranged as a mix of the most extreme components from preschool and school: free play and workbooks (Eriksen Hagtvet 2003).

Studies of transition from preschool to school stress the importance of providing continuity for children's learning processes, but this does not necessarily mean that the practices children move to have to be identical to those they left. On the contrary, studies drawing on children's perspectives show that they often appreciate a marked transition and new challenges (Garpelin 2003; Sandberg 2012). One aspect that has proven to be important for continuity for children's learning processes is that teachers from preschools and schools collaborate on curricula and thus prevent a break in the children's learning process (Athola et al. 2010; Peters 2010, 2014). Peters used the concept of borderlands, referring to a common sphere of understanding, a 'shared space between the early childhood and school' (Peters 2010, p. 81), which is created between the teachers who transmit and receive a child at a transition between different stages. The creation of the preschool class was an attempt by the Swedish government to create such a space, physically as well as epistemologically.

15.3 Theoretical Perspectives

Bronfenbrenner's (1979) ecological system has been useful in understanding transitions and their importance for children. In this model, children's development and learning are considered a consequence of factors and circumstances from micro to macro level. According to this theory, a transition is characterised by changes in activities, relationships and roles.

Another analytical term that has been applied is 'rites of passage' (Fabian and Dunlop 2007; Garpelin 2014; van Gennep 1908/1997). This term refers to the culturally bound rituals that may be related to different developmental and life crises in connection with transitions between different stages in individuals' lives. Van Gennep divided rites of passage into three phases: preliminal/separation, liminal/transition and postliminal/incorporation. According to the rites of passage theory, the individual can handle the different transitions more easily if they occur in the company of other people.

Corsaro and Molinari (2000) developed the notion of 'priming events' to describe and analyse activities in which children, through their involvement, attend prospectively to ongoing or expected changes in their lives. Teachers and children together create a community in which the children make friends, socialise and develop by taking an active part in, and contributing to, cultural production and change (interpretive reproduction). The concept of priming events has been used as an analytic tool in our studies.

A transition from one pedagogical setting to another entails changes in one way or another and leads to opportunities, as well as challenges, for children. Providing and promoting continuity in children's learning processes during these transitions are of major importance. Closely related to continuity in learning is Vygotsky's (1934/1986) theory on the zone of proximal development. According to this theory, teachers should consider where the child is situated in terms of learning and development and offer practical support in the learning process.

In order to understand transitions as social and cultural historical events, 'activity theory' (Engeström 1987) has been useful. It is also useful in order to understand different practices and how they function as systems in which the children play different types of roles and are given different opportunities. These systems need to be understood to be able to understand the transitions between them. Drawing on this theoretical base, research interest has attended to actions carried out by teachers as they organise pedagogical environments and transitory activities. There may be many, sometimes divergent, motives for an activity system – motives reflecting the social struggle and the differing interests within a society. Understanding practitioners' actions, therefore, requires an examination of the way they interpret the activities they are involved in (Hundeide 2003). Instruments are used to achieve the objectives of activity systems (Engeström and Sannino 2010). Instruments may be symbolic tools, such as language, or material tools, such as pencils or computers. In preschool education, they could include educational methods, ways of organising work, disposal of time and space and so on.

Adults' encounters with the children, and the purposes behind these, are regarded as important instruments in transitory activities. It is here assumed that children entering a new class also enter a new culture with new instruments to master and that this is a part of the transitory process as well as a part of the learning process. The study of instruments, in other words, is a study of educational framings because as Rogoff (2003, p. 6) claims, 'What people in community do depends in important ways on the cultural meaning given to the event'.

15.4   Method

In our research, we applied an interpretive approach (Erickson 1986; Garpelin 1997) with its roots in hermeneutics and phenomenology (Dilthey 1883/1976; Ödman 2007). Using an interpretive approach, we chose methods for gathering and analysing data commonly applied in qualitative research in general and ethnographic research in particular (Erickson 1986; Hammersley and Atkinson 1995; Walford 2008). The studies referred to in this chapter focus on the activities arranged in the preschool for 3–5-year-olds, the preschool class and the first year of primary school and the transitions between these school forms. The empirical data consist of interviews with teachers and classroom observations in the three school forms. Data have been transcribed and analysed in various ways, including content analyses, analyses of teachers' perspectives with inspiration from hermeneutic perspectives and analyses of activity systems.

Ethics is a critical aspect of ethnographic research. There are many ethical issues that need to be taken into account when entering other people's everyday environments as a researcher, especially when there are children involved. In our research, project issues concerning informed consent, confidentiality and management of data were carefully considered, applying rules and guidelines from the regulations for research specified by the Swedish Research Council (2015).

15.5 Three School Forms in Children's Learning Journeys

In this chapter, some findings will be presented concerning the transitions from preschool, via the preschool class, to school. As noted earlier, the complex structure of Swedish early childhood education, with three different school forms, created challenges for the children and their learning journeys.

15.5.1 Preschool

The Swedish preschool offers full-time day care for children aged 1–5 years. In 2013, 84.2 % of all Swedish children aged between one and five and 94.6 % of those aged between four and five were enrolled in a preschool (The Swedish National Agency for Education 2013). In Sweden, it is mandatory for municipalities to provide preschool education for children from the age of 1 year if the parents are studying or employed. All children have the right to preschool education from the age of 3 years (The Swedish National Agency for Education 2013).

Preschool education is tax subsidised and financed by additional parental fees. Normally, a formal specialised education at either upper secondary education level (children's nurse) or university level (preschool teacher) is required to work in preschool education. Thus, in 2012, 91.4 % of employees in preschools possessed such formal qualifications (The Swedish National Agency for Education 2013). The national curriculum for preschool education was revised in 2010, specifying more precise requirements concerning the contents of learning. The curriculum states:

> The preschool should stimulate children's development and learning and offer secure care. Activities should be based on a holistic view of the child and his or her needs and be designed so that care, socialisation and learning together form a coherent whole. (The Swedish National Agency for Education 2010, p. 4)

The curriculum is built on a child-centred tradition. It states that the child's curiosity, initiative and interests should be encouraged and their will and desire to learn should be stimulated. It also states that children should have the opportunity to explore an issue of their own in greater depth and to search for their own answers and solutions to problems and questions.

15.5.1.1 Preschool in Practice

The first example of pedagogical practice in this area came from a cooperative preschool, owned by the employees, in which the teachers were working with 22 children aged 3–5 years. In the cooperative there was a strong, shared vision concerning objectives and curriculum content. The preschool worked thematically and tried to integrate the theme throughout the working day with the explicit purpose of developing every child's abilities, as declared in their programme:

> Our theme, the senses, should permeate our environments where diversity of materials and modes of expression allow, challenge and develop children's abilities.

In this preschool, themes were being explored over a long period of time, with the children reporting on what they had done in the project as a recurrent activity. In planned activities, the children's participation was regarded as important. For the remaining time, the children had a considerable amount of freedom to play independently and to explore and work with different kinds of aesthetic subjects, but with responsibilities for each other and materials. Circle time was mainly used to organise project work and to recapitulate what had happened during the activities. The children's interests were captured through documentation and discussed by the team. Issues raised by the children during activities were also discussed in the work team and with the children. At the time of this research, the preschool was working with the theme 'senses', and the children's abilities in relation to the senses were examined in many different ways. The themes were supposed to provide the opportunity to explore the senses in depth and breadth, with many different opportunities for learning. However, the teachers stressed that the purpose was also to strengthen group solidarity. Children's own exploration and activity were regarded as important. They initiated new issues and exerted an influence on what happened. The teachers, whose social constructivist approach to knowledge was essential, led the process by providing information, guidance and challenges. As one teacher noted, they tried to invent projects related to the children's questions:

> The kids had a theory that you hear better if you have hair in your ears. So first, the kids got to listen to some everyday sounds without hair in the ears. Then they had to try out different "hair" in their own ears. They were given the choice of human hair, cotton or wool. They came to the conclusion that they actually hear better without hair in their ears.

There was great variation in the preschool in the way in which the theme was implemented. The teachers and children conducted studies and worked with different aesthetic expressions, both individually and in groups. A variety of materials were used. The teachers often provided feedback and asked if the children remembered what they did and what happened. They asked comparative questions of the children and negotiated with them about what was happening and what to do. In the following year, when the preschool teachers planned the theme 'our senses', they drew on the children's interest in working with aesthetic expression and introduced the children to the theme by visiting an art museum. The children drew and talked about their experiences. Their stories were recorded in writing beside their pictures. As a follow-up, over a long period, the children produced dragons similar to those they had seen at the art museum, which resulted in their own exhibition at the preschool. They made another visit to the museum and saw an exhibition that was made up of mirrors. The teachers built a mirror corner in a room at the nursery. The mirror corner was constructed by different variations of mirrors on the floor, walls and ceiling. Then the children got to explore, first in small groups and then as they wished.

Staff at another preschool for children aged 4–5 years worked in a similar way with the theme of 'water'. The teachers in this setting stated in documentation that:

> In discussions with the children, we concluded that water is transparent when it comes from the tap but it is blue in the sea and in the river. We agreed that we should go and fetch water from the river and compare with our tap water. One of the children had a theory that we should not fetch water from the shore where the water is transparent; we must go further out and retrieve the blue water. We also thought about the smell and taste: it smells like nothing, was the general opinion, and it tastes like cold or hot. Otherwise it tastes like "just water". Jessica also asked where water is available. There is the sea, lake, river, stream, tap, puddle, the clouds, the rain, the bathtub, toilet, waterfall, stream, pipe, on the beach, bathhouse, fire truck and in the river.

In both of these preschools, there was criticism among the preschool teachers concerning how the collaboration with the school and work around preparation for, and receiving children to, preschool class had been organised previously. Initiatives had been taken by the principals to develop a programme to prepare for the transition and to bridge the gap between the preschool and the preschool class. The programme had been developed through collaboration between preschool teachers and teachers in the preschool class. This programme was implemented for the first time during the time of our project. The programme included planned visits by the receiving teacher at the preschools as well as visits by the children to the preschool class. The jointly drafted document contained provisions on how information would be provided for parents, by whom, when and in what form. It also specified the information to be transferred from preschool to preschool class.

To summarise, these preschools were characterised by educational practice that emphasised children's own activities and meaning making. The educational environment aimed to promote children's independence and responsibility. The children's learning was mainly mediated by teacher organisation of learning activities based on experiments and investigations in which the children's experiences were taken as points of departure. The children and teachers tested and discussed ideas collectively.

15.5.2 Preschool Class

Since 1998, Swedish municipalities have been required to provide all 6-year-olds with a place in a preschool class, which is a voluntary school form, free of charge. Almost all Swedish children attend the preschool class. It is common that the teachers working in the preschool class are qualified preschool teachers with professional experiences from preschool. The preschool class is usually located in the same building as the Grade 1 school class and the after-school childcare centre. The preschool class was founded to bridge the gap between preschool and primary school in such a way that a synthesis of these seemingly different pedagogical environments and traditions was achieved. There were also financial and practical incentives to the founding of this form of school (Persson 2008). The curriculum for compulsory school, preschool class and after-school care centre, LGR 11 (The Swedish National Agency for Education 2011), applies to preschool classes. This curriculum is divided into three parts. The first part of the curriculum concerns the school's fundamental values and tasks, emphasising the democratic foundation of education and the opportunities for a lifelong desire to learn:

> The task of school is to encourage pupils to discover their own uniqueness as individuals and thereby be able to participate in the life of society by giving their best in responsible freedom. (The Swedish National Agency for Education 2011, p. 9)

In the second part of the curriculum, overall goals and guidelines for education are presented and divided into eight areas: norms and values, knowledge, responsibility and influence of pupils, school and home, transition and cooperation, the school and the surrounding world, assessment and grading and the responsibility of the principal. The third part of the curriculum includes the syllabus, outlining the aims and core content for subjects and knowledge requirements stated after Grades 3, 6 and 9. It does not apply to the preschool class.

15.5.2.1 Preschool Class in Practice

The teachers from the preschool class in our study said that the most essential aim of the activities was supporting the children's self-esteem, social participation and well-being, leading to the outcome that the children would develop social skills and learn how to respect and trust each other. The preschool class was thus supposed to provide children with a good socio-emotional foundation to lean on before facing the expectations and challenges of school:

> The most important task for me is creating a stable group, characterised by good relationships and well-being among the children. The stable group makes it possible for them to focus schoolwork in Grade 1. (Teacher in preschool class)

Further, the teachers claimed that the year in preschool class was preparatory; it prepared the children to become pupils in school. The children became familiar with the school environment and they learned how to behave in different school contexts. The preparation was also about meeting the demands of school that require concentration and focus – 'sitting on a chair and working with a pencil in your hand', as one of the teachers interviewed in the study said. The preschool classes in the study arranged lessons in which these skills were practised, known as school-work. With regard to academic learning and development, all the teachers repeated that the preschool class was not school, so, for example, drilling letters or numbers would not occur in their classrooms. The preschool class was regarded as a place where the children had the opportunity to meet and investigate reading, writing and mathematics through playful and creative activities:

> When children start in preschool class, many of them say that when you start school you should read, write and do mathematics. And what is mathematics? The children expect it to be counting: 4 and 2 is 6. So there are many children who come to us with the attitude that this is what we should do. As one of the girls said to me: "We are not doing mathematics for real!"' We are working with concepts and preparatory mathematics on the basis of play. And for the girl, this is not real maths. (Teacher in preschool class)

The views expressed in the quotation above are in line with the way the activities related to literacy and numeracy were planned and arranged in the preschool classes examined. There was a strong focus on play and games to stimulate and prepare for future learning, in combination with tasks on worksheets such as the one described below. The activities aimed at stimulating academic learning such as literacy and numeracy were not individualised; thus, all of the children were given the same tasks, regardless of where they were in their learning process:

> The circle time opens with a 'good morning song' sung in Swedish, English, German, French and Finnish. Tuesday is mathematics day and one of the two teachers shows a 12-sided dice to the children and puts it in a jar. Then all of the children pull the dice from the jar and go out and find as many stones as the number they got. When they return inside they put the stones in front of them, compare them and play with them for a while. One of the teachers then puts a tray in the middle of the circle and asks the children who has the largest and the smallest stone to put them on the tray and then she initiates a discussion about the concepts big, small and in between. After the circle time the children are given a worksheet. The task is to paint as many things as the given number indicates. (From an observation in preschool class)

In addition to the preparatory aspects, great emphasis was placed on children's free play. Free play in this context means that the children chose activities and play-mates themselves. From observations it appeared that free play was an activity that was used in different ways. In the case studies, teachers expressed the value of free play as a rich ground for the children's learning and not least for their social development. Another aspect of free play was as a kind of reward, with the children allowed to play after finishing their work. Free play also sometimes seemed to be the time when the teachers could do something else, such as take a break, put things away, talk with parents or prepare new activities.

The activities in preschool class were, to a great extent, characterised by preparation for primary school. However, at the end of the last term in preschool class, the school preparation activities increased. As an example, the children in preschool class visited Grade 1 and met their future teacher. Before the start of school, the teachers conducted a screening of the children's literacy and numeracy knowledge.

To summarise, the activities in preschool classes reflected traditions and practices from preschool as well as from school, but there was not a synthesis. It could be better described as a school form with two different traditions, play and formal instruction, which run parallel, like two streams. The children's learning activities were mediated by playful means and by using worksheets that did not take into account the variation in the children's experiences. The tasks given to the children were constructed from a view of knowledge as something essential. The tasks given to the children were often not very stimulating or challenging. This raised questions about the school form: was it a real bridge or was it holding the children in limbo?

15.5.3   Primary School

Generally, Swedish children start primary school in August the year they turn seven. Teachers working in Grade 1 are qualified primary school teachers and usually follow the same group of children up to Grade 3. The preschool class and the first 3 years of school are usually organised in cooperation with the after-school care centre, often sharing the same premises. In some schools, students attending Grades 1–3 are divided into mixed-aged classes. From Grade 1, the syllabuses and knowledge requirements formulated in the Swedish compulsory school curriculum (The Swedish National Agency for Education 2011) are applied. In this part of the curriculum, the core content and knowledge requirements for Grades 1–3 are specified for each school subject (such as music, mathematics, science and Swedish).

15.5.3.1   Primary School in Practice

Activities in Grade 1 were, to a great extent, structured into lessons in the various school subjects with a great emphasis placed on literacy and numeracy. The teachers considered it vital to identify where children were in their learning process in order to provide tasks at an appropriate level for each one of them in the classroom. This was achieved by using qualitative and quantitative types of mapping. The work, for example, in literacy or mathematics, was organised in a mix of joint activities (lectures, discussions, play) and individual desk work.

Two strategies for organising individual work emerged from the empirical data; the first was structured around the idea that children should work according to their own preconditions and at their own pace. Thus, the children, to a considerable degree, planned their own work, and a large amount of time was spent on individual work. The other visible teaching strategy was a strong focus on a shared community in terms of joint activities and discussions. The work in the classroom included a base for everyone to work with, complemented by additional tasks on the individual level:

> The lesson starts on the carpet in the middle of the room where the teacher and the children sit together in a circle. After some small talk, they play *A ship comes carrying …* and then the teacher initiates a discussion about how to construct a sentence. After that the children

go to their desks and work with a given task related to the shared activity about sentences. Gradually, as they are finished, the children choose individual tasks: Adam and Bob play a game where you must match the images with the first letter. Cilla, David and Eric are playing a reading game together on the carpet. Felix, Greta and Harriet are working with reading tasks in a self-instruction book called Apple. Inez is doing a reading puzzle and Jason is reading books from his individual list of books. Karen is reading a book together with the teacher. (From an observation in Grade 1)

Of course, there were other activities for the learners in Grade 1, such as music and science. The school day was structured by lessons, breaks and lunch. Free play took place during the breaks and after school in the after-school care centre, to which most of the children went. Although there was great emphasis on academic skills, teachers in Grade 1 underlined their work with social relationships among the children and the way the two interacted: 'learning and togetherness are inter-twined' (Teacher, Grade 1).

To summarise, the activities in Grade 1 of primary school were, to a great extent, affected by the new demands imposed concerning learning for the individual child and were thus organised in accordance with school subjects and lessons. The teaching in Grade 1 was characterised by pluralism and variation. One example was the teachers' perspectives on reading and writing instruction, which represented a range of approaches based on different theoretical standpoints, all aimed at promoting learning and development. In addition to the emphasis on academic learning in Grade 1, great importance was attached to children's social participation and competence.

15.6   Discussion

The three school forms for children aged 3–8 years examined in this research project revealed different pedagogical practices and ways of providing opportunities for children to learn and to participate. In accordance with other studies (Einarsdóttir 2006; Mackenzie 2014; Peters 2010), preschool practice, in broad terms, could be described using hallmarks such as care, play and children's interests and experiences, investigations and knowledge construction as a basis for teaching. The pedagogical practice in primary school is characterised by school subjects, knowledge, assessments and compulsory participation in ongoing activities. The Swedish preschool class is both metaphorically and literally placed in between preschool and primary school. This finding can be compared with the picture given by Eriksen Hagtvet (2003) of the new Grade 1 for 6-year-olds in Norway, interpreted as a mix of the two extremes from preschool and school, free play and formalised tasks.

The differences in activities between the three pedagogical school forms that emerged in our research could be related to the national curricula. According to Hellblom-Thibblin (2004), a curriculum can be used as an analysis tool with the intention of clarifying the relationship between curricula and teachers' perceptions. In Sweden, activities in the preschool are regulated by the curriculum for preschool,

Lpfö 98 (The Swedish National Agency for Education 2010). The curriculum for compulsory school, preschool class and the after-school care centre, LGR 11 (The Swedish National Agency for Education 2011), applies to the preschool class and Grade 1 in primary school. The two curricula rest on similar fundamental values, tasks for preschool/school, goals and guidelines. However, there are differences between the curricula. The curriculum for primary school includes syllabus and knowledge requirements in a number of subjects, which exerts a major influence on the way activities are designed. In the curriculum for preschool, there are guidelines on the preschool teachers' responsibility to promote children's learning in different areas, as illustrated by one example: 'An ability to make use of, interpret and talk about pictures, texts and different media' (The Swedish National Agency for Education 2010, p. 10). This has a corresponding description in the third part of the curriculum for primary school, which stipulates that education in Grades 1–3 must contain 'texts that combine words and pictures, such as films, interactive games and web texts' (The Swedish National Agency for Education 2011, p. 212). This example of continuity between the two curricula is about literacy, but the same occurs in numeracy, science, nature and technology. As shown in our research, the position of preschool class, being 'in between', is valid in relation to the curricula. The third part of the curriculum (LGR 11), containing syllabus and knowledge requirements, does not apply to the preschool class. In practice, this means that teachers in the preschool class do not have any guidelines for what their activities should include except that they should fulfil the more overall aims of school. This contributes to the creation of a school form that does not serve as a bridge to school but rather creates a ditch, or perhaps even a place of limbo, for some children.

Given the picture emerging from the practices examined, the conclusion is that there are significant differences between the three school forms in terms of organisation, content and teaching methods. The demands and guidelines in the curricula exert a major impact on the way practices take shape, but there are other factors of importance as well. Traces from different theories and epistemological traditions could be found in the way teachers created the educational settings. This circumstance on its own may not be critical for children's learning journeys. With reference to earlier research (Corsaro and Molinari 2000; Garpelin 2003), a new setting providing new and different challenges as well as opportunities can be both positive and beneficial for children's learning and well-being.

Even though the difference between the three educational settings can be experienced as positive from an actor perspective, there are some more problematic aspects that appeared from the empirical data. One was the lack of connection, in terms of teachers' pedagogical and didactical cooperation, between the three school forms. There did not seem to be any common ground for the teachers' sharing, discussion or development of teaching strategies. This is an important factor, addressed in earlier studies, with regard to creating continuity for children's learning during an educational transition (Athola et al. 2010; Mackenzie 2014; Peters 2010, 2014). Another problematic aspect is identified if the new setting is less demanding, and in some respects less qualified, than the previous one. From our research, it appeared that this may have been the case for some of the children, especially during the transition from preschool to the preschool class. In preschool, the activities mediating learning were more complex than they were in the preschool class. They were also constructed on the basis of the children's experiences and took different children's knowledge levels into account. This was not the case in the preschool class. With reference to the theory on the zone of proximal development (Vygotsky 1934/1986), this could have a negative effect on the continuity of the children's learning journeys, meaning that the learning activities provided in the preschool class were often not very challenging. Preschools and schools in Sweden arrange the transition from one setting to another in many different ways as a consequence of, for example, municipality regulation, practical reasons or pedagogical beliefs. Something clearly apparent is that Swedish children pass through two pedagogical transitions in just over a year. According to Bronfenbrenner (1979), an ecological transition takes place when 'a person's position in the ecological environment is altered as a result of change in role or setting or both' (p. 45). For the children in the research project, such a transition took place when they started the preschool class and then again when they started Grade 1.

One issue that could be discussed on a more general level is whether or not it is a good idea to try to fill a gap between two educational settings by inventing a new setting between the two. As shown in this chapter, such a construction may function as a ditch or as place of limbo, instead of as a bridge. Both preschool and school have long traditions. They have existed for different reasons and their underlying purposes have been different. Consequently, they have historically created different kinds of instruments to execute their given tasks. One of the problems of creating a new kind of school form to take the best from two others to make something new, without giving clear guidelines in curricula, is that the objectives become unclear and so do the instruments suitable for achieving those objectives. With reference to the studies in our project, there may be better ways to build bridges between different pedagogical settings and thus enhance children's learning journeys. One approach is to develop teachers' pedagogical cooperation in spaces such as the borderland and thus extend teachers' knowledge and understanding of each other's practices. Another important factor is that the curriculum for one school form should link closely to the curriculum for the next.

References

Athola, A., Silinskas, G., Poikonen, P.-L., Kontoniemi, M., Niemi, P., & Nurmi, J.-E. (2010). Transition to formal schooling: Do transition practices matter for academic performance? *Early Childhood Research Quarterly, 26*, 295–302.

Bronfenbrenner, U. (1979). *The ecology of human development. Experiments by nature and design.* London: Harvard University Press.

Bulkeley, J., & Fabian, H. (2006). Well-being and belonging during early educational transitions. *International Journal of Transitions in Childhood, 2*, 18–30.

Corsaro, W. A., & Molinari, L. (2000). Priming events and Italian children's transition from preschool to elementary school: Representations and action. *Social Psychology Quarterly, 63*(1), 16–33.

252   G. Sandberg et al.

Dilthey, W. (1883/1976)! *Selected writings* (H. P. Rickman, Trans. to English). Cambridge: Cambridge University Press.

Dockett, S., & Perry, B. (2007). *Transitions to school. Perceptions, expectations, experiences.* Sydney: University of New South Wales Press.

Einarsdóttir, J. (2006). From pre-school to primary school: When different contexts meet. *Scandinavian Journal of Educational Research, 50*(2), 165–184.

Engeström, Y. (1987). *Learning by expanding: An activity-theoretical approach to developmental research.* Helsinki: Orienta-konsultit.

Engeström, Y., & Sannino, A. (2010). Studies of expansive learning: Foundations, findings and future challenges. *Research Review, 5*(1), 1–24.

Erickson, F. (1986). Qualitative methods in research on teaching. In M. C. Wittrock (Ed.), *Handbook of research on teaching* (pp. 119–161). New York: Macmillan.

Eriksen Hagtvet, B. (2003). Skriftspråkstimulering i første klasse: faglig innhold og didaktiske angrepsmåter [Stimulating written language in year 1. Subject content and didactical approach]. In I. K. Klette (Ed.), *Klassrommets praksisformer etter Reform 97* (pp. 173–223). Oslo: Det utdanningsvitenskaplige fakultet.Universitetet i Oslo.

Fabian, H. (2007). Informing transitions. In A.-W. Dunlop & H. Fabian (Eds.), *Informing transitions in the early years: Research, policy and practice* (pp. 3–20). Maidenhead: Open University Press.

Fabian, H., & Dunlop, A.-W. (2007). *Outcomes of good practice in transition processes for children entering primary school. Working papers in early childhood development, 42.* The Hague: Bernard van Leer Foundation.

Garpelin, A. (1997). *Lektionen och livet* [Lesson and life] (Uppsala studies in education 70). Uppsala: Acta Universitatis Upsaliensis.

Garpelin, A. (2003). *Ung i skolan* [Young in school]. Lund: Studentlitteratur.

Garpelin, A. (2014). Transition to school: A rite of passage in life. In B. Perry, S. Dockett, & A. Petriwskyj (Eds.), *Transitions to school: International research, policy and practice* (pp. 117–128). Dordrecht: Springer.

Hammersley, M., & Atkinson, P. (1995). *Ethnography: Principles in practice.* London: Routledge.

Hellblom-Thibblin, C. (2004). *Kategorisering av barns"problem" i skolans värld. En undersökning av skolhälsovårdsrapporter läsåren 1944/45-1988/89* [Categorization of children's problems in school. A study of health care reports 1944/45-1988/89] (Uppsala studies in education no. 106). Uppsala: Acta Universitatis Upsaliensis.

Hundeide, K. (2003). *Barns livsverden: sosiokulturelle rammer for barns utviklin g* [Children's life worlds: Socio-cultural rammer]. Oslo: Cappelen.

Karlsson, M., Melander, H., Pérez Prieto, H., & Sahlström, F. (2006). *Förskoleklassen – ett tionde skolår?* [Preschool class- a tenth year of school?]. Stockholm: Liber.

Lam, M., & Pollard, A. (2006). A conceptual framework for understanding children as agents in the transition from home to kindergarten. *Early Years, 26*(2), 123–141. doi:10.1080/09575140600759906.

Mackenzie, N. (2014). Transition and emergent writers. In B. Perry, S. Dockett, & A. Petriwskyj (Eds.), *Transitions to school: International research, policy and practice* (pp. 89–102). Dordrecht: Springer.

Ödman, P.-J. (2007). *Tolkning, förståelse, vetande: Hermeutik i teori och praktik* [Interpretation, understanding, knowledge: Hermeneutics in theory and practice]. (2 uppl.). Stockholm: Norstedts akademiska förlag.

Persson, S. (2008). *Forskning om villkor för yngre barns lärande i förskola, förskoleklass och fritidshem* [Research about children's learning in preschool, preschool class and recreation centre] (Vetenskapsrådets rapportserie, 1651–7350, 2008:11.). Stockholm: Vetenskapsrådet.

Peters, S. (2010). Shifting the lens: Re-framing the view of learners and learning during the transition from early childhood education to school in New Zealand. In D. Jindal-Snape (Ed.), *Educational transitions: Moving stories from around the world* (pp. 68–84). New York: Routledge.

Peters, S. (2014). Chasms, bridges and borderlands: A transitions research 'across the border' from early childhood education to school in New Zealand. In B. Perry, S. Dockett, & A. Petriwskyj (Eds.), *Transition to school: International research, policy and practice* (pp. 105–116). Dordrecht: Springer.

Rogoff, B. (2003). *The cultural nature of human development*. New York: Oxford University Press.

Sandberg, G. (2012). *På väg in i skolan. Om villkor för olika barns delaktighet och skriftspråkslärande* [On their way into school. About conditions for participation and learning] (Studia Didactica Upsaliensia 6). Uppsala: Acta Universitatis Upsaliensis.

Sandberg, G., Hellblom-Thibblin, T., & Garpelin, A. (2014). Transition to school: A Swedish perspective. *Early Childhood Folio, 18*(2), 15–21.

The Swedish National Agency for Education. (2010). *Lpfö98. Läroplan för förskolan* [Curriculum for the preschool]. Stockholm: The Swedish National Agency for Education.

The Swedish National Agency for Education. (2011). *Lgr11. Läroplan för grundskolan, förskoleklassen och fritidshemmet* [Curriculum for compulsory school, preschool class and recreation centre]. Stockholm: The Swedish National Agency for Education.

The Swedish National Agency for Education. (2013). *Skolverket* [The Swedish national agency for education]. http://www.skolverket.se. Accessed 18 July 2015.

The Swedish Research Council. (2015). *CODEX, rules and guidelines for research*. http://www.codex.vr.se. Accessed 4 Nov 2015.

van Gennep, A. (1908/1997). *Rites of passage* (M. B. Vizedom & G. L. Caffee, Trans.). London: Routledge & Kegan Paul.

Vygotsky, L. (1934/1986). *Thought and language*. (A. Kozulin, Trans. and Ed.). Cambridge, MA: The MIT Press.

Walford, G. (2008). The nature of educational ethnography. In G. Walford (Ed.), *How to do educational ethnography* (pp. 1–15). London: Tufnell Press.

Part V
Into the Future

Chapter 16
Transitions as a Tool for Change

Aline-Wendy Dunlop

This chapter interrogates contemporary perspectives on transitions and their potential to be seen as tools for change. It conceptualises 'Transitions as a tool for change' as a novel concept that embraces the perspectives of practitioners, children and families. 'Transitions as a tool for change' has been generated by and developed in the Scottish POET project through three themes: children's learning journeys, professional beliefs and practices and family engagement. Using these themes, we explore understandings of transition, consider a wider literature that may inform the concept of 'transitions as a tool for change' and draw from our own research to bring insight to the concept, which has a potential to inform future research directions and policy decisions.

16.1 Introduction

The growing number of publications focusing on early childhood transitions attests to the fact that this has become a recognised field of research and practice enquiry. Authors use metaphors such as journeys, bridges and landscapes to denote that there are often significant changes as children move from one educational setting to another.

A focus on transitions between settings in a study of children's behaviour as they navigated the journey into childcare, on to preschool and into school (Dunlop et al. 2008), gave rise to discussion at the pilot stage of the Scottish project about the terminology used. Three questionnaires had been designed to ask about parental and staff perceptions of children's social behaviour and competence in the process of transition and used the titles 'transition into out-of-home settings', 'transitions

A.-W. Dunlop (✉)
University of Strathclyde, Glasgow, UK
e-mail: a.w.a.dunlop@strath.ac.uk

© Springer International Publishing Switzerland 2017
N. Ballam et al. (eds.), *Pedagogies of Educational Transitions*, International
Perspectives on Early Childhood Education and Development 16,
DOI 10.1007/978-3-319-43118-5_16

within settings' and 'transition to primary school'. Given the opportunity to ask questions and provide feedback at the pilot stage of the study, parents asked what was meant by 'transitions'. Once explained, they asked, almost with one voice, 'Why don't you just call it change?' We did, but at the same time this raised an important question for the research team: Why did we refer to these moves for children as 'transition'? Why not just call these moves 'change'?

In later work, Dunlop (2015a) answered this question by saying:

> For some time now there has been a growing recognition that attending to change as a process, rather than as an event, means thinking of changes, even everyday changes, as transitions that children and their families are moving through rather than one-off happenings. Using the term 'transition' brings a renewed emphasis to this change process. (p. 143)

In this chapter, we build on from seeing transitions as something to be bridged and navigated, with gaps narrowed: valid and productive as these ways of seeing transitions are. Rather it is about recognising that until we change systems so that children are not faced by change at an age, or stage or life circumstance when such change might be challenging, it may be more productive to use the term 'transitions' instrumentally. By making transitions into sites of change, we can make them work for children, families and practitioners in positive ways, and using them instrumentally may help us move towards changing systems.

What tools do we have at our disposal to make transitions themselves into tools of change? In the three themes – children's learning journeys, professional beliefs and practices and family engagement – there is a range of helpful tools. First, the Scottish context for this work needs to be explained.

16.2 The Scottish Context

Scotland is a country in transition. The political landscape is volatile and changing. Scots want change, if not yet independence. One of the changes most spoken about is the desire for social justice and equity. Arguably, the biggest issue facing Scotland is poverty (Scottish Government 2014b). Nevertheless, the Scottish Government is ambitious and 'wants to make Scotland the best place for children and young people to grow up, from giving them the best start in life to ensuring they have the opportunities to thrive and develop into healthy, confident individuals, ready to succeed' (Scottish Government 2012a).

In Scotland, all children have access to a free educational entitlement of 16 h a week for all 3- and 4-year-olds, for 2 years prior to school entry, and for 'vulnerable twos' – that is, children whose family economic circumstances render them eligible (This entitlement rises to 30 free hours per week or 1140 per annum by 2021) The 2-year entitlement is well established and the take-up is high, but there is stress on the system to find appropriate patterns of attendance, flexibility of attendance and enough appropriately qualified staff. Too many children continue to experience poverty, abuse and marginalisation despite these systems of early learning and childcare. The focus must be on quality and on entry points and processes for children and families, as well as on equipping the work force appropriately.

The Early Years Framework (Scottish Government 2008) has been the flagship policy and is the foundation for much of the current early childhood work in Scotland. The Framework is driven by four key principles:

- We want all to have the same outcomes and the same opportunities.
- We identify those at risk of not achieving those outcomes and take steps to prevent that risk materialising.
- Where the risk has materialised, we take effective action.
- We work to help parents, families and communities to develop their own solutions, using accessible, high-quality public services as required.

The leading practice approaches that together contribute to the change in Scotland are the *Early Years Framework* (Scottish Government 2008), *Getting it Right for Every Child* (Scottish Government 2012b), *Pre-birth to Three* (Education Scotland 2010), *Curriculum for Excellence Early Level* (Education Scotland 2007), *The Early Years Collaborative* (Scottish Government 2014c) and *Building the Ambition* (Scottish Government 2014a) and guidelines supporting the *Children and Young People (Scotland) Act* (Scottish Government 2014b), as well as raising the qualifications and registering of practitioners in the early years (Dunlop 2015b). Dunlop described these policies and frameworks as a 'toolbox'. Transitions provide the key for change. This ambition for change was captured in a recent statement from Scotland's first minister:

> I want us to determine now that a child born today in one of our most deprived communities will, by the time he or she leaves school, have the same chance of going to university as a child born in one of our least deprived communities. (Scottish Government 2015)

A fifth to a quarter of all Scottish children live in poverty and at the margins of Scottish society, and this affects the children's material well-being, health, education, behaviours and risks, as well as housing and environment (United Nations Children's Fund [UNICEF] 2013). Appropriate relationally based intervention and prevention is the best chance of changing outcomes for children in high-risk families and communities. The professional–parent partnership may be identified as being the single most important factor in delivering effective programmes (Barlow et al. 2007).

The Early Years Collaborative (EYC) Programme (Scottish Government 2014c) aims to improve children's life chances by ensuring that all children reach certain developmental milestones by age 30 months and just prior to school. Given that too many children in Scotland were starting school already disadvantaged in comparison to the competences of their peers, the EYC identified the following 'key change' themes: early support for pregnancy and beyond; attachment, child development and learning; continuity of care in transitions; a 27–30-month child health review; parenting skills and family engagement to support learning; addressing child poverty;

and children's health, well-being and play. Each of the EYC themes contributes to the overall aim, and the 'continuity of care in transitions' theme may be translated through the three themes of 'transitions as a tool for change', with a focus on children's learning journeys, changes in professional values and practices and family engagement as priorities.

16.3   Theorising Transitions

The *Transition to School: Position Statement* (Educational Transitions and Change [ETC] Research Group 2011) that was developed by an international research, policy and practice group defined transition to school as a dynamic process of continuity and change as children move into the first year of school. The process of transition to school occurs over time, beginning before children start school and extending to the point where children and families feel a sense of belonging at school and when educators support this sense of belonging (Dockett and Perry 2014). The impact of early childhood transitions and the transitions ease, resilience and transition capital acquired through positive transitions have been proposed as important to subsequent transitions (Dunlop 2013a) and later school success as a learner (European Commission 2015).

Transitions tend to be theorised through an ecological systems approach. Bronfenbrenner stressed the interaction between systems and human development in context (Bronfenbrenner and Ceci 1994). It is a natural step to recognise the importance of the interrelationships of the people who populate the contexts or situations through which children travel on their educational journey.

Edwards (2010) brought a particular focus to relational agency in interprofessional work. This focus is relevant to the complex professional task of working towards common understandings in situations where different practices intersect, such as at times of transition between educational sectors. Environment also plays its part in transitions and carries affordances, or lack of such affordances, in ways that influence the relational experiences of all involved. Understanding about the importance of the home learning environment has grown (Siraj-Blatchford 2010). Lenz-Taguchi's (2010) work highlighted the potential of pedagogical documentation as a means of learning and change in preschool and primary school, within and between given contexts, and offers the notion of an intra-active pedagogy that pays attention to the affordances of materials and the environment, as well as to the human resources. Thus, it is possible to populate an ecological theorising of transitions with a variety of thinking (Dunlop 2014).

In addressing human development in context over time, Bronfenbrenner (1977) offered several hypotheses that showed the challenge and opportunity of transitions. Here, we include two of these hypotheses, which emphasise the importance of making transitions in company and of sharing information between settings:

> The developmental potential of a setting in a mesosystem is enhanced if the person's initial transition into that setting is not made alone. (Hypothesis 27, p. 211)

> Upon entering a new setting, the person's development is enhanced to the extent that valid information, advice and experience relevant to one setting are made available on a continuing basis, to the other. (Hypothesis 42, p. 217)

Bronfenbrenner (1977) also highlighted that 'An ecological transition occurs whenever a person's position in the ecological environment is altered as a result of a change in role, setting or both' (Definition 6, p. 26). Thus the intra-action within the child and the interaction between the interrelated elements of that child with a consequent new role, entering a new setting and learning about the people and the practices of that new setting, bring about an ecological transition. The potential in the intersections that occur – in information sharing, in children's early experiences, in forms of learning, in curriculum, in pedagogy, in environment and in relationships – each demands attention.

When these intersections are positive and relational agency (Edwards 2010) is engaged, the practices during transitions are more likely to be helpful to the child. A focus on Dweck's (2006) growth mindsets; a shift from skills, that Claxton and Lucas (2015) are so wary of, to understanding fostered by first-hand experience; joint creation of meaning (Dunlop 2003a), and the development of children's own working theories (Ministry of Education 1996) support children to make sense of their world. Transitions knowledge in these areas provides tools to support the changes that children, parents and professionals need to navigate. This highlights transitions practices in learning and childcare environments as a quality issue.

The impact of early childhood transitions is often claimed to have an effect on subsequent transitions and later school success as a learner (Fabian and Dunlop 2007). It is important to consider what is meant by 'positive' transitions and to reflect on the many variables that may contribute to them. Positive early experiences, linked to well-considered transitions, may equip children with tools to support them at times of change. Dunlop (2013a) coined the concepts of 'transitions ease', 'transitions capital' and 'transitions readiness' acquired through positive experiences and more recently has stressed the importance of 'transitions networks' (Dunlop 2015a). These concepts may inform practitioner support for children's learning journeys, which may be fostered through the relationships between early educators, statutory schooling, parents and families.

16.4 The State of Play

Transitions are widely conceptualised as times of change for the various stakeholders, particularly for children (ETC Research Group 2011). There is a sizeable multidisciplinary literature (Dunlop 2014) on ways to support the child in transition. The literature provides guidance on:

- How to facilitate continuity of learning at school start
- How to involve parents in this process
- How to affect greater alignment between sectors

while helping children to build on strengths, adjust to differences, build recipro-cal social relationships and cope with any discontinuities.

Fabian and Dunlop (2007) reviewed literature from 20 countries and considered outcomes of good practice in transition processes for children entering primary school. They asserted that this particular transition is among early childhood's big-gest challenges and that many researchers suggest that the way transition is experi-enced initially may have an impact in terms of later school success. If this transition is positive, both socially and academically, then that sense of success can influence subsequent transitions in education. Dunlop (2007) termed the incremental nature of positive experiences in transition as 'transitions capital', focusing on Bourdieu's (1991) 'symbolic capital' and Woolcock's (2001) 'bridging and bonding social cap-ital'. Transitions can be a tool for recognising, valuing and potentially increasing the child's and family's cultural capital (Miller et al. 2014), which can be shaped by socio-demographic differences and cultural gaps between home and school.

The Fabian and Dunlop review (2007) also reminded us that a child's transition does not occur in isolation, but through interlocking systems including home, prior-to-school and school. The key agents in these settings include the child and chil-dren's agency as well as family, practitioners, curriculum, policy drivers and structures. These elements contribute to the notion of 'transitions as a tool for change' in which not only children's learning journeys but also family engagement and professional beliefs and practices play a key part in the interplay of well-being and learning. Looking at transitions as tools for change means going beyond the way transitions could be transformed to understanding the potential of transitions themselves to create change.

From the literature reviewed above, it appears that there has been little direct focus on how the process of transition may be used to effect change, to engage stakeholders in change or to identify what those sought-after changes might be. In the next section, transitions are conceptualised differently – not as navigation or adjustment, but as an impetus for identifying the opportunities for change that the transition process itself may foster.

One of the overarching aims of the POET project was 'to expand knowledge and understanding of the significance of educational transition for young children, their families and communities in national and international contexts' (European Commission 2015). It was expected that POET would also generate new thinking and new concepts in the field of transitions. The formulation of 'transitions as a tool for change' in this chapter is an attempt to fulfil this expectation.

16.5 A Proposition: Conceptualising Transitions as a Tool for Change

Against the background of little direct focus on the concept of transitions as a tool for change, the Scottish POET group arrived at a single driving question: *How can transitions be best handled to support positive change for all involved?* The group explored positive views of transitions through three strands of enquiry.

The first of these was the learning journeys that children make through prior-to-school and school settings. Here, we are currently investigating: *What part do transitions play in children's learning journeys from early childhood to the first year in school as they traverse settings and curricula?*

Young children's transitions may be understood as processes rather than events (Peters 2010a), with each process building or undermining transitions capital (Dunlop 2007). The processes that children are engaged in are recognised as learning journeys (Peters 2010b), and particular events may shape these journeys. The nature of children's learning, and their involvement in it, is rarely static. It is influenced by parental and professional models of the child and pedagogical approaches that can differ from setting to setting. In capturing the day-to-day experiences of children, a better understanding of what happens for them as they move through early childhood provision and the impact of transitions on that process will be developed. These journeys are accompanied by practitioner and family journeys and create an opportunity to consider the relationships between transition journeys and various curricula (Dunlop 2013b), while understanding curriculum as a tool. In some jurisdictions, preschool and primary curricula are linked in both tightly and loosely coupled early childhood–school systems, to align early education with statutory school systems (Nelson 2000; Education Review Office 2013).

The second strand of thinking around transitions as tools for change focuses on professional beliefs and practices. New concepts of early childhood pedagogy and early childhood specialism are emerging. Here, we ask the question: *What is the relationship between staff qualities and effective transitions for children?* The need for specialist knowledge of early-year approaches applies equally in the early stages in primary school. Internationally, the age of school start can be as young as 4 years and a few months (England) or as late as 7 years (some Nordic countries). Writing about 'relational agency', Edwards (2007, 2011) provided a key to effecting knowledge in practice. She wrote of practitioners sharing their knowledge with others and through effective interaction, people with different expertise distributing their knowledge, sharing and trusting the expertise of others and valuing the emerging 'common knowledge' that helps in turn to solve problems of practice. The ensuing collaboration comes about by each practitioner adjusting their practice to reflect others' strengths and needs, as well as their own. In this way, networks of expertise are built up. In preschool settings, there is a long history of people holding different qualifications and of bringing together two disciplines – care and education – to provide children and families within a network of expertise.

In many countries, the professional backgrounds differ for work in preschool and in primary education. This highlights the importance of developing a mutual ground and shared understandings to cross over the cultural and ideological difference between these education levels. Practitioner preparation and threads of thinking about the impact of their own professional learning on educational transitions can therefore make a vital contribution to the experience of children and families.

Family engagement in education is the third element considered as part of transitions as a tool for change. The third question generated is *What roles could be played by parents and families in affecting positive transitions for children?* From the time of becoming a parent, all the way through witnessing the changes that occur in their children, adults undergo a constant repositioning in relation to their child's emotional, social and learning journeys. While often being highly aware of the changes with which their children are coping, parental experience runs in parallel to the known challenges, discontinuities, dips and adjustments that children are known to experience during educational transitions (Dunlop and Grogan 2009).

Children's transitions are also opportunities for parents. The 'transitions as a tool for change' project suggests that transitions practices could profitably focus on opportunities for a renewed engagement in learning for adults as well as for their children. While longitudinal evidence shows that the quality of preschool remains a significant influence on children's performance to age 16, there are also important effects from the home learning environment experienced in the early years and from family characteristics such as the qualification level of the mother or being in a household with multiple disadvantages (Taggart et al. 2015).

Parental engagement with their own and their child's education can be fostered through an intergenerational approach into the transitions that families and children experience in the first years of a child's life. We see children's educational transitions prior to school, at school entry and through the school system as creating opportunities for family engagement. The co-construction of the child's transitions by family members and practitioners (Griebel and Niesel 2002) creates new opportunities for children and family members to engage in education. The engagement of the family's older adults in younger people's learning has also been found to make a significant difference on matters such as barriers to involvement and influential types of empathetic relationships (Bissland and Ford 2015).

The three aspects of early experiences – learning journeys, professional reflection on beliefs and practices and family engagement – resonate across the country projects in this book. Well-being can be achieved through curriculum processes seeking continuity in children's learning, developing family engagement (of which well-being is a part), adapting curriculum and facilitating professional qualities to combat poverty, which remains one of the dominant factors that mitigates against school success (Dunlop 2015b). Throughout, we stress the importance of relationships, perspectives and practices, and the next section focuses on educator practices, collaborations and mutual understanding as transitions tools.

16.6 Working Together Towards Shared Professional Beliefs and Practices

16.6.1 Relationships Among Educators

Collaboration and good relationships are at the core of positive transitions. Relationships are important between parents and educators, among educators at different school levels as well as between children and other children. To create a smooth transition for children advancing from preschool to primary school, educators have to work together. Collaborations between institutions with different cultural and historical roots, as well as between professionals with different views and ideologies, can be problematic. To work together on producing successful transitions for children (which may be defined as experiences that, in the new context they are joining, allow children to cope with change and show what they are interested in, know and are capable of), educators need to be open to different views and practices and be willing to change.

This is not to say that children or parents are passive at times of transition. They, too, can be agents of change (Dunlop 2003a, b). A Vygotskian framework links cognitive change to collaboration both for children and for adults. The interactions between adults stand to affect their mutual understanding of transitions work, while for children, working in partnership with other children and moving between settings with paired others are likely to enhance the experience of transition. Rogoff et al. (2001) also emphasised the learning partnerships of adults and children in school communities. Transitions may be thought about in terms of communities of transitions learners or what Dunlop (2015a) called 'transitions networks'.

Edwards (2005, 2010) introduced the concept of 'relational agency' to describe the relationship between professionals who work together and build on the expertise of both parties involved. This means working with each other towards negotiated outcomes, which involves being able to adjust one's thoughts and practices to align with those of others, in order to interpret and address problems of practice. It means recognising that another person may be a valuable resource and that work needs to be done to elicit, recognise and negotiate the use of that resource in order to align oneself in joint action (Edwards 2005).

Preschools and primary schools are historically and culturally constructed, and the practices of these institutions differ. Children's educational environments change when they move between school levels, usually from a child-centred play and learning environment to more goal-oriented learning and teacher-directed instruction. Educators in these two different environments bring to the table not only different views on practices and education but also different views of children and childhood. By working purposefully together, negotiating meaning, using the resources that each specialist brings with him or her and drawing on common knowledge, successful transition practices can be achieved for the benefit of children and their families. The concept of 'relational-turn' in professional practice offers the opportunity for an enhanced form of practice, which is potentially more beneficial to professionals than claims of individual autonomy might be. Relational expertise is in addition to one's core expertise. It allows the expertise and resources offered by others to surface and be used. To avoid the idea that specialist knowledge is to be downplayed in relational work, Edwards (2010) distinguished between the ability to recognise and work with what matters for others and being able to do what they do.

16.6.2 Collaboration of Preschool and Primary School Teachers

Until now, there has been little Scotland-specific evidence of the contribution of registered teachers working in early childhood. A recent study has developed an important evidence base (Dunlop et al. 2016). Teachers registered with the General

Teaching Council of Scotland are currently the only 'on-the-floor' professionals who are able to span preschool and early primary education and work in both contexts. Depth of knowledge about children's learning and teaching approaches and knowledge of both sectors, including transition to school and leadership of learning, are important qualities of the qualified teacher. The childhood practice graduates are registered with the Scottish Social Services Council. They work predominantly with children aged between birth and 5 years who are in preschool services as well as children aged between 5 and 14 years who are attending out-of-school care.

Increasingly, early childhood educators in the preschool sector and in early primary school in Scotland are collaborating at times of transition. Most children visit the new setting they will attend before they start; sometimes educators make home visits, and often there is a sharing of information between the sectors. For the first time in Scotland, there is now a curriculum that spans preschool and school and forms the framework for education of children aged between 3 and 18 years (Education Scotland 2015).

16.6.3 Parents' and Practitioners' Shared Transition Themes

In the *Positive Behaviour in the Early Years Study* (Dunlop et al. 2008), practitioners and parents shared a number of themes in their responses. Both groups recognised that when children make transitions, their families do as well. Practitioners reported a good level of awareness of what parents might be feeling as their children start in out-of-home care or education, and the settings were providing support and making policy a reality.

Overall, the data from the staff transitions questionnaires showed this as an aspect of practice in which staff were thoughtful, looking for solutions and more than prepared to collaborate between sectors and with children and families. In both parental and staff returns, the major focus was on social and emotional support for children. While not absent in their returns, much less emphasis was placed on continuity and progression in learning and on bridging the curriculum between settings. This remains an important area for investigation.

16.6.4 Transitions Focus: Nursery to P1 Progress Records in a Sample of Settings

Further insight into transitions for young children was provided during the Positive Behaviour study by examining transition records (Dunlop et al. 2008). This form of documentation differs from the running documentation that adults and children co-produce as a learning tool. It can, however, be argued to be a tool with performative agency (Lenz-Taguchi 2010). Such documents describe a reality from the perspective of one or more stakeholders, but in recording that reality, the documentation also shapes and changes the social reality and may be differently interpreted by different readers. Typically in Scotland, such records are passed from preschool to school as children enter primary education. They facilitate the school start and can be understood as agents of transition through documentation. The timing and follow-up of this exchange of information varies from area to area, but provides an opportunity for staff groups on either side of the transition to school to bridge children's experiences in positive ways. Such documentation brings together the three elements highlighted in this chapter – children's learning journeys, professional beliefs and practices and how they are enacted and family engagement – as contributing to the exchange of information.

The influence of such documentation goes far beyond the process of writing it, and it may become a vehicle to assist in the navigation of change leading up to school start. It is a tool for change that reflects children's dispositions, interests, coping strategies, their sense of well-being as well as their relationships and learning. The records emphasise the relational nature of early childhood practice and link this to transitions for young children. Research shows that the building of professional relationships between sectors is an important site for change (Dunlop 2003a; Dunlop et al. 2008), but these studies, like Hopps (2004, 2014), have emphasised that there is nothing automatic about successful communication and relational agency between different professional groups.

16.7   Discussion of Transitions as a Tool for Change

We have considered each strand of the 'transitions as a tool for change' model and focused mostly on the instrumentalism of the practitioner. Now we turn to reflections on how each of these strands may become a site for change.

16.7.1   Changes in Children's Learning Journeys

Research has focused on children's voice and children's perspectives as being important as children transition to school, but it remains uncertain as to what extent children have agency in practice (Harcourt et al. 2011). Continuities and discontinuities, the nature of the links between home and school, curriculum, play, relationships and dispositions were each emphasised in Peters' (2010b) transition review. She wrote: 'Analysis of success is most usefully looked at over time, considering long-term learning trajectories rather than focusing solely on initial skills and adjustments' (p. 1). Learning may be affected by transitions issues (Peters 2010b): the situated nature of learning may mean that the child does not immediately connect with learning in a different sector. At the same time, curriculum differences and the changes in pedagogy between sectors can lead to different interpretations of learning needs. Transition to school is therefore a site to consider change through which gaps can be bridged or narrowed. As Petriwskyj et al. (2005) identified, it is important that any definition of successful transition goes beyond the immediate settling-in period, to consider trajectories in the longer term.

16.7.2   Changes in Professional Beliefs and Practices

There is plenty of evidence to show that professionals need to engage differently in transitions and communicate more effectively with each other to benefit children (Fabian and Dunlop 2007). Little training for working with parents may mean staff bring preconceived ideas about families who are different from their own. Disparate outcomes mean that transitions done well provide an opportunity to build family cultural and school capital through respectful engagement. Transitions are, in this sense, a tool for change. Practitioners need to be aware of the inequities that affect families' capacity to support their children in relation to school (Siraj-Blatchford 2012), which may then reduce these children's opportunities for good outcomes.

Professional profiles may be linked to particular fields of work and stages of the system. At the transitions stage, there is less often a professional whose profile includes taking a leadership role in both preschool and in school. *The CoRe Report* (Urban et al. 2011) highlighted fears regarding the 'schoolification' of early childhood at the expense of play, an issue highlighted by Broström (2006) in Denmark, where relational pedagogy ensures content is secondary to interaction. It may be that there is a need to consider further what have been called playful pedagogies and reflection on play as a tool for facilitating transitions (Fabian and Dunlop 2015).

The CoRe Report (Urban et al. 2011) also described practice and training developments that are sympathetic to bridging ECEC settings. For example, they described the development of a transition class designed to bridge preschool and school, accompanied by especially designed transitions courses for staff. The introduction of the 'preschool class' in Sweden and Denmark, for example, attempts to retain the school entry age at 7 years, while meeting the challenge of introducing literacy and numeracy foci sooner than in the past. Equally, the governance of the early childhood sector needs to competently balance agreed standards with space for innovation in professionalism. It is this sense of innovation that is proposed as part of promoting transitions as a tool for professional change.

16.7.3   Changes in Family Engagement

Research has indicated that optimal parent involvement in their children's learning exerts positive effects for their children, educators and themselves. Parental engagement is strongly associated with children's later academic success, completion of high school, socio-emotional development and adaptation in society (Galindo and Sheldon 2012; Henderson and Mapp 2002; Organisation for Economic Cooperation and Development [OECD] 2012a, b; Siraj-Blatchford et al. 2008). The home learning environment is now recognised to be important, but it matters more what parents do rather than what they have materially. At the same time, what Miller et al. (2014) call 'school connectedness' is stronger when families bring cultural capital to home–school relationships and when it is recognised and respected by the schools.

The nature and quality of interactions among parents, teachers and children during transitions to school influence the children's educational trajectories. In this sense, parents act as important links in successful transitions to school and as critical partners in providing continuity as children move between school levels (Clarke 2007; Dockett and Perry 2014; McIntyre et al. 2007). It may be argued that parents and families are the guardians of continuity of experience for their children. Work with army, migrant and newly arrived children (Fabian and Dunlop 2015) attests to this. Continuity may be conceived as both positive and negative, depending on the child's experience.

Extending parental inclusion to the co-construction of the transition to school aims mainly to improve the situation for children. Evidence suggests that positive parental engagement has a sustained impact on children's aspirations (Gorard et al. 2012). Griebel and Niesel (2009) showed that parental engagement in the transition to school also brings changes in family identity. When parents and teachers collaborate during the transition process, there is a strong chance that this change in cooperation and engagement will foster longer-term, two-way relationships between family and school.

16.8   Conclusions

This chapter has interrogated contemporary perspectives on transitions and their potential to be seen as tools for change. It has conceptualised transitions as a tool for change as a novel concept, which embraces the potential to enhance well-being and achieve positive outcomes from the transitions process from the perspectives of practitioners, children and families. The concept of transitions as a tool for change has been illustrated through discussion of the literature, examples from research and discussion of the three themes of professional beliefs and practices, children's learning journeys and family engagement.

The importance of relational approaches has been proposed as a core element of positive transitions, while parental participation in transitions processes is believed to lead to greater confidence in families and strong relationships between parents, children and educators. With attention paid to relational approaches and parental participation, transition networks can be established for the child, through which useful exchanges of information and shared decision-making can lead to transitions ease for children.

In identifying three themes or arenas for embracing the tools available to us for change, this chapter builds on work started in 2010 when working with colleagues, many of whom were to become part of the POET venture. My list for future directions then (Dunlop 2014) included:

> ... unpicking curriculum for early childhood as a cultural script; ... [paying attention] to the place of children who find themselves at the margins of family and society; safeguarding children through transitions by equipping them to build transitions capital ...; engaging with parenting processes, ... [participation and] transitions; and building on understandings of transitions to challenge policy makers in their design of educational systems, curriculum and social supports for children and families, and embracing the differential impact of transitions by asking why this is still so. (pp. 43–44)

By focusing on transitions as tools for change, this chapter has illustrated how an increased focus on children's learning journeys helps to ensure approaches that foster well-being and the agency of children to influence what happens to them. A new focus in research participation brings about thoughtful reflection on existing approaches, to change the beliefs and practices of educators in children's favour, so supporting the child's journey. Shifts and changes in adult practices, relational agency between practitioners with different roles and responsibilities and from different sectors and engagement of and with parents allow the reframing of transitions as positive opportunities, which become tools to change the experience of the child.

References

Barlow, J., Tennant, R., Goons, C., Stewart-Brown, S., & Day, C. (2007). *A systematic review of reviews of interventions to promote mental health and prevent mental health problems in children and young people.* Coventry: University of Warwick.

Bissland, V., & Ford, C. (2015). *Older adults' engagement in younger people's learning.* Paper presented at the UALL (Universities Association for Lifelong Learning) Conference, University of Strathclyde, Glasgow, 11–15 March 2015.

Bourdieu, P. (1991). *Language and symbolic power.* Cambridge, MA: Harvard University Press.

Bronfenbrenner, U. (1977). *The ecology of human development. Experiments by nature and design.* Cambridge, MA: Harvard University Press.

Bronfenbrenner, U., & Ceci, S. J. (1994). Nature-nurture reconceptualized in developmental perspective: A bioecological model. *Psychological Review, 101*(4), 568–586.

Broström, S. (2006). Curriculum in preschool. *International Journal of Early Childhood, 38*(1), 65–76.

Clarke, C. (2007). Parent involvement in the transition to school. In A.-W. Dunlop & H. Fabian (Eds.), *Informing transitions in the early years* (pp. 120–136). Maidenhead: Open University Press.

Claxton, G., & Lucas, B. (2015). *Educating Ruby: What our children really need to learn.* Carmarthen: Crown House Publishing.

Dockett, S., & Perry, B. (2014). *Continuity of learning: A resource to support effective transition to school and school age care.* Canberra: Australian Government Department of Education.

Dunlop, A.-W. (2003a). Bridging early educational transitions in learning through children's agency. *European Early Childhood Education Research Journal, Transitions Themed Monograph Series, 1,* 67–86.

Dunlop, A.-W. (2003b). Bridging children's early education transitions through parental agency and inclusion. *Education in the North, 11,* 55–76.

Dunlop, A.-W. (2007). Bridging research policy and practice. In A.-W. Dunlop & H. Fabian (Eds.), *Informing transitions in the early years* (pp. 151–168). Maidenhead: Open University Press.

Dunlop, A.-W. (2013a).*What happens if you're not ready for school? The troublesome concept of school readiness.* Individual paper presented at the European early childhood research association conference, Tallinn, August.

Dunlop, A.-W. (2013b). Curriculum as a tool for change in transitions practices: Transitions practices as a tool for changing curriculum. In K. Margetts, & A. Kienig (Eds.), *International perspectives on transitions to school: Reconceptualising beliefs, policy and practice* (pp.135–146). London: Routledge.

Dunlop, A.-W. (2014). Thinking about transitions: One framework or many? Populating the theoretical model over time. In B. Perry, S. Dockett, & A. Petriwskyj (Eds.), *Transitions to school: International research, policy and practice* (pp. 31–46). Dordrecht: Springer.

Dunlop, A.-W. (2015a). The developing child in society: Making transitions. In M. Reed, & R. Walker (Eds.), *A critical companion to early childhood.* London: Sage.

Dunlop, A.-W. (2015b). Aspiration and actions: Early childhood from policy to practice in Scotland. *International Journal of Early Years Education.* http://dx.doi.org/10.1080/09669760.2015.1074559. Accessed 15 Feb 2015.

Dunlop, A-W., & Grogan, D. (2009). *Ten families study: Five years on.* Unpublished report. Glasgow: University of Strathclyde.

Dunlop, A.-W., Lee, P., Fee, J., Hughes, A., Grieve, A., & Marwick, H. (2008). *Positive behaviour in the early years: Perceptions of staff, service providers and parents in managing and promoting positive behaviour in early years and early primary settings.* Edinburgh: Scottish Government.

Dunlop, A.-W., Frame, K., Goodier, J., Miles, C., Renton, K., Small, M., with Adie, J., & Ludke, K. (2016). *The contribution of the GTCS-registered teachers as part of the early childhood learning and care workforce in Scotland. Audit Report.* Edinburgh: The Child's Curriculum Group.

Dweck, C. S. (2006). *Mindset: The new psychology of success.* New York: Random House.

Education Review Office. (2013). Priorities for children's learning in early childhood services. http://www.ero.govt.nz/National-Reports/Priorities-for-Children's-Learning-in-Early-Childhood-Services-May-2013/Background. Accessed 15 Nov 2015.

Education Scotland. (2015). What is curriculum for excellence? http://www.educationscotland.gov.uk/learningandteaching/thecurriculum/whatiscurriculumforexcellence/. Accessed 15 Feb 2015.

Educational Transitions and Change (ETC) Research Group. (2011). Transition to school: Position statement. Albury, Australia: RIPPLE, Charles Sturt University. http://www.csu.edu.au/faculty/educat/edu/transitions/publications/Position-Statement.pdf. Accessed 15 Feb 2015.

Edwards, A. (2005). Let's get beyond community and practice: The many meanings of learning by participating. *The Curriculum Journal, 16*(1), 53–69.

Edwards, A. (2007). Relational agency in professional practice: A CHAT analysis. *Action: An International Journal of Human Activity Theory, 1*, 1–17.

Edwards, A. (2010). Learning how to know who: Professional learning for expansive practice between organisations. In S. Ludvigsen, A. Lund, I. Rasmussen, & R. Saljo (Eds.), *Learning across sites* (pp. 17–32). London: Routledge.

Edwards, A. (2011). Building common knowledge at the boundaries between professional practices: Relational agency and relational expertise in systems of distributed expertise. *International Journal of Educational Research, 50*, 33–39.

European Commission. (2015). Periodic report summary 1 – POET (Pedagogies of Educational Transitions). http://cordis.europa.eu/result/rcn/169030_en.html. Accessed 23 Nov 2015.

Fabian, H., & Dunlop, A.-W. (2007). *Outcomes of good practice in transition processes for children entering primary school* (Working paper 42). The Hague: Bernard van Leer Foundation.

Fabian, H., & Dunlop, A.-W. (2015). Personalising transitions: How play can help 'newly arrived children' settle into school. In J. Moyles (Ed.), *Excellence of play* (4th ed., pp. 172–183). Maidenhead: Open University Press.

Galindo, C., & Sheldon, S. B. (2012). School and home connections and children's kindergarten achievement gains: The mediating role of family involvement. *Early Childhood Research Quarterly, 27*, 90–103.

Gorard, S., Huat See, B., & Davies, P. (2012). *The impact of attitudes and aspirations on educational attainment and participation*. York: Joseph Rowntree Foundation.

Griebel, W., & Niesel, R. (2002). Co-constructing transition into kindergarten and school by children, parents and teachers. In H. Fabian & A.-W. Dunlop (Eds.), *Transitions in the early years: Debating progression and continuity for children in early education* (pp. 64–75). London: RoutledgeFalmer.

Griebel, W., & Niesel, R. (2009). A developmental psychology perspective in Germany: Co-construction of transitions between family and education system by the child, parents and pedagogues. *Early Years, 29*(1), 59–68.

Harcourt, D., Perry, B., & Waller, T. (Eds.). (2011). *Researching young children's perspectives: Ethics and dilemmas of educational research with children*. London: Routledge.

Henderson, A. T., & Mapp, K. L. (2002). *A new wave of evidence: The impact of school, family and community connections on student achievement*. Austin: National Center for Family and Community Connections with Schools.

Hopps, K. (2004). Teacher communication across the preschool-school boundary. *Australian Journal of Early Childhood, 29*(1), 8–13.

Hopps, K. (2014). Preschool + school + communication = What for educator relationships? *Early Years, 34*(4), 405–419. doi:10.1080/09575146.2014.963032.

Lenz-Taguchi, H. (2010). *Going beyond the theory/practice divide in early childhood education: Introducing and intra-active pedagogy*. London: Routledge.

McIntyre, L. L., Eckert, T. L., Fiese, B. H., DiGennaro, F. D., & Wildenger, L. K. (2007). The transition to kindergarten: Family experiences and involvement. *Early Childhood Education Journal, 35*, 83–88.

Miller, K., Hilgendorf, A., & Dilworth-Bart, J. (2014). Cultural capital and home-school connections in early childhood. *Contemporary Issues in Early Childhood, 15*(4), 329–345.

Ministry of Education. (1996). *Te Whāriki. He Whāriki Mātauranga mō ngā Mokopuna o Aotearoa. Early childhood curriculum*. Wellington: Ministry of Education.

Nelson, R. F. (2000). Aligning preschool and elementary school curricula through a collaborative professional development model. *Journal of Early Childhood Teacher Education, 21*(1), 59–63.

Organisation for Economic Cooperation and Development (OECD). (2012a). *ECEC for children from disadvantaged backgrounds: Findings from a European literature review and two case studies*. Final Report. European Commission. OECD Publishing.

Organisation for Economic Cooperation and Development (OECD). (2012b). Encouraging quality in early childhood education and care (ECEC) strategies to tackle challenges in ECEC, Stage 2 – curriculum alignment for continuous child development. http://www.oecd.org/education/school/48419081.pdf. Accessed 22 Aug 2015.

Peters, S. (2010a). Shifting the lens: Re-framing the view of learners and learning during the transition from early childhood education to school in New Zealand. In D. Jindal-Snape (Ed.), *Educational transitions: Moving stories from around the world* (pp. 68–84). New York: Routledge.

Peters, S. (2010b). Literature review: Transition from early childhood education to school, Report to the Ministry of Education. Wellington: NZ Ministry of Education. http://lnxweb1.manukau.ac.nz/__data/assets/pdf_file/0008/85841/956_ECELitReview.pdf. Accessed 5 Dec 2014.

Petriwskyj, A., Thorpe, K. J., & Tayler, C. P. (2005). Trends in construction of transition to school in three western regions 1990–2004. *International Journal of Early Years Education, 13*(1), 55–69.

Rogoff, B., Turkanis, C. G., & Bartlett, L. (Eds.). (2001). *Learning together: Children and adults in a school community*. Oxford: Oxford University Press.

Education Scotland. (2007). *Building the curriculum 2: Active learning in the early years.* Glasgow: Education Scotland.

Education Scotland. (2010). *Pre-birth to three: Positive outcomes for Scotland's children and families.* Glasgow: Education Scotland.

Scottish Government. (2008). The early years framework. http://www.scotland.gov.uk/Publications/2009/01/13095148/0. Accessed 9 Oct 2014.

Scottish Government. (2012a). *Children and young people (Scotland) bill.* Edinburgh: Scottish Government.

Scottish Government. (2012b). Getting it right for every child. http://www.scotland.gov.uk/Topics/People/Young-People/getingitright/national-practice-model. Accessed 9 Oct 2014.

Scottish Government. (2014a). Building the ambition. http://www.scotland.gov.uk/Resource/0045/00458455.pdf. Accessed 9 Oct 2014.

Scottish Government. (2014b). Child poverty strategy for Scotland: Our approach. http://www.scotland.gov.uk/Resource/0044/00445863.pdf. Accessed 14 Jan 2015.

Scottish Government. (2014c). The early years collaborative. http://www.scotland.gov.uk/Topics/People/Young-People/early-years/about. Accessed 14 Jan 2015.

Scottish Government. (2015). Commission on widening access, Nicola Sturgeon, First Minister of Scotland, www.commissiononwideningaccess.co.uk. Accessed 14 Jan 2015.

Siraj-Blatchford, I. (2010). Learning in the home and at school: How working class children 'succeed against the odds'. *British Educational Research Journal, 36*(3), 463–482. http://dx.doi.org/10.1080/01411920902989201.

Siraj-Blatchford, I. (2012). *Succeeding against the odds.* Keynote address at the Scottish Educational Research Association Conference, 22nd November 2012, Ayr.

Siraj-Blatchford, I., Taggart, B., Sylva, K., Sammons, P., & Melhuish, E. (2008). Towards the transformation of practice in early childhood education: The Effective Provision of Preschool Education (EPPE) project. *Cambridge Journal of Education, 38*(1), 23–36.

Taggart, B., Sylva, K., Melhuish, E., Sammons, P., & Siraj-Blatchford, I. (2015). *Effective preschool, primary and secondary education project (EPPSE 3-16+): How preschool influences children and young people's attainment and developmental outcomes over time.* Research Brief. London: UCL Institute of Education.

United Nations Children's Fund (UNICEF). (2013). *Child well-being in rich countries: A comparative overview* (Innocenti report card 11). Florence: UNICEF Office of Research.

Urban, M., Vandenbroeck, M., Van Laere, K., Lazzari, A., & Peeters, J. (2011). *Competence requirements in early childhood education and care. Final report.* London/Brussels: European Commission. Directorate General for Education and Culture.

Woolcock, M. (2001). The place of social capital in understanding social and economic outcomes. *Isuma: Canadian Journal of Policy Research, 2*(1), 1–17.

Chapter 17
Pedagogies of Educational Transition: Current Emphases and Future Directions

Sue Dockett, Bob Perry, Anders Garpelin, Jóhanna Einarsdóttir, Sally Peters, and Aline-Wendy Dunlop

In exploring the pedagogies of educational transitions, the chapters in this book reflect both the personal and collective nature of transitions. While transitions are experienced by individuals, they occur within social, educational, community, political, economic and institutional frames, involving children and families in expanding sets of relationships. Examining experiences of transition not only illuminates the potential influences in individual lives but also contributes to our collective understandings of transition. As a result, we can highlight the journeys of transition for individual children and families and discuss the shared transition experiences of children in Sweden as they move from preschool to the preschool class and then to school, challenges in recognising diversity and promoting inclusion in different contexts, the experiences of Indigenous children as they start school in Australia and New Zealand, implications for children as they experience different pedagogical and curriculum approaches across preschool and school in Iceland and the potential of transitions as a focus for change in Scotland.

S. Dockett (✉)
Charles Sturt University, Albury, NSW, Australia
e-mail: sdockett@csu.edu.au

B. Perry
Research Institue for Professional Practice, Learning and Education (RIPPLE),
Charles Sturt University, Albury, NSW, Australia

A. Garpelin
Mälardalen University, Västerås, Sweden

J. Einarsdóttir
University of Iceland, Reykjavik, Iceland

S. Peters
University of Waikato, Hamilton, New Zealand

A.-W. Dunlop
University of Strathclyde, Glasgow, UK

© Springer International Publishing Switzerland 2017
N. Ballam et al. (eds.), *Pedagogies of Educational Transitions*, International
Perspectives on Early Childhood Education and Development 16,
DOI 10.1007/978-3-319-43118-5_17

17.1   Introduction

Just as the experiences of individuals contribute to our understanding of collective transitions, so too do the individual chapters in this book contribute to our deepening understanding of the phenomenon of educational transitions, particularly the transition to school and the pedagogies that surround this. The sociocultural positioning of educational transitions is at the heart of the issues identified throughout the book. We begin this chapter by outlining the working definitions of transition used throughout the book, before exploring the implications of these for examining pedagogies of educational transition. An overview of each of the sections of this book – *Borders, bridges and rites of passage; Diversity and inclusion; Transitions to school for Indigenous children; Continuity and change as children start school;* and *Into the future* – follows. From this, we examine the themes that emanate from the collection of chapters and synthesise these into directions for future research under the Pedagogies of Educational Transition (POET) umbrella.

17.2   Transition

The term 'transition' has many meanings. Across educational contexts, transition has been used to refer both to the experiences of people and to changes in institutions, such as educational systems (Hviid and Zittoun 2008). In this book, we have focused primarily on the transitions made by individuals between institutions: between home and/or early childhood education and care (ECEC) settings and school. Transition experiences, in this sense, involve physical movement between contexts as well as processes of adjustment for children, families and communities. However, educational transitions involve more than a change in physical context; they also involve changes in identity and role, as individuals navigate new social environments and relationships (Crafter and Maunder 2012). Educational transitions involve processes of continuity and change (Educational Transitions and Change [ETC] Research Group 2011). They are located within a specific time and require ongoing negotiation and navigation, as individuals and those close to them reorient their modes of engagement and build new relationships.

The transition to school generates points of contact between different contexts, such as home, ECEC and school. Across several chapters, these points of contact have been described as borders or boundaries. Bridges can be built to provide safe passage and promote some forms of continuity across borderlands and boundary spaces. Bridges, in both a physical and metaphorical sense, can assist movement to a new, unfamiliar space while also retaining connections with the more familiar environment. While many individuals may use the same bridge, each transition involves 'a range of interactions and processes over time, experienced in different ways by different people in different contexts' (Dockett et al. 2014, p. 3). These considerations of transition underpin the chapters in this book, positioning educational transition as a 'dynamic process of continuity and change' (ETC Research Group 2011, p. 1), experienced by individuals within a specific social context.

17.3 Pedagogies of Educational Transition

The authors of each chapter have utilised several lenses to explore pedagogies of educational transition. In Chap. 12, this term is defined by Dockett et al. as encompassing:

> … the interactive processes and strategies that enable the development of opportunities, aspirations expectations and entitlements for children, families, educators, communities and educational systems around transition to school, together with the theories, beliefs, policies and controversies that shape them. (Davies 2014)

This definition draws on both pedagogical theory in early childhood education (Alexander 2008; Siraj-Blatchford et al. 2006) and the *Transition to School: Position Statement* (ETC Research Group 2011), to which several of the chapter authors contributed. Integral to this definition are recognition that interpretations of pedagogies differ across settings and among those who enact them; acknowledgement that pedagogies are influenced by the environments in which they are enacted – physical, cultural, social and political; and understanding that pedagogies are shaped by interactions and relationships.

The *Transition to School: Position Statement* synthesises 'a wide range of transitions research, policy and practice' into a statement designed to 'inform and guide future research, policy and practice in the area of transition to school' (Dockett and Perry 2014b, p. 277). In an educational climate in which discourses of readiness and assessment feature prominently in discussions, the position statement reconceptualises transition to school in terms of opportunities, aspirations, expectations and entitlements for all involved. Inclusion of these four pillars within explorations of pedagogies of educational transition emphasises the interdependence of relationships, beliefs and pedagogical approaches. For example, educators who regard transition as a time of opportunity are likely to build relationships and enact pedagogies that reflect these.

Each of the chapters in this book has invoked elements of this approach to pedagogies of educational transition. Several chapters have acknowledged the importance of context in pedagogies, noting particularly the differences between prior-to-school and school contexts (Garðarsdóttir and Ólafsdóttir, Chap. 10; Sandberg et al., Chap. 15; Garðarsdóttir et al., Chap. 13), as well as some differences among prior-to-school settings (Karlsdóttir and Perry, Chap. 11). These chapters have highlighted links between curriculum and pedagogy, but also cautioned against a simple dichotomy that characterises ECEC and school educational environments only in terms of difference.

Several chapters have explored teachers' beliefs, attitudes, knowledge and approaches to collaboration as shapers of pedagogy (Sandberg et al., Chap. 15; Hellblom-Thibblin and Marwick, Chap. 2; Dealtry et al., Chap. 8; Dunlop, Chap. 16), reiterating the notion that pedagogies are relationship-based interactions. The importance of relationships and interactions with family and community, as well as with children, across periods of transition has also been highlighted by Hohepa and Paki in Chap. 7.

This focus on relationships has been extended by addressing issues of inclusion and exclusion. Peters and Sandberg (see Chap. 14) argued that effective pedagogies of educational transition recognise and value the perspectives of all learners. The inclusive educational environments described in Part I (Mitchell et al., Chap. 3; Hellblom-Thibblin et al., Chap. 4; Wilder and Lillvist, Chap. 5) were characterised by relationships of cooperation and complementary pedagogies that built upon the strengths and funds of knowledge of all involved. Culturally inclusive pedagogies that foster and respect Indigenous culture and seek to 'nurture and surround the child through their funds of knowledge' (Hohepa and Paki, p. 117) have been highlighted in Part II. Such pedagogies emphasise processes of transition that impact on the 'whole' child, as well as on the family and community. The policy contexts in which Indigenous children, their families and communities make the transition to school (Hohepa and McIntosh, Chap. 6), as well as practices that position Indigenous children as they start school (Dealtry et al., Chap. 8), have also been explored in detail.

Further attention to policy has been directed towards the development of prior-to-school and school curriculum (Dockett et al., Chap. 12), highlighting the relationships between curriculum and pedagogy. While chapters have noted consistent calls for continuity across prior-to-school and school settings, recognition of the disparate histories, philosophies and approaches of the different sectors has resulted in efforts to build 'bridges' (Peters and Sandberg, Chap. 14). Many potential forms of continuity can be promoted (Dockett and Einarsdóttir, Chap. 9). However, the importance of change during transition has also been emphasised.

Research under the POET project umbrella reflects the complex, multifaceted nature of educational transitions. Following an overview summary of the parts of this book, we build on these to offer some directions for future research.

17.3.1   Diversity and Inclusion

Diversity and inclusion have long been concepts of crucial importance when considering pedagogies of educational transition. This importance extends to the policy level, as well as among teachers, parents and children engaged with preschools and schools. Steering documents, such as the *United Nations Convention on the Rights of the Child* (United Nations 1989), the *Salamanca Declaration* (UNESCO 1994) and the *Education for All* document (UNESCO 2015), have played important roles in supporting children's rights in general with reference to diversity and inclusion in particular. The impact of these documents can be seen in a range of national curricula (e.g. National Agency for Education 2010, 2011) and educational acts (Ministry of Education 2015).

On the policy level, there is general support for the rights of all children to an equivalent education. However, the closer we come to the practical level, the more challenging it is to sort out how this will be accomplished. Inclusive education in theory is easy, but in practice, different perspectives and interests intersect. Teachers, as well as school leaders, experience daily dilemmas as they acknowledge diversity and implement approaches to inclusive education.

Across the four chapters in the section of the book on diversity and inclusion, researchers from three countries have presented research overviews and results from their own studies of diversity and inclusion at the time of transition to school. In the overview chapter (Hellblom-Thibblin and Marwick, Chap. 2), the concepts of diversity and inclusion were presented with reference to various aspects of children and young people's growth and development. A leading theme was the way children with their individual 'virtual backpacks' – their unique prior experiences and funds of knowledge – met different challenges in preschool and school, as well as in the transition between these school forms. The other chapters reported separate research studies. One of them had teaching and learning for refugee children and their families in early childhood education as its focus (Mitchell et al., Chap. 3). Another focused on the way children (with their individual 'backpacks') are perceived and understood in their meeting with different forms of school, with special reference to obstacles and challenges (Hellblom-Thibblin et al., Chap. 4). The third study explored aspects of diversity and inclusion, discussed in the context of young children with intellectual disabilities and their transition from preschool to school (Wilder and Lillvist, Chap. 5).

Inclusive education builds on the idea that all children, regardless of their capabilities and experiences, should be able to participate in the school setting, in a context in which differences are seen as assets or the natural variation of different individuals in an inclusive setting, rather than a reason for exclusionary practice (Bines and Lei 2011). These chapters explored the daily dilemmas of educational practice and the controversial link between diversity on the one hand and inclusion on the other. Further research is needed to scrutinise this area, especially from the perspective of the differences between children in educational environments.

Researchers have the potential to influence both policy and practice around diversity and inclusion, particularly in relation to pedagogies of educational transition. Areas for future research include examination of the ways in which preschools and primary schools meet and challenge all children, not only in relation to learning and development in school subjects but also in social relationships. Research exploring the balance between individual and group needs could make a major contribution to our understanding of educational transitions. In practice, it is well known that solutions, with reference to diversity and inclusion, often build on a mixture of different interests of the teacher and of each child: an optimal solution for one child might be devastating for another; another solution might destabilise the social structure and the conditions for teaching; some parents might disagree and take their children out of school. Research that helps to explore these situations from a range of perspectives can make a significant addition to policy and practice that promotes diversity and inclusion.

Following on from this, it is important to investigate the ways transitions between educational institutions are organised, particularly drawing on perspectives of vulnerability and victimisation (Garpelin 2004). It is essential that we continue to explore the ways individual children, with their 'virtual backpacks', experience the challenges they encounter in preschool and primary school, as well as in the transition between these school forms.

17.3.2 Transitions to School for Indigenous Children

The three chapters in this part of the book provided an overview of current issues in research, policy and practice for Indigenous children's transition to school. This was achieved through an overview chapter written by Indigenous members of the POET group from Aotearoa New Zealand and Australia and resting heavily, though not exclusively, on research emanating from those two countries. The components of two research projects, one each from Aotearoa New Zealand and Australia, which have formed major components of the POET alliance, were described and analysed. In this section of the final chapter in this book, the key ideas from these three chapters are used to point to future directions in this important field of educational transition research.

One of the key underlying ideas in all three of these chapters was the need for a change of emphasis from the rhetoric of 'closing the gap' for Indigenous children to one of recognising, celebrating and enhancing the strengths these children have, particularly as they make the transition to school. We know there is a 'gap' as measured by standardised 'Western' instruments, but we also know there are many strengths displayed by young Indigenous children. For example, Dockett et al. (2010, p. 10) noted that 'assessments of the skills and knowledge of individual children consistently indicate that Indigenous children in Australia perform at lower levels on cognitive and language tasks than their non-Indigenous peers at school entry'. However, many authors (Martin 2007; Nakata 2007; Peters 2010; Simpson and Clancy 2001) have pointed to the strengths that all children, including Indigenous children, bring with them to school as part of their cultural and experiential 'toolkit'. Added to the strengths of the children involved as they start school, it is very important to consider that all of the other players – early childhood educators, school teachers, families and communities – bring their strengths to the task of making the children's transition to school as effective as possible.

Another key idea in all of the chapters in this section was that, wherever possible, Indigenous researchers should be leading, or at least be part of, research teams investigating Indigenous children's transition to school. All three chapters discussed the need for appropriate, culturally respectful protocols when undertaking transition research with Indigenous people. In Sect. 6.4 of Chap. 6, Hohepa and McIntosh made the following important observation:

Negative feelings that Māori and other Indigenous peoples have about research are well documented. These include critiques of research processes, outcomes and its complicity in undermining Indigenous cultural integrity and viability, not to mention alienation of physical and environmental resources. (p. 94)

One of the key protocols discussed was the close and early involvement of the Indigenous communities in designing and implementing the research projects in which their communities will participate. This culturally respectful protocol is part of *Kaupapa Māori* methodology as well as the Wiradjuri and Tharawal protocols on which the studies described in this section were based.

In the Aotearoa New Zealand study, Māori researchers and communities had banded together to investigate the learning journeys of Māori children from a Māori-medium prior-to-school setting (*kōhanga reo*) to a Māori-medium school (*kura kaupapa*) setting. The importance of culture, language, relationships and identity was highlighted in this study.

The development of identity was one of the many challenges investigated by the *Gudaga goes to school study* from which Chap. 8 was drawn. *Gudaga goes to school* is the first comprehensive longitudinal study of urban Aboriginal children and their families in Australia as the children start and pass through the first few years of school. By focusing on the interview data from school educators, this chapter considered the way Aboriginal children were positioned by these educators as they started school.

Both the Aotearoa New Zealand and the Australian studies highlighted important aspects of Indigenous children's transitions to school. They stressed the importance of recognising the cultural and experiential characteristics of the children, including language and identity, as well as the characteristics of the communities from and into which the transitions were occurring. As well, the ways in which the children, their families and communities were perceived by the educators in the schools in which the children were developing their identity as (Indigenous) school children could facilitate or limit the children's chances of effective transitions to school.

As highlighted in the chapters comprising the *Transitions to school for Indigenous children* section of this book, a great deal is already known about how to make these transitions effective. It is important to consider the strengths that all the stakeholders, including the children, bring to the enterprise; to recognise the different lenses, including social justice lenses, that are used by different people at different times during the transition process; and to develop culturally and linguistically sensitive transition practices appropriate to the local context in which the transitions take place. However, more work still needs to be done.

One of the challenges for researchers of Indigenous children's transition to school is to consider the research and literature drawn from fields beyond those in which they are working. At this stage, in spite of strong international Indigenous education research groups such as the Native American and Indigenous Studies Association (NAISA) and the American Educational Research Association's

Indigenous Peoples of the Pacific Special Interest Group, Aotearoa New Zealand researchers use mainly Aotearoa New Zealand research, and Australian researchers use mainly Australian research. While there are cultural arguments for this, it may close off opportunities for insights that are not available from the local work.

17.3.3   Continuity and Change as Children Start School

Internationally, there has been an ongoing discussion about transitions and continuity between different stages in the school system, especially between preschool and primary school – two educational systems that emerged from different traditions and with different intentions. The continuity of children's learning and experiences and their transitions are now recognised as central to the quality of young children's experiences and well-being (Vogler et al. 2008). The Organisation for Economic Co-operation and Development (OECD) (2006) report on early childhood education emphasised the importance of transitions in the early years, urging that a more unified approach to learning should be adopted in both early childhood education and primary school systems and that attention should be given to transition challenges faced by young children as they enter school.

All five chapters in this section discussed continuity and change as children move from preschool to primary school. The chapters have given examples from Australian and Icelandic contexts that illustrate the dissimilarities between preschool and primary school evident in the different curricular emphases of the two sectors. Bringing curricula together across sectors and aligning preschools and elementary schools have proven to be far from easy in praxis. Across the world, attempts to provide continuity between school levels have resulted in the curriculum of primary schools being pushed down to the preschools and play being replaced by more formal methods. For example, in spite of the emphasis on continuity in policy documents in Iceland, there is a tendency to move the primary school curriculum down to the preschool (Einarsdóttir 2006), and preschool teachers seem keen on adopting the primary school structure and teaching methods. This may indicate that it is easier to change policy than to change practice and that practice lags behind policy.

Educational systems have multiple layers of infrastructure that have accumulated over time (Gutiérrez and Penuel 2014). In preschools and primary schools, these infrastructures and traditions differ. Possible ways to change and improve these systems and to create continuity between them include in-service and pre-service teacher education in which methods and values are taught and discussed. Further ways of achieving this may include research collaboration with teachers who want to improve their practice. Thus, future transition research may focus on teacher education and on including practitioners in research efforts to transform the system.

Much attention has been paid to notions of continuity and ways to 'smooth' the transition to school for children. However, transitions are also times of change.

Indeed, Zittoun (2008) argues that change is the prompt for transition. Rather than focusing only on ways to promote continuity, chapters in this section have reflected also on change and the significance of change for those making the transition. Children note their changed identity as they become school students (Crafter and Maunder 2012), just as parents note their changed role and status as 'parents of a school student' (Griebel and Niesel 2009). Future research directions include opportunities to explore notions of change and the importance of change in identity, status, roles, relationships and knowledge during educational transitions.

The first goal of the *Education for All* (UNESCO 2015) strategy describes the importance of expanding and improving comprehensive early childhood care and education, especially for vulnerable groups. Several political, economic, cultural and social factors influence children's access to quality early childhood education (Vogler et al. 2008). While evidence related to children from backgrounds described as complex or disadvantaged indicates that a positive start to school influences positive life trajectories, it is also the case that these children may experience – or may be expected to experience – a more problematic transition to school than their more advantaged peers (Dockett and Perry 2007, 2014a). Exploring the experiences of those considered vulnerable, and the ways in which pedagogies of educational transition can both recognise their strengths and build upon these, will continue to be an important area for research. Transition research has the potential to disentangle the factors that explain why some children have successful transitions and do well in school, while others do not. It also offers opportunities to understand the impact of transitions on educational and life trajectories (Vogler et al. 2008).

17.3.4 Borders, Bridges and Rites of Passage

In each of the countries participating in POET projects, children make a number of moves in their educational journeys. While the age at which these moves are made differs, children across the five countries usually attend preschool before moving to a preschool class (Sweden) or school (Australia, New Zealand, Iceland, Scotland). These moves contribute to children's educational trajectories.

In their explorations of borderlands, bridges and rites of passage, researchers from New Zealand and Sweden acknowledged that individuals experience moves between and across educational settings. They positioned transitions as times of movement and opportunity, attending to the notions of 'becoming' in a transition (Hörschelmann 2011) and the new roles that are adopted and enacted.

Transitions are also recognised as times of potential crisis and challenge, especially when a familiar role or context is left and the transition sits as a threshold between what was and what is to come (Ackesjö 2014). Viewing transition to school as a rite of passage (van Gennep 1977) provides one possible lens for considering transition experiences and how they might be marked, celebrated and understood, while also paying attention to the wider sociocultural contexts in which they occur.

Chapters in this section and throughout the book have outlined some of the traditional differences between early childhood education and school that help to shape the nature of pedagogies in these two contexts and, hence, the nature of continuity and change inherent in transitions across settings. In considering borderlands, bridges and rites of passage, we have explored the ways in which these traditional differences can create separate cultures, or territories, leading to potential borders between the sectors. Moves to blur these boundaries have included efforts to form borderlands to support the connections between sectors with metaphorical bridges. Both chapters in this section considered the Swedish example of the preschool class for 6-year-olds as a potential year-long 'bridge' between preschool and school. This has been compared with the New Zealand example of children moving from prior-to-school settings to school on their fifth birthday and research in which teachers have attempted to form borderlands between early childhood education and care and school, to support this move.

The bridges or connections between ECEC and school can take many forms, ranging from functional linkages (Boyle and Petriwskyj 2014), in which the focus is on early childhood settings preparing children for school, to transformative relationships that have the potential to revolutionise each setting (Moss 2013). Sandberg and her colleagues (see Chap. 15) have noted that the Swedish preschool classes were established with the aim of melding together the two different pedagogical traditions from preschool and school. Begun in 1998, they were intended as an alternative to following the example of Norway, which reduced the school starting age from 7 to 6 years (Kaga 2007; Taguma et al. 2013). Interestingly, given that in many countries children start school at age 4 or 5 years, in Sweden it was 'claimed that lowering the entry age would mean taking away a part of childhood – considered a golden time of life – and feared that schooling at 6 would have a negative impact on children' (Kaga 2007, p. 1).

Kaga (2007) indicated that the Swedish prime minister at the time recommended that preschool pedagogy should influence the early years of compulsory school. The intention was that preschool classes should integrate the approaches from both sectors and support the transition from 'one educational stage to the next' (p. 1). However, while this idea appeared to have promise in gradually transitioning between the pedagogy and curriculum of early childhood centres and those of school, by 2007 it seemed that school practices were dominating the preschool class (Kaga 2007). In Chap. 15, the Swedish team wrote about the preschool class being a year spent learning to be a student. While, in many respects, the preschool class did seem to offer the intended mix of pedagogies, the team concluded that these seemed to run as two silos rather than being integrated. In this sense, the preschool class seemed to share issues with the Norwegian practice it sought to avoid, with Hagtvet (2003) indicating that the first year of school for six-year-olds in Norway offered an uneasy mix of the most extreme components from preschool and school.

This book has captured some of the international research being conducted on educational transitions, especially the transition to school. Although there has been a wealth of research that has led to many improvements in practice, it seems that there are still issues related to enhancing children's learning journeys as they navigate a range of educational transitions. Chapters in this section have identified one abiding area of contention as the learning goals for children aged 4–7 years and the related issues around appropriate pedagogies to achieve these goals. This is not an isolated concern: in their review of early childhood curricula, Taguma et al. (2013) outlined early childhood curriculum frameworks in a range of countries, noting that irrespective of the curriculum approaches, or the age at which children make the transition to school, there are potential challenges in navigating pathways between and across settings. The construction of bridges and/or meeting places to connect settings is one strategy to address this.

However, it is important to note that major political moves, such as creating the preschool class in Sweden, seem not to have ameliorated the challenges posed by transition to school. It is timely to look more closely at what is involved in the last years of prior-to-school settings and the first years of school and seek a contextualised understanding of what shapes practices and what changes might assist both the transition and the long-term learning journeys of all children. The five POET countries, with their different ages for school entry and different practices surrounding this, are well positioned to explore what children aged 4–7 years experience in each country, not just at the policy level but in practice in their learning experiences within settings.

17.3.5 Into the Future

Conceptualising transitions as a tool for change has been the focus for the Scottish POET project since 2012. This was driven by the concerns about children on the margins of society, in particular, children whose lives are affected by poverty and related disadvantages. This concern has led to debates about the ways the timing and processes of transition might offer opportunities to children, families and professionals for changes beyond those usually expected at times of educational transition. Thinking, to date, embraces three distinct but related strands: children's learning journeys, family engagement, and professional beliefs and practices. A strong focus in all of these themes is the well-being of children, as defined by relationships, behaviours, identity, interaction and the nature of engagement in activities and learning. The new roles that children take on, the ways in which adults share information and provide for children, and the alignment of pedagogy and curriculum across settings and sectors each present possible tools to effect change. The purpose of such change must be equity for all children.

Emerging from the emphasis on transitions as a tool for change is a need for research to focus strongly on what creates well-being for all children, but especially those considered vulnerable; what enhances learning and development; and how transitions provide a different lens to view the perspectives of children, families and professionals, which can be used to inform policy and practice through research and vice versa.

In a practical way, 'Transitions are now recognized as central to young children's experiences and well-being, as well as a powerful integrative framework for research' (Vogler et al. 2008, p. 1). Conceptualising transitions as a tool for change suggests broadening perspectives on transitions to include understandings of how professional beliefs intersect with children's experience, how participation of parents and children together in transitions can introduce ways to engage families and how educators and policy makers can understand better what works for families and children on the edges of society. Each of these offers potential to influence for the better the ways transitions are structured in policy and practice. Children and the adults surrounding them need to be active participants in these processes; transitions are a site for such change. Thinking about transitions as tools for change recognises the potential of this 'powerful integrative framework' and supports the ambition of increased well-being for all concerned.

17.4   Emerging Threads for Further Research

A number of threads are woven throughout the chapters of this book. Identifying these threads provides a means to draw together our individual projects and to present a collective stance that describes the state of our current knowledge about pedagogies of educational transition and identifies future research priorities. We enter this discussion by outlining the different – but interwoven – threads.

17.4.1   Transition as a Social Experience

The transition to school involves both individual and social experiences. The importance of recognising the social dimension of transition has been noted throughout the chapters, as the roles of peers, adults and community have been emphasised. Interactions with others provide individuals with access to social knowledge – clues to appropriate ways of acting, interacting and reacting, in new situations. Social relationships also help foster a sense of belonging in the new environment.

While the focus on journeys of 'becoming' features in a range of transition research (Cuconato and Walther 2015; Hörschelmann 2011), there are also opportunities to explore notions of 'belonging' within transitions. Recognising many dimensions of belonging, and the 'multiplicity of interconnected belongings' (Sumsion and Wong 2011, p. 33), there is potential to explore the influence of transitions across areas such as *emotional belonging*, which includes feeling liked and respected within a setting, feeling 'suitable' (Broström 2003), and demonstrating a sense of emotional comfort; *social belonging*, characterised by acceptance within a group and participation in the practices of that group; and *cultural belonging*, evidenced by participation within a group that is connected through shared histories, knowledge and practices and the demonstration of expected ways of acting and interacting in specific contexts (Sumsion and Wong 2011). Interrogation of these areas could explore the dynamic and ongoing processes of belonging as individuals engage with, and navigate, social interactions and contexts. In other words, such research could promote an integrated focus on individual and social processes.

The social environment not only provides support but also a range of resources on which those making the transition may draw. However, the social context of transitions also generates constraints, as the social structures in which individuals are embedded are themselves subject to varying levels of resources and opportunities (Tikkanen et al. 2015). Educational structures, such as the organisation, standardisation and stratification of educational systems, influence the educational choices available, the ways transitions are effected, the impact of these and the educational trajectories of those involved. Individual, social and structural factors are central to experiences of transition and to the evaluation of its effectiveness (Walther et al. 2015). Recognising the potential for structural inequalities at times of educational transition opens up the need for transition research that moves beyond the individual level to consider broader social, cultural, political and economic contexts in our quest to examine why some children thrive in school, while others do not.

17.4.2   Individual Change and Transition Journeys

With considerable attention to promoting continuity across educational transitions, reflected in efforts to 'smooth transition', much less emphasis has been directed to the importance of processes of change. This is despite change being an inherent component of transition. In Zittoun's (2008) definition, processes of transition are generated by change – in her terms, 'ruptures' that interrupt 'usual processes' and require 'the production of newness' (p. 165). Starting school can be conceptualised as an event that interrupts patterns of action, requiring that all involved develop new ways of being, operating and interacting. Children starting school experience changes in identity as they encounter new environments, meet different expectations and are repositioned as 'school students'. Changes in knowledge acquisition are noted as children are expected to embrace the knowledge and skills associated with schools and to reflect this in their engagement as a member of the school or class group. Changes in sense-making occur as children interpret and make sense of their new environment and their role and place within it (Zittoun 2008). Rather than regarding change as problematic, a nuanced understanding of the complexity of transitions may be generated by attention to the nature and import of change during transition. In this vein, Crafter and Maunder (2012, p. 16) note, '… the transition journey is just as important for the individual as the outcome. Despite the uncertainty, unfamiliarity and feelings of discomfort associated with change, learning to navigate this process is personally constructive and identity shaping'.

The transition journeys of children starting school, and the families, communities and educators who make the journey with them, are the focus of much of the work of the POET group. Whether these journeys are conceptualised as rites of passage, journeys over a bridge, or in some way, as forays into the borderlands, all children making the transition to school are moving towards new environments, new ways of being and new expectations. The nature of the pathways that promote this, and the ways in which learning goals and directions are created and supported, continues to be a fruitful and important line of research. Alongside an awareness of the multiple pathways that constitute transition journeys, recognition of the spaces occupied by different educational institutions, such as preschool, preschool class and school, can put the spotlight on boundaries and the strategies of boundary maintenance (or their breaching) that support these.

17.4.3 *Transition and Precariousness*

In her discussions of transitions though the life course, Hörschelmann (2011, p. 378) urges reconceptualisation of transition to capture its 'precariousness, unpredictability and diversity without ignoring the structuring effects of state regulation and institutionalization'. This reference to the precariousness of life transitions prompts similar thinking about educational transitions.

Approaches to transition have the potential to position some groups of children as 'vulnerable' (Dockett 2014; Perry 2014). This often includes children 'from financially disadvantaged families, Indigenous families, families with children who have a disability, and culturally and linguistically diverse (CALD) families' (Rosier and McDonald 2011, p. 1). In responding to such positioning, we have chosen to question what is meant by vulnerability and how decisions about, as well as responses to, vulnerability are made.

Work examining the Occupy movement and other political protests (Butler 2004) has emphasised the theme of precarity, which has been defined as 'the condition of living without security or predictability' (Chinnery 2015, p.1). Entwined with this definition is a conceptualisation of vulnerability and the 'ways in which some people are rendered more vulnerable – and their lives more precarious – than others ... whose social, economic, or political status renders them more vulnerable, more precarious, than others' (p. 2).

Collectively, the research of our POET group has engaged with groups described as vulnerable or marginalised, including those experiencing poverty, homelessness, chronic unemployment and/or major health issues; refugee families; children with diverse abilities and needs; Indigenous children and families; and families from diverse cultural and linguistic backgrounds. Rather than expecting children from such groups to experience educational difficulties, Chinnery (2015) argued for close examination of the prevailing social, economic and political contexts that underpin such circumstances. She calls for action whereby:

> ... instead of blaming children for the detrimental effects of circumstances and experiences beyond their control, we need to start holding to account the adults who could in fact make a difference to those children's lives ... mov[ing] away from prevailing discourses of cul-

tural deprivation and deficit … to the recent scholarship on vulnerability and precarity in order to reframe our conception of pedagogical responsibility …. (p. 1)

In current contexts, where many children, families and communities face multiple dislocations, we do not need to look hard to identify insecurity borne out of an 'unequal distribution of vulnerability' (Butler 2012). When considering the educational transitions of young people, Chinnery (2015) argued that as educators and researchers, we have an ethical and pedagogical responsibility for the educational engagement and trajectories of those who are designated as vulnerable. This responsibility encompasses both individual and broader social elements. It requires us to:

… examine educational systems, policies and practices that render some students unnecessarily vulnerable, and which categorise certain ways of being as inherently at risk. It is not about denying difference, but rather what we do with these differences. (Chinnery 2015, pp. 7–8)

17.4.4 Pedagogical Responsibility

Viewed in this way, we argue that we have a relationship of responsibility – an ethical and pedagogical responsibility – to promote equity and social justice in educational transitions. Key directions for our future research involve questioning how we engage with both individual and broader encounters that examine vulnerability and precarity, exploring ways to move transition research beyond deficit views and deficit expectations and emphasising positive and potential transitions and trajectories. The generation of the *Transition to School: Position Statement*, which frames transition as a time of opportunities, aspirations, expectations and entitlements, has already contributed to this framing of pedagogical responsibility. This is taken up in much of the work reported in this book, as researchers have addressed issues such as the importance of broad definitions of diversity; the daily dilemmas encountered by educators; the strengths of children, families and communities; the impact of policy contexts; the importance of pedagogies that connect with funds of knowledge; and the positioning of children and families in educational discourses.

17.5 Conclusion

The research reported in this book builds on a broad corpus of transition research undertaken in the five POET countries over many years. While there are contextual differences across the countries, there are also similar issues, debates and concerns and similar research results, particularly about the transition to school. The combined impact of the research reported provides a sound basis for recognising what we have learned and moving beyond this to address some of the enduring and contradictory issues evident in each of our contexts.

Exploring the commonalities of our research agendas helps to identify the research problems that are worthy of attention and unlikely to be resolved in any one context. Positioning our research in terms of pedagogical responsibility requires us to consider some of the 'wicked problems' in education – those that are difficult to resolve because of their complexity, entrenched nature and the intersection of multiple, overlapping challenges (Weber and Khademian 2008). Wicked problems generate multiple, often contradictory, views about appropriate responses. Our combined POET research, across different countries and contexts, utilising a range of theoretical frameworks and methodologies, has the potential to make a valuable contribution to such challenges.

References

Ackesjö, H. (2014). Children's transitions to school in a changing educational landscape: Borders, identities and (dis)continuities. *International Journal of Transitions in Childhood, 7*, 3–15.

Alexander, R. (2008). Pedagogy, curriculum and culture. In P. Murphy, K. Hall, & J. Soler (Eds.), *Pedagogy and practice: Culture and identities* (pp. 3–27). London: Sage.

Bines, H., & Lei, P. (2011). Disability and education: The longest road to inclusion. *International Journal of Educational Development, 31*, 419–424.

Boyle, T., & Petriwskyj, A. (2014). Transitions to school: Reframing professional relationships. *Early Years, 34*(4), 392–404. doi:10.1080/09575146.2014.953042.

Broström, S. (2003). Transitions from kindergarten to school in Denmark. In A.-W. Dunlop & H. Fabian (Eds.), *European early childhood education research journal -transitions* (Themed monograph series 1, pp. 5–14). Worcester: EECERA.

Butler, J. (2004). *Precarious life: The powers of mourning and violence*. London: Verso.

Butler, J. (2012). *Can one lead a good life in a bad life? Radical Philosophy, Adorno Prize Lecture.* http://www.egs.edu/faculty/judith-butler/articles/can-one-lead-a-good-life-in-a-bad-life/. Accessed 1 Sept 2015.

Chinnery, A. (2015). Precarity and pedagogical responsibility. *Journal of Educational Controversy, 9*(1). http://cedar.wwu.edu/jec/vol9/iss1/10. Accessed 1 Sept 2015.

Crafter, S., & Maunder, R. (2012). Understanding transitions using a sociocultural framework. *Educational and Child Psychology, 29*(1), 10–18.

Cuconato, M., & Walther, A. (2015). 'Doing transitions' in education. *International Journal of Qualitative Studies in Education, 28*(3), 283–296. doi:10.1080/09518398.2014.987851.

Davies. J. (2014). *Pedagogies of educational transitions: Continuity and change as children start school in rural areas*. Unpublished research proposal. Charles Sturt University.

Dockett, S. (2014). Transition to school: Normative or relative? In B. Perry, S. Dockett, & A. Petriwskyj (Eds.), *Transitions to school: International research, policy and practice* (pp. 187–200). Dordrecht: Springer.

Dockett, S., & Perry, B. (2007). *Transitions to school: Perceptions, expectations, experiences*. Sydney: UNSW Press.

Dockett, S., & Perry, B. (2014a). *Continuity of learning: A resource to support effective transition to school and school age care*. Canberra: Australian Government Department of Education.

Dockett, S., & Perry, B. (2014b). Research to policy: Transition to school position statement. In B. Perry, S. Dockett, & A. Petriwskyj (Eds.), *Transitions to school: International research, policy and practice* (pp. 277–294). Dordrecht: Springer.

Dockett, S., Perry, B., & Kearney, E. (2010). *School readiness: What does it mean for Indigenous children, families, schools and communities?* (Issues Paper No 2). Canberra: Closing the Gap Clearing-house.

Dockett, S., Petriwskyj, A., & Perry, B. (2014). Theorising transition: Shifts and tensions. In B. Perry, S. Dockett, & A. Petriwskyj (Eds.), *Transitions to school: International research, policy and practice* (pp. 1–18). Dordrecht: Springer.

Educational Transitions and Change (ETC) Research Group. (2011). *Transition to school: Position statement.* http://www.csu.edu.au/faculty/educat/edu/transitions/publications/Position-Statement.pdf. Accessed 12 Nov 2014.

Einarsdóttir, J. (2006). From pre-school to primary school: When different contexts meet. *Scandinavian Journal of Educational Research, 50*(2), 165–184.

Garpelin, A. (2004). Accepted or rejected in school. *European Educational Research Journal, 3*(4), 729–742.

Griebel, W., & Niesel, R. (2009). A developmental psychology perspective in Germany: Co-construction of transitions between family and education system by the child, parents and pedagogues. *Early Years, 29*(1), 59–68.

Gutiérrez, K. D., & Penuel, W. R. (2014). Relevance to practice as a criterion for rigor. *Educational Researcher, 43*(1), 19–23.

Hagtvet, B. E. (2003). Skriftspråkstimulering i første klasse: faglig innhold og didaktiske an-grepsmåter [Stimulating written language in Year 1. Subject content and didactical ap-proach]. In I. K. Klette (Ed.), *Klassrommets praksisformer etter Reform 97* (pp. 173–223). Oslo: Det utdanningsvitenskaplige fakultet.Universitetet i Oslo.

Hörschelmann, K. (2011). Theorising life transitions: Geographical perspectives. *Area, 43*(4), 378–383.

Hviid, P., & Zittoun, T. (2008). Editorial introduction: Transitions in the process of education. *European Journal of Psychology of Education, 23*(2), 121–130.

Kaga, Y. (2007). *Preschool class for 6-year-olds in Sweden: A bridge between early childhood and compulsory school* (UNESCO Policy Brief on Early Childhood, No. 38). http://unesdoc. unesco.org/images/0015/001508/150815e.pdf. Accessed 29 Sept 2015.

Martin, K. (2007). Ma(r)king tracks and reconceptualising Aboriginal early childhood education: An Aboriginal Australian perspective. *Childrenz Issues, 11*(1), 15–20.

Ministry of Education. (2015). *Skollag* [Education Act]. *Svensk författningssamling 2010:800.* Stockholm: Ministry of Education.

Moss, P. (2013). The relationship between early childhood and compulsory education: A proper political question. In P. Moss (Ed.), *Early childhood and compulsory education: Reconceptualising the relationship* (pp. 2–49). London: Routledge.

Nakata, M. (2007). *Disciplining the savages: Savaging the disciplines.* Canberra: Aboriginal Studies Press.

National Agency for Education. (2010). *Lpfö98. Läroplan för förskolan* [Curriculum for the pre-school]. Stockholm: The National Agency for Education.

National Agency for Education. (2011). *Lgr11. Läroplan för grundskolan, förskoleklassen och fritidshemmet* [Curriculum for compulsory school, preschool class and recreation centre]. Stockholm: The National Agency for Education.

Organisation for Economic Co-operation and Development (OECD). (2006). *Starting strong II: Early childhood education and care.* Paris: OECD.

Perry, B. (2014). Social justice dimensions of starting school. In B. Perry, S. Dockett, & A. Petriwskyj (Eds.), *Transitions to school: International research, policy and practice* (pp. 175–186). Dordrecht: Springer.

Peters, S. (2010). *Literature review: Transition from early childhood education to school. Report commissioned by the Ministry of Education.* Wellington: Ministry of Education. http://www. educationcounts.govt.nz/publications/ece/78823. Accessed 22 Sept 2015.

Rosier, K., & McDonald, M. (2011). *Promoting positive education and care transitions for children.* Communities and Families Clearinghouse Resource Sheet. http://www.aifs.gov.au/cafca/ pubs/sheets/rs/rs5.html. Accessed 22 Sept 2015.

Simpson, L., & Clancy, S. (2001). Context and literacy: Young Aboriginal learners navigating early childhood settings. *Journal of Australian Research in Early Childhood Education, 8*(1), 81–92.

Siraj-Blatchford, I., Sylva, K., Muttock, S., Gilden, R., & Bell, D. (2006). Review of the literature on effective pedagogy. In R. Parker-Rees & J. Willan (Eds.), *Early years education: Major themes in education* (Vol. 3, pp. 283–305). London: Routledge.

Sumsion, J., & Wong, S. (2011). Interrogating 'belonging' in Belonging, Being and Becoming: The early years learning framework for Australia. *Contemporary Issues in Early Childhood, 12*(1), 28–45. doi:10.2304/ciec.2011.12.1.28.

Taguma, M., Litjens, I., & Makowiecki, K. (2013). *Quality matters in early childhood education and care Sweden.* OECD. http://www.oecd.org/edu/school/SWEDEN%20policy%20profile%20%20published%2005-02-2013.pdf. Accessed 29 Sept 2015.

Tikkanen, J., Bledowski, P., & Felczak, J. (2015). Education systems as transition spaces. *International Journal of Qualitative Studies in Education, 28*(3), 297–310. doi:10.1080/09518398.2014.987853.

UNESCO. (1994). *The Salamanca statement and framework for action on special needs education.* Paris: UNESCO.

UNESCO. (2015). *Education for all 2000–2015: Achievements and challenges.* Paris: UNESCO.

United Nations. (1989). *Convention on the rights of the child.* http://www.unicef.org/crc/crc. Accessed 22 Sept 2015.

van Gennep, A. (1977). *The rites of passage.* London: Routledge.

Vogler, P., Crivello, G., & Woodhead, M. (2008). *Early childhood transitions research: A review of concepts, theory, and practice* (Working Paper No. 48). The Hague: Bernhard van Leer Foundation.

Walther, A., Warth, A., Ule, M., & du Bois-Reymond. (2015). 'Me, my education and I': Constellations of decision-making in young people's educational trajectories. *International Journal of Qualitative Studies in Education, 28*(3), 349–371. doi:10.1080/09518398.2014.987850.

Weber, E. P., & Khademian, A. M. (2008). Wicked problems, knowledge challenges, and collaborative capacity builders in network settings. *Public Administration Review, 68*(2), 334–349.

Zittoun, T. (2008). Learning through transitions: The role of institutions. *European Journal of Psychology of Education, 23*(2), 165–181.

Appendix

This added material provides a background to the Pedagogies of Educational Transition (POET) international alliance in terms of ongoing research on educational transitions, the genesis of the alliance in the 2010 transition to school invited conference in Australia and the funding of the alliance. Details of the successful bid for funds to the Marie Curie International Research Staff Exchange Scheme (IRSES) and individual country schemes are presented. The overall purpose and vision for the POET alliance is explained in terms of the five major aims of the project.

A.1 Background to the POET International Alliance

The POET international alliance was originally developed by six experienced transition to school researchers from the five countries involved: Initial information about the people and countries involved and the early interactions among these researchers is provided in Sect. 1.4 of this book. Further detail concerning the development and activities of POET is provided in the remainder of this Appendix.

A.1.1 Transition to School Conference, Australia, 2010

In October 2010, 14 researchers from eight countries met in Albury, New South Wales (NSW), Australia, to explore current directions in transition research and how their own considerable bodies of research contributed to, and extended, these directions. The six future POET international alliance leaders were integral to this meeting. Funding for this meeting came from a number of sources, including Charles Sturt University, the Ian Potter Foundation, NSW Department of Education

© Springer International Publishing Switzerland 2017
N. Ballam et al. (eds.), *Pedagogies of Educational Transitions*, International Perspectives on Early Childhood Education and Development 16, DOI 10.1007/978-3-319-43118-5

and Training, Victorian Department of Children and Youth Services, South Australian Department of Education and Children's Services and Department of Education, Employment and Workplace Relations.

The researchers exchanged information with six higher-degree research students who were also investigating specific aspects of transition; 35 policymakers representing local, state and national organisations with direct responsibilities for transition to school; and approximately 100 practitioners, employed in both prior-to-school and early-years-of-school settings. These exchanges included written papers, roundtable discussions, written and oral critiques, informal conversations and input on current research from all participants.

One of the aims of this transition conference was to synthesise the wide range of transition research, policy and practice into a position statement that would, in turn, inform and guide future research, policy and practice in the area of transition to school (Dockett and Perry 2014; Educational Transitions and Change Research Group [ETC] 2011). Another of the aims was to produce an edited volume arising from the papers that the researchers had prepared for the conference (Perry et al. 2014). All of the future POET leaders have a chapter in this volume.

While the conference was held in Australia, the contributions of research participants from Australia, Finland, Hong Kong, Iceland, New Zealand, Sweden, the UK and the USA ensured that the discussions encompassed issues and approaches that were of international relevance and significance. In addition, the involvement of both practitioners and policymakers promoted a focus not only on the research but also the ways in which it was, and could be, interpreted and applied. The engagement of the policymakers and practitioners meant that the research discussions were tempered through their application to policy and practice. Collaborative involvement offered the opportunity for researchers, policymakers and practitioners to generate a common language around issues related to transition, consider ways in which research could influence policy and practice and create pathways such that issues of transition policy and practice could generate new approaches to research.

At this meeting, some of the European researchers had information about the Marie Curie IRSES (European Commission 2013), and they canvassed the possibility of an ongoing group of researchers continuing to meet to explore issues and challenges in educational transitions, if funds could be won from this scheme. Out of this idea grew the POET international alliance.

A.1.2 Funding the POET Alliance Activities

In 2010 and 2011, POET researchers in each of the member countries were (or were planning to be) involved in a number of high-profile, nationally funded research projects. While the six POET leaders led most of these projects, there were many other educational transition researchers from the five universities, including middle- and early-career researchers and doctoral candidates. The initial purpose of the proposed POET alliance was to bring all of these people together, not to do the research, but to share, critique, improve and extend the research already being done. To do this, POET needed funding for staff exchanges, and the Marie Curie IRSES seemed appropriate, at least to fund the European researchers to travel to the Antipodes (Australia and New Zealand):

> The Marie Curie International Research Staff Exchange Scheme is an action that aims to strengthen research partnerships through staff exchanges and networking activities between European research organisations and research organisations from countries with which the European Union has an S&T [Science and Technology] agreement or is in the process of negotiating one. (European Commission 2013, p. 5)

The initial application to IRSES was made by the five organisations in the 2011 round. It sought funding over a 4-year period (2011–2015) for biannual exchanges among the POET members, firstly each year, in either Australia or New Zealand, and, later, around the time of the EECERA conference in one of the European partner countries. This initial proposal to IRSES was unsuccessful. However, useful feedback from the assessors and from each of the five universities gave the POET leaders enough confidence to try again in the 2012 round. After a great deal of work by all the leaders throughout 2011 and an intensive week in Glasgow in January, 2012, a new proposal was created. The statement of aims was expanded and sharpened since the previous proposal:

The five overarching project aims for POET are:

- To facilitate the development of diverse research skills and expertise among the researchers;
- To promote collaboration among early-career and established researchers around the topic of pedagogies of educational transition;
- To build sustainable research collaborations between the universities that will be maintained and extended, leading to proposals for major international research projects around early years education and educational transitions;
- To expand knowledge and understanding of the significance of educational transition for young children, their families and communities in national and international contexts; and
- To generate knowledge transfer among and between researchers, educators, other professionals and policymakers involved in educational transitions. (European Commission 2015)

The research projects being conducted in each of the five countries were to provide the content and context on which the exchanges would rely. They were drawn together through the placemat of themes shown in Fig. A.1.

The 2012 POET application was successful, and €222 600 became available to fund four exchanges, between 2013 and 2016, by the European POET members to either Australia or New Zealand. However, the project as approved required another four exchanges in Europe, for which IRSES could not be used. Additionally, there were requirements on the Australian and New Zealand POET members for 'equivalent exchange quantum' in Europe and for travel to each other's exchanges over the 4 years.

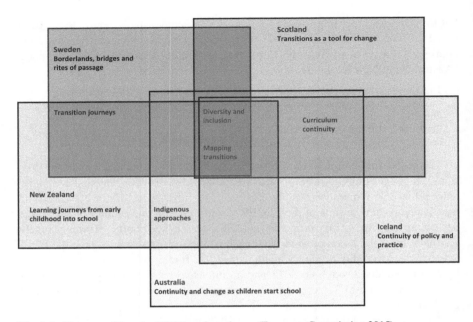

Fig. A.1 Themes guiding the POET work packages (European Commission 2015)

The New Zealand POET group was successful in gaining funding from the Royal Society of New Zealand. No such funding was available to the Australian group, so they have paid for their involvement in the POET exchanges through some support from the Charles Sturt University Global Alliance fund, along with judicious use of research funds. For each country, what is not covered by IRSES and other funds has been met from personal resources, sometimes requiring substantial supplementation. At the time of writing this book, the POET international alliance is nearing the completion of its funded exchange programme.

A.2   POET International Alliance Vision and Purpose

POET was built around detailed planning for each of the work packages (exchanges), with work between these work packages supplementing the intensive exchange periods (see Table A.1).

While intensive work was planned, instigated, undertaken and sometimes completed during the staff exchanges to each university, much was expected to happen between these exchanges:

The work packages included a series of reciprocal staff exchanges, each for periods of 1–3 months. Each work package involves experienced, early-career researchers and doctoral candidates from each of the partner institutions in:

Table A.1 Details of work packages (WP)

	Title	Host organisation	Period
WP1	Introduction	University of Strathclyde	July–October, 2012
WP2	Mapping transition research and practice	Charles Sturt University	March–June, 2013
WP3	Diversity and inclusion	Mälardalen University	July–October, 2013
WP4	Indigenous approaches	University of Waikato	March–June, 2014
WP5	Curriculum continuity	University of Iceland	July–October, 2014
WP6	Transition journeys	University of Waikato	March–June, 2015
WP7	Transitions as a tool for change	University of Strathclyde	July–October, 2015
WP8	Into the future	Charles Sturt University	February–April, 2016

- preliminary work on each country project as well as readings and specific activities to be shared during the staff exchange;
- staff exchanges including: research symposia reporting country projects; identification and discussion of issues; intensive skills development workshops around identified themes/processes; collaborative writing; reflection; theorising; and opportunities to engage with local practitioners, researchers and policymakers to promote both knowledge transfer and understanding of the local contexts of educational transitions; and
- follow-up work including: finalising projects from the work package/staff exchange; preparation and planning for the following work package; and collaborative writing. (European Commission 2015)

The overall vision and purpose for the POET alliance are represented through two underlying components: relational aspects and engagement with knowledge and understandings about educational transitions. These components interact with and complement each other, and within these lie the possibilities for sustainable research in this field.

Relational aspects of the POET collaboration are powerful in that they move beyond the momentary networking opportunities that can occur at traditional academic conferences or symposia. The biannual POET exchanges offer consistent and regular opportunities to build robust and meaningful relationships within and between country groups, at both professional and personal levels. One distinctive feature of the alliance was the bringing together of early-career and experienced researchers, which resulted in unique mentoring opportunities and sharing of expertise. As is common for any long-term project, the 4-year exchange programme also coincided with significant personal life changes for some participants, including doctorate completions, promotions, births and the loss of loved ones. The bond formed among the POET participants through these personal events over the exchange period has served to strengthen the collaboration overall.

Another important relational aspect of the POET alliance is purposeful networking and partnering with other stakeholders. Educational practitioners, policymakers and other professionals participated in various seminars, presentations and discussions with the POET country teams at each exchange. This provided significant opportunities to learn from and share with one another in an ongoing way. While each country team has core members who participated in the majority of the POET exchanges, a benefit of meeting in a different location for each exchange was that peripheral researchers and students, who may have been unable to travel elsewhere, could also participate in POET activities in their respective universities.

The second underlying component of the vision and purpose for the POET alliance is engagement with knowledge and understandings about educational transitions. In many ways, this component occurred in a more focused manner because of the strength of the existing relationships between the alliance's team leaders and the establishment of solid relationships between the participants early in the exchange programme. The initial exchanges focused on becoming familiar with each country's context, the existing country projects and individual projects related to educational transitions. This sharing of rationales and ways of working, and the ensuing workshops and discussions, undoubtedly contributed to the development of diverse research skills and expertise among the POET exchange participants.

One of the benefits of the POET alliance has been having a wider, international foundation of expertise to provide input into country-based projects. This input includes critique and interrogation of individual work, as well as the capacity to pose and address questions at comparative level. Approximately halfway through the 4-year exchange programme, there was a distinct shift in focus, when it became evident that a depth of bonding and rigorous exploration of research projects had occurred. At this point, more substantial plans about moving collective knowledge and understandings about educational transitions forwards began to unfold, and this book comes as a result of this.

It is intended that ongoing networking and collaborative work in the area of educational transitions will continue among POET participants after the 4-year exchange programme is completed. The final chapter of this book, written by the POET country team leaders, outlines their vision for future directions for research in the area of educational transitions.

References

Dockett, S., & Perry, B. (2014). *Continuity of learning: A resource to support effective transition to school and school age care*. Canberra: Australian Government Department of Education.

Educational Transitions and Change (ETC) Research Group. (2011). *Transition to school: Position statement*. http://www.csu.edu.au/faculty/educat/edu/transitions/publications/Position-Statement.pdf. Accessed 12 Nov 2014.

European Commission. (2013). *Marie Curie actions, guide for applicants: International Research Staff Exchange Scheme*. http://ec.europa.eu/research/mariecurieactions/documents/about-mca/actions/irses/m_gfa_irses_2013_en.pdf. Accessed 11 Nov 2015.

European Commission. (2015). *Periodic report summary 1 – POET (Pedagogies of Educational Transitions)*. http://cordis.europa.eu/result/rcn/169030_en.html. Accessed 11 Nov 2015.

Perry, B., Dockett, S., & Petriwskyj, A. (Eds.). (2014). *Transitions to school: International research, policy and practice*. Dordrecht: Springer.

CPI Antony Rowe
Chippenham, UK
2017-10-05 06:15